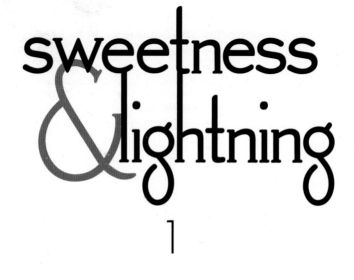

sweetness & lightning

1

Gido Amagakure

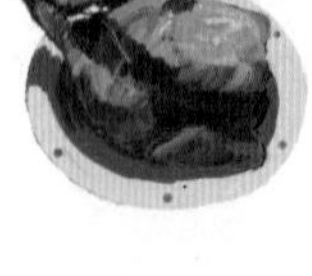

c o n t e n t s

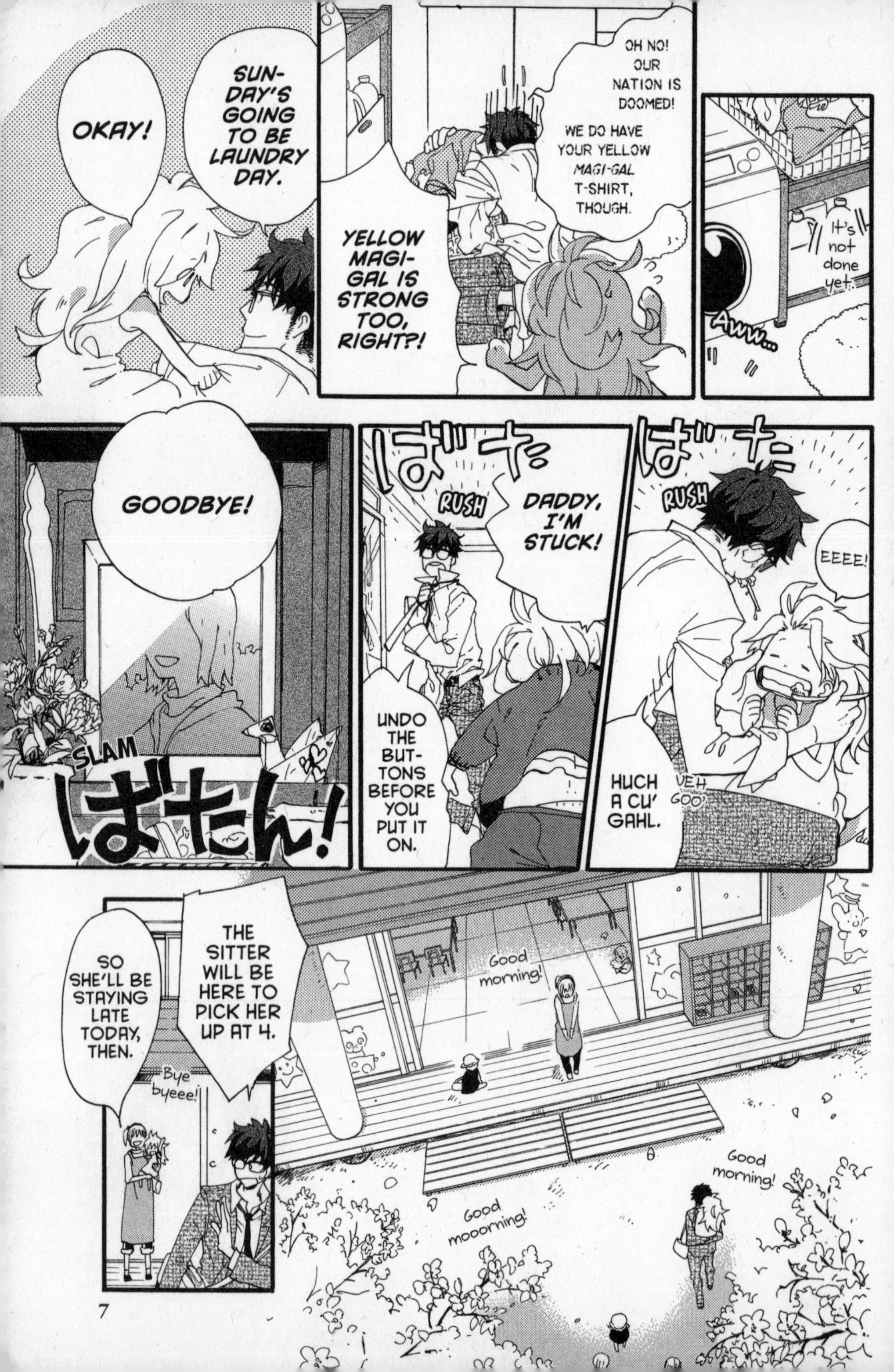
It's not done yet.
Aww...
OH NO! OUR NATION IS DOOMED!
WE DO HAVE YOUR YELLOW MAGI-GAL T-SHIRT, THOUGH.
YELLOW MAGI-GAL IS STRONG TOO, RIGHT?!
SUN-DAY'S GOING TO BE LAUNDRY DAY.
OKAY!
ばたばた
RUSH
EEEE!
VEH GOO'
HUCH A CU' GAHL.
ばたばた
RUSH
DADDY, I'M STUCK!
UNDO THE BUT-TONS BEFORE YOU PUT IT ON.
GOODBYE!
SLAM
ばたん!
Good morning!
Good morning!
Good mooorning!
THE SITTER WILL BE HERE TO PICK HER UP AT 4.
SO SHE'LL BE STAYING LATE TODAY, THEN.
Bye byeee!

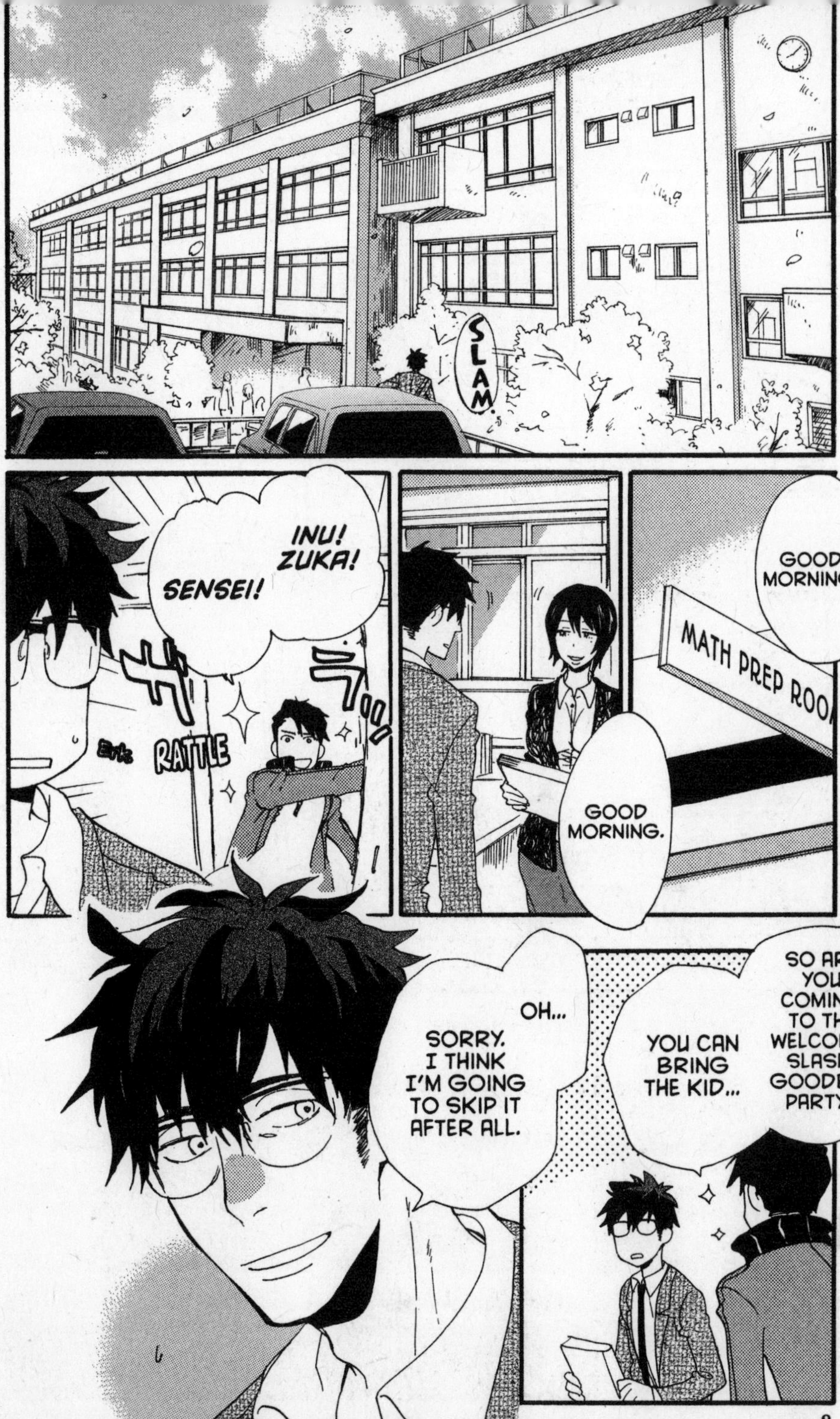
SLAM
GOOD MORNING.
MATH PREP ROO
GOOD MORNING.
INU! ZUKA! SENSEI!
RATTLE
SO ARE YOU COMING TO THE WELCOME-SLASH-GOODBYE PARTY?
YOU CAN BRING THE KID...
OH...
SORRY. I THINK I'M GOING TO SKIP IT AFTER ALL.

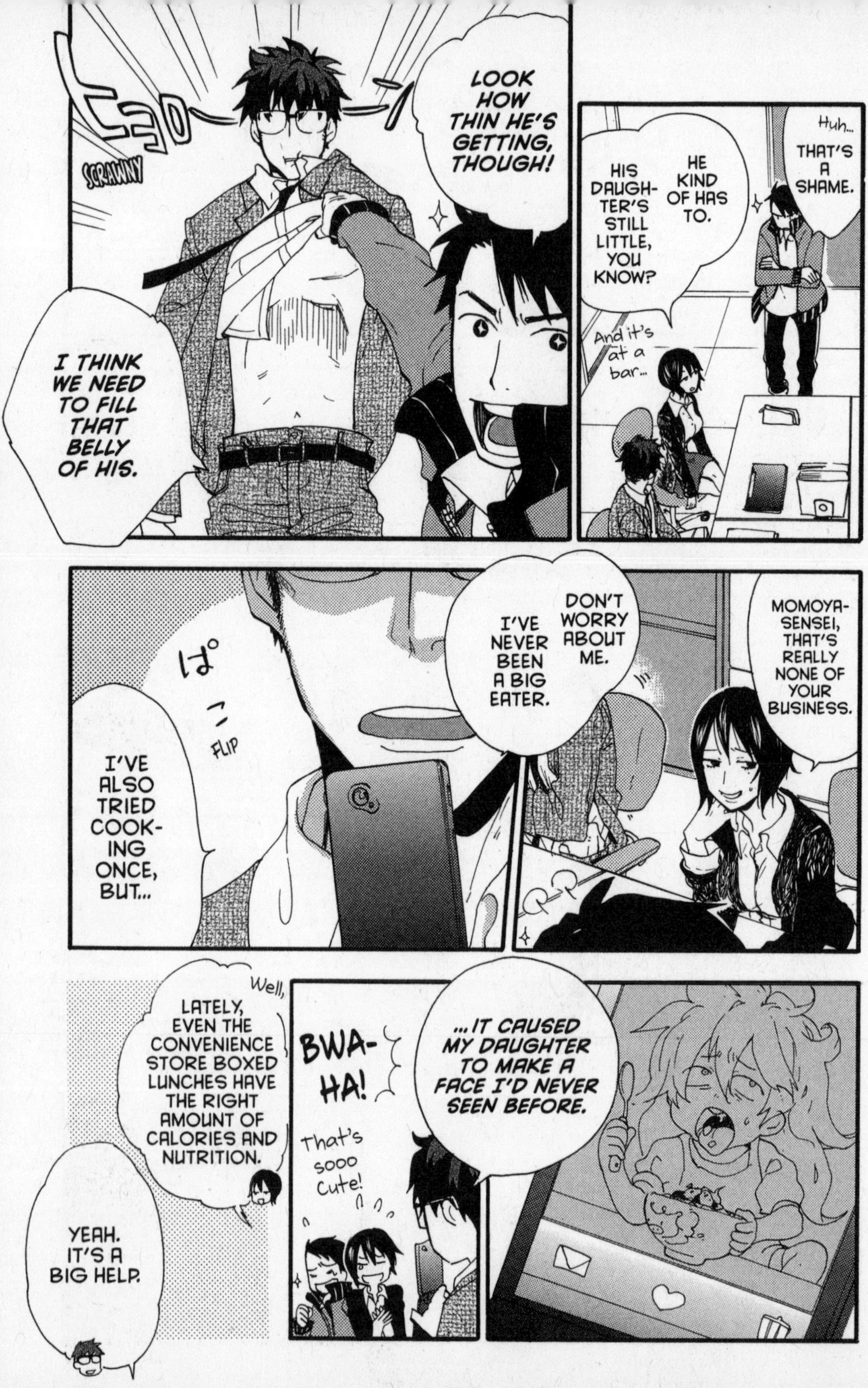
Huh... THAT'S A SHAME.
HE KIND OF HAS TO.
HIS DAUGHTER'S STILL LITTLE, YOU KNOW?
And it's at a bar...
LOOK HOW THIN HE'S GETTING, THOUGH!
SCRAWNY
I THINK WE NEED TO FILL THAT BELLY OF HIS.
MOMOYA-SENSEI, THAT'S REALLY NONE OF YOUR BUSINESS.
DON'T WORRY ABOUT ME.
I'VE NEVER BEEN A BIG EATER.
ぱこ
FLIP
I'VE ALSO TRIED COOKING ONCE, BUT...
...IT CAUSED MY DAUGHTER TO MAKE A FACE I'D NEVER SEEN BEFORE.
BWA-HA!
That's sooo cute!
Well,
LATELY, EVEN THE CONVENIENCE STORE BOXED LUNCHES HAVE THE RIGHT AMOUNT OF CALORIES AND NUTRITION.
YEAH. IT'S A BIG HELP.

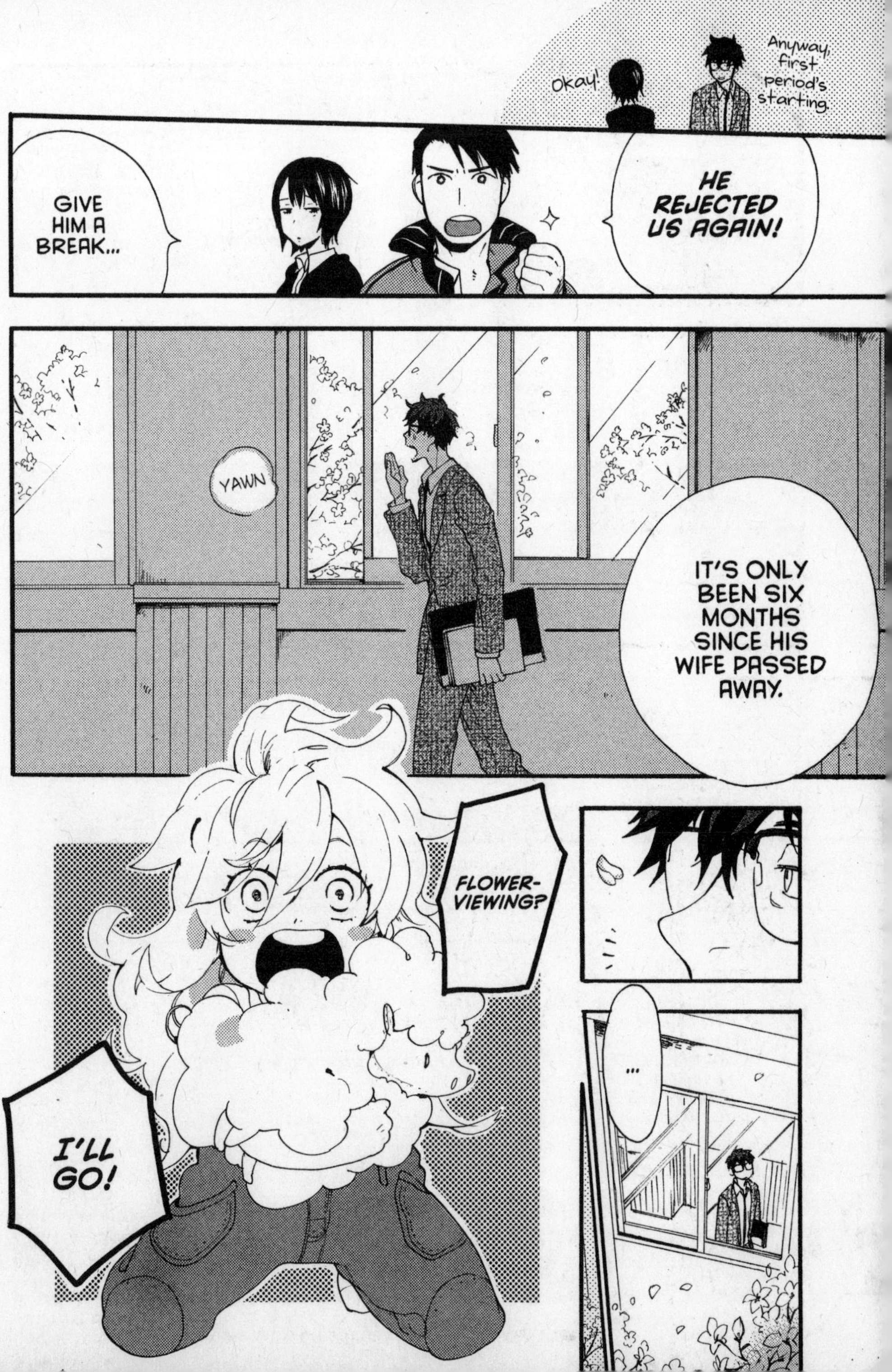
Anyway, first period's starting.
Okay!
HE REJECTED US AGAIN!
GIVE HIM A BREAK...
IT'S ONLY BEEN SIX MONTHS SINCE HIS WIFE PASSED AWAY.
YAWN
...
FLOWER-VIEWING?
I'LL GO!

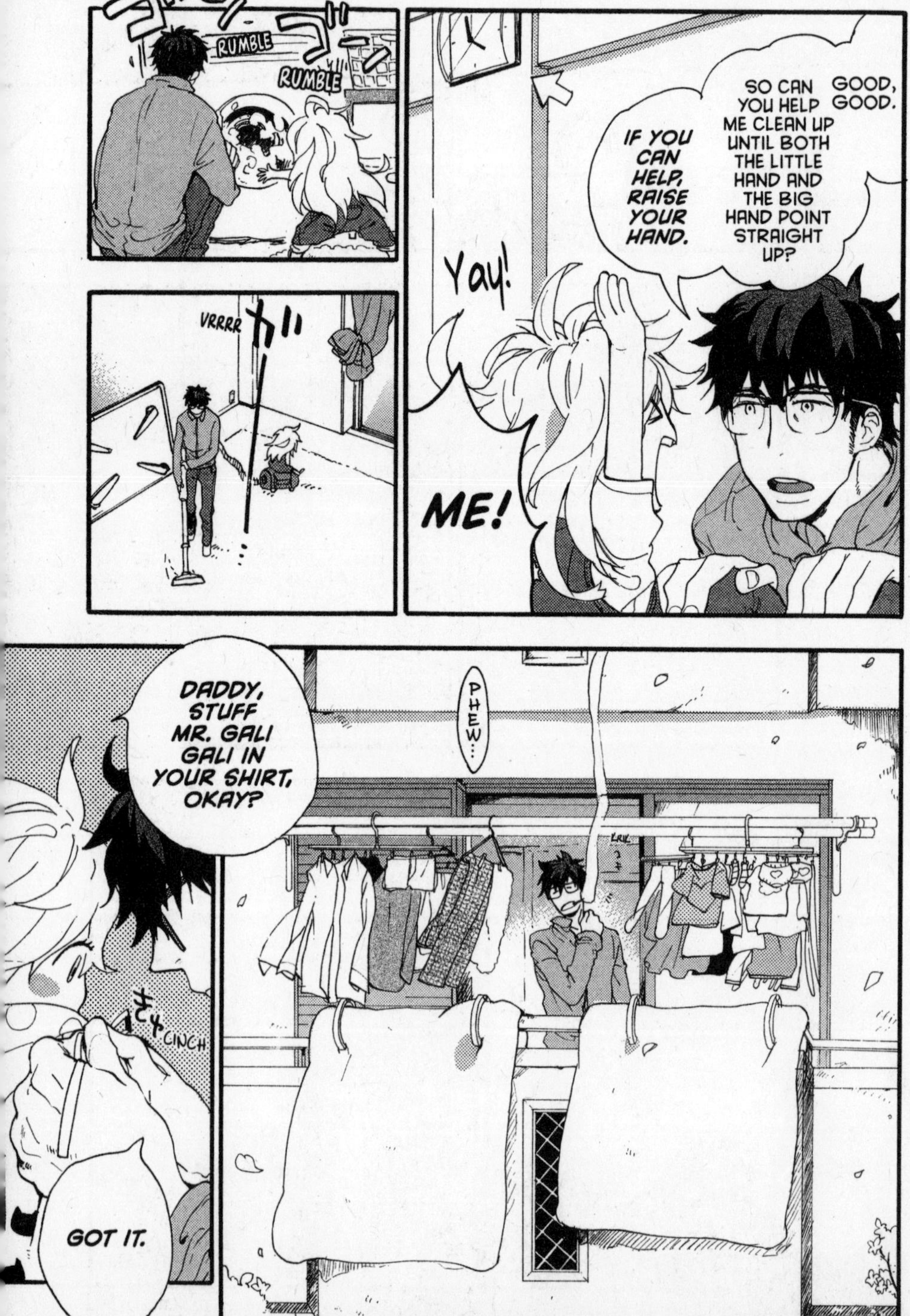
GOOD, GOOD.
SO CAN YOU HELP ME CLEAN UP UNTIL BOTH THE LITTLE HAND AND THE BIG HAND POINT STRAIGHT UP?
IF YOU CAN HELP, RAISE YOUR HAND.
Yay!
ME!
RUMBLE
RUMBLE
VRRRR
PHEW...
KRIK
DADDY, STUFF MR. GALI GALI IN YOUR SHIRT, OKAY?
CINCH
GOT IT.

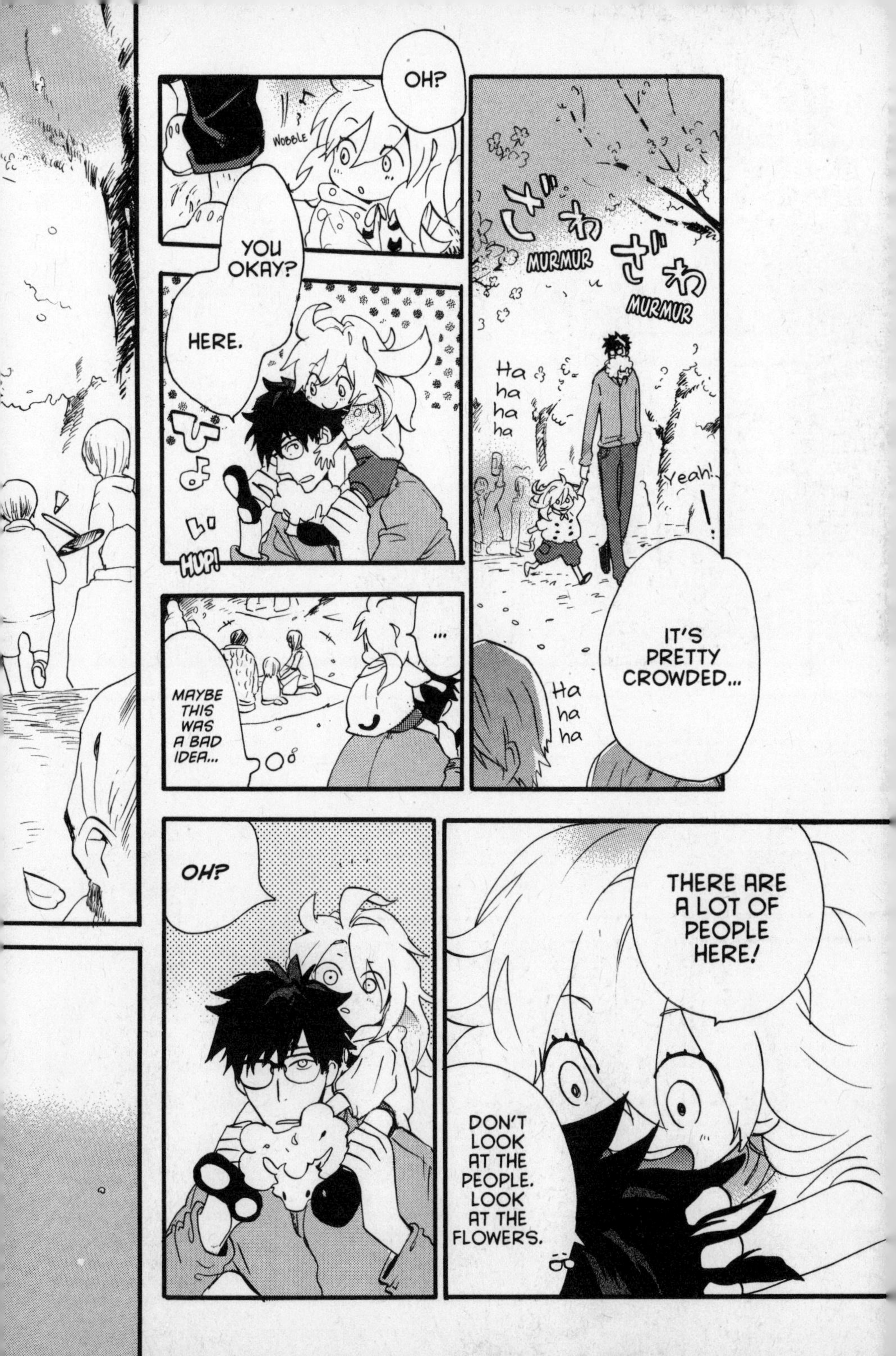

ざわ
MURMUR
ざわ
MURMUR
Ha ha ha ha
Yeah!
IT'S PRETTY CROWDED...
Ha ha ha
OH?
WOBBLE
YOU OKAY?
HERE.
ひょい
HUP!
...
MAYBE THIS WAS A BAD IDEA...
THERE ARE A LOT OF PEOPLE HERE!
DON'T LOOK AT THE PEOPLE. LOOK AT THE FLOWERS.
OH?

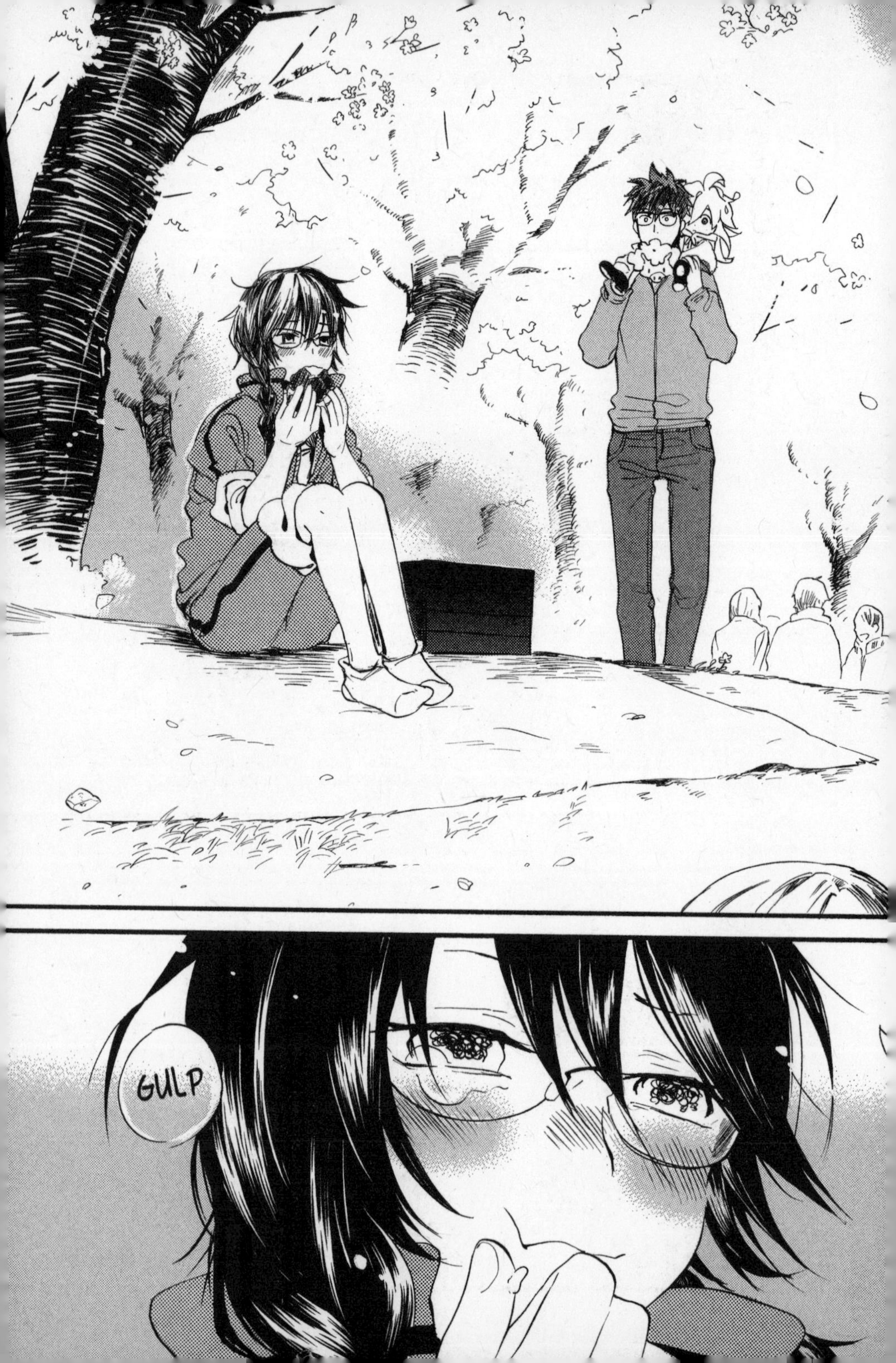
GULP

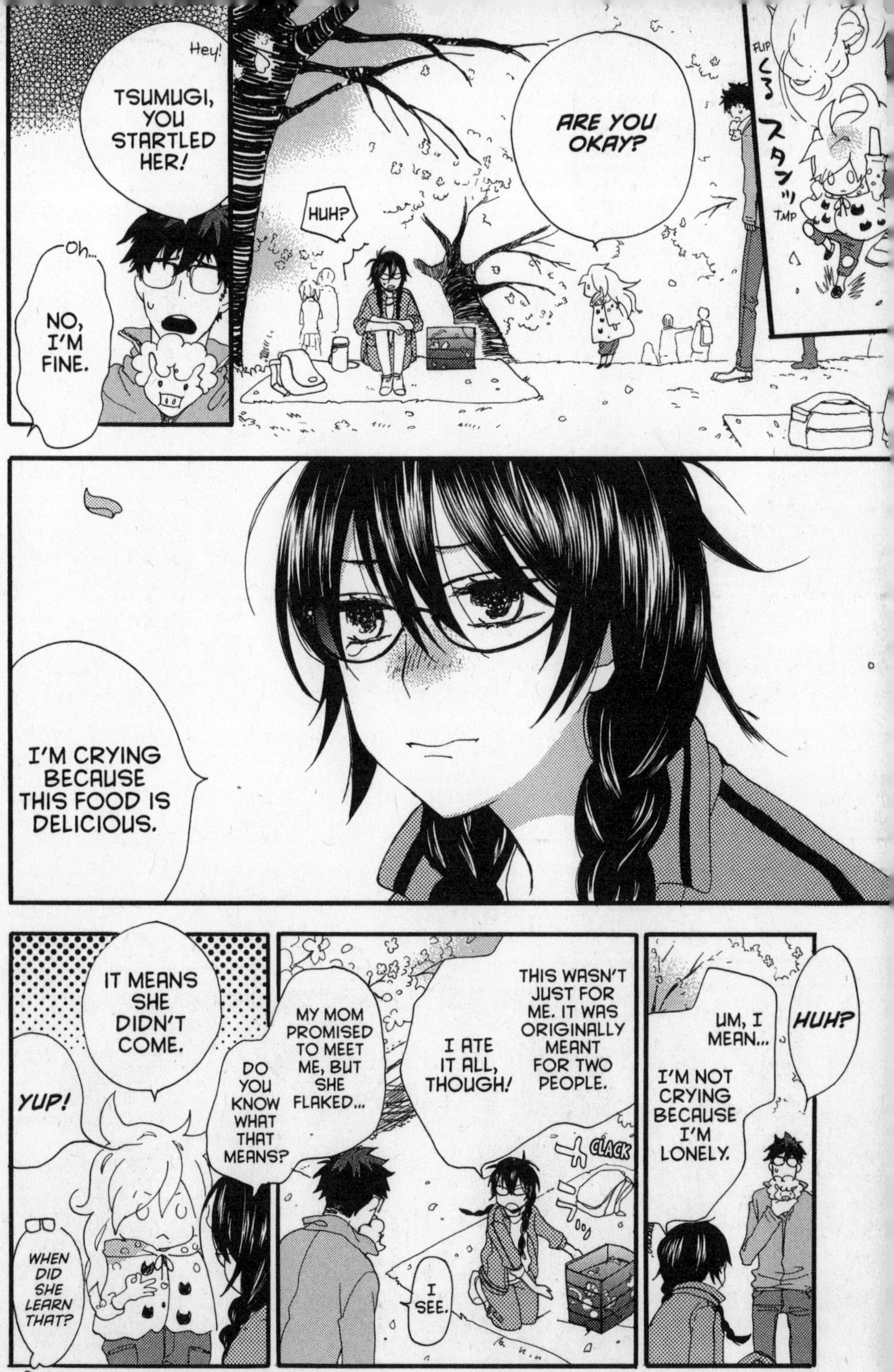
FLIP くる
スタンッ TMP
ARE YOU OKAY?
HUH?
Hey!
TSUMUGI, YOU STARTLED HER!
Oh...
NO, I'M FINE.
I'M CRYING BECAUSE THIS FOOD IS DELICIOUS.
HUH?
UM, I MEAN...
I'M NOT CRYING BECAUSE I'M LONELY.
THIS WASN'T JUST FOR ME. IT WAS ORIGINALLY MEANT FOR TWO PEOPLE.
I ATE IT ALL, THOUGH!
CLACK
I SEE.
MY MOM PROMISED TO MEET ME, BUT SHE FLAKED...
DO YOU KNOW WHAT THAT MEANS?
IT MEANS SHE DIDN'T COME.
YUP!
WHEN DID SHE LEARN THAT?

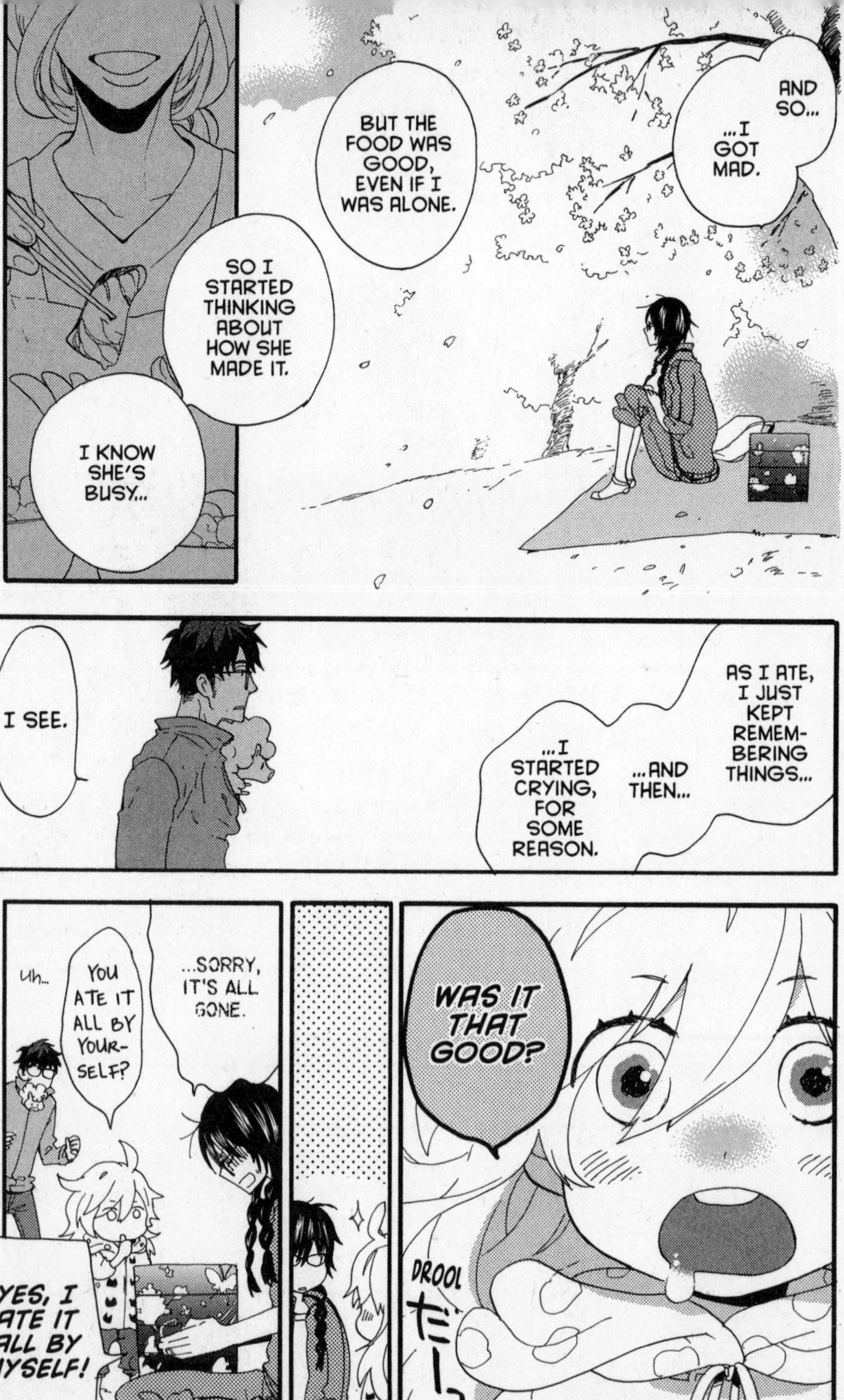
AND SO...
...I GOT MAD.
BUT THE FOOD WAS GOOD, EVEN IF I WAS ALONE.
SO I STARTED THINKING ABOUT HOW SHE MADE IT.
I KNOW SHE'S BUSY...
AS I ATE, I JUST KEPT REMEMBERING THINGS...
...AND THEN...
...I STARTED CRYING, FOR SOME REASON.
I SEE.
WAS IT THAT GOOD?
DROOL
だー
...SORRY, IT'S ALL GONE.
YOU ATE IT ALL BY YOURSELF?
Uh...
YES, I ATE IT ALL BY MYSELF!

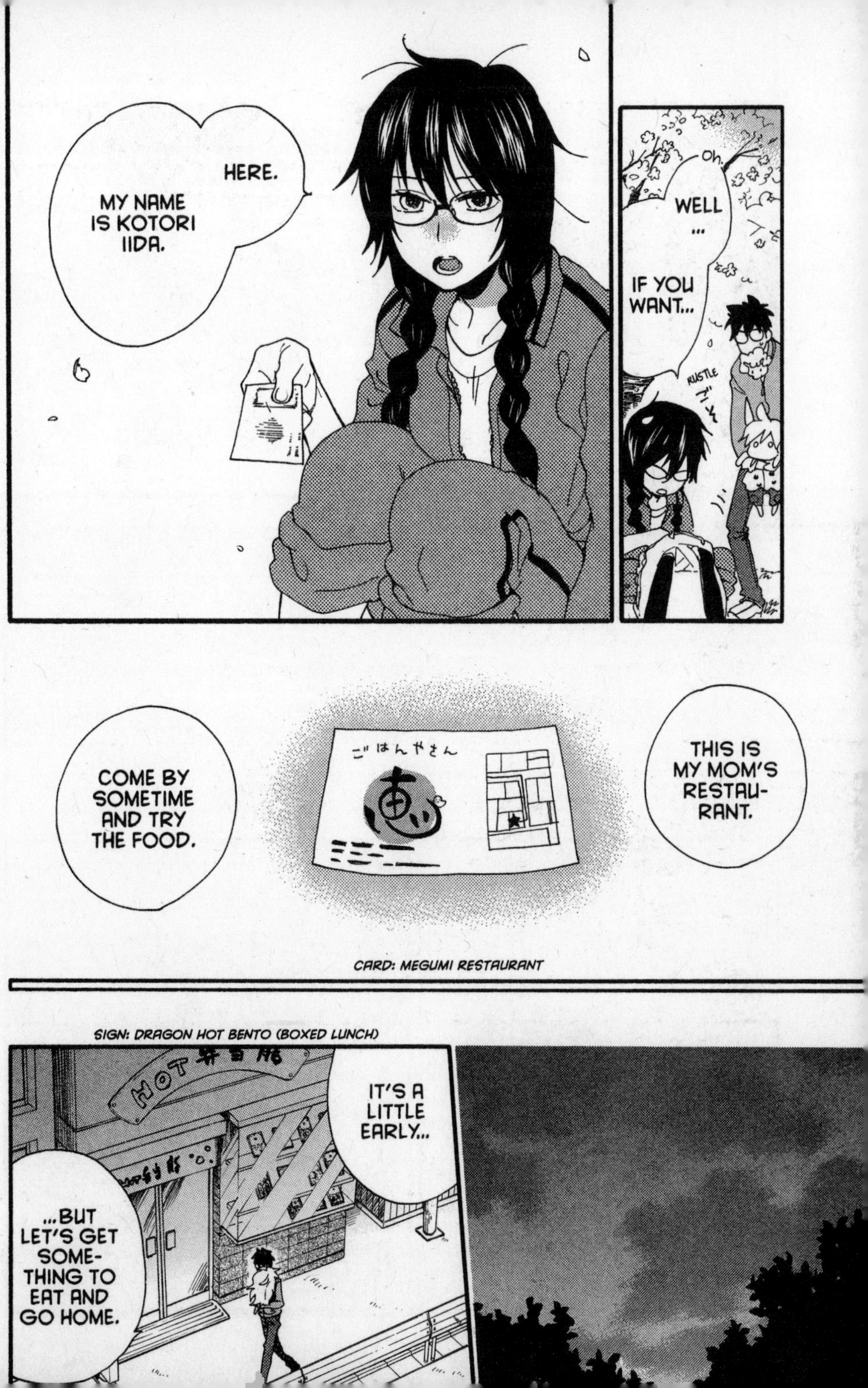
Oh.
WELL ...
IF YOU WANT...
RUSTLE
HERE.
MY NAME IS KOTORI IIDA.
THIS IS MY MOM'S RESTAU-RANT.
ごはんやさん
COME BY SOMETIME AND TRY THE FOOD.
CARD: MEGUMI RESTAURANT
SIGN: DRAGON HOT BENTO (BOXED LUNCH)
HOT
IT'S A LITTLE EARLY...
...BUT LET'S GET SOME-THING TO EAT AND GO HOME.

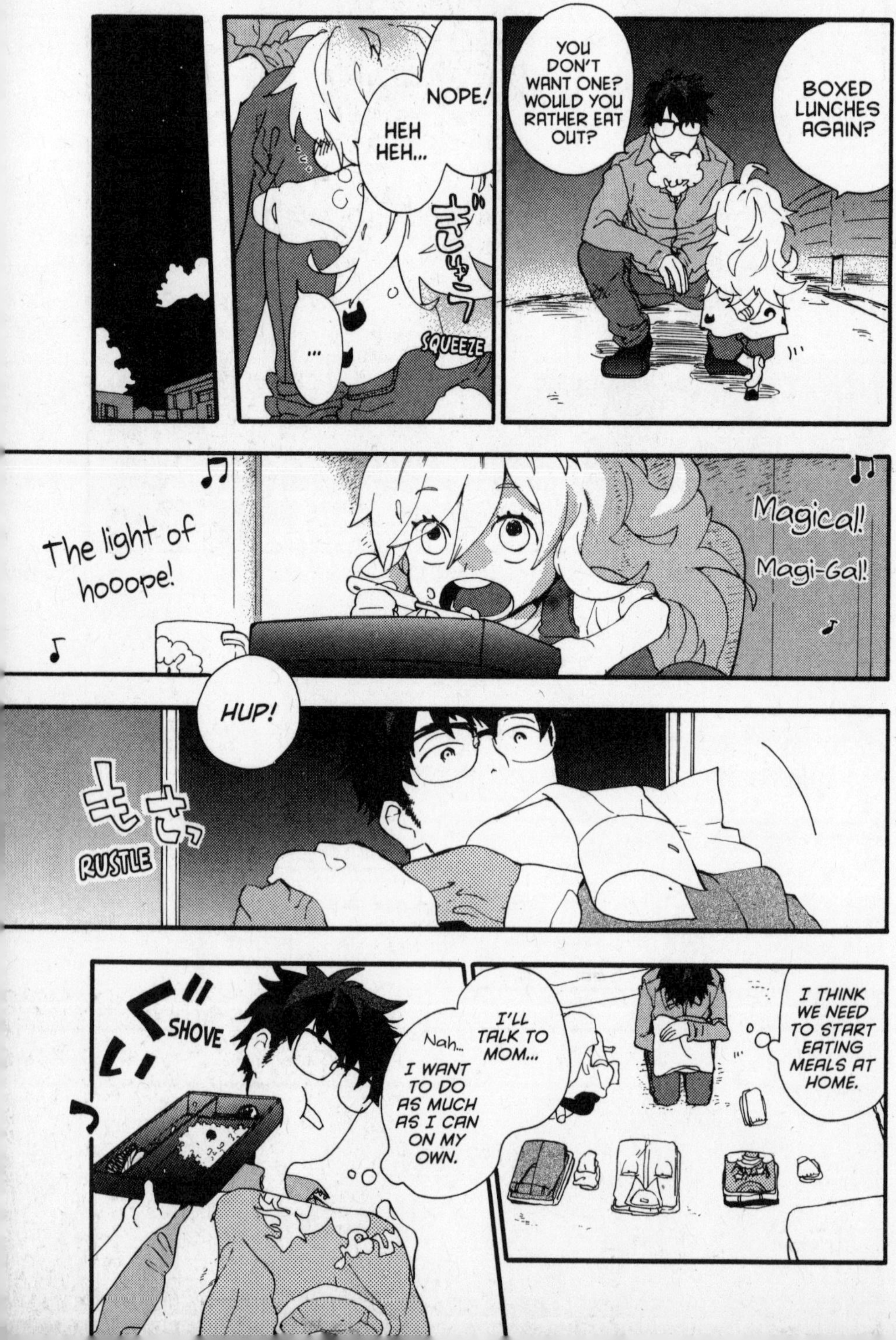
BOXED LUNCHES AGAIN?
YOU DON'T WANT ONE? WOULD YOU RATHER EAT OUT?
NOPE!
HEH HEH...
ぎゅっ
SQUEEZE
...
Magical!
Magi-Gal!
The light of hooope!
HUP!
もさっ
RUSTLE
I THINK WE NEED TO START EATING MEALS AT HOME.
I'LL TALK TO MOM...
Nah... I WANT TO DO AS MUCH AS I CAN ON MY OWN.
ぐいっ
SHOVE

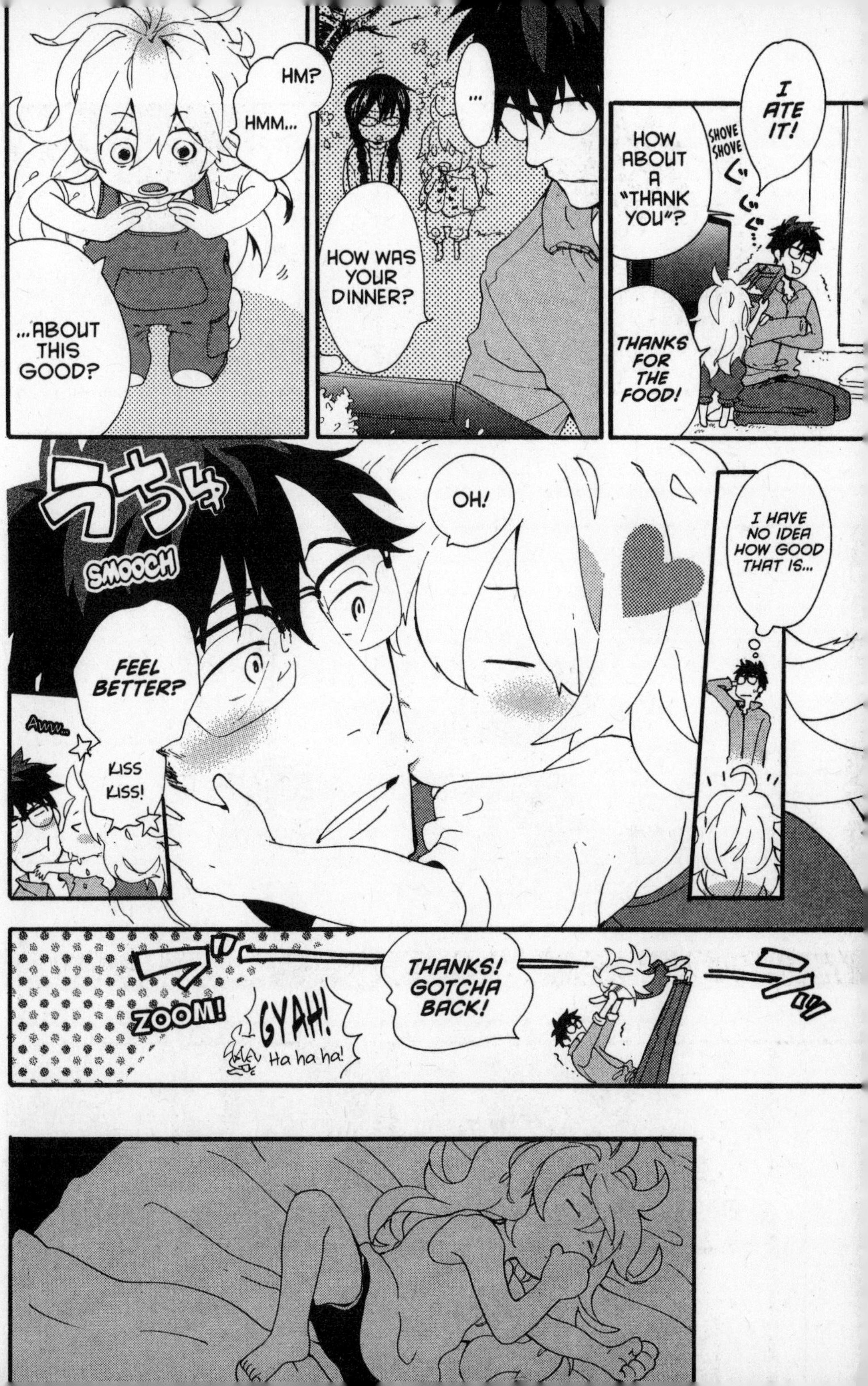
I ATE IT!
SHOVE SHOVE
HOW ABOUT A "THANK YOU"?
THANKS FOR THE FOOD!
...
HOW WAS YOUR DINNER?
HM?
HMM...
...ABOUT THIS GOOD?
I HAVE NO IDEA HOW GOOD THAT IS...
OH!
SMOOCH
FEEL BETTER?
Aww...
KISS KISS!
THANKS! GOTCHA BACK!
GYAH!
Ha ha ha!
ZOOM!

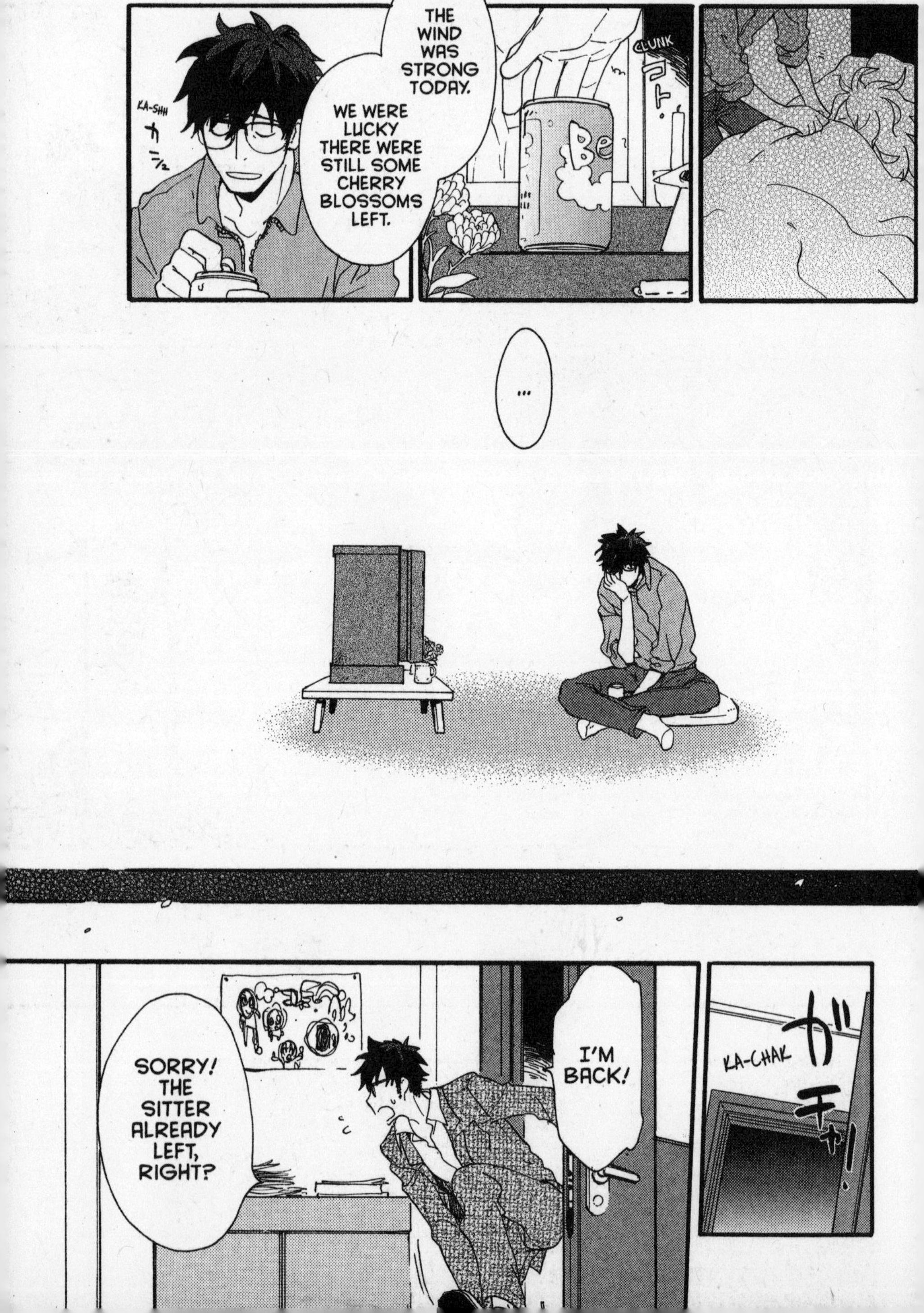
CLUNK
コト
THE WIND WAS STRONG TODAY.
WE WERE LUCKY THERE WERE STILL SOME CHERRY BLOSSOMS LEFT.
KA-SHH
...
KA-CHAK
ガチャ
I'M BACK!
SORRY! THE SITTER ALREADY LEFT, RIGHT?

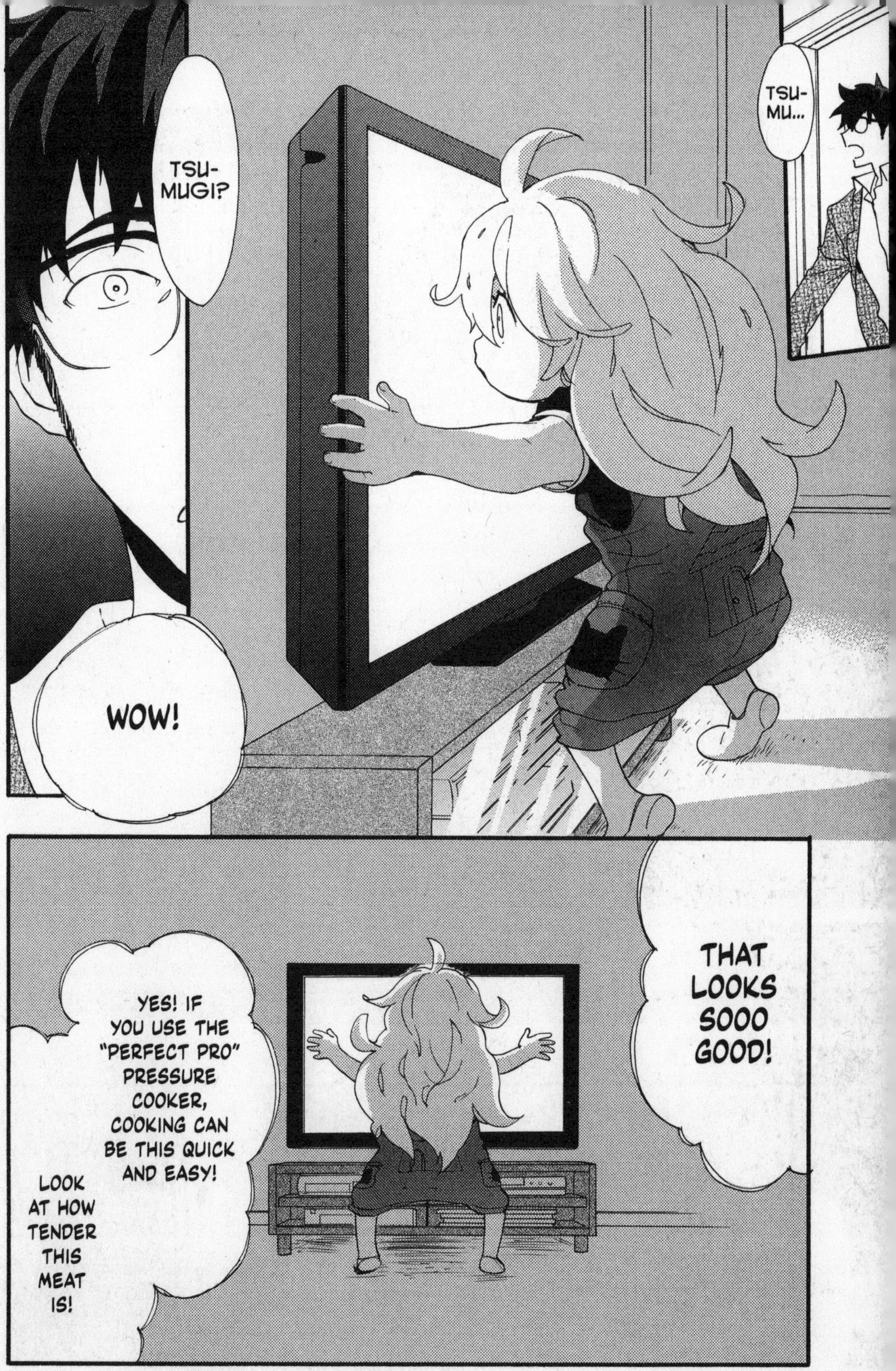
TSU-MU...
TSU-MUGI?
WOW!
THAT LOOKS SOOO GOOD!
YES! IF YOU USE THE "PERFECT PRO" PRESSURE COOKER, COOKING CAN BE THIS QUICK AND EASY!
LOOK AT HOW TENDER THIS MEAT IS!

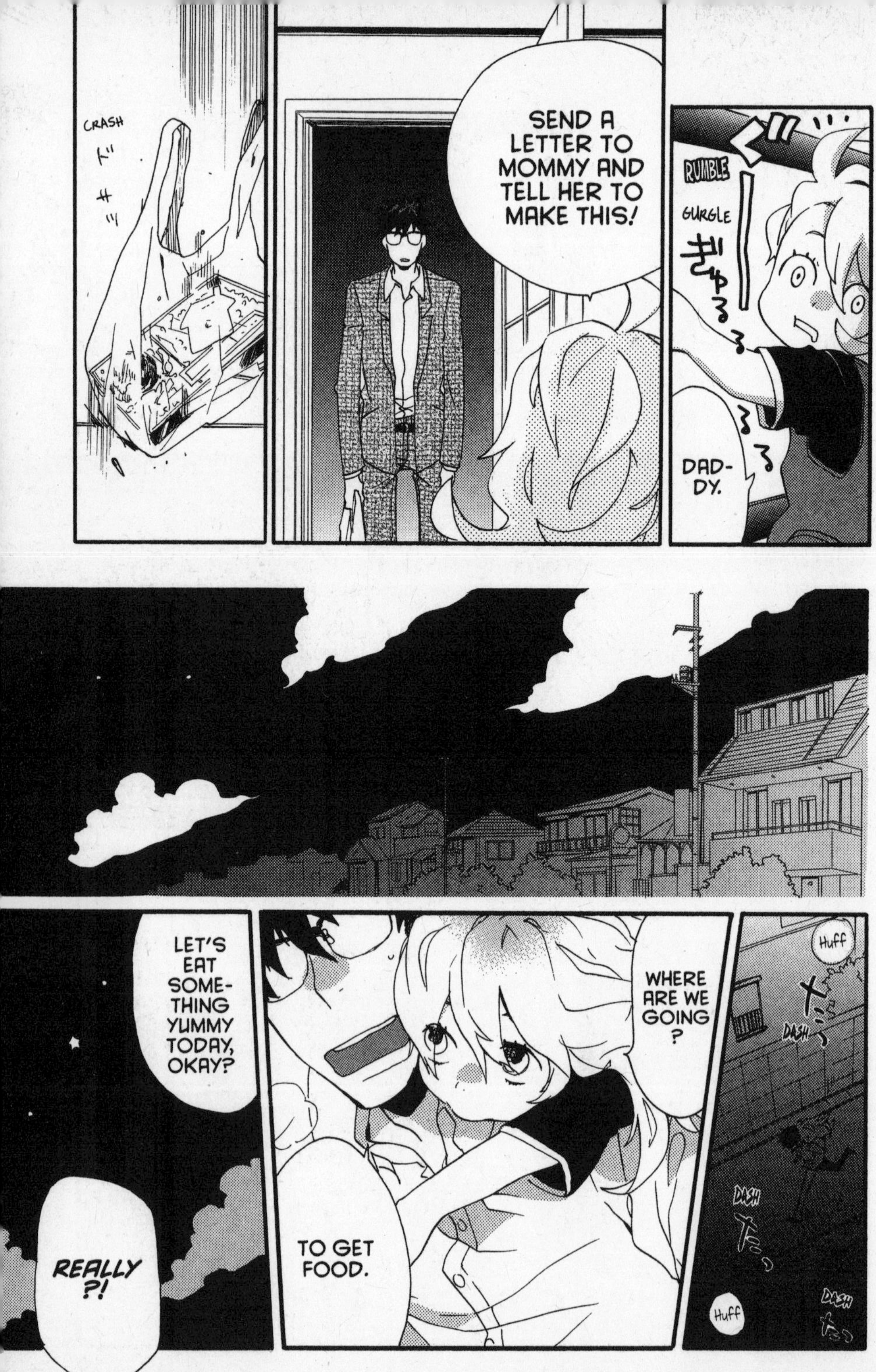
RUMBLE
GURGLE
DADDY.
SEND A LETTER TO MOMMY AND TELL HER TO MAKE THIS!
CRASH
Huff
DASH
DASH
Huff
DASH
WHERE ARE WE GOING?
TO GET FOOD.
LET'S EAT SOMETHING YUMMY TODAY, OKAY?
REALLY?!

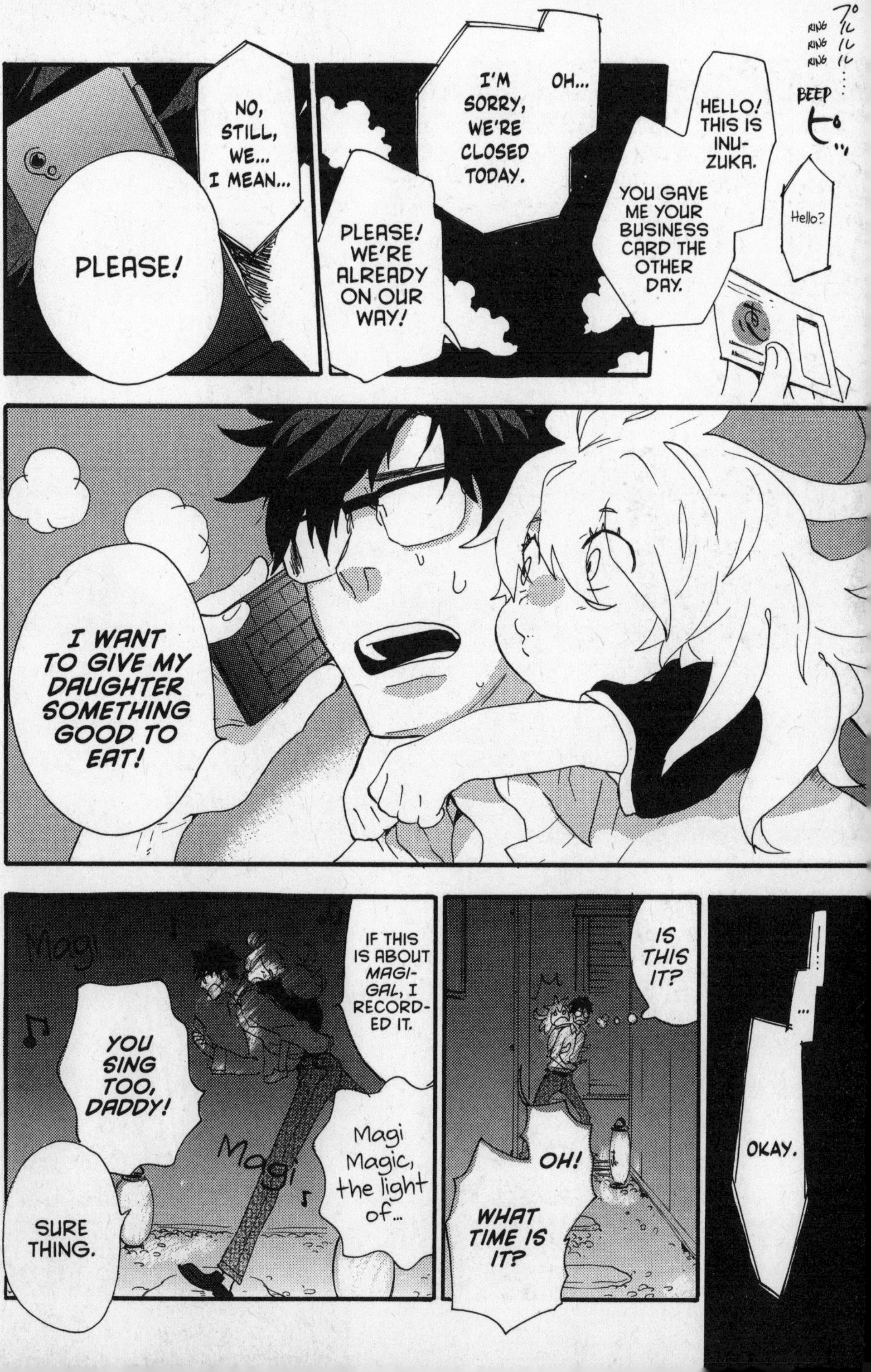
RING
RING
RING
BEEP
Hello?
HELLO! THIS IS INU-ZUKA.
YOU GAVE ME YOUR BUSINESS CARD THE OTHER DAY.
OH...
I'M SORRY, WE'RE CLOSED TODAY.
PLEASE! WE'RE ALREADY ON OUR WAY!
NO, STILL, WE... I MEAN...
PLEASE!
I WANT TO GIVE MY DAUGHTER SOMETHING GOOD TO EAT!
!...
...
OKAY.
IS THIS IT?
OH!
WHAT TIME IS IT?
IF THIS IS ABOUT MAGI-GAL, I RECORDED IT.
Magi
YOU SING TOO, DADDY!
Magi
Magi Magic, the light of...
SURE THING.

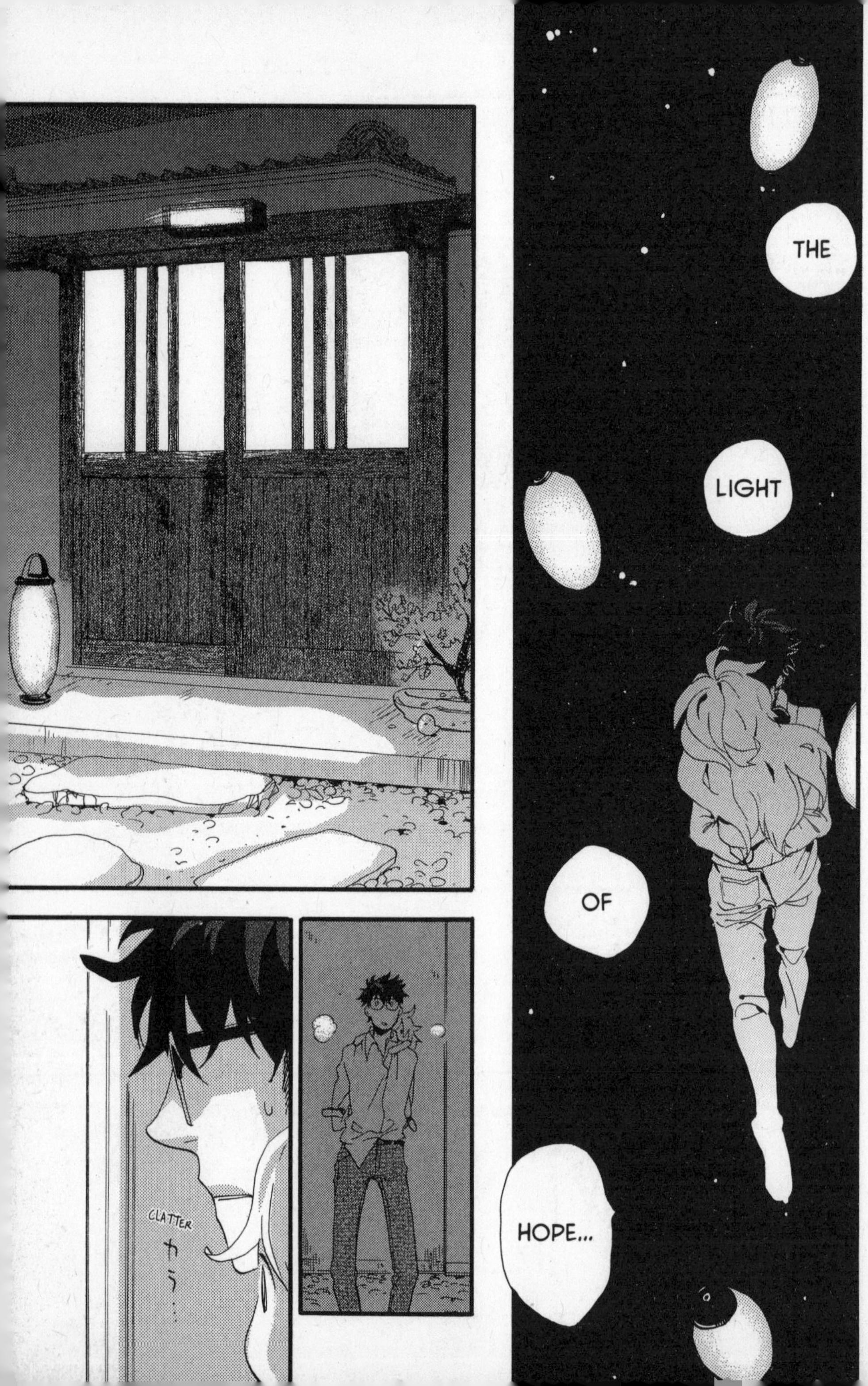
THE
LIGHT
OF
HOPE...
CLATTER
カラ…

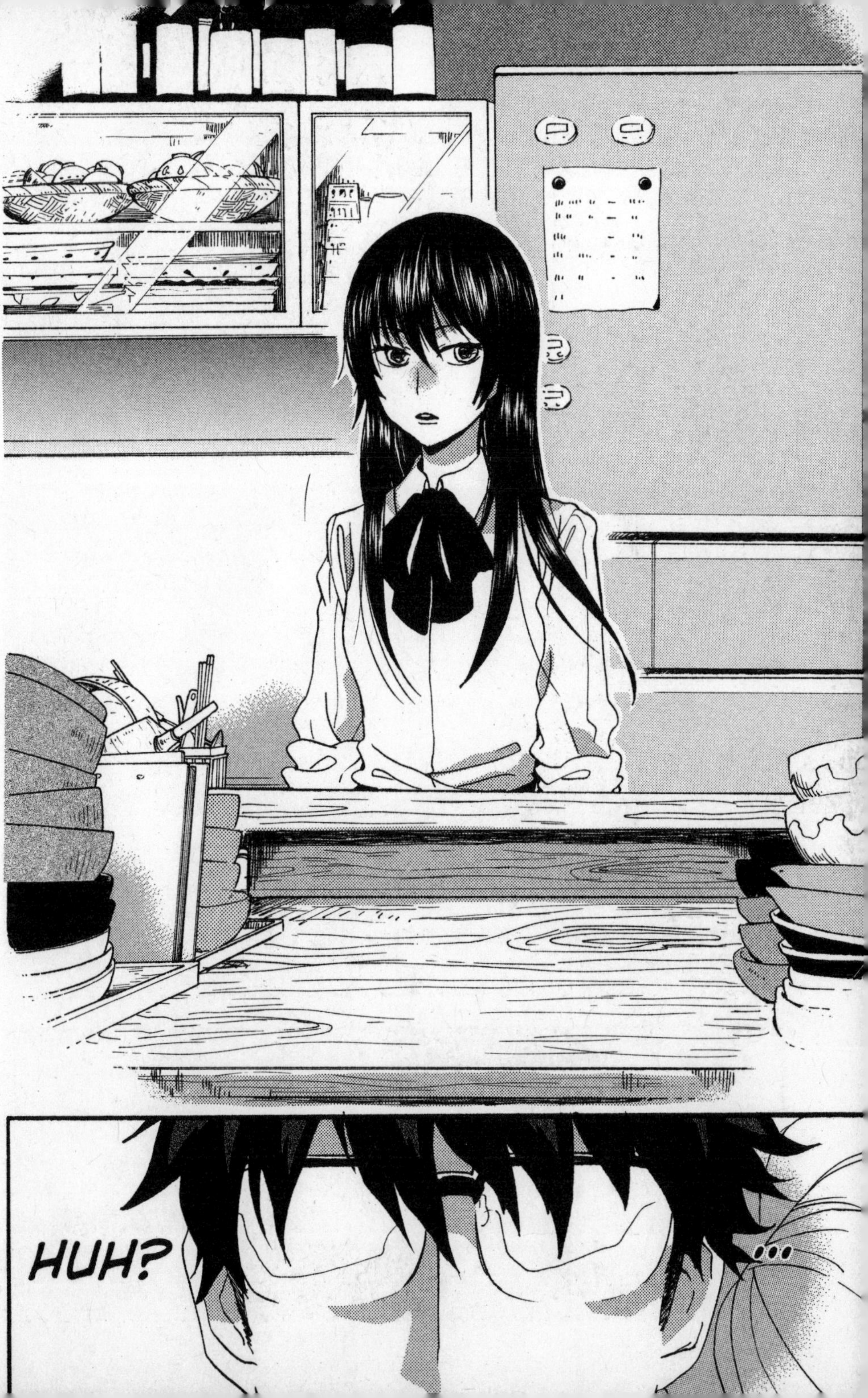
...
HUH?

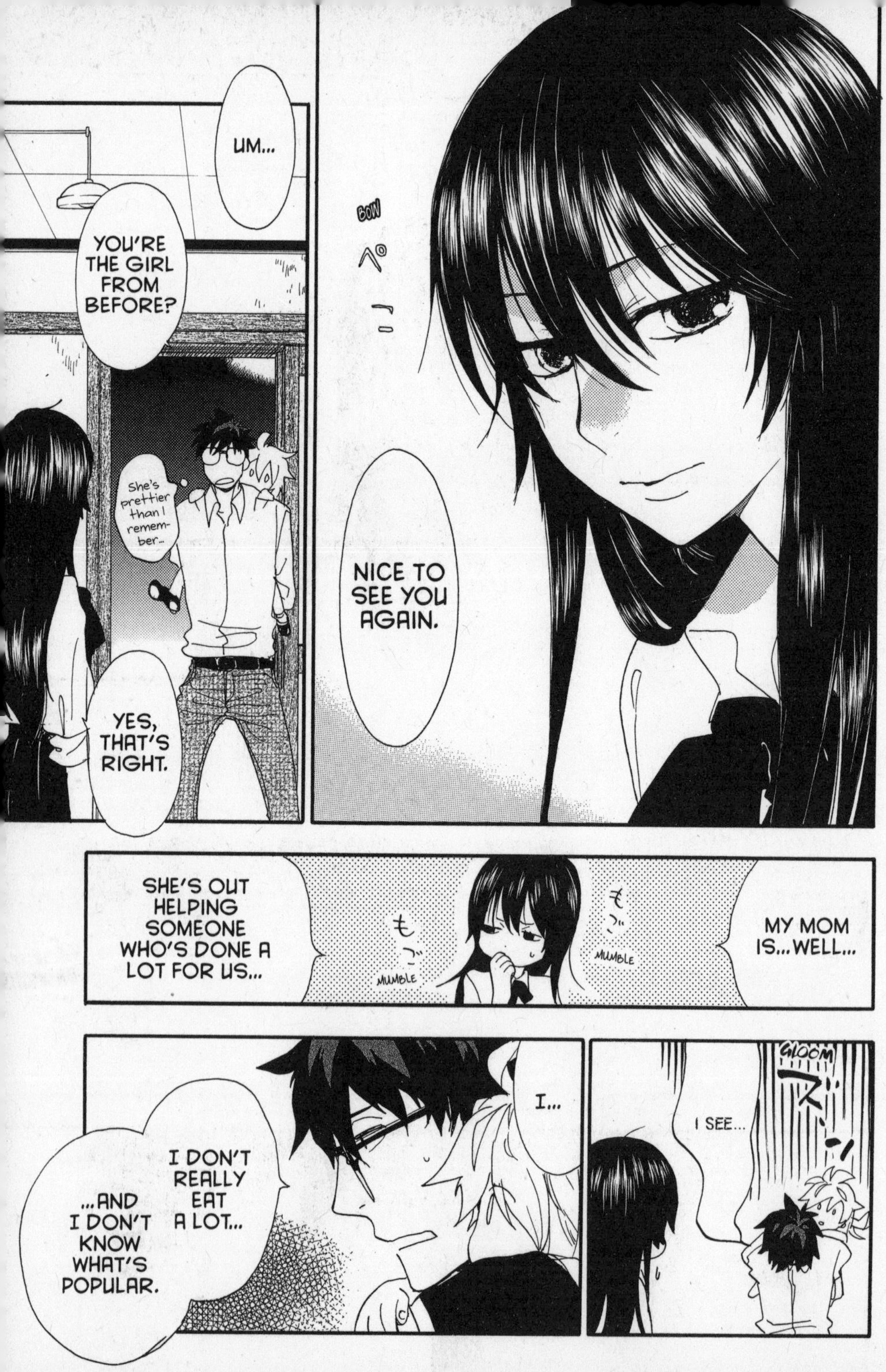
BOW
NICE TO SEE YOU AGAIN.
UM...
YOU'RE THE GIRL FROM BEFORE?
She's prettier than I remember...
YES, THAT'S RIGHT.
MY MOM IS...WELL...
MUMBLE
MUMBLE
SHE'S OUT HELPING SOMEONE WHO'S DONE A LOT FOR US...
GLOOM
I SEE...
I...
I DON'T REALLY EAT A LOT...
...AND I DON'T KNOW WHAT'S POPULAR.

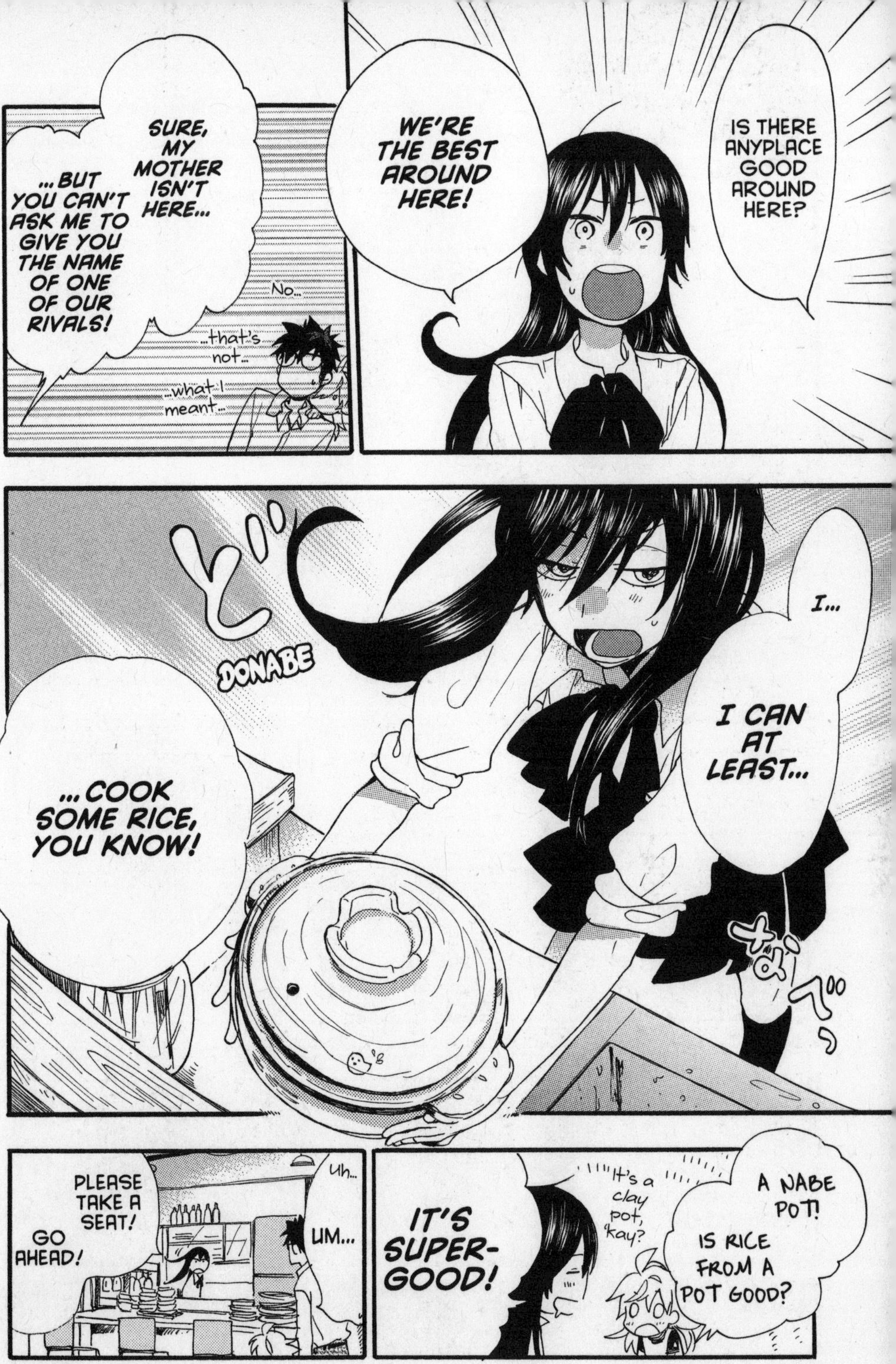
IS THERE ANYPLACE GOOD AROUND HERE?
WE'RE THE BEST AROUND HERE!
SURE, MY MOTHER ISN'T HERE...
...BUT YOU CAN'T ASK ME TO GIVE YOU THE NAME OF ONE OF OUR RIVALS!
No...
...that's not...
...what I meant...
I...
I CAN AT LEAST...
DONABE
...COOK SOME RICE, YOU KNOW!
A NABE POT!
IS RICE FROM A POT GOOD?
It's a clay pot, 'kay?
IT'S SUPER-GOOD!
Uh...
UM...
PLEASE TAKE A SEAT!
GO AHEAD!

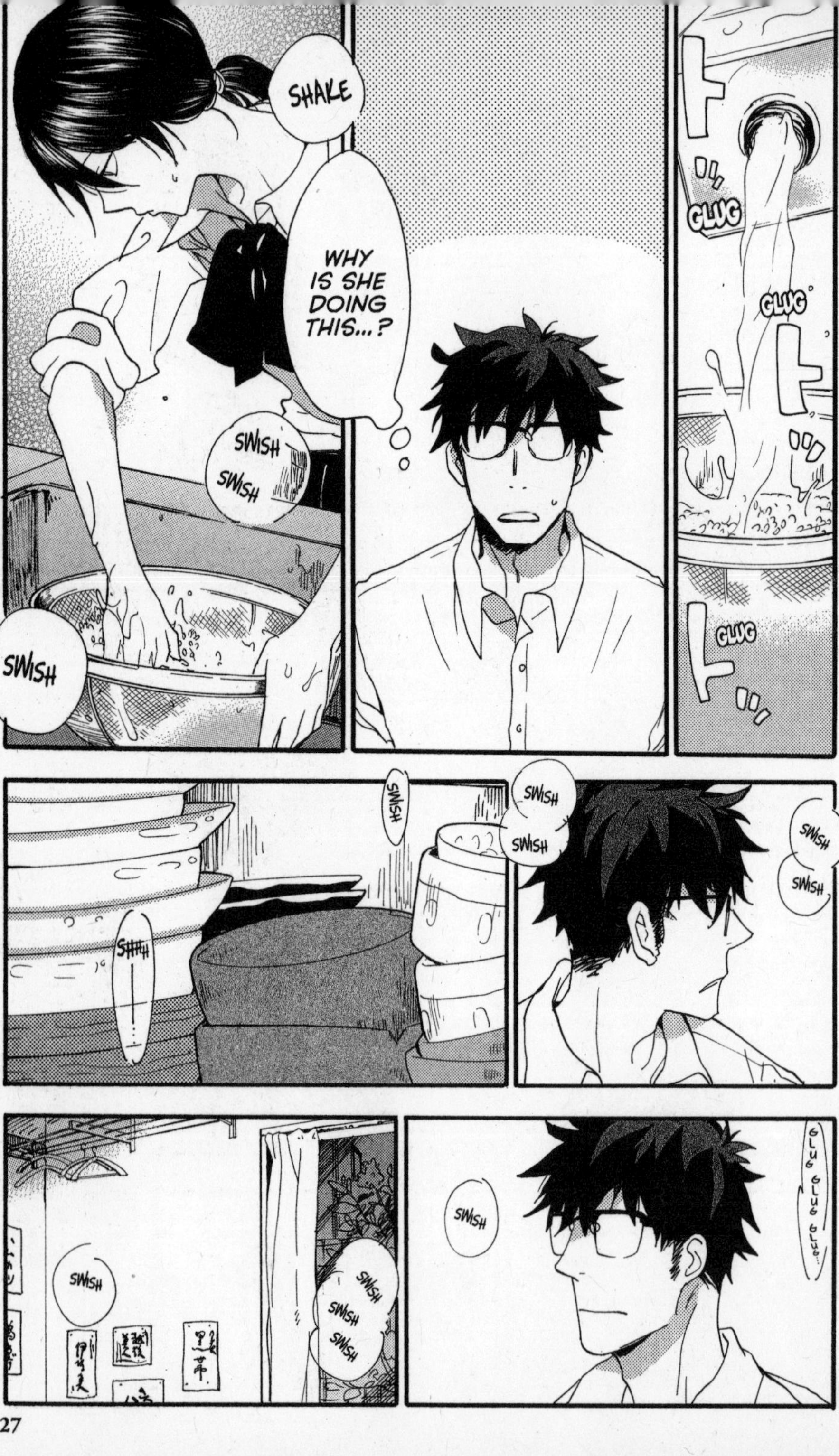
GLUG
GLUG
GLUG
WHY IS SHE DOING THIS...?
SHAKE
SWISH SWISH
SWISH
SWISH
SWISH
SWISH
SWISH
SWISH
SHHH
GLUG GLUG GLUG GLUG...
SWISH
SWISH SWISH SWISH
SWISH

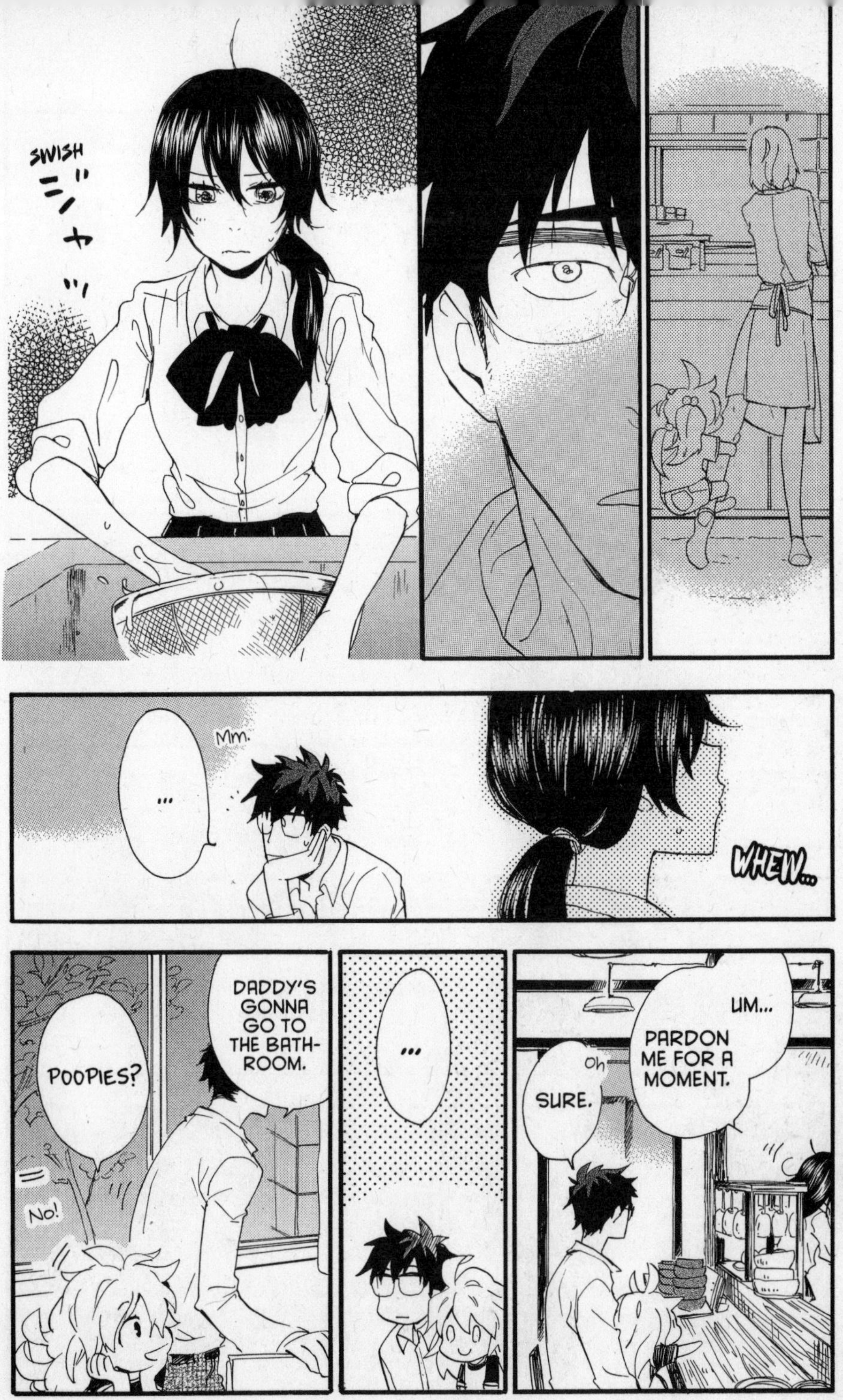
SWISH
ジャッ
WHEW...
Mm.
...
UM... PARDON ME FOR A MOMENT.
Oh
SURE.
...
DADDY'S GONNA GO TO THE BATH-ROOM.
POOPIES?
No!

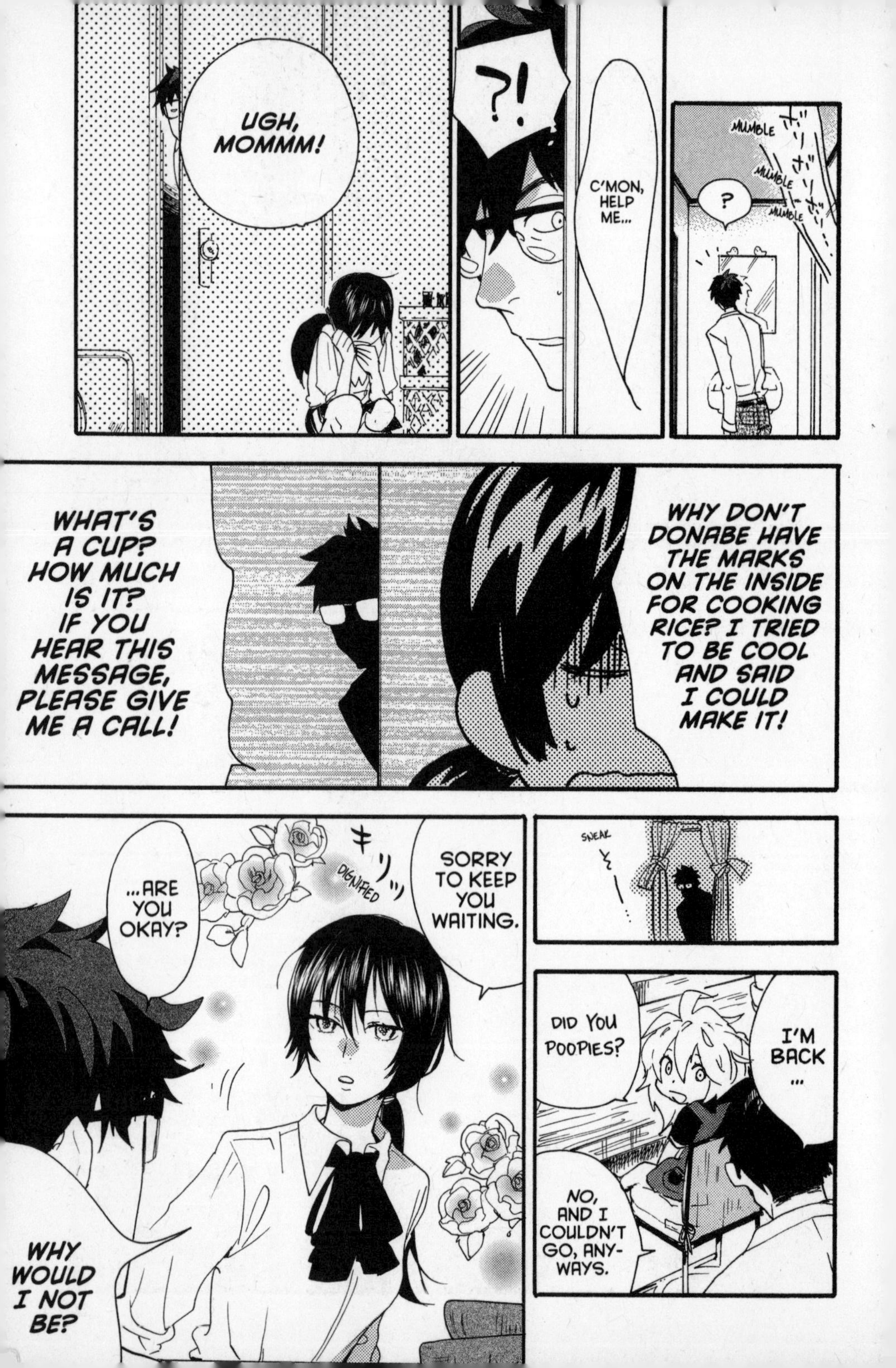
MUMBLE
MUMBLE
MUMBLE
?
?!
C'MON, HELP ME...
UGH, MOMMM!
WHY DON'T DONABE HAVE THE MARKS ON THE INSIDE FOR COOKING RICE? I TRIED TO BE COOL AND SAID I COULD MAKE IT!
WHAT'S A CUP? HOW MUCH IS IT? IF YOU HEAR THIS MESSAGE, PLEASE GIVE ME A CALL!
SNEAK
I'M BACK ...
DID YOU POOPIES?
NO, AND I COULDN'T GO, ANY-WAYS.
SORRY TO KEEP YOU WAITING.
DIGNIFIED
...ARE YOU OKAY?
WHY WOULD I NOT BE?

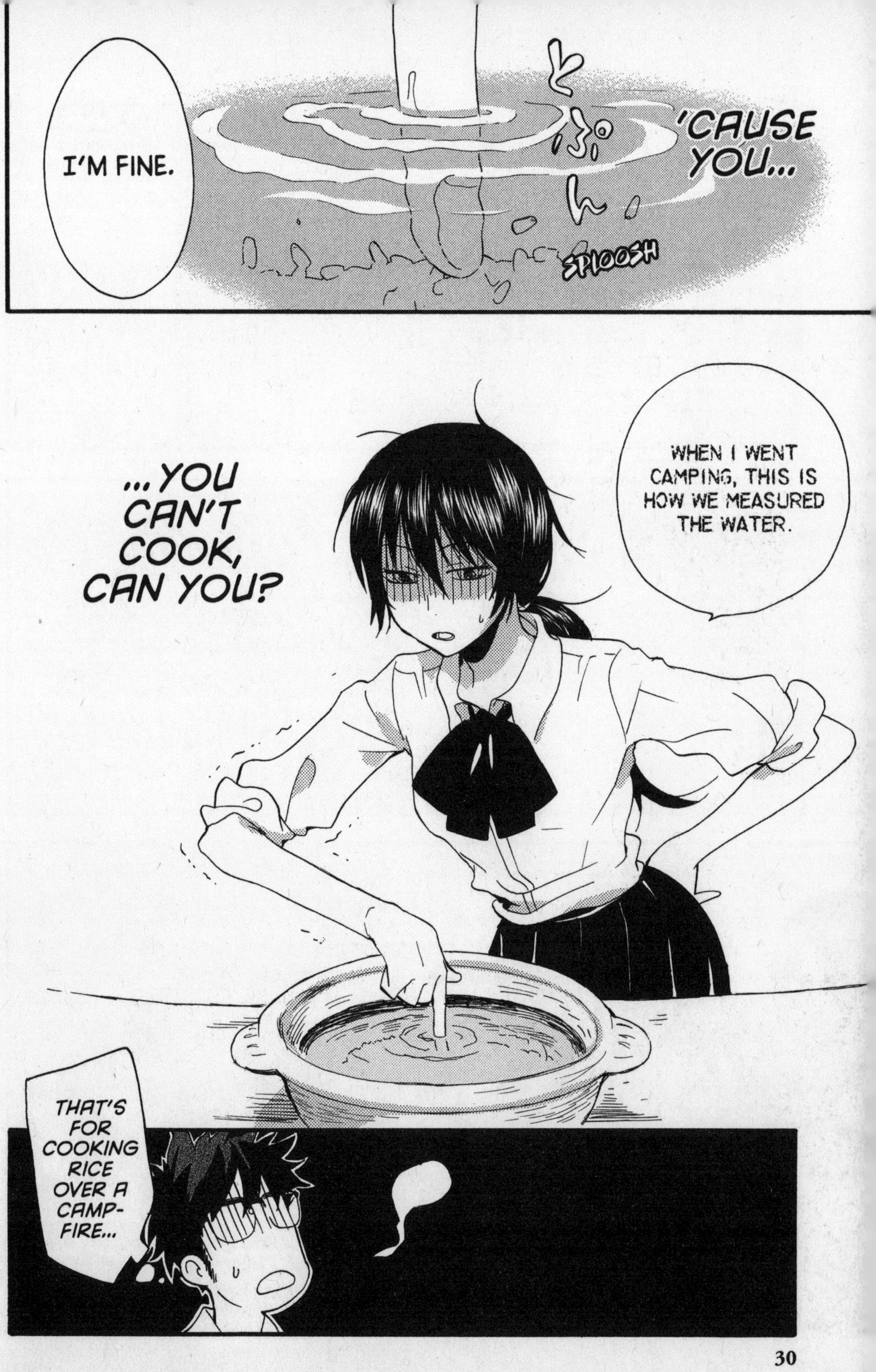
'CAUSE YOU...
とぷん
SPLOOSH
I'M FINE.
WHEN I WENT CAMPING, THIS IS HOW WE MEASURED THE WATER.
...YOU CAN'T COOK, CAN YOU?
THAT'S FOR COOKING RICE OVER A CAMP-FIRE...

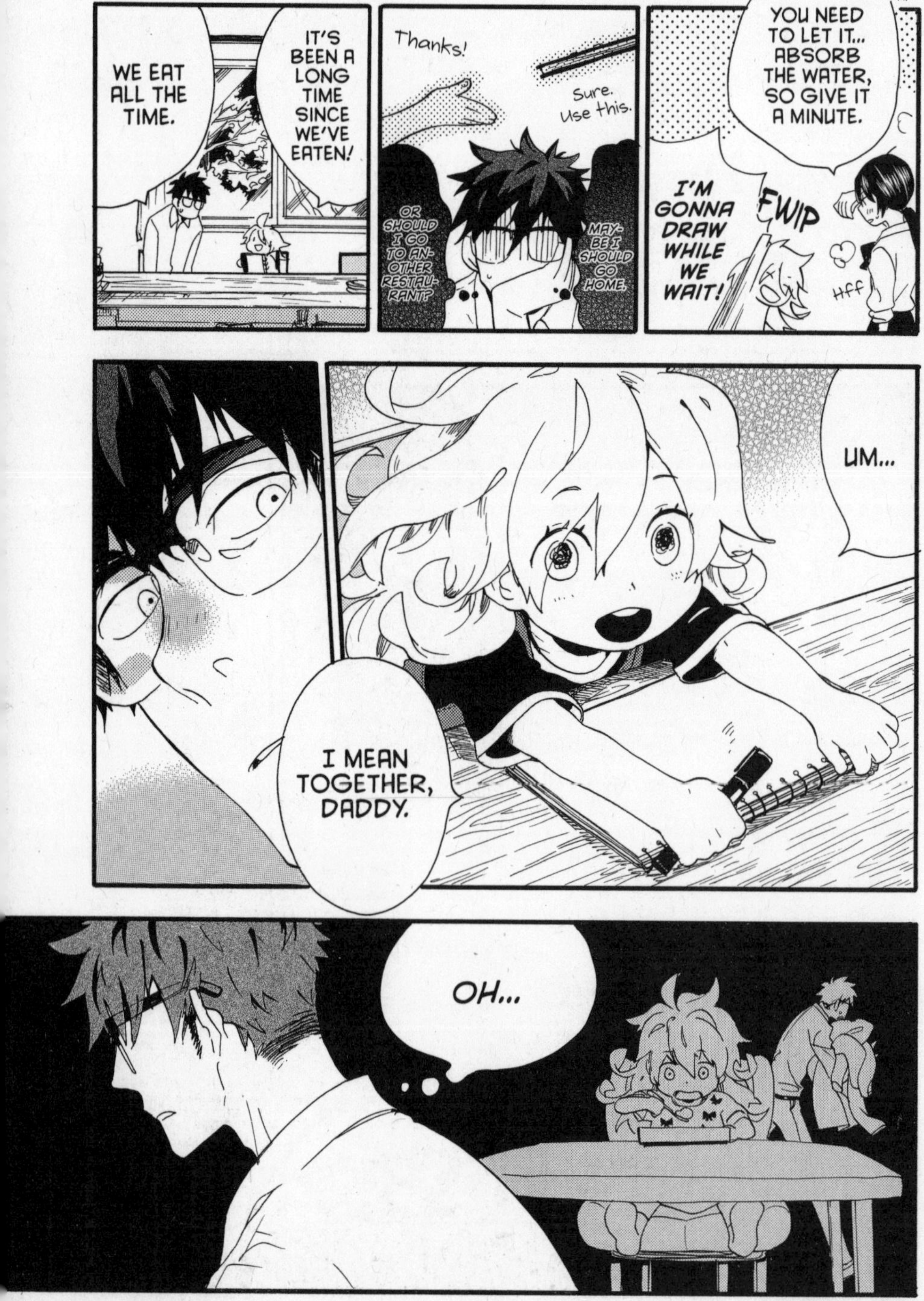
Uhhh...
YOU NEED TO LET IT... ABSORB THE WATER, SO GIVE IT A MINUTE.
FWIP
I'M GONNA DRAW WHILE WE WAIT!
Hff
Thanks!
Sure. Use this.
MAYBE I SHOULD GO HOME.
OR SHOULD I GO TO ANOTHER RESTAURANT?
IT'S BEEN A LONG TIME SINCE WE'VE EATEN!
WE EAT ALL THE TIME.
UM...
I MEAN TOGETHER, DADDY.
OH...

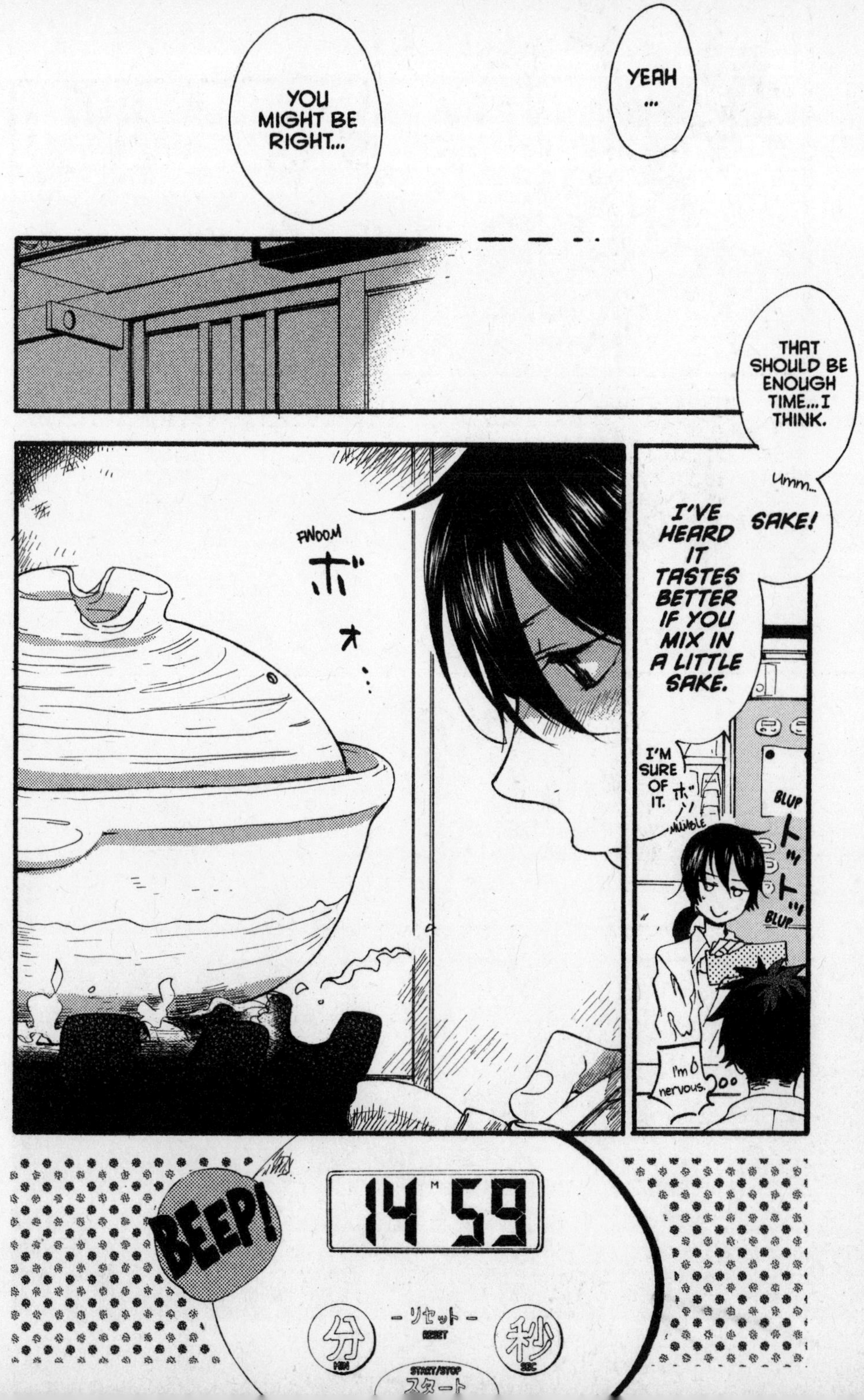
YEAH ...
YOU MIGHT BE RIGHT...
THAT SHOULD BE ENOUGH TIME... I THINK.
Umm... SAKE!
I'VE HEARD IT TASTES BETTER IF YOU MIX IN A LITTLE SAKE.
BLUP
I'M SURE OF IT.
MUMBLE
BLUP
I'm nervous.
FWOOM
ボォ…
BEEP!
14 M 59
− リセット −
RESET
分
MIN
秒
SEC
START/STOP
スタート

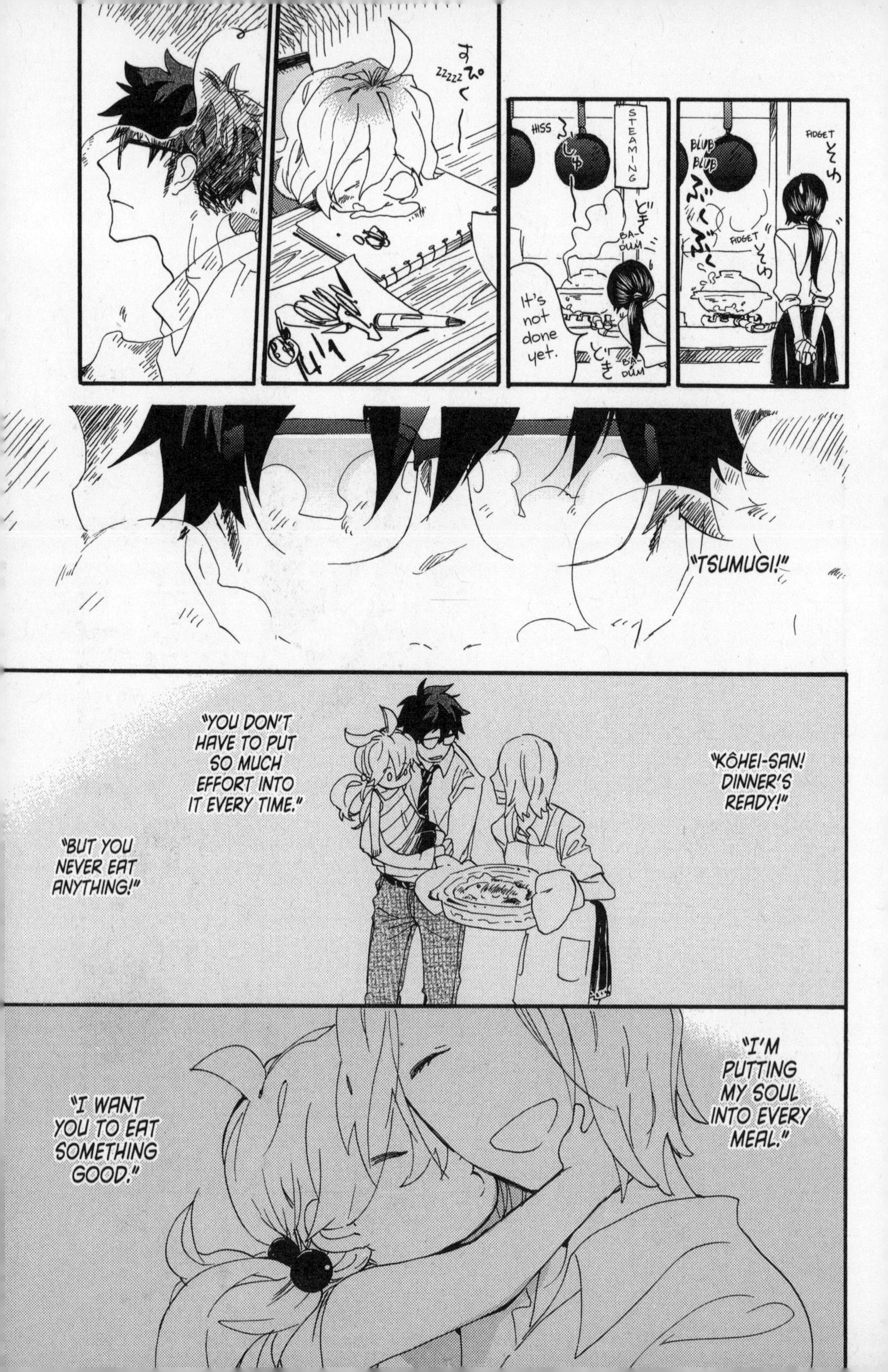
FIDGET そわ
BLUB BLUB
ぶくぶく
FIDGET そわ
STEAMING
HISS ふしゅ〜
どき BA-DUM
It's not done yet.
どき BA-DUM
すぴ〜
zzzzz
"TSUMUGI!"
"KÔHEI-SAN! DINNER'S READY!"
"YOU DON'T HAVE TO PUT SO MUCH EFFORT INTO IT EVERY TIME."
"BUT YOU NEVER EAT ANYTHING!"
"I'M PUTTING MY SOUL INTO EVERY MEAL."
"I WANT YOU TO EAT SOMETHING GOOD."

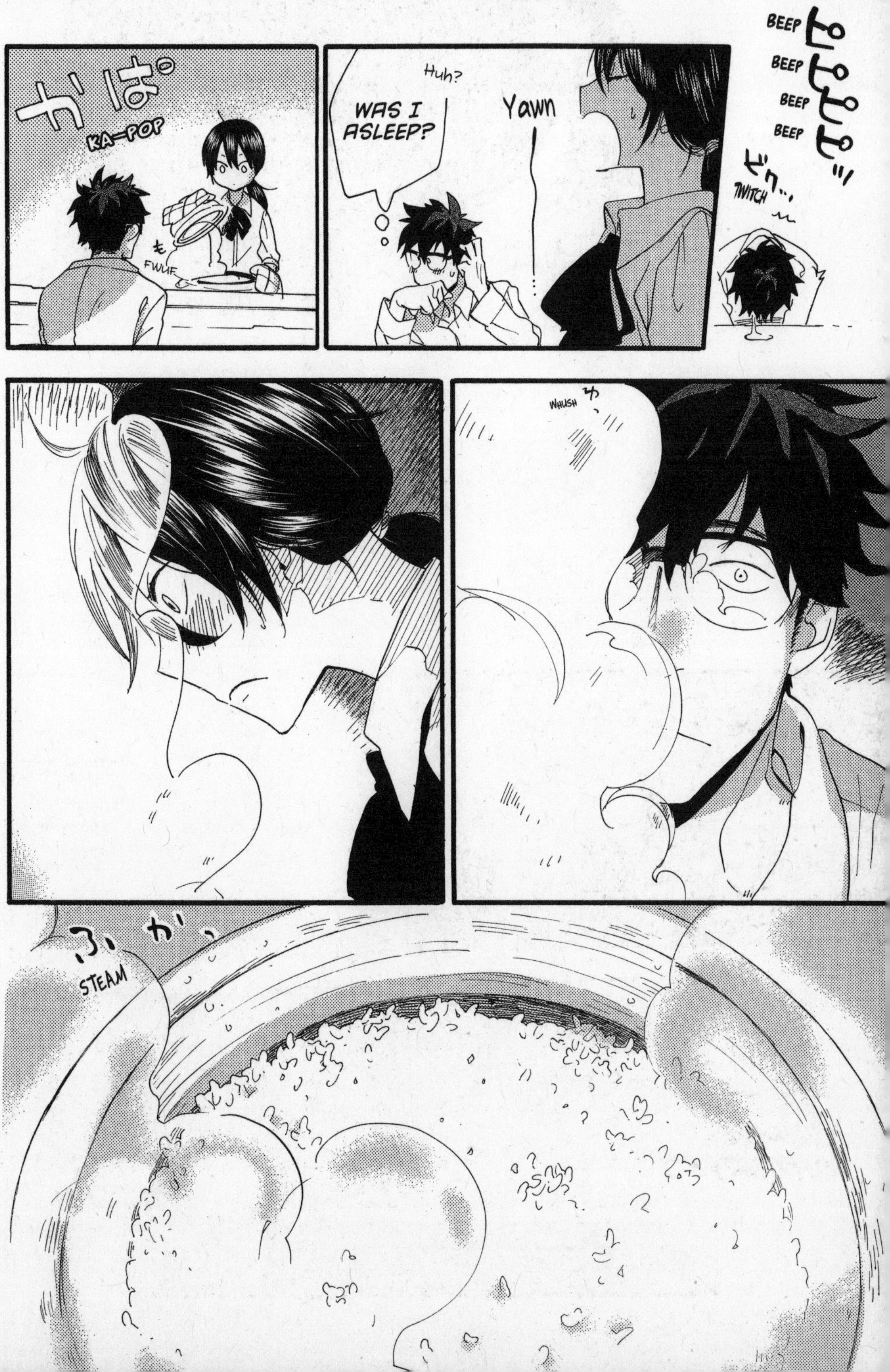

BEEP BEEP BEEP BEEP
TWITCH
Yawn
Huh?
WAS I ASLEEP?
KA-POP
FWUF
WHUSH
STEAM

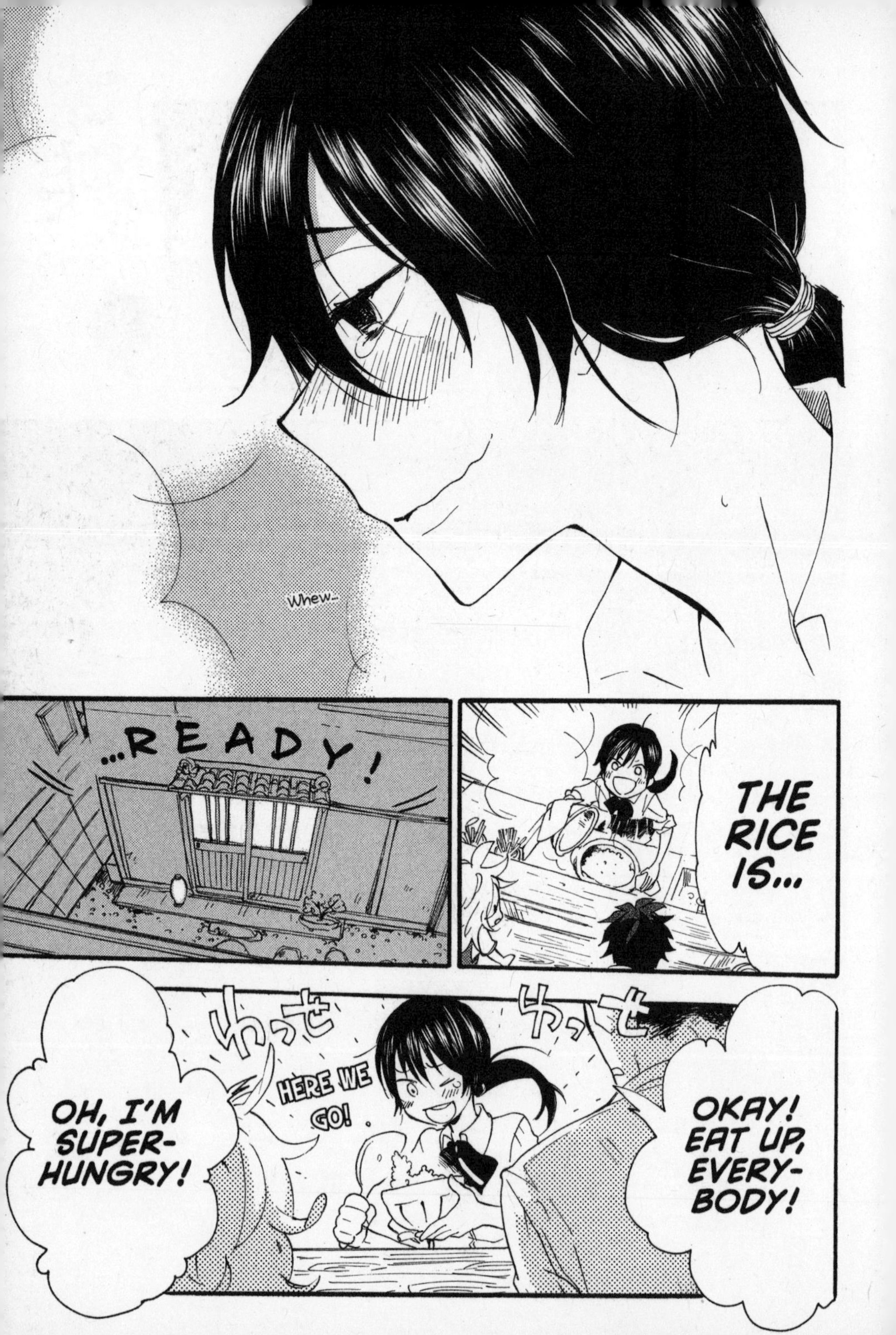
Whew...
THE RICE IS...
...READY!
OKAY! EAT UP, EVERY-BODY!
やっせ
わっせ
HERE WE GO!
OH, I'M SUPER-HUNGRY!

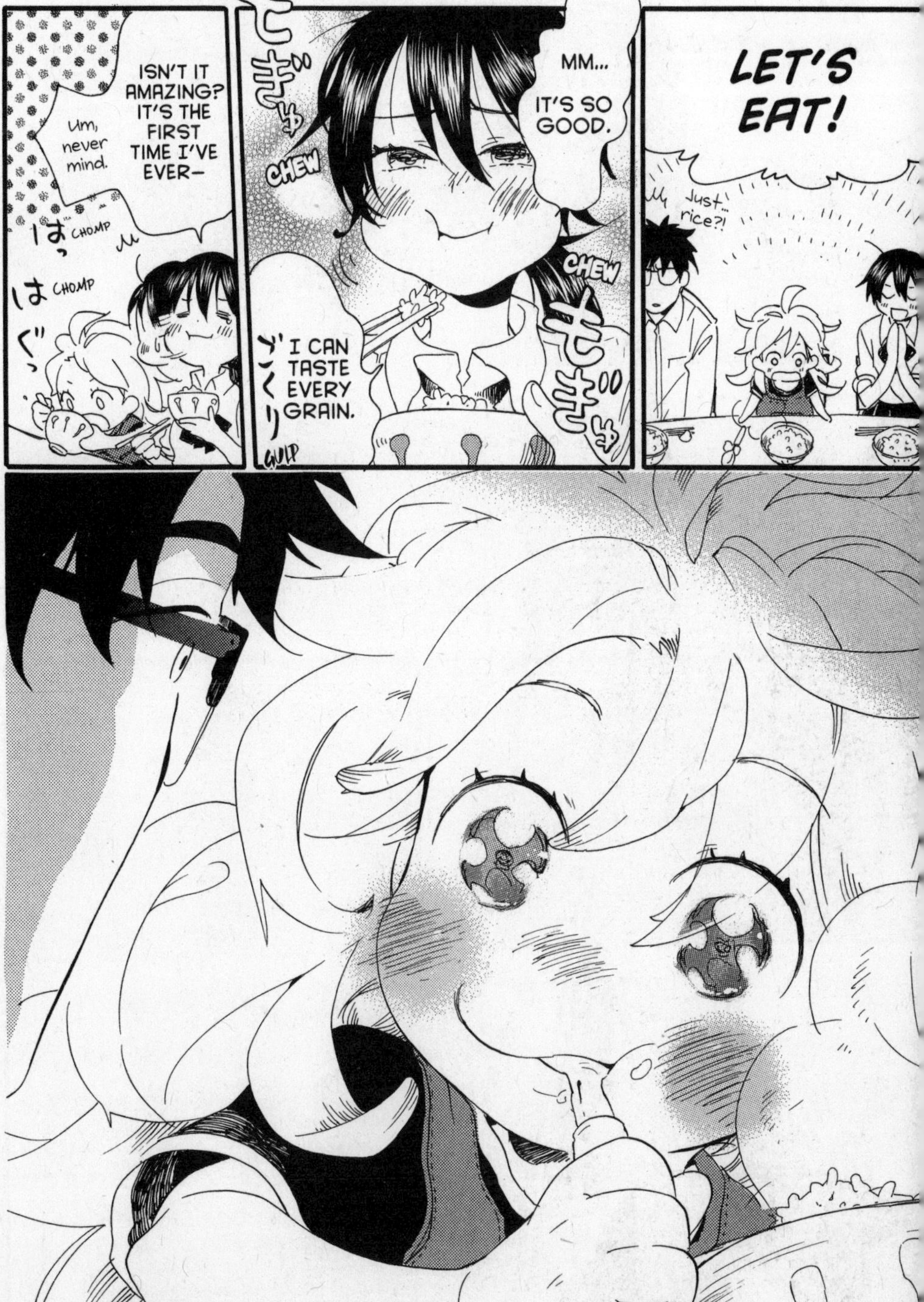
LET'S EAT!
Just... rice?!
MM... IT'S SO GOOD.
もぎゅ
CHEW
もぎゅ
CHEW
I CAN TASTE EVERY GRAIN.
ゴくり
GULP
ISN'T IT AMAZING? IT'S THE FIRST TIME I'VE EVER—
Um, never mind.
はっ
CHOMP
はぐっ
CHOMP

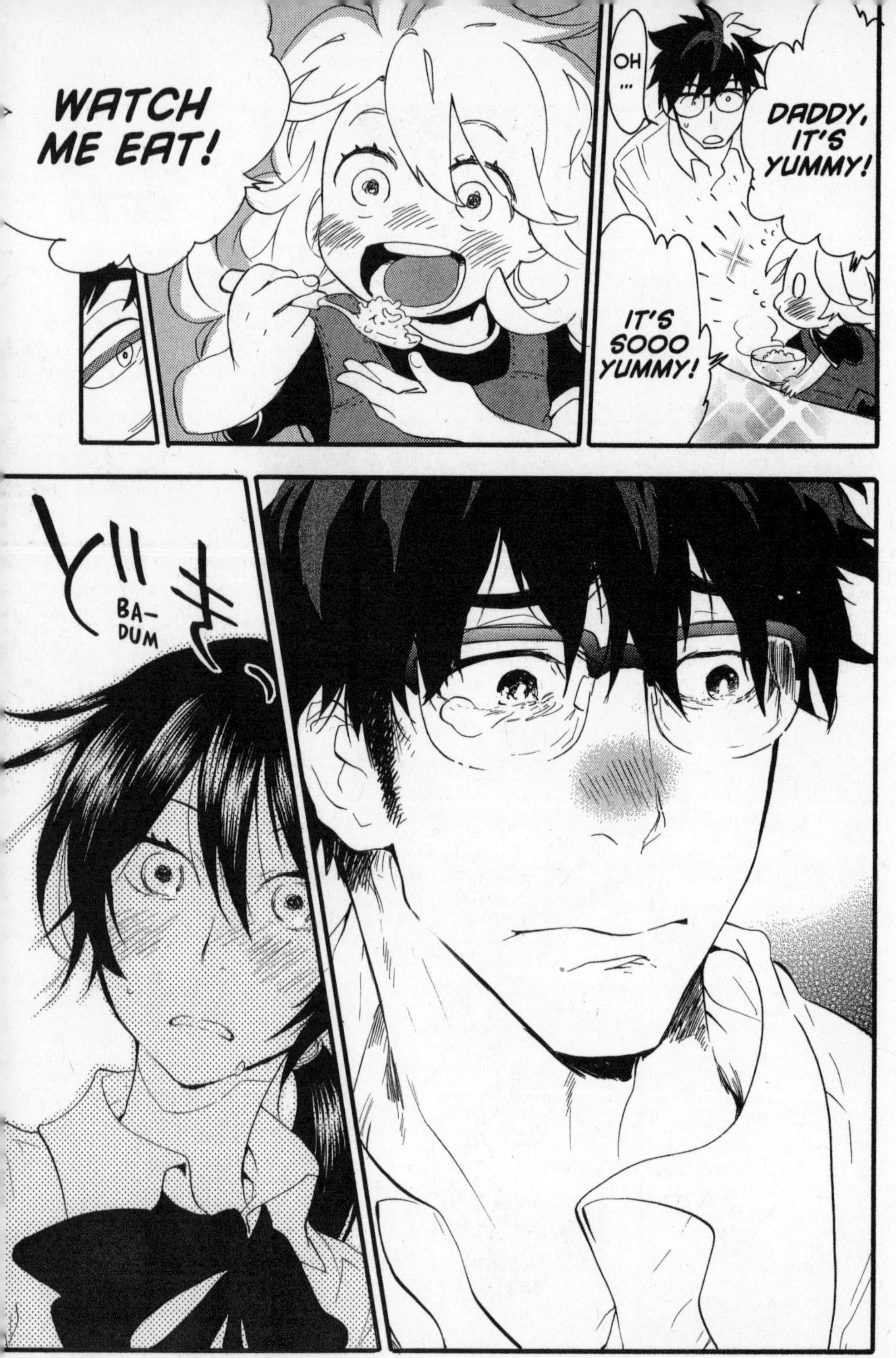
DADDY, IT'S YUMMY!
OH ...
IT'S SOOO YUMMY!
WATCH ME EAT!
BA-DUM

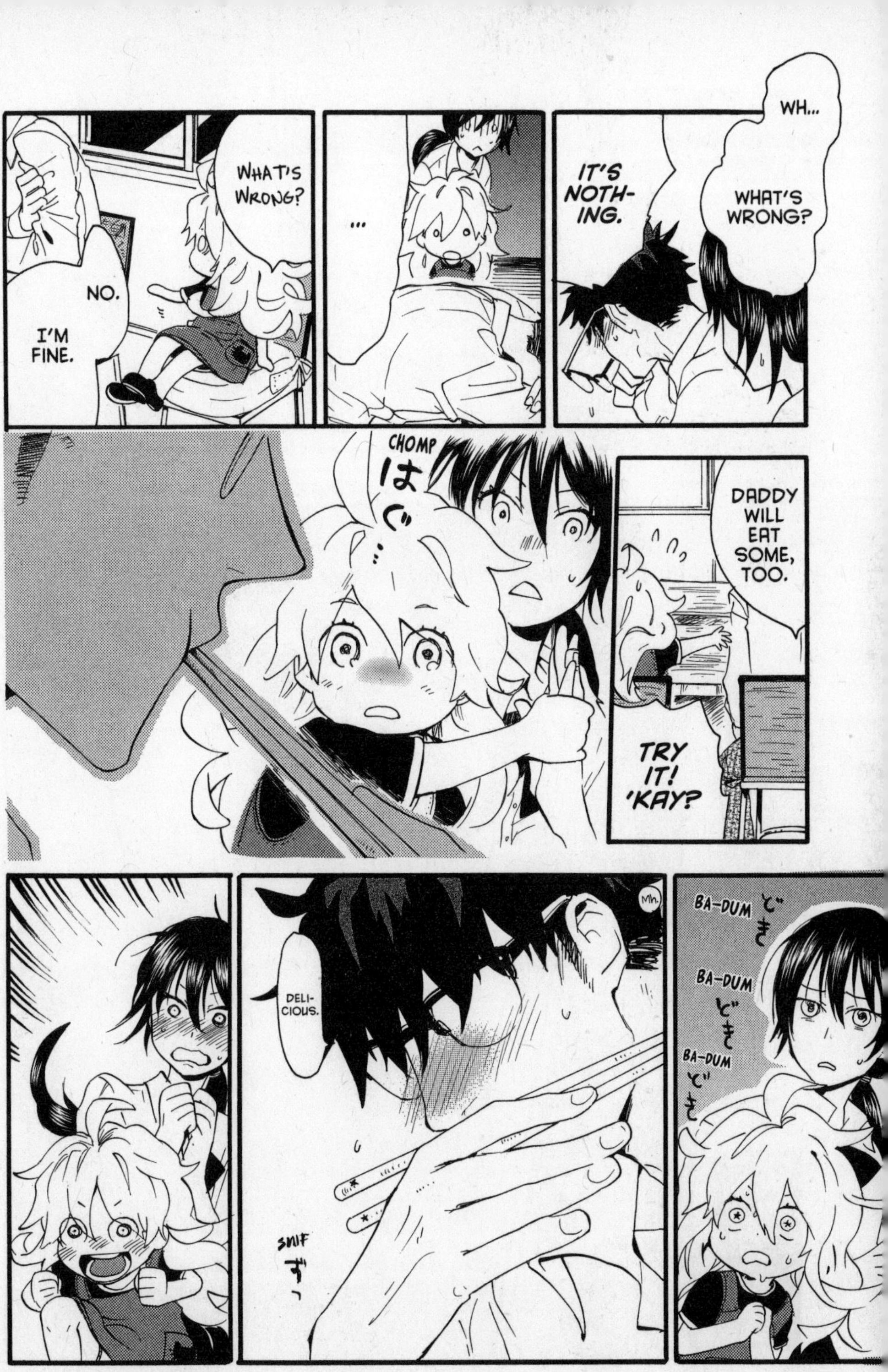
WH...
WHAT'S WRONG?
IT'S NOTH-ING.
...
WHAT'S WRONG?
NO.
I'M FINE.
DADDY WILL EAT SOME, TOO.
TRY IT! 'KAY?
CHOMP
はぐ…
BA-DUM どき
BA-DUM どき
BA-DUM どき
Mh.
DELI-CIOUS.
SNIF
ずっ

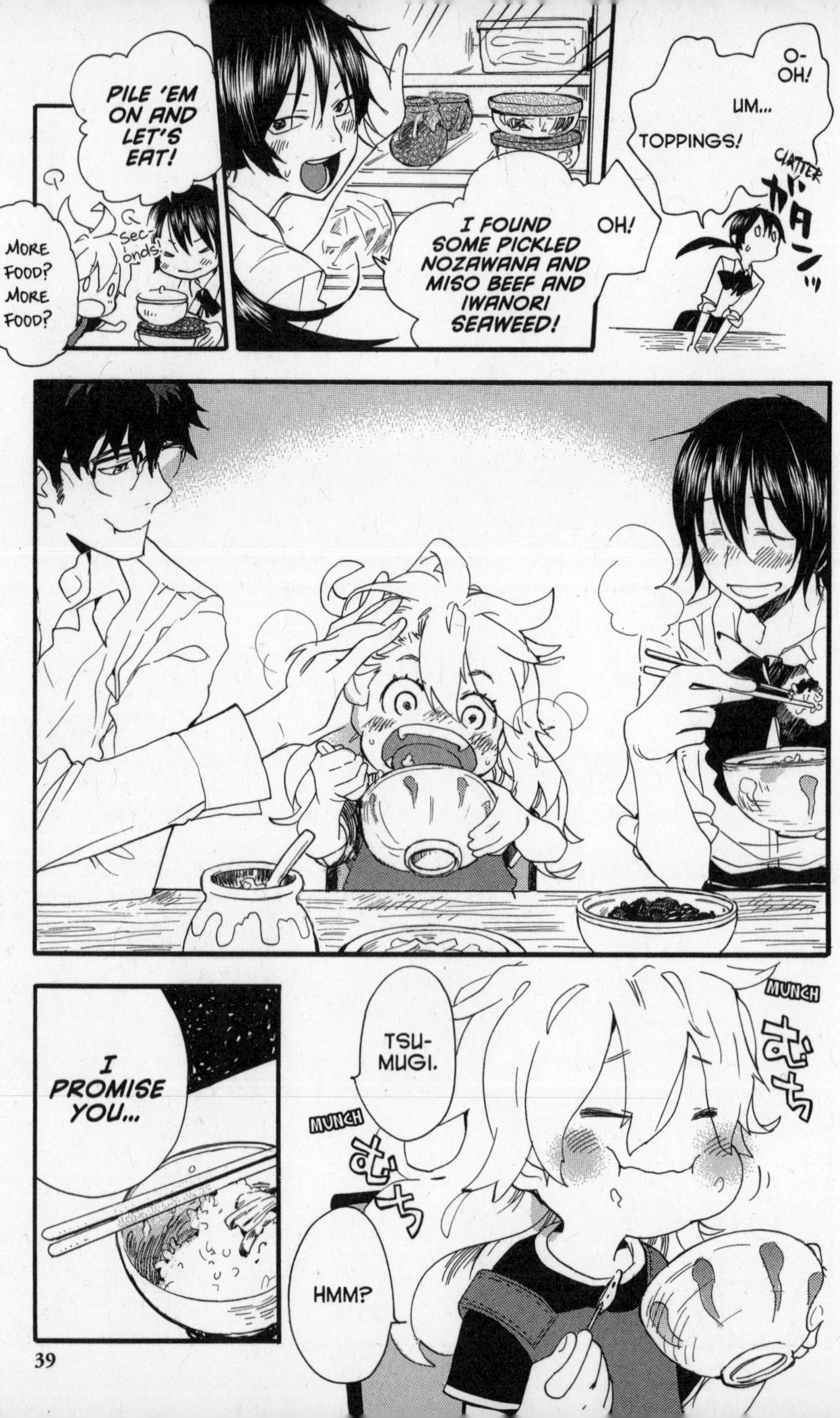
O-OH!
UM...
TOPPINGS!
CLATTER
OH!
I FOUND SOME PICKLED NOZAWANA AND MISO BEEF AND IWANORI SEAWEED!
PILE 'EM ON AND LET'S EAT!
Sec-onds!
MORE FOOD? MORE FOOD?
MUNCH
TSU-MUGI.
MUNCH
HMM?
I PROMISE YOU...

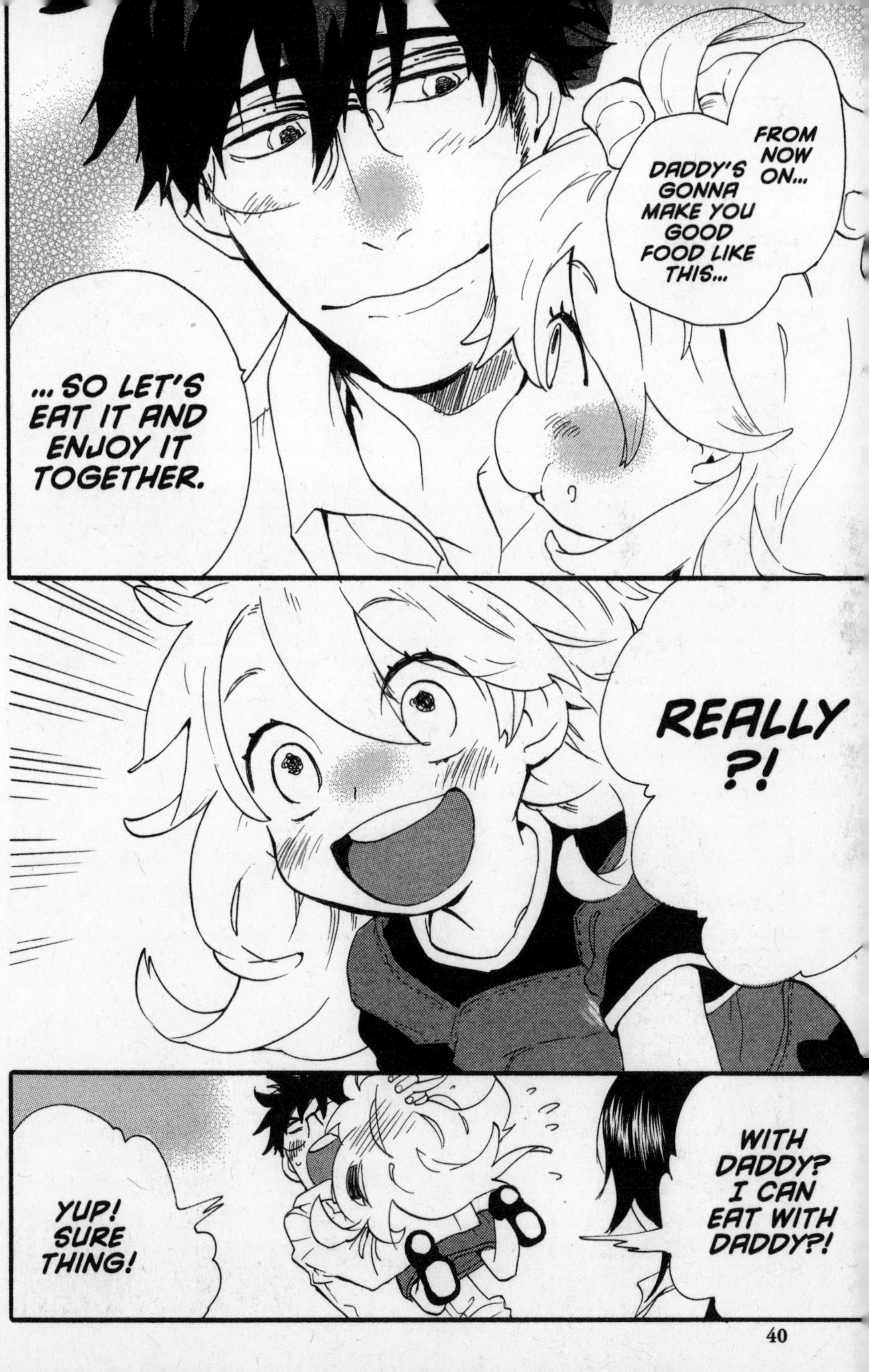
FROM NOW ON... DADDY'S GONNA MAKE YOU GOOD FOOD LIKE THIS...
...SO LET'S EAT IT AND ENJOY IT TOGETHER.
REALLY ?!
WITH DADDY? I CAN EAT WITH DADDY?!
YUP! SURE THING!

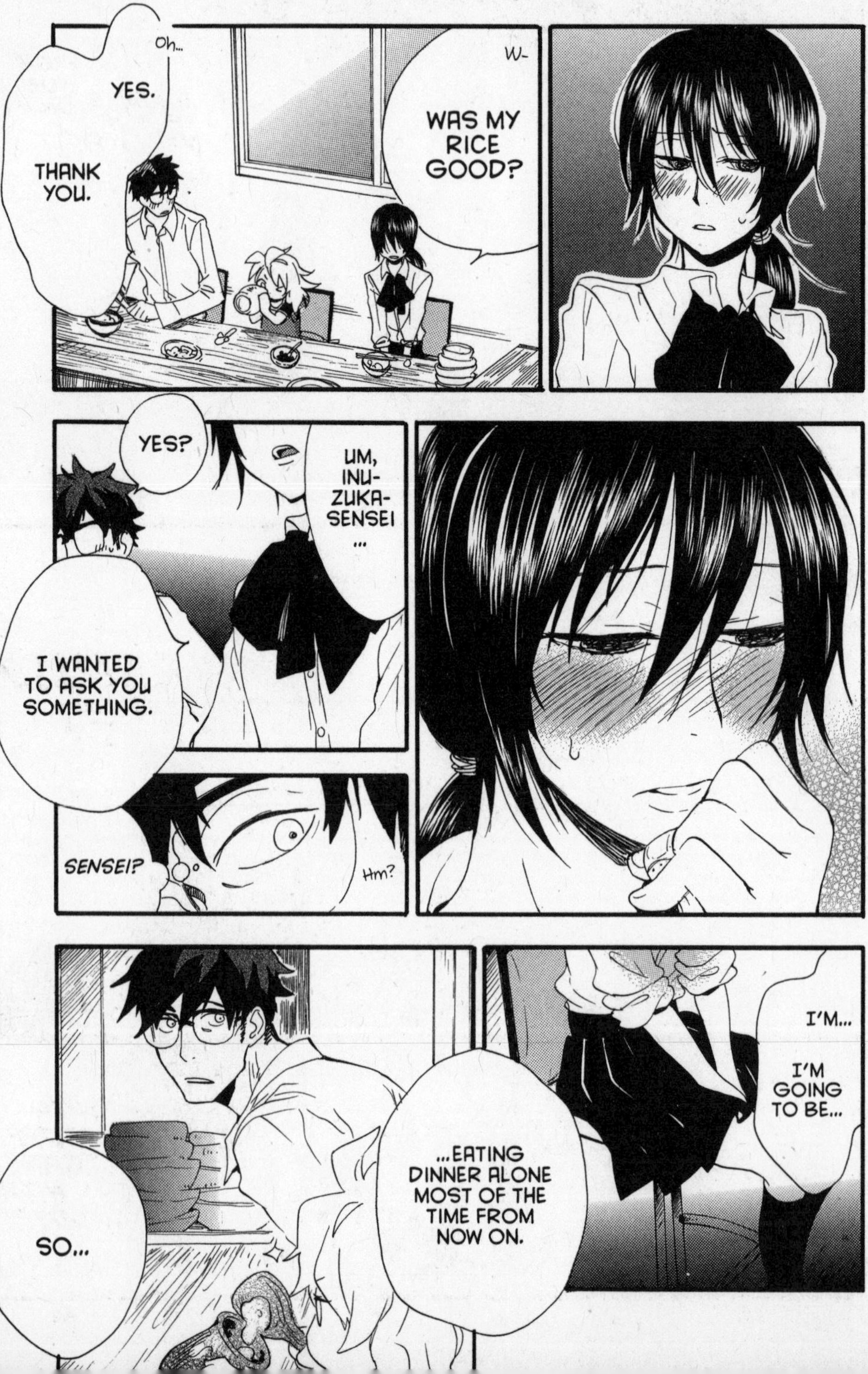
W-
WAS MY RICE GOOD?
Oh...
YES.
THANK YOU.
UM, INUZUKA-SENSEI ...
YES?
I WANTED TO ASK YOU SOMETHING.
Hm?
SENSEI?
I'M...
I'M GOING TO BE...
...EATING DINNER ALONE MOST OF THE TIME FROM NOW ON.
SO...

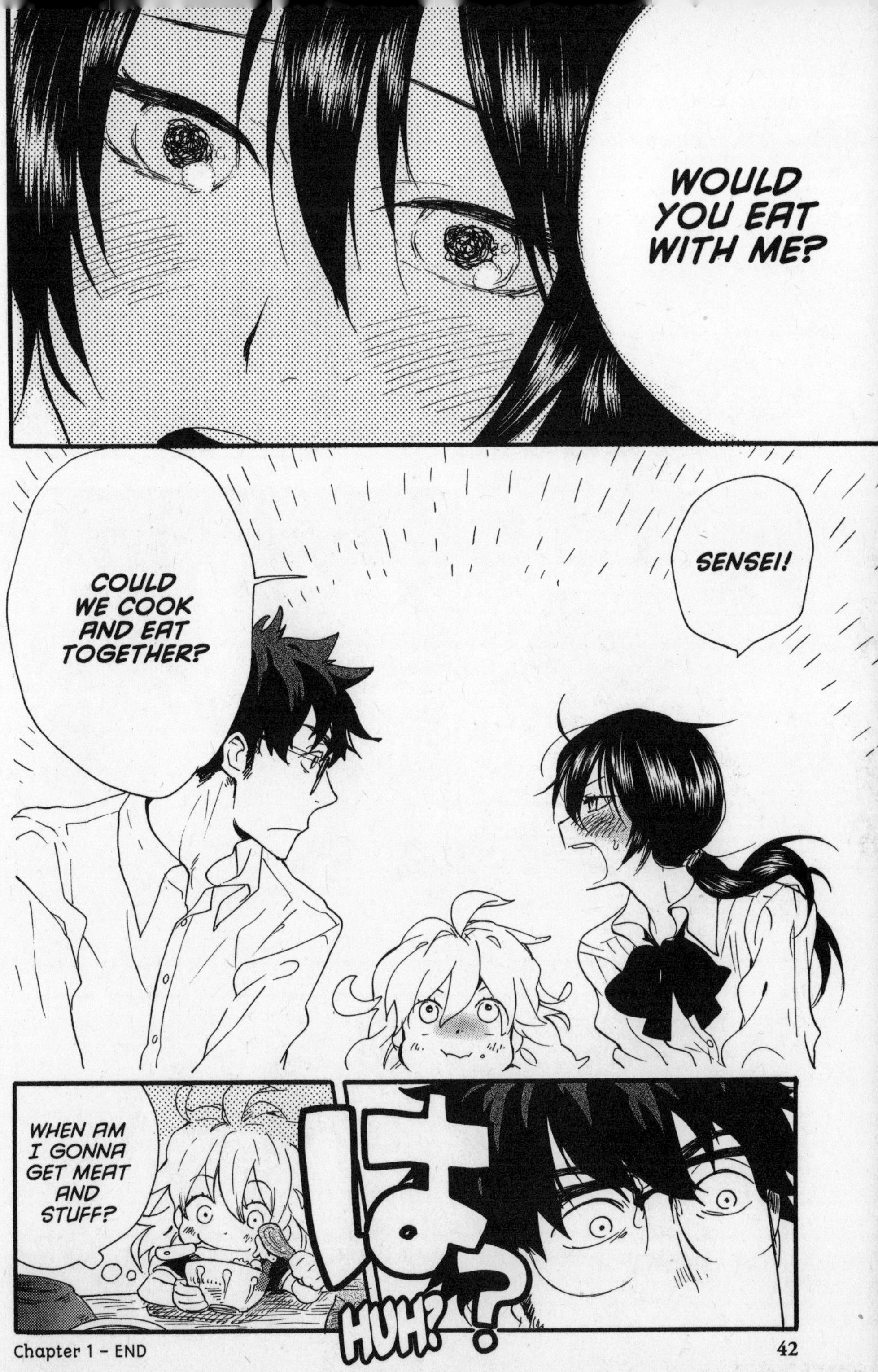
WOULD YOU EAT WITH ME?
SENSEI!
COULD WE COOK AND EAT TOGETHER?
は?
HUH?
WHEN AM I GONNA GET MEAT AND STUFF?

Chapter 1 - END

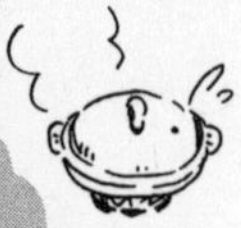

DONABE RICE

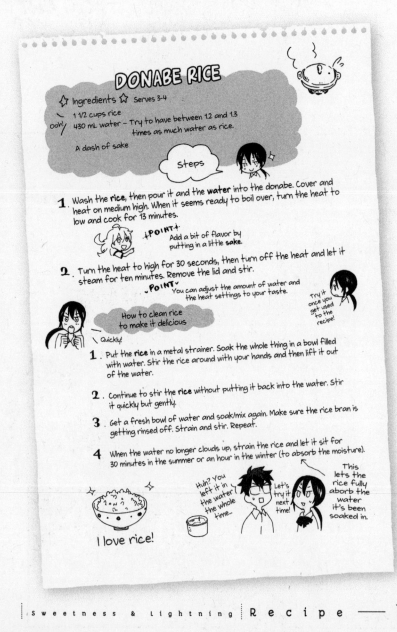

☆ Ingredients ☆ Serves 3-4

1 1/2 cups rice

430 mL water – Try to have between 1.2 and 1.3 times as much water as rice.

A dash of sake

Ooh!

Steps

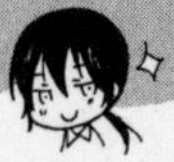

1. Wash the **rice**, then pour it and the **water** into the donabe. Cover and heat on medium high. When it seems ready to boil over, turn the heat to low and cook for 13 minutes.

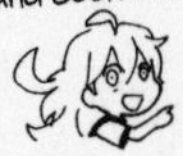

POINT: Add a bit of flavor by putting in a little **sake**.

2. Turn the heat to high for 30 seconds, then turn off the heat and let it steam for ten minutes. Remove the lid and stir.

POINT: You can adjust the amount of water and the heat settings to your taste.

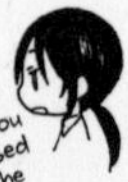
Try it once you get used to the recipe!

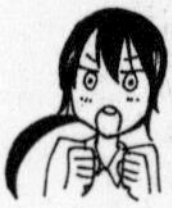
Quickly!

How to clean rice to make it delicious

1. Put the **rice** in a metal strainer. Soak the whole thing in a bowl filled with water. Stir the rice around with your hands and then lift it out of the water.
2. Continue to stir the **rice** without putting it back into the water. Stir it quickly but gently.
3. Get a fresh bowl of water and soak/mix again. Make sure the rice bran is getting rinsed off. Strain and stir. Repeat.
4. When the water no longer clouds up, strain the rice and let it sit for 30 minutes in the summer or an hour in the winter (to absorb the moisture).

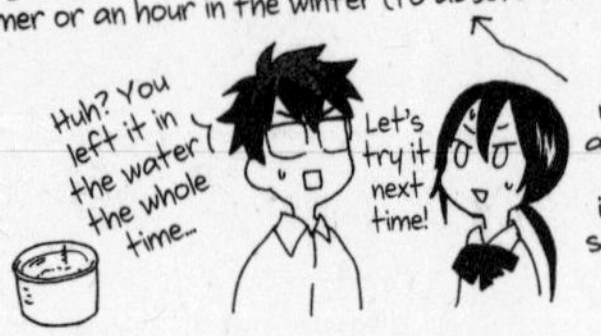
This lets the rice fully aborb the water it's been soaked in.
Let's try it next time!
Huh? You left it in the water the whole time...

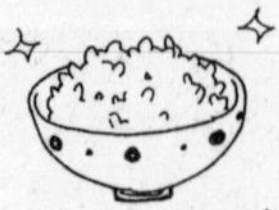

I love rice!

CONVERSION NOTES:
430 ML WATER = ABOUT 1 3/4 CUPS

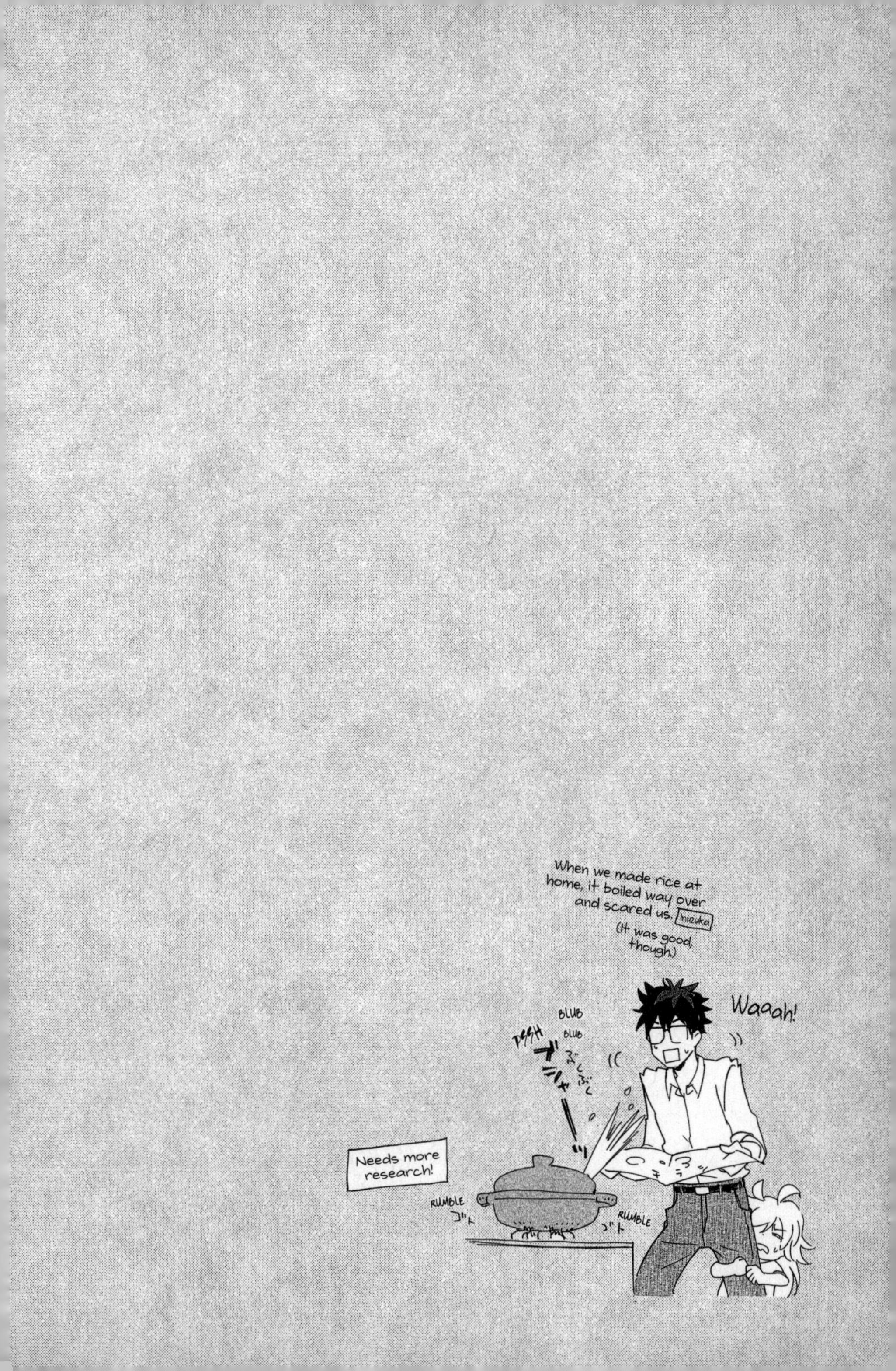
When we made rice at home, it boiled way over and scared us. Inuzuka
(It was good, though.)
Waaah!
BLUB BLUB
DSSSH
RUMBLE
RUMBLE
Needs more research!

Chapter 2 | Pork Miso Soup and Restaurant Lights

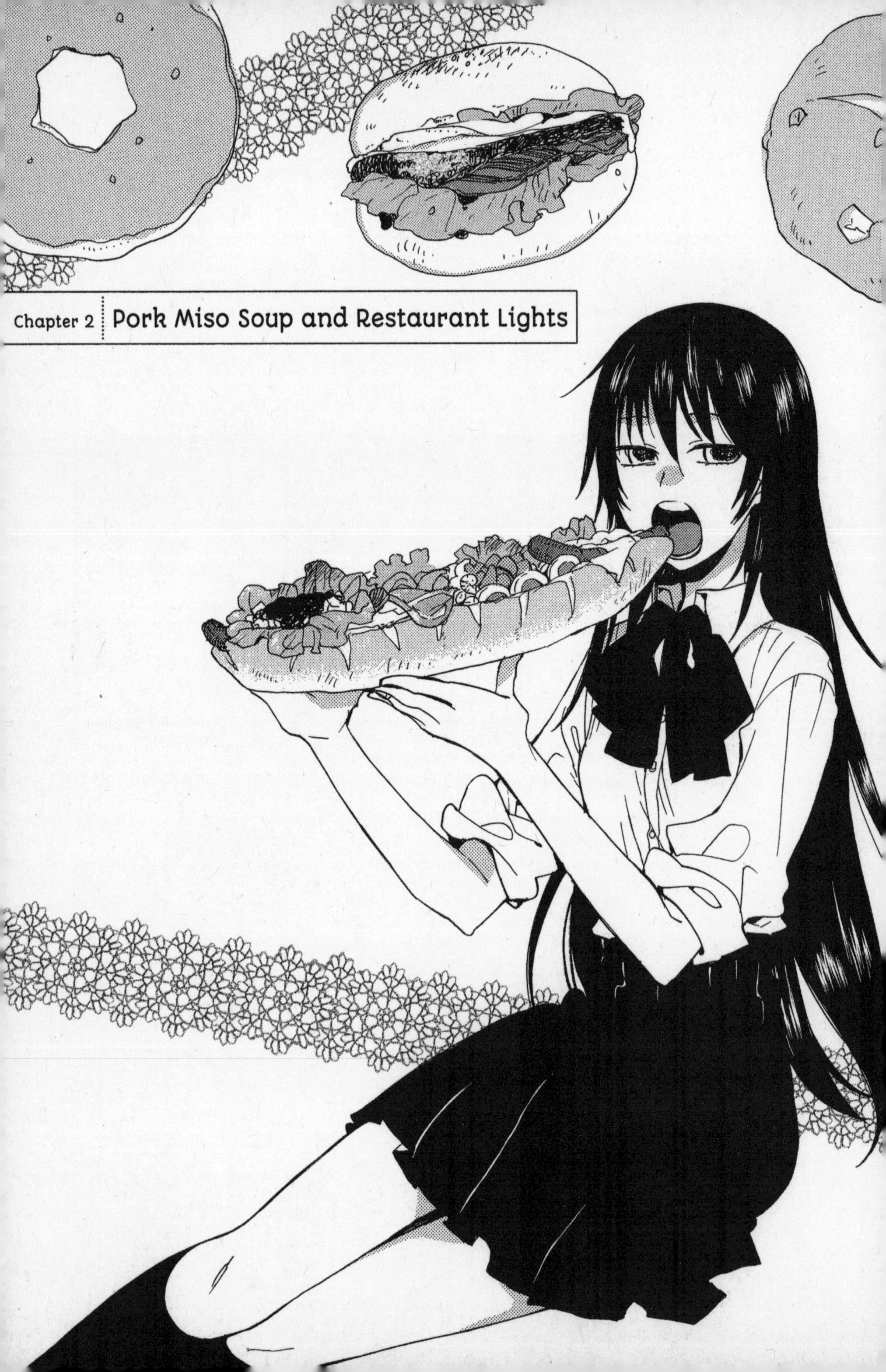

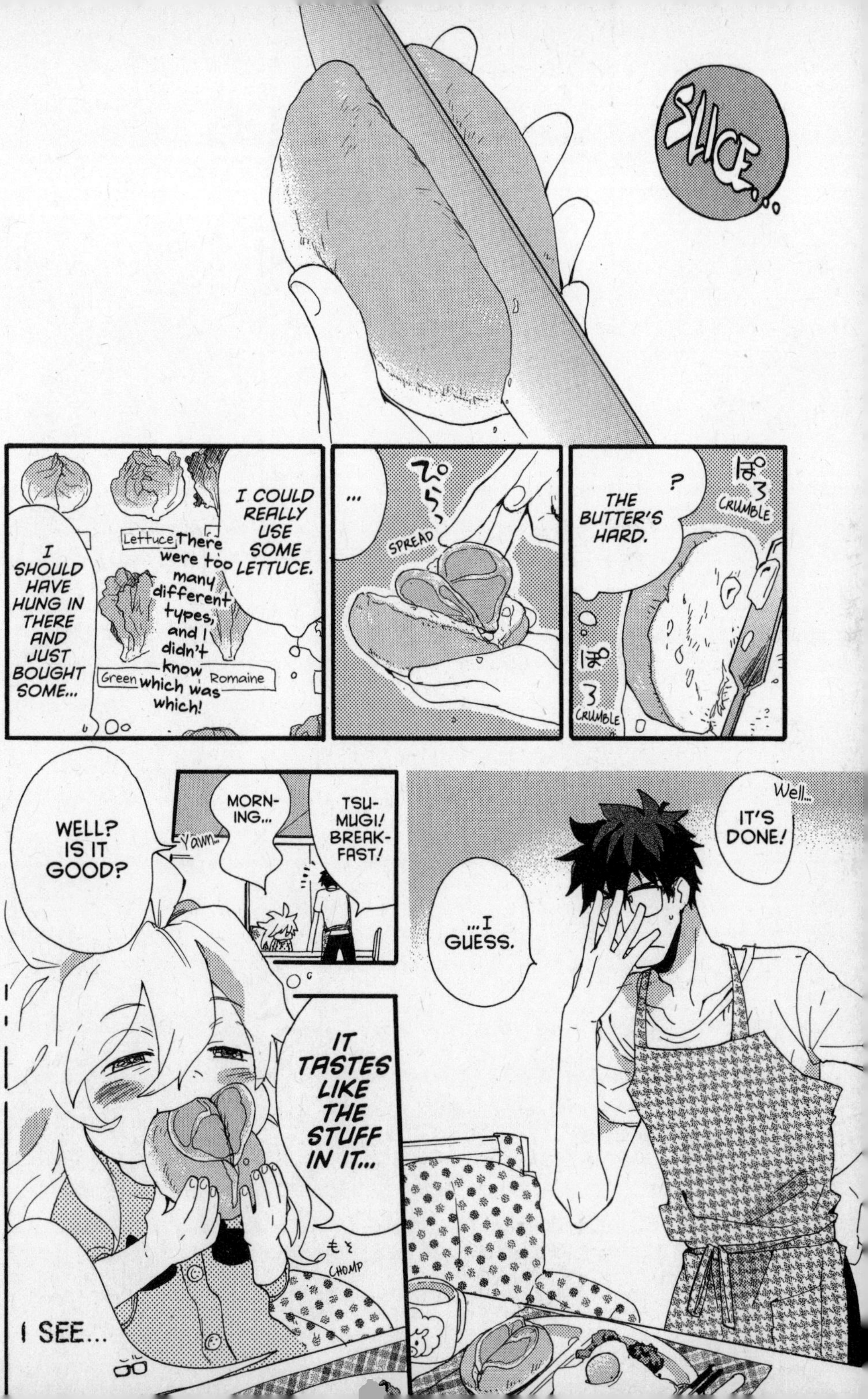
SLICE...
?
THE BUTTER'S HARD.
ぽろ
CRUMBLE
ぽろ
CRUMBLE
...
ぴらっ
SPREAD
I COULD REALLY USE SOME LETTUCE.
There were too many different types, and I didn't know which was which!
Lettuce
Green
Romaine
I SHOULD HAVE HUNG IN THERE AND JUST BOUGHT SOME...
Well...
IT'S DONE!
...I GUESS.
TSUMUGI! BREAKFAST!
MORNING...
Yawn...
WELL? IS IT GOOD?
IT TASTES LIKE THE STUFF IN IT...
CHOMP
I SEE...

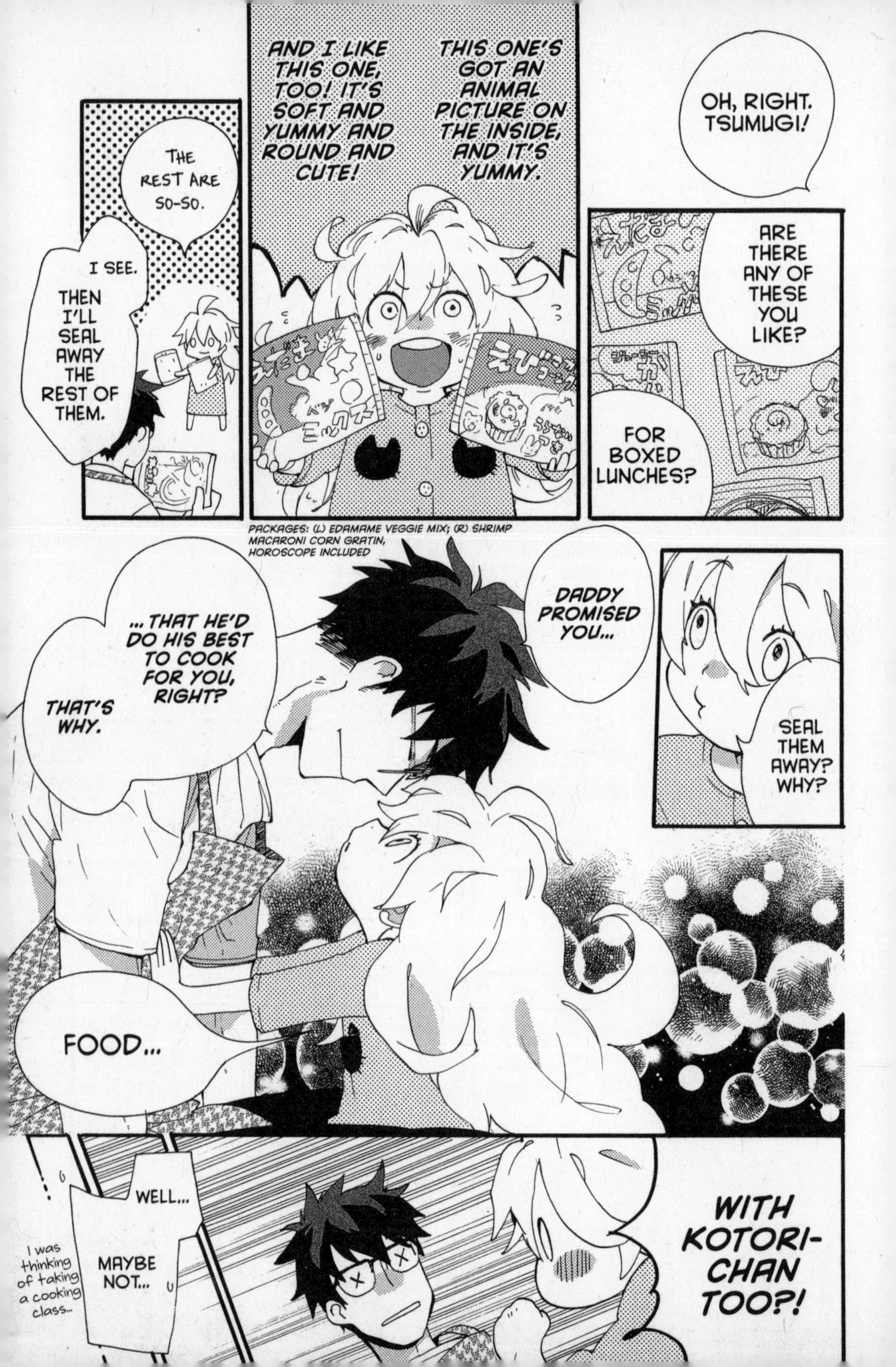
OH, RIGHT. TSUMUGI!
ARE THERE ANY OF THESE YOU LIKE?
FOR BOXED LUNCHES?
THIS ONE'S GOT AN ANIMAL PICTURE ON THE INSIDE, AND IT'S YUMMY.
AND I LIKE THIS ONE, TOO! IT'S SOFT AND YUMMY AND ROUND AND CUTE!
THE REST ARE SO-SO.
I SEE.
THEN I'LL SEAL AWAY THE REST OF THEM.
PACKAGES: (L) EDAMAME VEGGIE MIX; (R) SHRIMP MACARONI CORN GRATIN, HOROSCOPE INCLUDED
SEAL THEM AWAY? WHY?
DADDY PROMISED YOU...
...THAT HE'D DO HIS BEST TO COOK FOR YOU, RIGHT?
THAT'S WHY.
FOOD...
WITH KOTORI-CHAN TOO?!
WELL...
MAYBE NOT...
I was thinking of taking a cooking class...

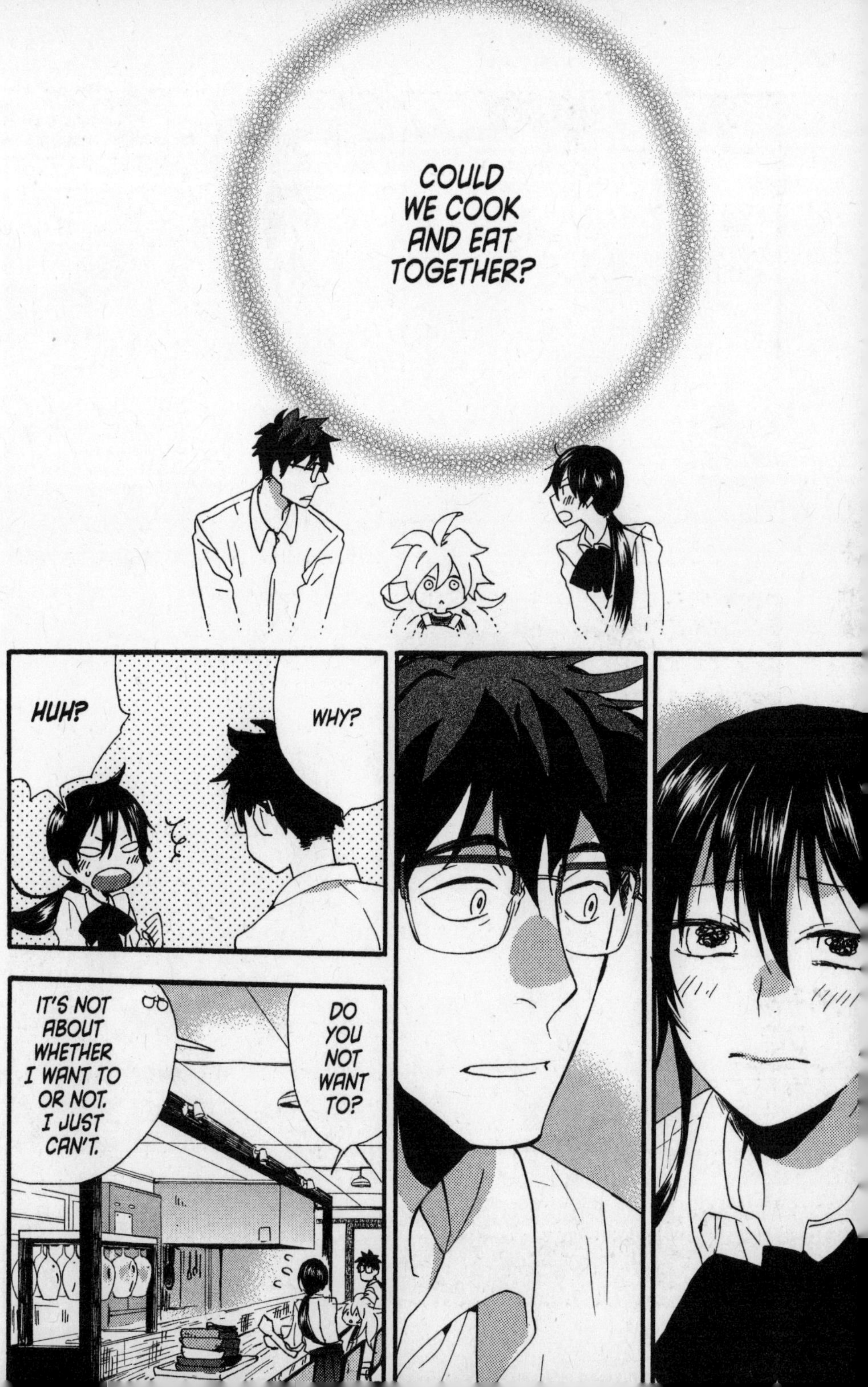
COULD WE COOK AND EAT TOGETHER?
WHY?
HUH?
DO YOU NOT WANT TO?
IT'S NOT ABOUT WHETHER I WANT TO OR NOT. I JUST CAN'T.

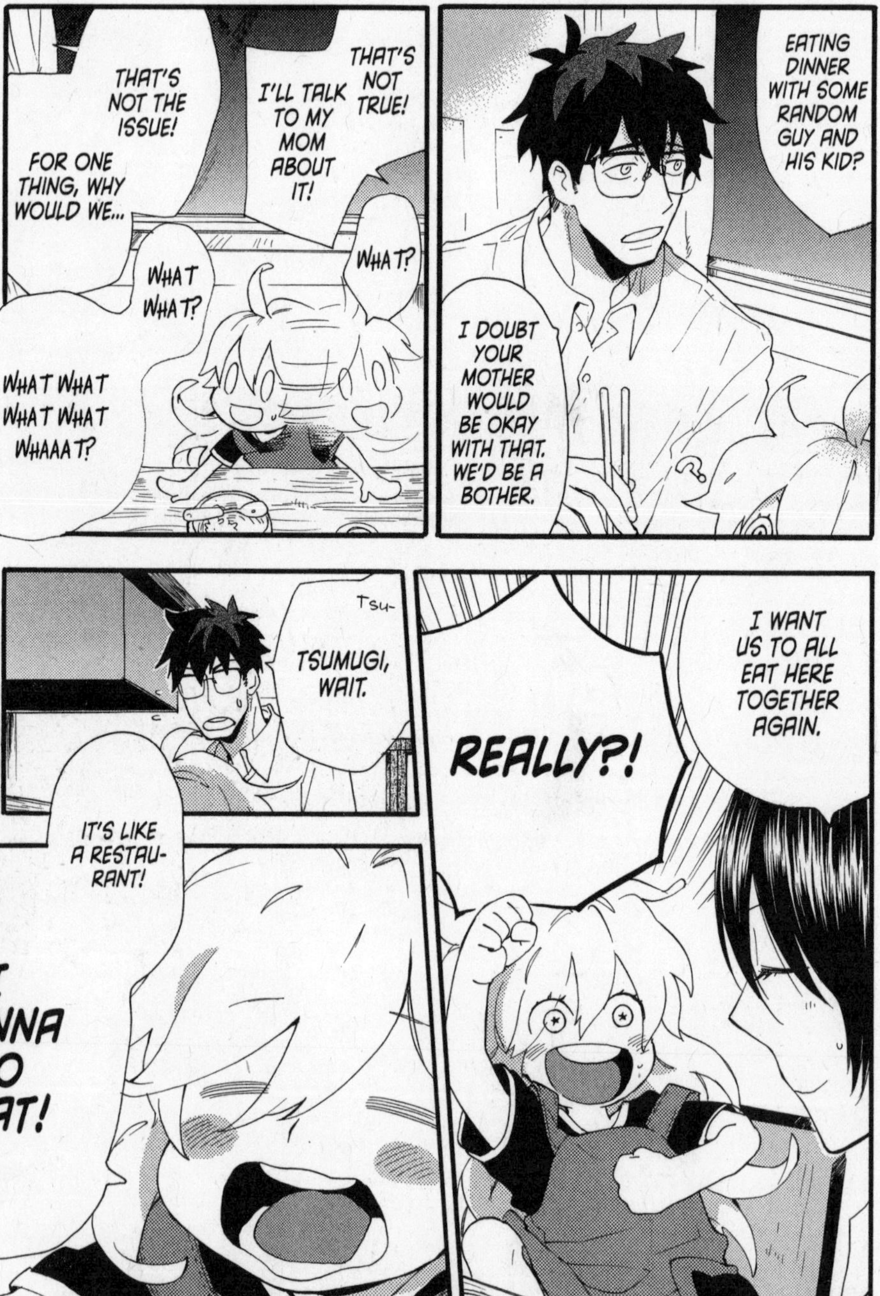
EATING DINNER WITH SOME RANDOM GUY AND HIS KID?
I DOUBT YOUR MOTHER WOULD BE OKAY WITH THAT. WE'D BE A BOTHER.
THAT'S NOT TRUE!
I'LL TALK TO MY MOM ABOUT IT!
THAT'S NOT THE ISSUE!
FOR ONE THING, WHY WOULD WE...
WHAT?
WHAT WHAT?
WHAT WHAT WHAT WHAT WHAAAT?
I WANT US TO ALL EAT HERE TOGETHER AGAIN.
REALLY?!
TSU-
TSUMUGI, WAIT.
IT'S LIKE A RESTAU-RANT!
I WANNA DO THAT!

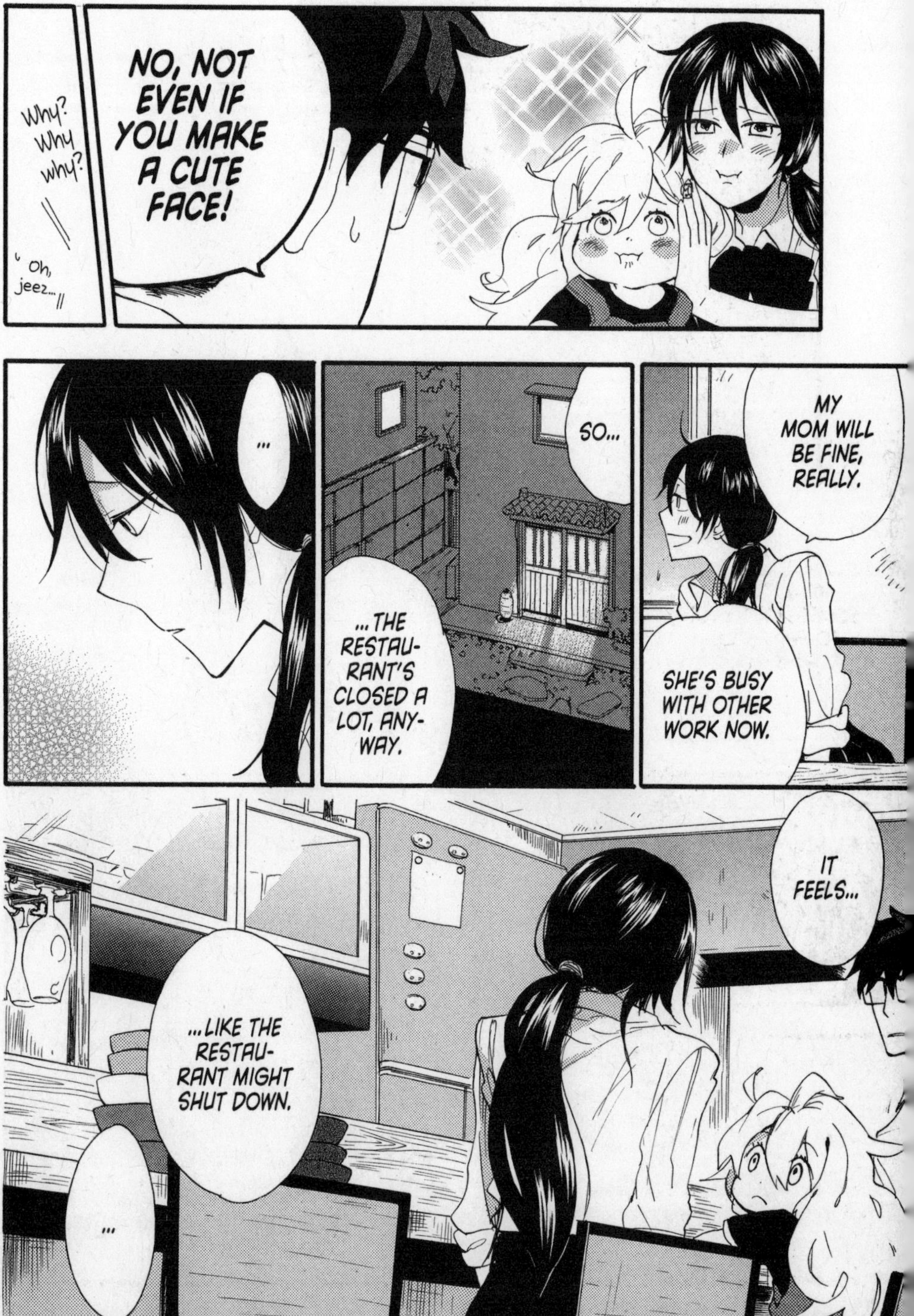
NO, NOT EVEN IF YOU MAKE A CUTE FACE!
Why? Why why?
Oh, jeez...
MY MOM WILL BE FINE, REALLY.
SHE'S BUSY WITH OTHER WORK NOW.
SO...
...THE RESTAU-RANT'S CLOSED A LOT, ANY-WAY.
...
IT FEELS...
...LIKE THE RESTAU-RANT MIGHT SHUT DOWN.
...

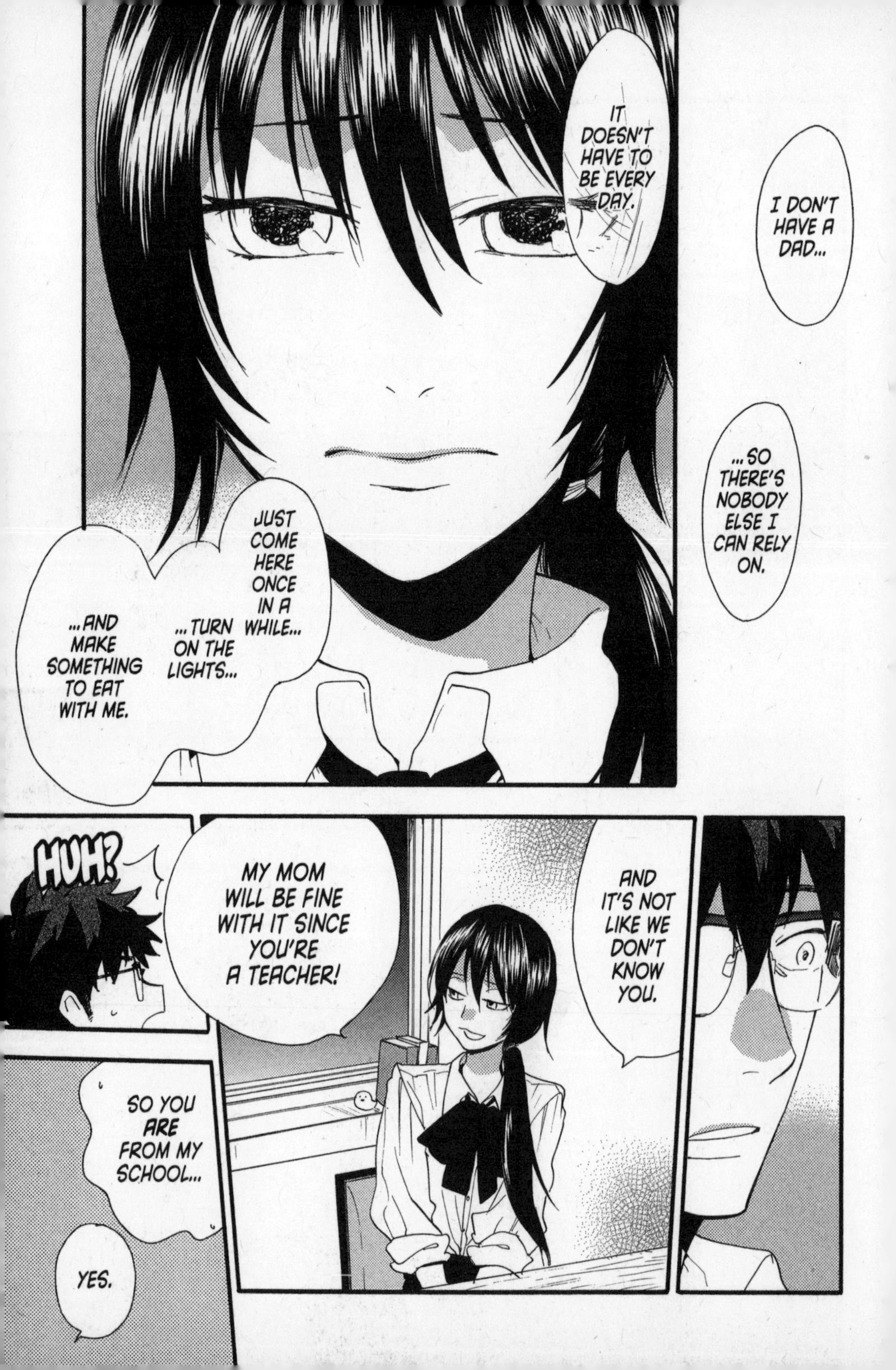
I DON'T HAVE A DAD...
...SO THERE'S NOBODY ELSE I CAN RELY ON.
IT DOESN'T HAVE TO BE EVERY DAY.
JUST COME HERE ONCE IN A WHILE...
...TURN ON THE LIGHTS...
...AND MAKE SOMETHING TO EAT WITH ME.
AND IT'S NOT LIKE WE DON'T KNOW YOU.
MY MOM WILL BE FINE WITH IT SINCE YOU'RE A TEACHER!
HUH?
SO YOU ARE FROM MY SCHOOL...
YES.

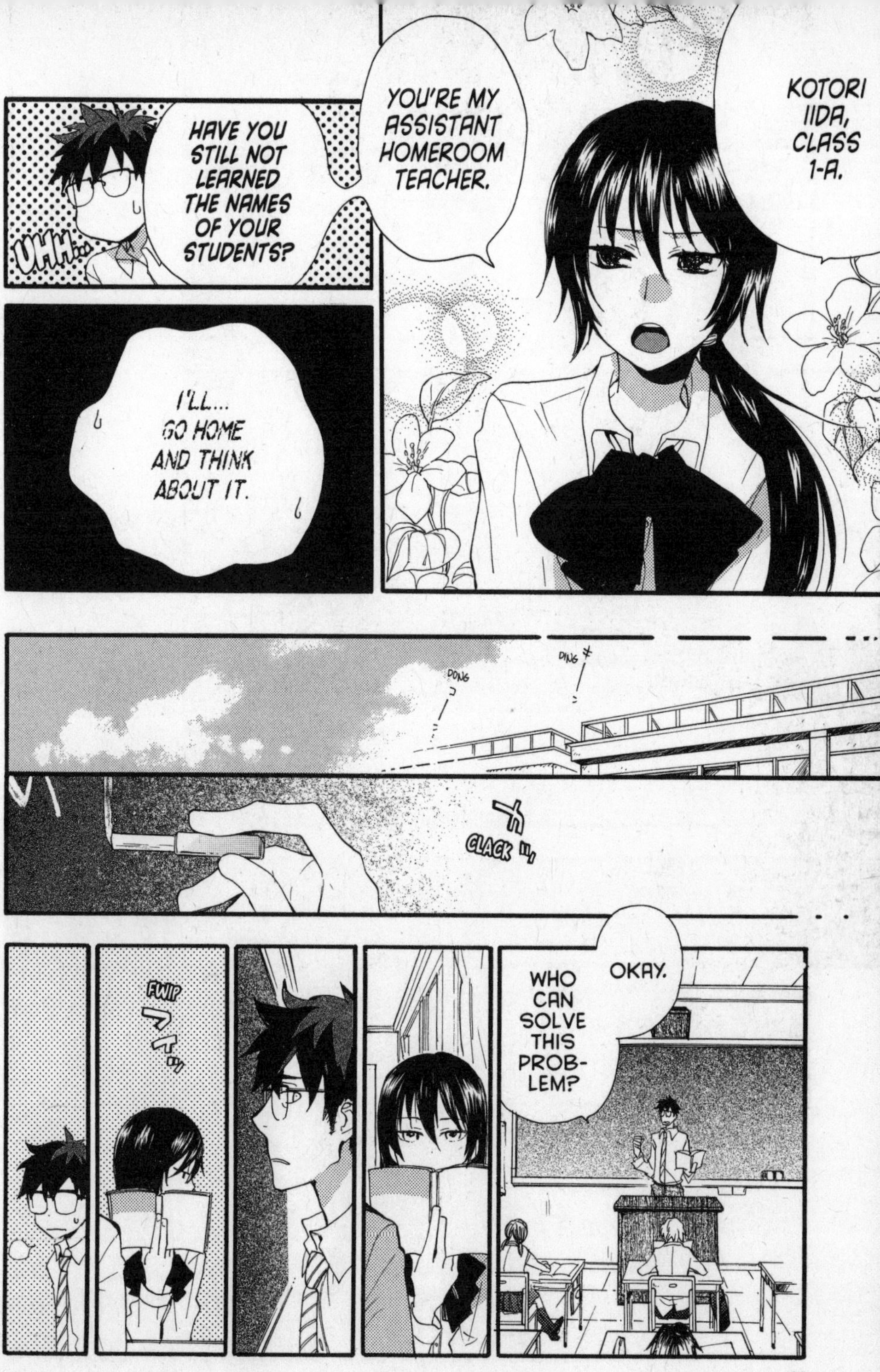
KOTORI IIDA, CLASS 1-A.
YOU'RE MY ASSISTANT HOMEROOM TEACHER.
HAVE YOU STILL NOT LEARNED THE NAMES OF YOUR STUDENTS?
UHH...
I'LL... GO HOME AND THINK ABOUT IT.
DING
DONG
CLACK
OKAY.
WHO CAN SOLVE THIS PROB-LEM?
FWIP

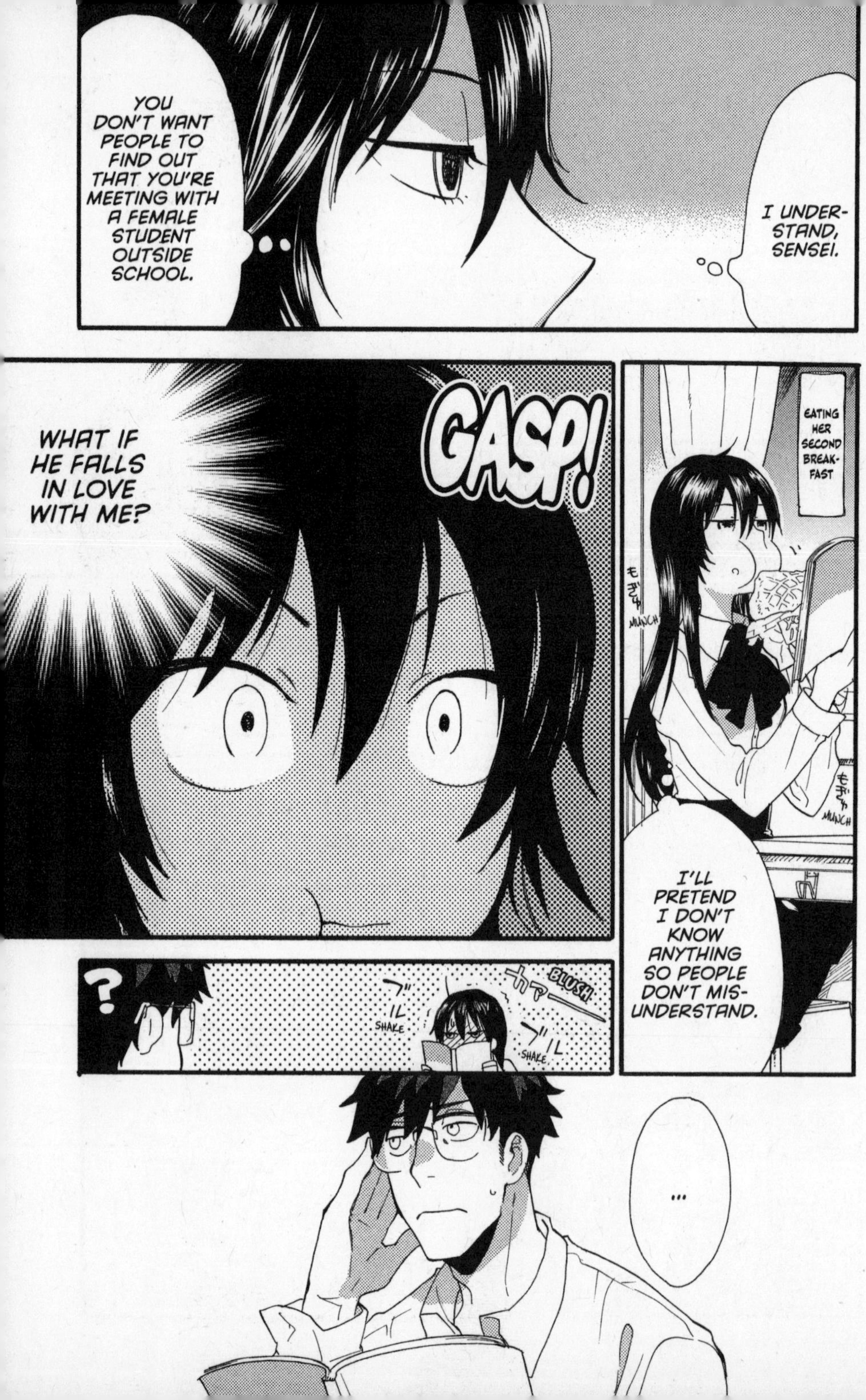
I UNDER-STAND, SENSEI.
YOU DON'T WANT PEOPLE TO FIND OUT THAT YOU'RE MEETING WITH A FEMALE STUDENT OUTSIDE SCHOOL.
EATING HER SECOND BREAK-FAST
MUNCH
MUNCH
I'LL PRETEND I DON'T KNOW ANYTHING SO PEOPLE DON'T MIS-UNDERSTAND.
GASP!
WHAT IF HE FALLS IN LOVE WITH ME?
BLUSH
SHAKE
SHAKE
?
...

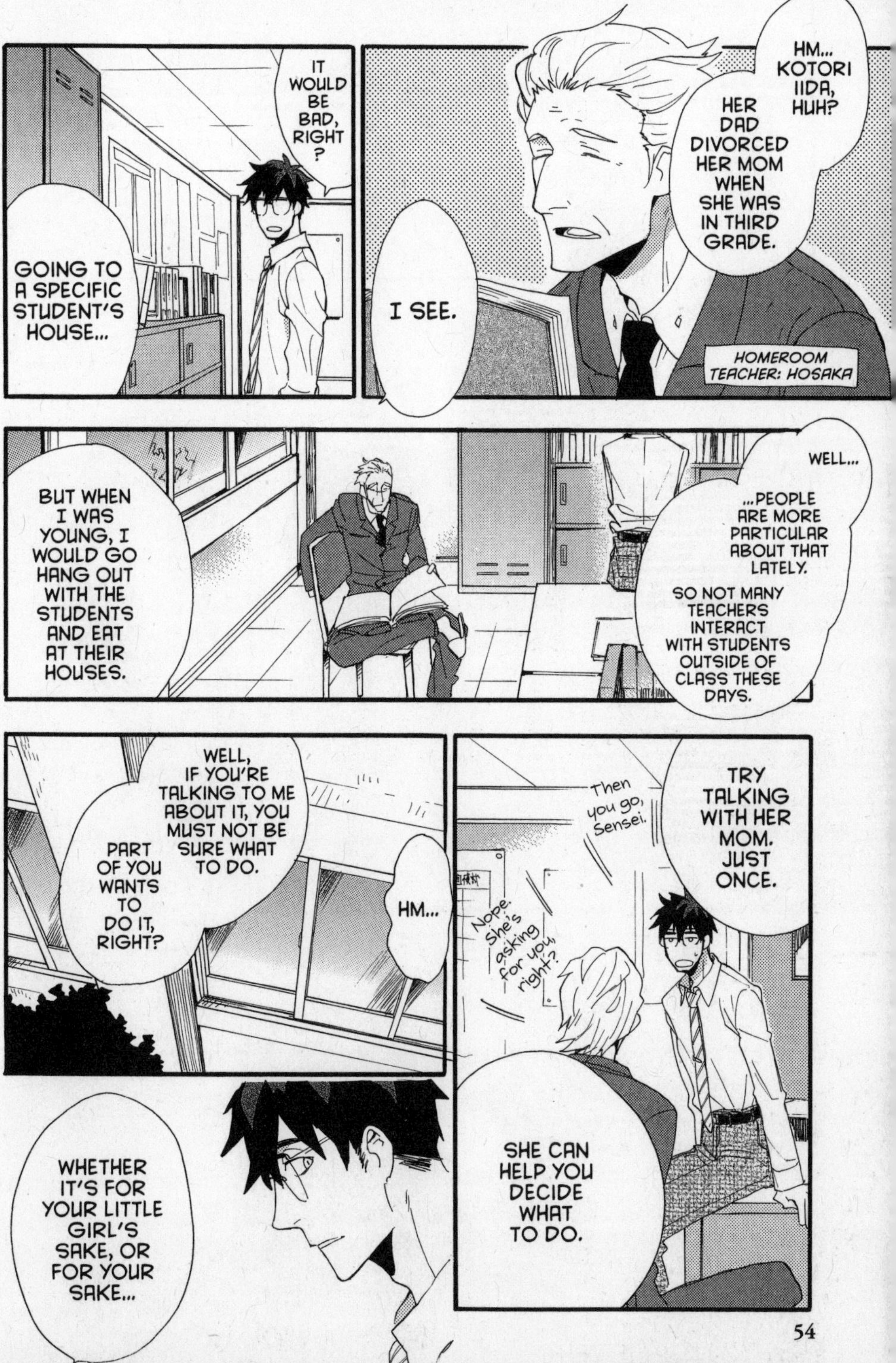

HM... KOTORI IIDA, HUH?
HER DAD DIVORCED HER MOM WHEN SHE WAS IN THIRD GRADE.
HOMEROOM TEACHER: HOSAKA
I SEE.
IT WOULD BE BAD, RIGHT?
GOING TO A SPECIFIC STUDENT'S HOUSE...
WELL...
...PEOPLE ARE MORE PARTICULAR ABOUT THAT LATELY.
SO NOT MANY TEACHERS INTERACT WITH STUDENTS OUTSIDE OF CLASS THESE DAYS.
BUT WHEN I WAS YOUNG, I WOULD GO HANG OUT WITH THE STUDENTS AND EAT AT THEIR HOUSES.
TRY TALKING WITH HER MOM. JUST ONCE.
Then you go, Sensei.
Nope. She's asking for you, right?
SHE CAN HELP YOU DECIDE WHAT TO DO.
HM...
WELL, IF YOU'RE TALKING TO ME ABOUT IT, YOU MUST NOT BE SURE WHAT TO DO.
PART OF YOU WANTS TO DO IT, RIGHT?
WHETHER IT'S FOR YOUR LITTLE GIRL'S SAKE, OR FOR YOUR SAKE...

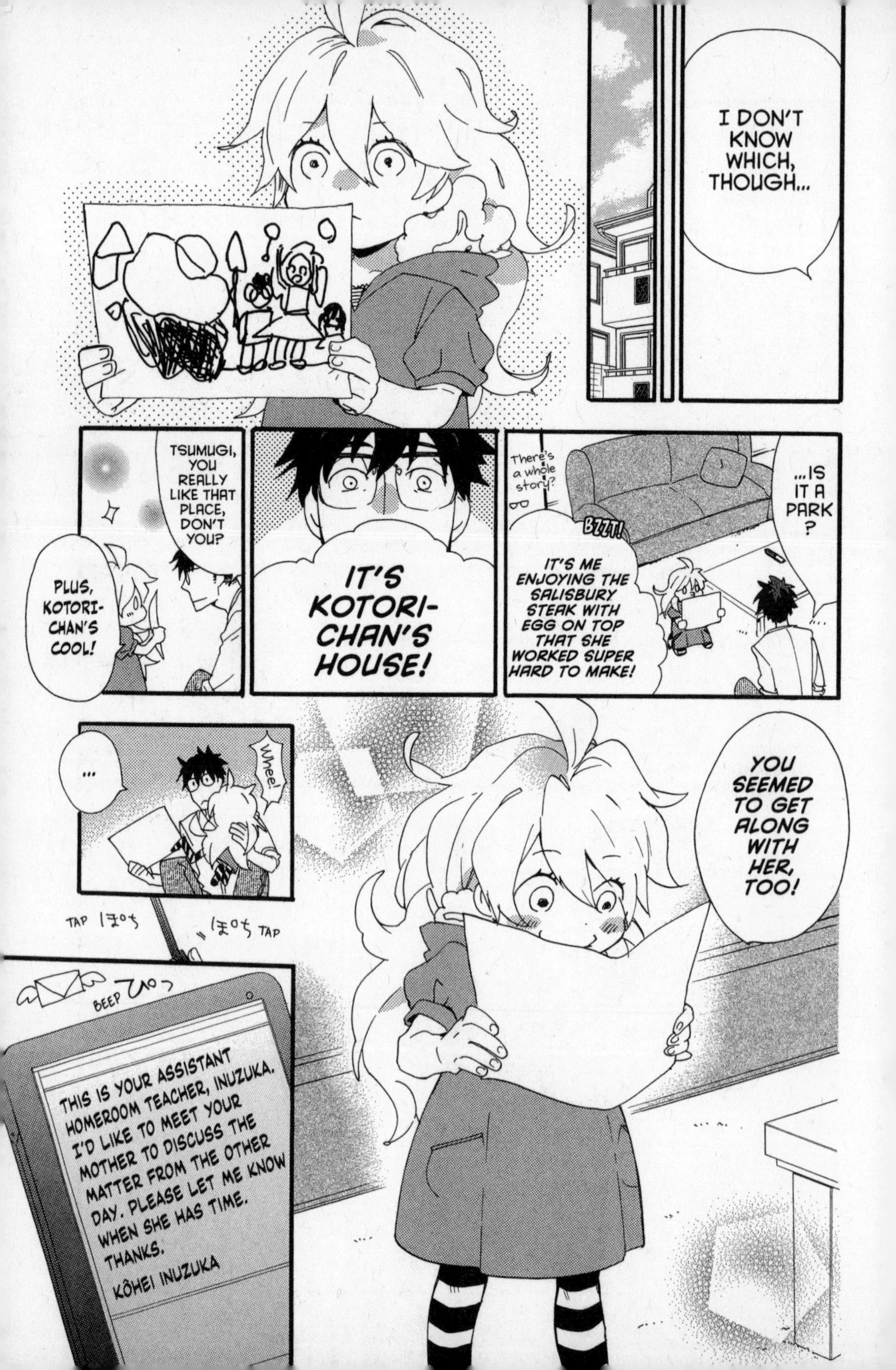
I DON'T KNOW WHICH, THOUGH...
...IS IT A PARK?
There's a whole story?
BZZT!
IT'S ME ENJOYING THE SALISBURY STEAK WITH EGG ON TOP THAT SHE WORKED SUPER HARD TO MAKE!
IT'S KOTORI-CHAN'S HOUSE!
TSUMUGI, YOU REALLY LIKE THAT PLACE, DON'T YOU?
PLUS, KOTORI-CHAN'S COOL!
YOU SEEMED TO GET ALONG WITH HER, TOO!
Whee!
...
TAP ぽち
ぽち TAP
BEEP ぴっ
THIS IS YOUR ASSISTANT HOMEROOM TEACHER, INUZUKA. I'D LIKE TO MEET YOUR MOTHER TO DISCUSS THE MATTER FROM THE OTHER DAY. PLEASE LET ME KNOW WHEN SHE HAS TIME. THANKS.
KŌHEI INUZUKA

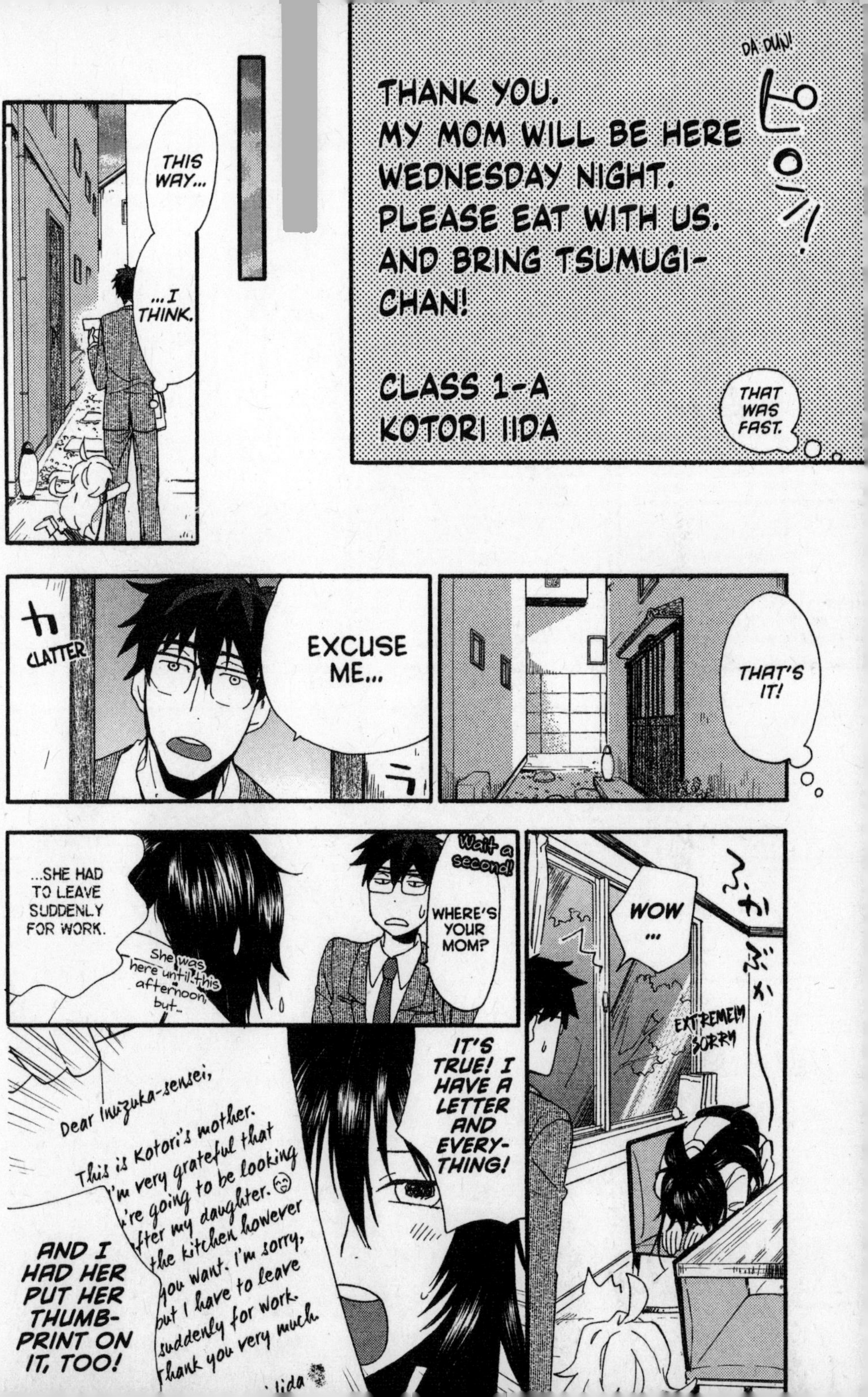

DA DUN!
THANK YOU.
MY MOM WILL BE HERE WEDNESDAY NIGHT.
PLEASE EAT WITH US.
AND BRING TSUMUGI-CHAN!
CLASS 1-A
KOTORI IIDA
THAT WAS FAST.
THIS WAY...
...I THINK.
THAT'S IT!
CLATTER
EXCUSE ME...
WOW...
EXTREMELY SORRY
Wait a second!
WHERE'S YOUR MOM?
...SHE HAD TO LEAVE SUDDENLY FOR WORK.
She was here until this afternoon, but..
IT'S TRUE! I HAVE A LETTER AND EVERYTHING!
Dear Inuzuka-sensei,
This is Kotori's mother.
'm very grateful that
u're going to be looking
fter my daughter.
the kitchen however
you want. I'm sorry,
but I have to leave
suddenly for work.
Thank you very much.
Iida
AND I HAD HER PUT HER THUMBPRINT ON IT, TOO!

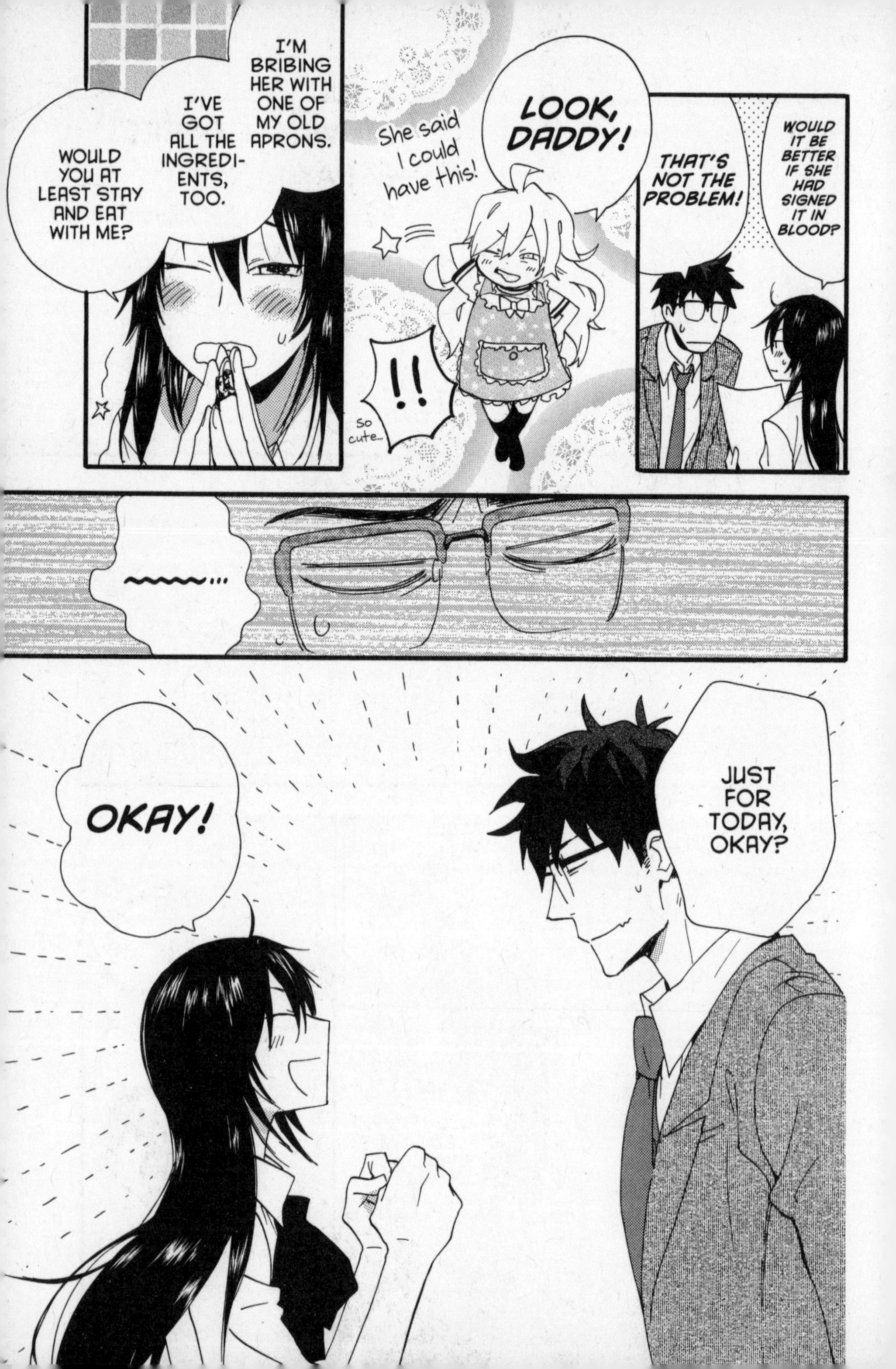
WOULD IT BE BETTER IF SHE HAD SIGNED IT IN BLOOD?
THAT'S NOT THE PROBLEM!
LOOK, DADDY!
She said I could have this!
!!
So cute...
I'M BRIBING HER WITH ONE OF MY OLD APRONS.
I'VE GOT ALL THE INGREDI-ENTS, TOO.
WOULD YOU AT LEAST STAY AND EAT WITH ME?
~~~~...
JUST FOR TODAY, OKAY?
OKAY!
~~~~

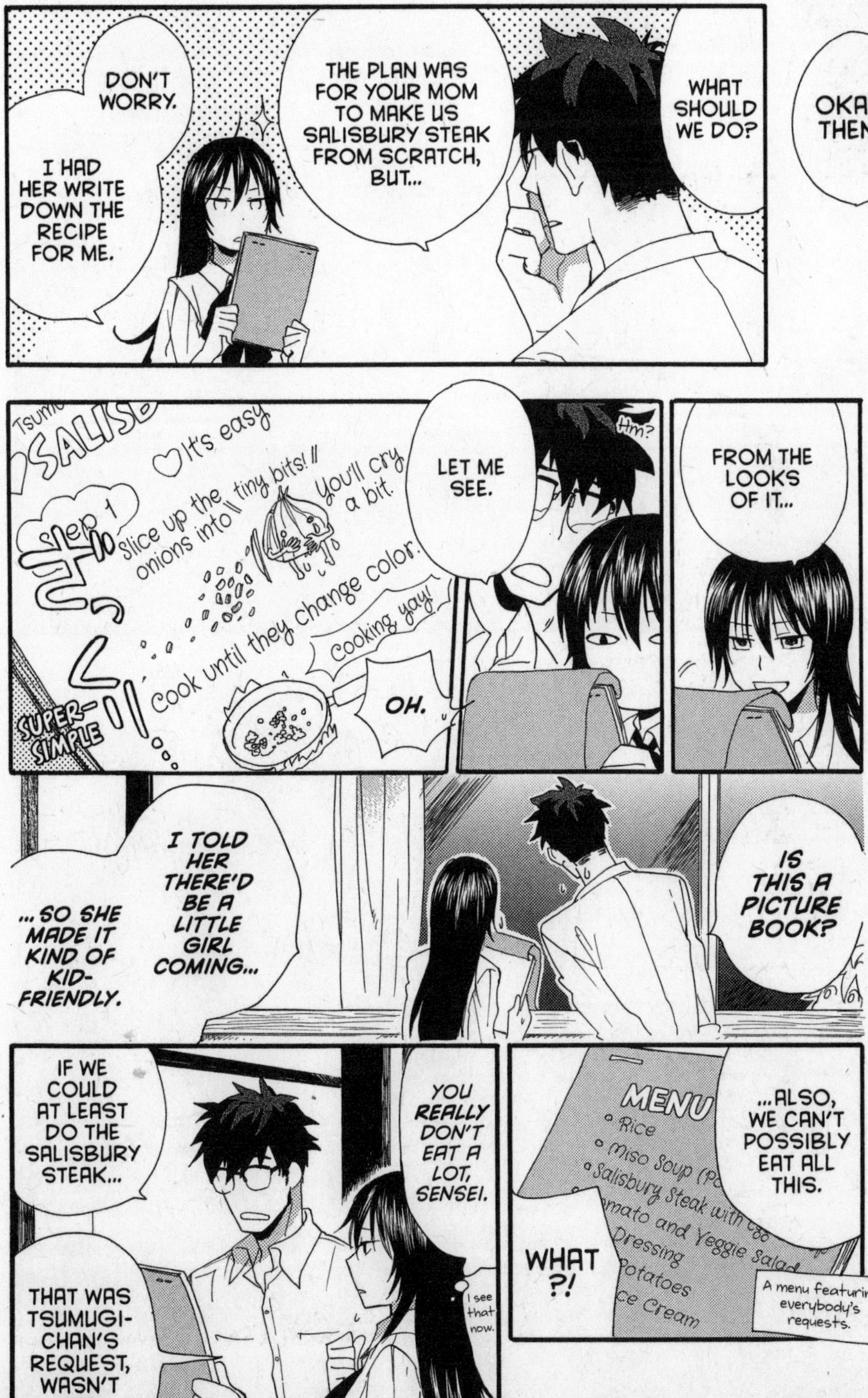
OKAY, THEN.
WHAT SHOULD WE DO?
THE PLAN WAS FOR YOUR MOM TO MAKE US SALISBURY STEAK FROM SCRATCH, BUT...
DON'T WORRY.
I HAD HER WRITE DOWN THE RECIPE FOR ME.
FROM THE LOOKS OF IT...
Hm?
LET ME SEE.
OH.
It's easy
Step 1
Slice up the onions into tiny bits!
You'll cry a bit.
Cook until they change color.
Cooking yay!
SUPER-SIMPLE
IS THIS A PICTURE BOOK?
I TOLD HER THERE'D BE A LITTLE GIRL COMING...
...SO SHE MADE IT KIND OF KID-FRIENDLY.
...ALSO, WE CAN'T POSSIBLY EAT ALL THIS.
MENU
Rice
Miso Soup
Salisbury Steak with
Dressing
Potatoes
WHAT?!
A menu featuring everybody's requests.
YOU REALLY DON'T EAT A LOT, SENSEI.
IF WE COULD AT LEAST DO THE SALISBURY STEAK...
THAT WAS TSUMUGI-CHAN'S REQUEST, WASN'T IT?
I see that now.

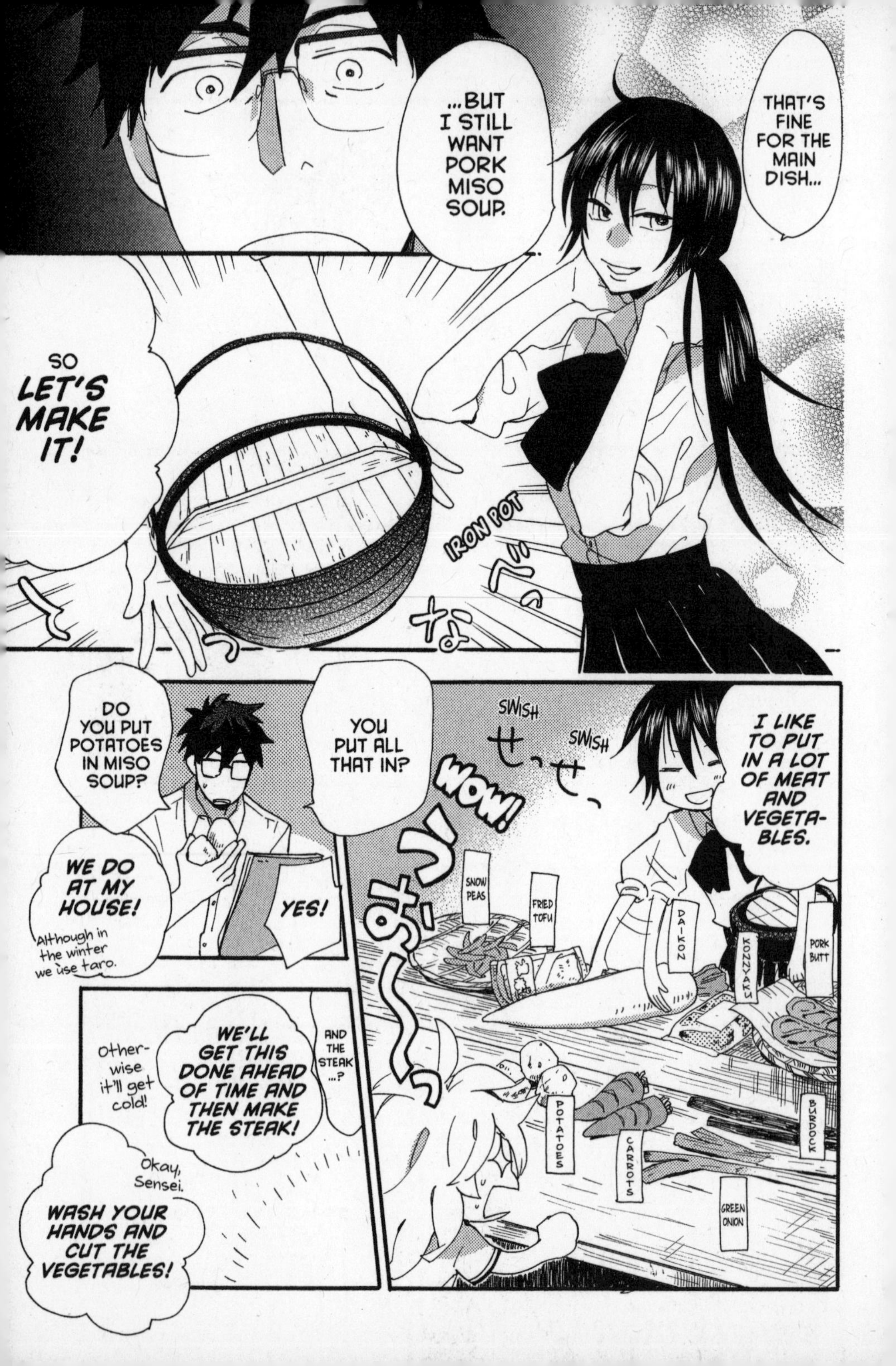
THAT'S FINE FOR THE MAIN DISH...
...BUT I STILL WANT PORK MISO SOUP.
SO LET'S MAKE IT!
IRON POT
I LIKE TO PUT IN A LOT OF MEAT AND VEGETABLES.
SWISH
SWISH
WOW!
YOU PUT ALL THAT IN?
PORK BUTT
KONNYAKU
DAIKON
FRIED TOFU
SNOW PEAS
BURDOCK
GREEN ONION
CARROTS
POTATOES
DO YOU PUT POTATOES IN MISO SOUP?
YES!
WE DO AT MY HOUSE!
Although in the winter we use taro.
AND THE STEAK ...?
WE'LL GET THIS DONE AHEAD OF TIME AND THEN MAKE THE STEAK!
Otherwise it'll get cold!
Okay, Sensei.
WASH YOUR HANDS AND CUT THE VEGETABLES!

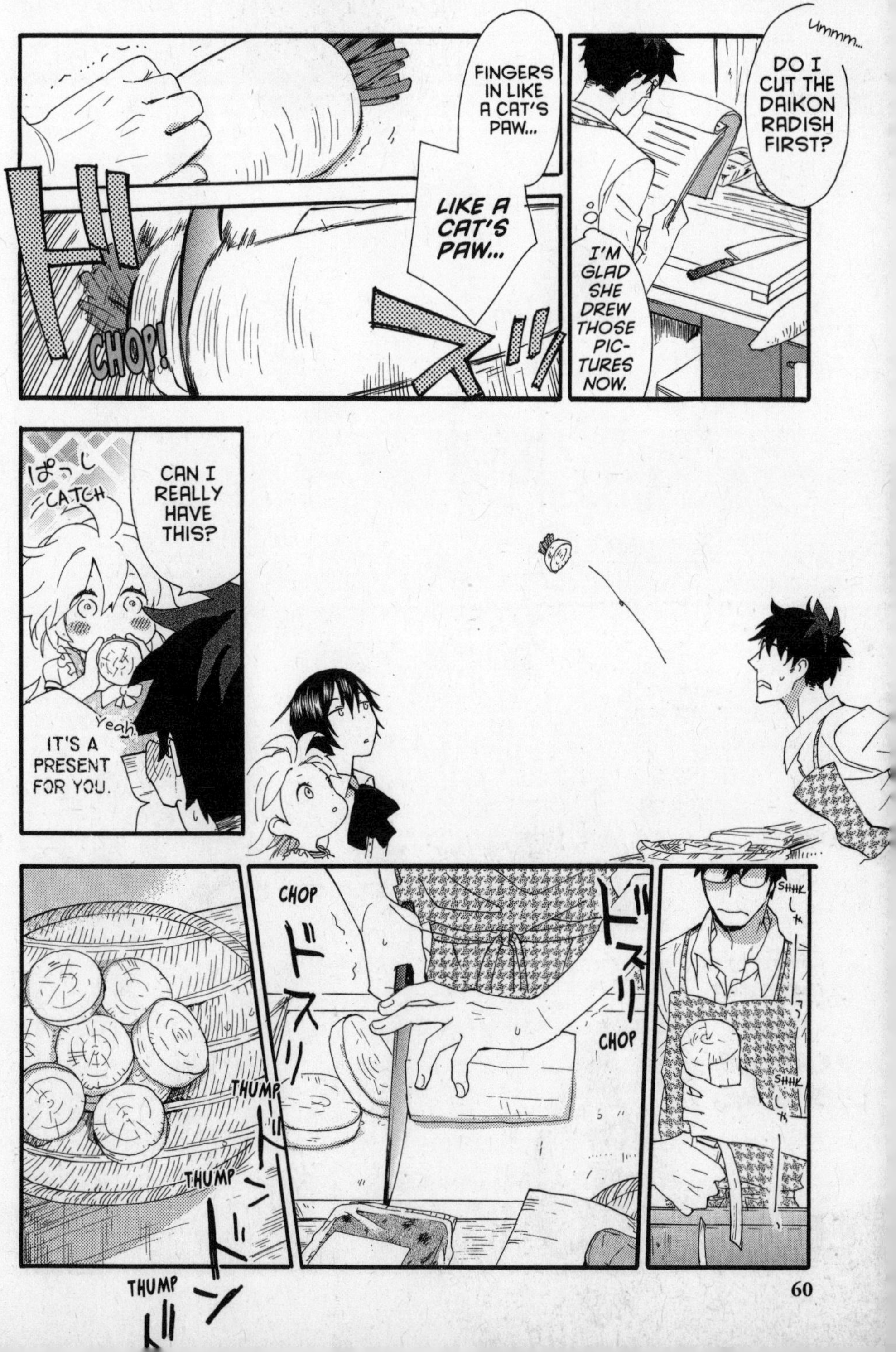

Ummm...
DO I CUT THE DAIKON RADISH FIRST?
I'M GLAD SHE DREW THOSE PICTURES NOW.
FINGERS IN LIKE A CAT'S PAW...
LIKE A CAT'S PAW...
CHOP!
CAN I REALLY HAVE THIS?
ぱっし
CATCH
Yeah.
IT'S A PRESENT FOR YOU.
SHHK
SHHK
CHOP
CHOP
THUMP
THUMP
THUMP

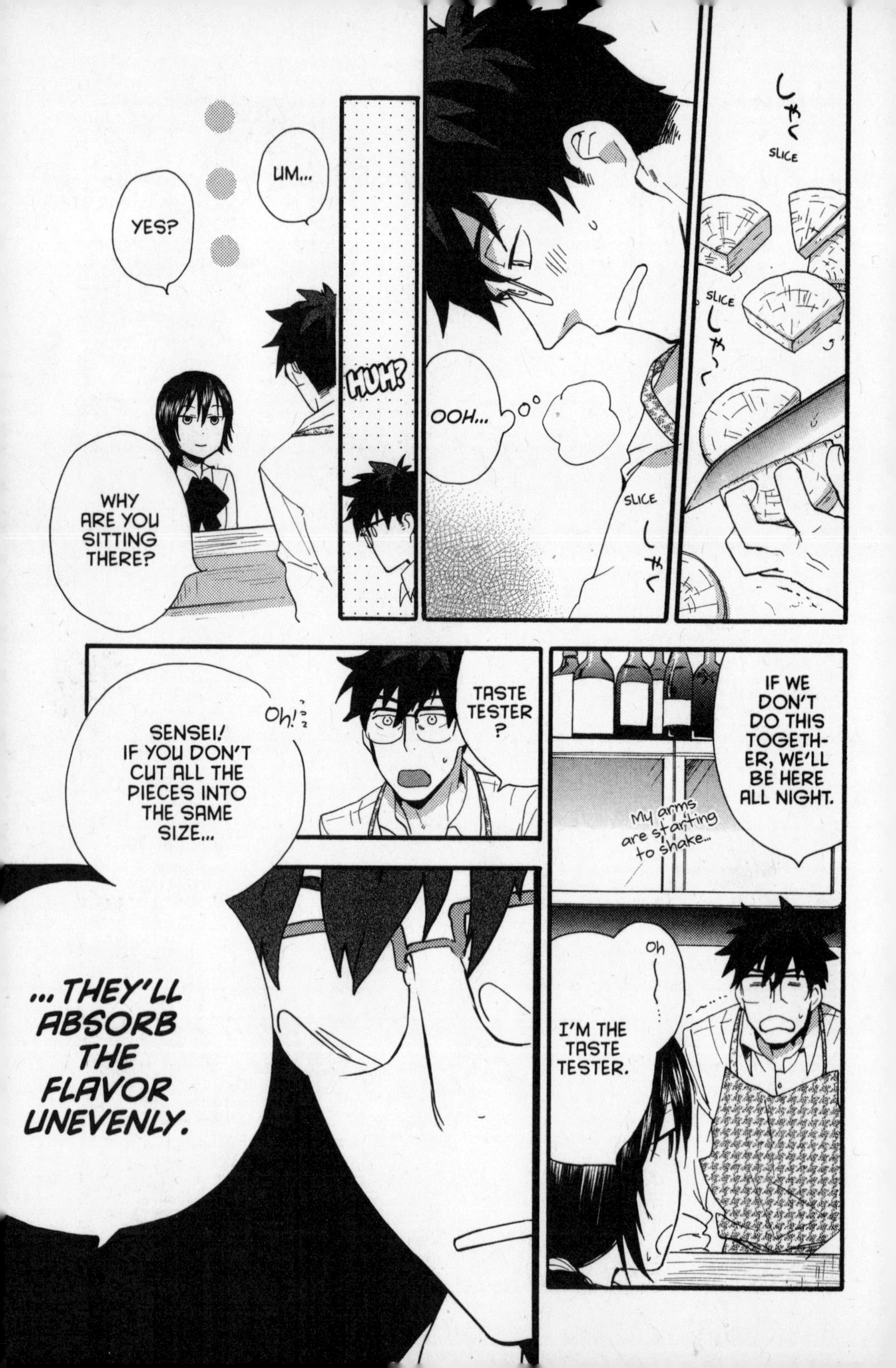
しゃく
SLICE
SLICE
しゃく
SLICE
しゃし
OOH...
HUH?
UM...
YES?
WHY ARE YOU SITTING THERE?
IF WE DON'T DO THIS TOGETHER, WE'LL BE HERE ALL NIGHT.
My arms are starting to shake...
Oh!
TASTE TESTER?
Oh~...
I'M THE TASTE TESTER.
SENSEI! IF YOU DON'T CUT ALL THE PIECES INTO THE SAME SIZE...
...THEY'LL ABSORB THE FLAVOR UNEVENLY.

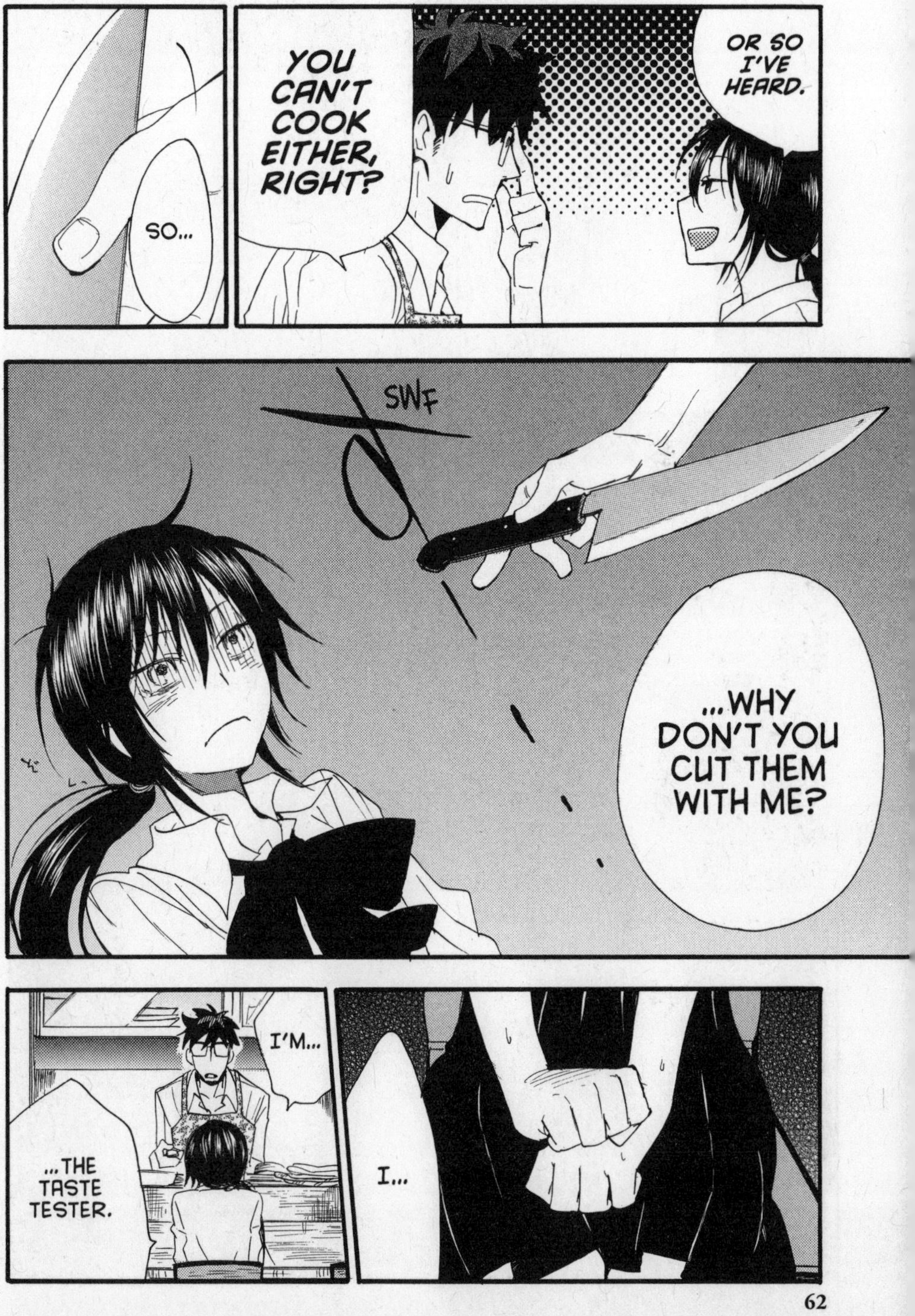

OR SO I'VE HEARD.
YOU CAN'T COOK EITHER, RIGHT?
SO...
SWF
...WHY DON'T YOU CUT THEM WITH ME?
I...
I'M...
...THE TASTE TESTER.

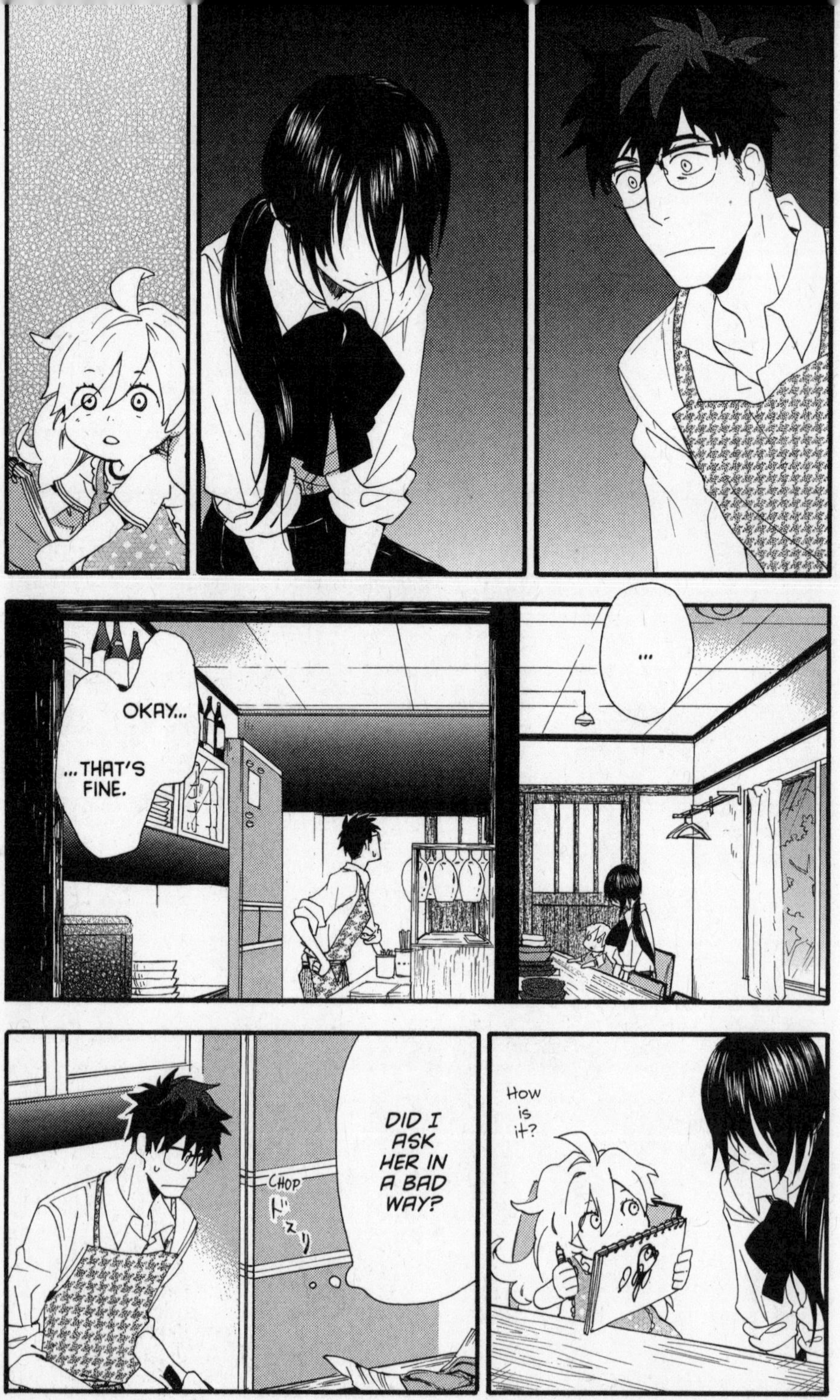
...
OKAY...
...THAT'S FINE.
How is it?
DID I ASK HER IN A BAD WAY?
CHOP
ドスリ

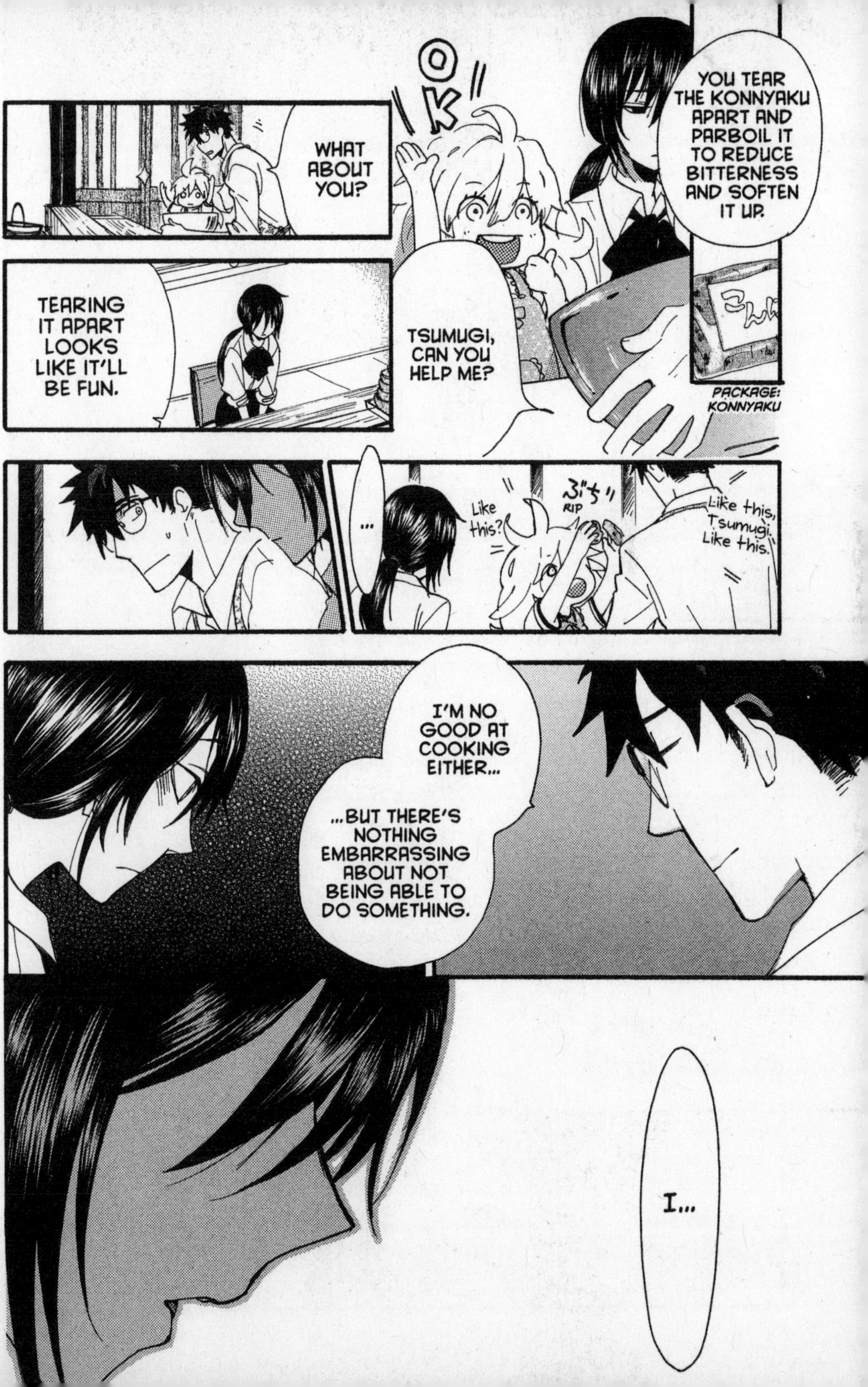
YOU TEAR THE KONNYAKU APART AND PARBOIL IT TO REDUCE BITTERNESS AND SOFTEN IT UP.
PACKAGE: KONNYAKU
OK
TSUMUGI, CAN YOU HELP ME?
WHAT ABOUT YOU?
TEARING IT APART LOOKS LIKE IT'LL BE FUN.
Like this, Tsumugi. Like this.
ぶち
RIP
Like this?
...
I'M NO GOOD AT COOKING EITHER...
...BUT THERE'S NOTHING EMBARRASSING ABOUT NOT BEING ABLE TO DO SOMETHING.
I...

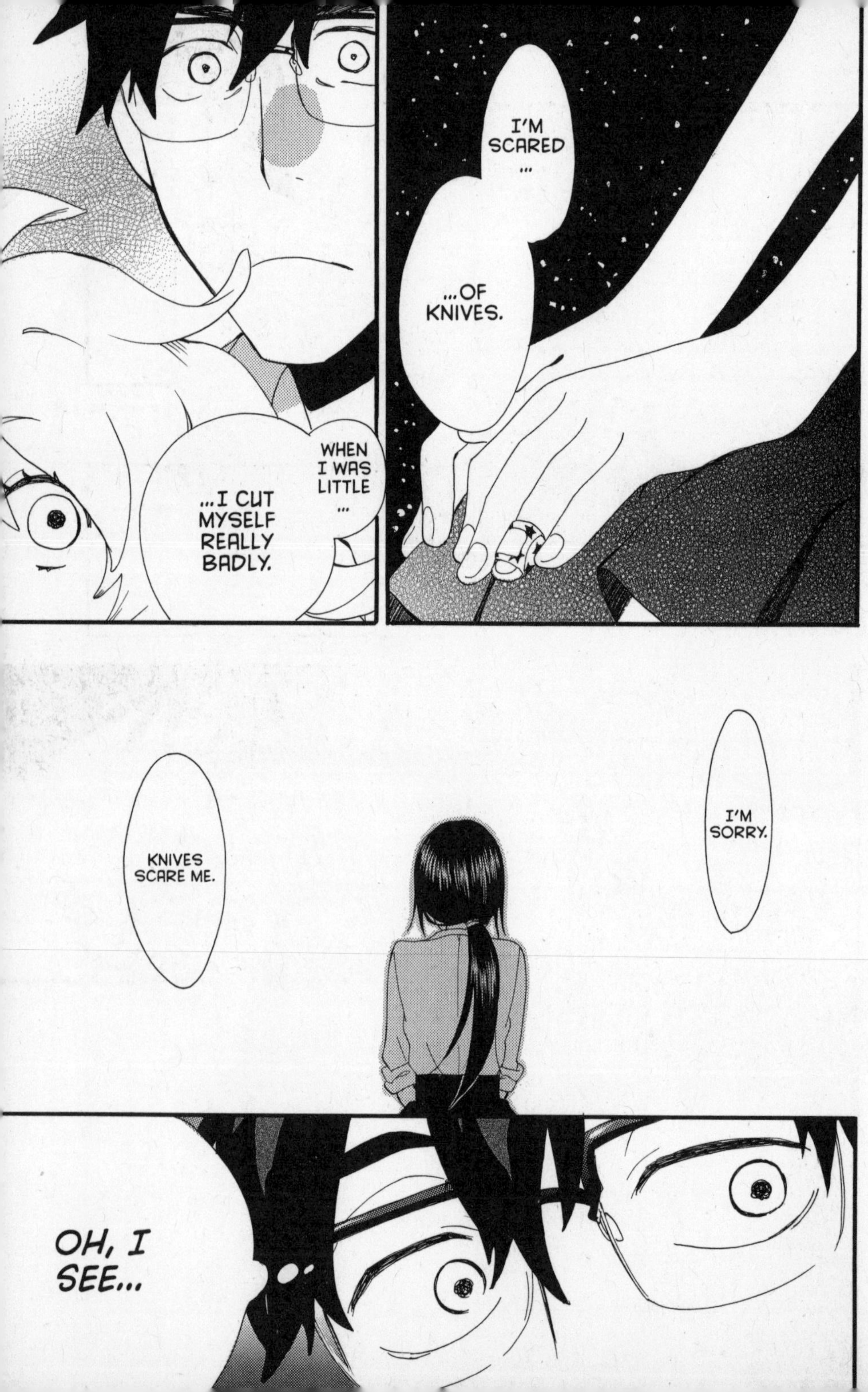
I'M SCARED ...
...OF KNIVES.
WHEN I WAS LITTLE ...
...I CUT MYSELF REALLY BADLY.
I'M SORRY.
KNIVES SCARE ME.
OH, I SEE...

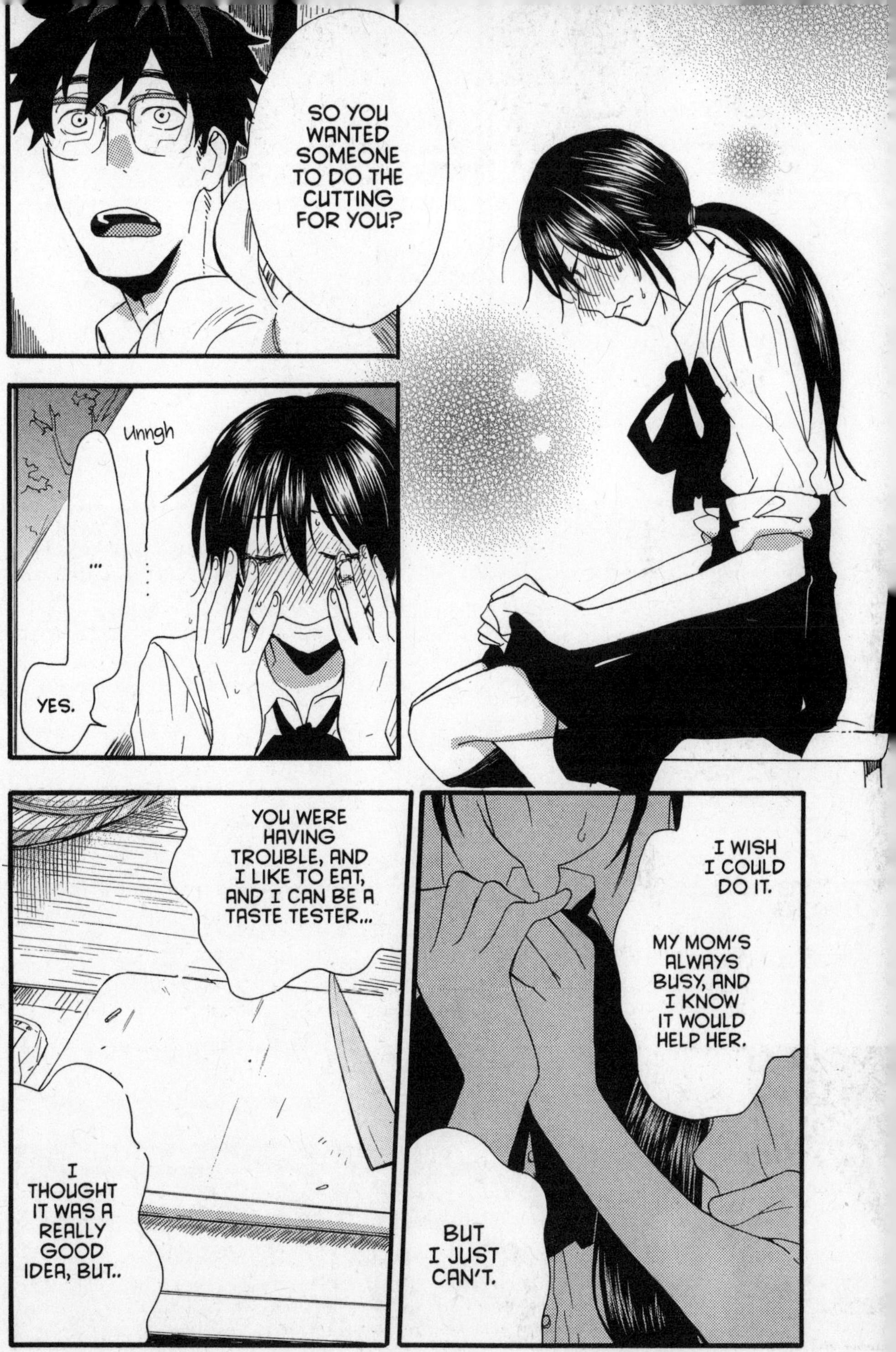

SO YOU WANTED SOMEONE TO DO THE CUTTING FOR YOU?
Unngh
...
YES.
I WISH I COULD DO IT.
MY MOM'S ALWAYS BUSY, AND I KNOW IT WOULD HELP HER.
BUT I JUST CAN'T.
YOU WERE HAVING TROUBLE, AND I LIKE TO EAT, AND I CAN BE A TASTE TESTER...
I THOUGHT IT WAS A REALLY GOOD IDEA, BUT..

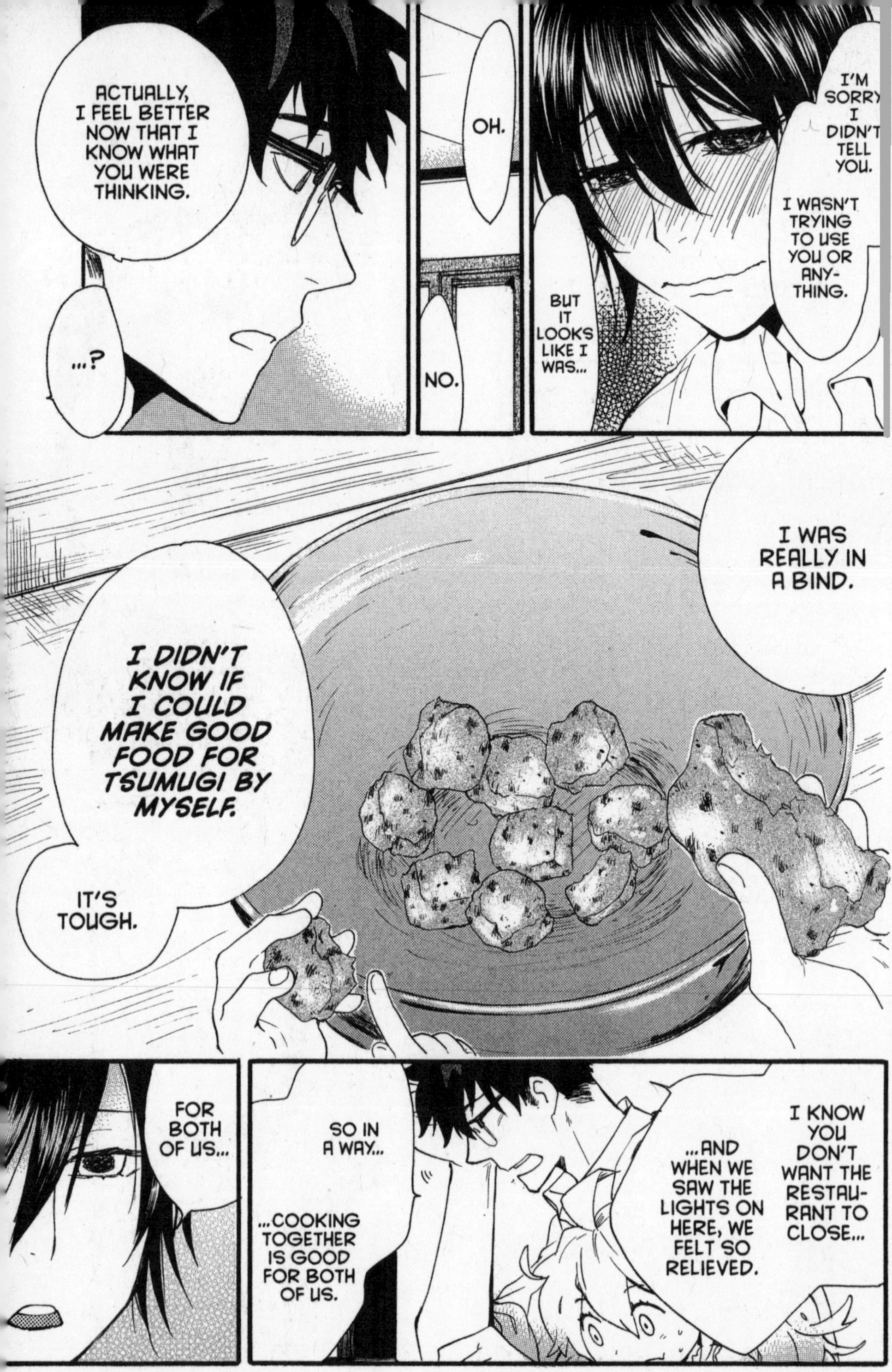
I'M SORRY I DIDN'T TELL YOU.
I WASN'T TRYING TO USE YOU OR ANY-THING.
BUT IT LOOKS LIKE I WAS...
OH.
NO.
ACTUALLY, I FEEL BETTER NOW THAT I KNOW WHAT YOU WERE THINKING.
...?
I WAS REALLY IN A BIND.
I DIDN'T KNOW IF I COULD MAKE GOOD FOOD FOR TSUMUGI BY MYSELF.
IT'S TOUGH.
I KNOW YOU DON'T WANT THE RESTAU-RANT TO CLOSE...
...AND WHEN WE SAW THE LIGHTS ON HERE, WE FELT SO RELIEVED.
SO IN A WAY...
...COOKING TOGETHER IS GOOD FOR BOTH OF US.
FOR BOTH OF US...

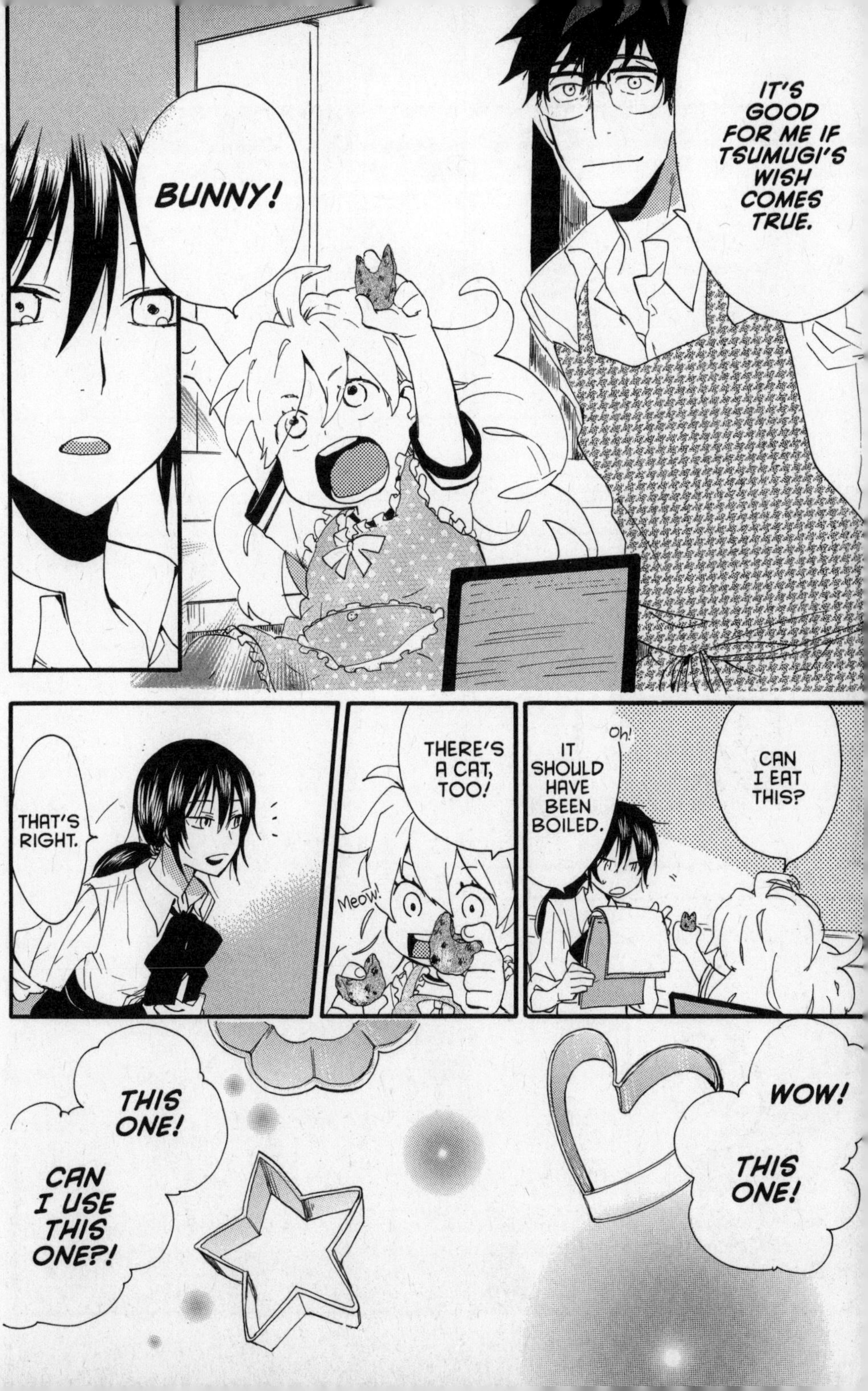
IT'S GOOD FOR ME IF TSUMUGI'S WISH COMES TRUE.
BUNNY!
CAN I EAT THIS?
Oh!
IT SHOULD HAVE BEEN BOILED.
THERE'S A CAT, TOO!
Meow!
THAT'S RIGHT.
WOW!
THIS ONE!
THIS ONE!
CAN I USE THIS ONE?!

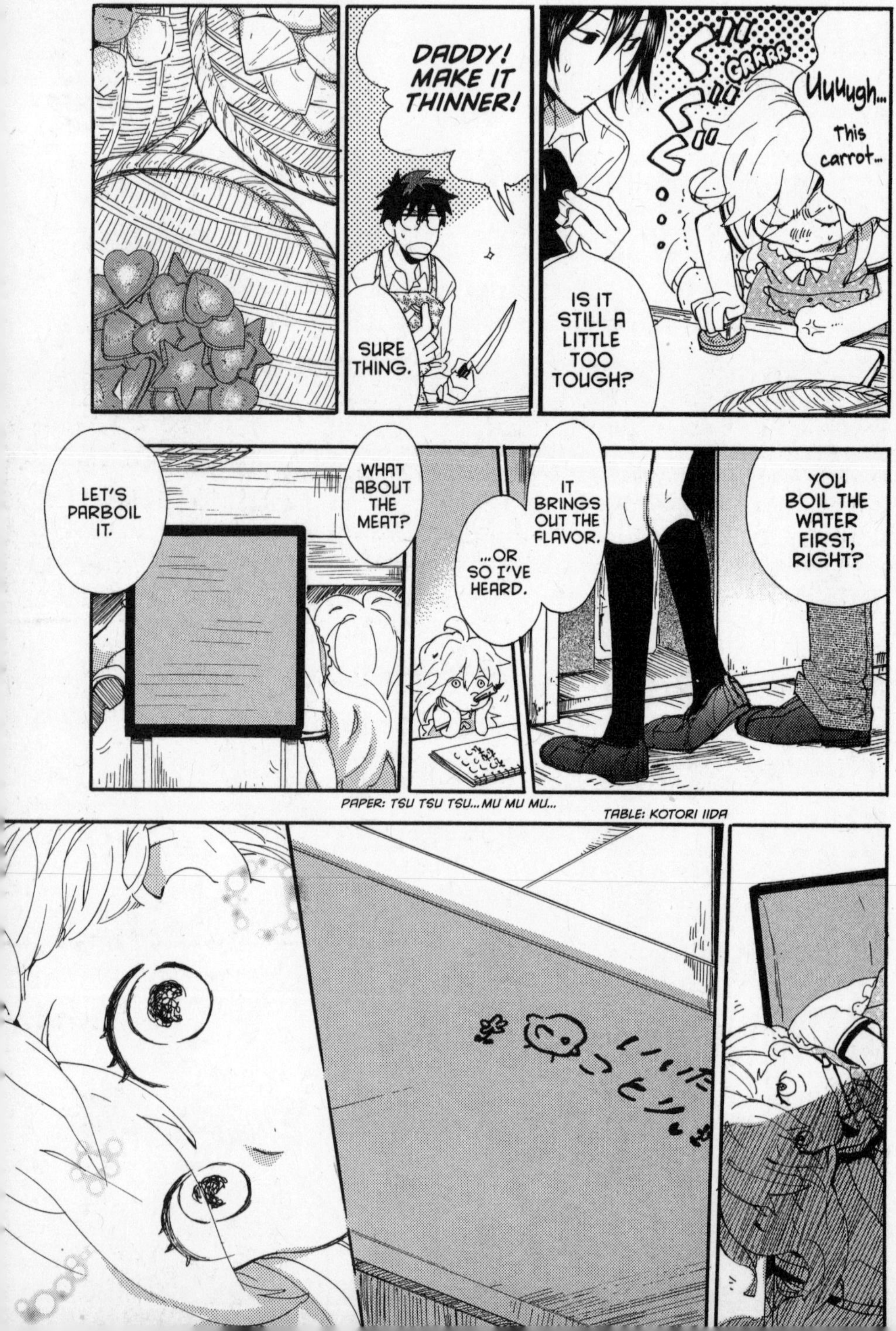
GRRRR
Uuuugh...
This carrot...
IS IT STILL A LITTLE TOO TOUGH?
DADDY! MAKE IT THINNER!
SURE THING.
YOU BOIL THE WATER FIRST, RIGHT?
IT BRINGS OUT THE FLAVOR.
...OR SO I'VE HEARD.
WHAT ABOUT THE MEAT?
LET'S PARBOIL IT.
PAPER: TSU TSU TSU...MU MU MU...
TABLE: KOTORI IIDA

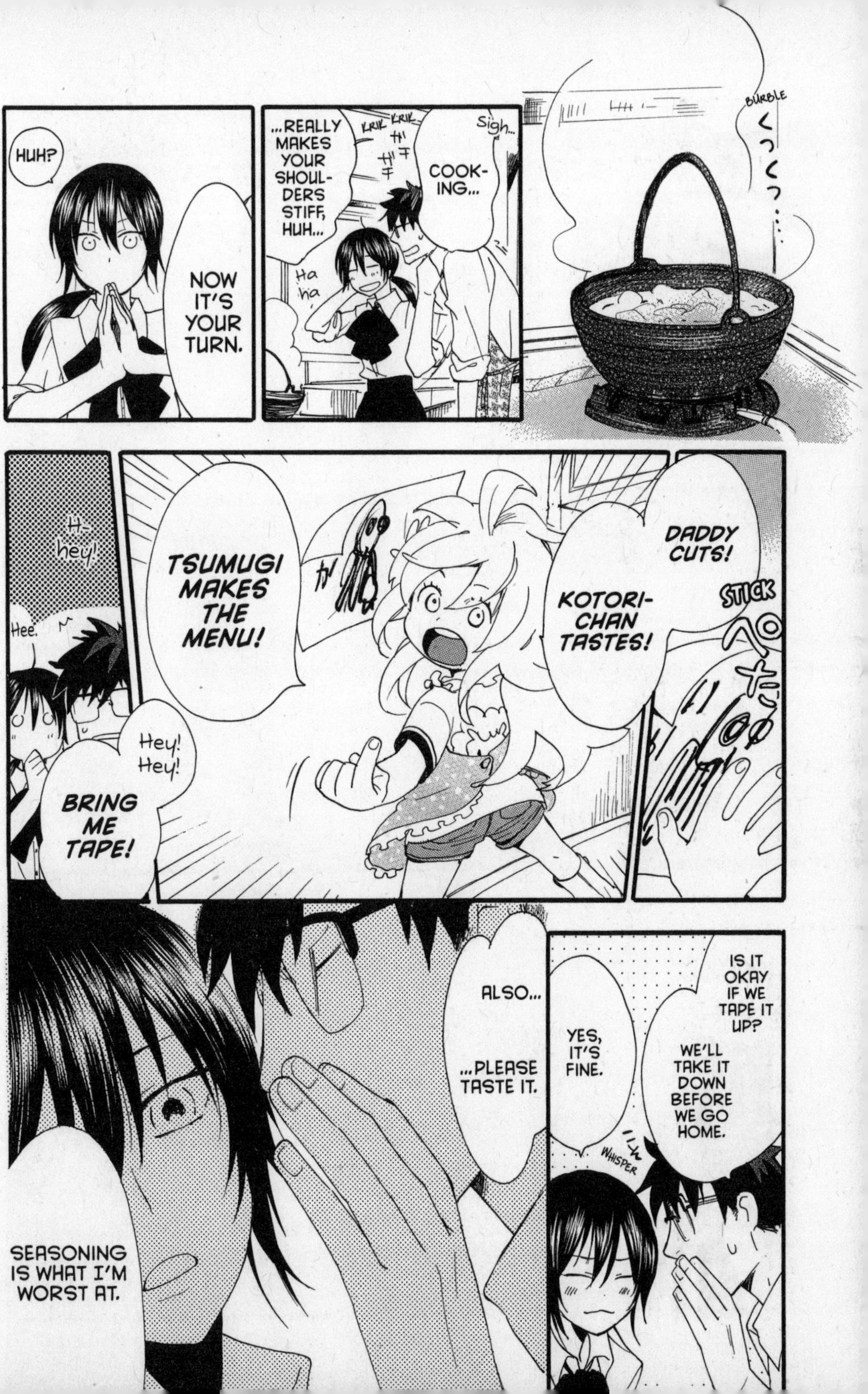
BURBLE
くつくつ…
Sigh…
COOK-ING…
KRIK KRIK
…REALLY MAKES YOUR SHOULDERS STIFF, HUH…
Ha ha
HUH?
NOW IT'S YOUR TURN.
STICK
DADDY CUTS!
KOTORI-CHAN TASTES!
TSUMUGI MAKES THE MENU!
H-hey!
Hee.
Hey! Hey!
BRING ME TAPE!
IS IT OKAY IF WE TAPE IT UP?
WE'LL TAKE IT DOWN BEFORE WE GO HOME.
YES, IT'S FINE.
WHISPER
ALSO…
…PLEASE TASTE IT.
SEASONING IS WHAT I'M WORST AT.

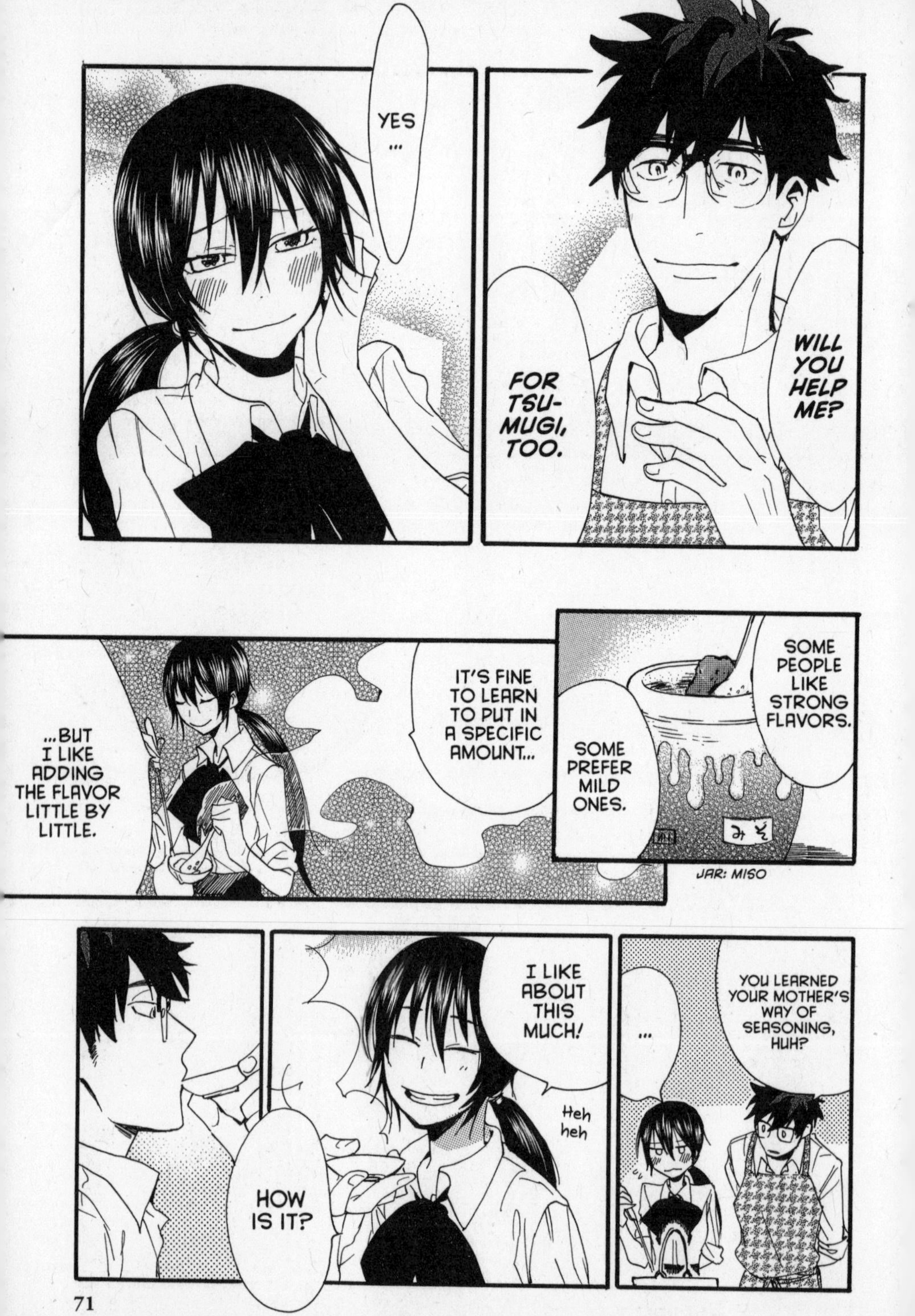
WILL YOU HELP ME?
FOR TSU-MUGI, TOO.
YES ...
SOME PEOPLE LIKE STRONG FLAVORS.
SOME PREFER MILD ONES.
JAR: MISO
IT'S FINE TO LEARN TO PUT IN A SPECIFIC AMOUNT...
...BUT I LIKE ADDING THE FLAVOR LITTLE BY LITTLE.
YOU LEARNED YOUR MOTHER'S WAY OF SEASONING, HUH?
...
I LIKE ABOUT THIS MUCH!
Heh heh
HOW IS IT?

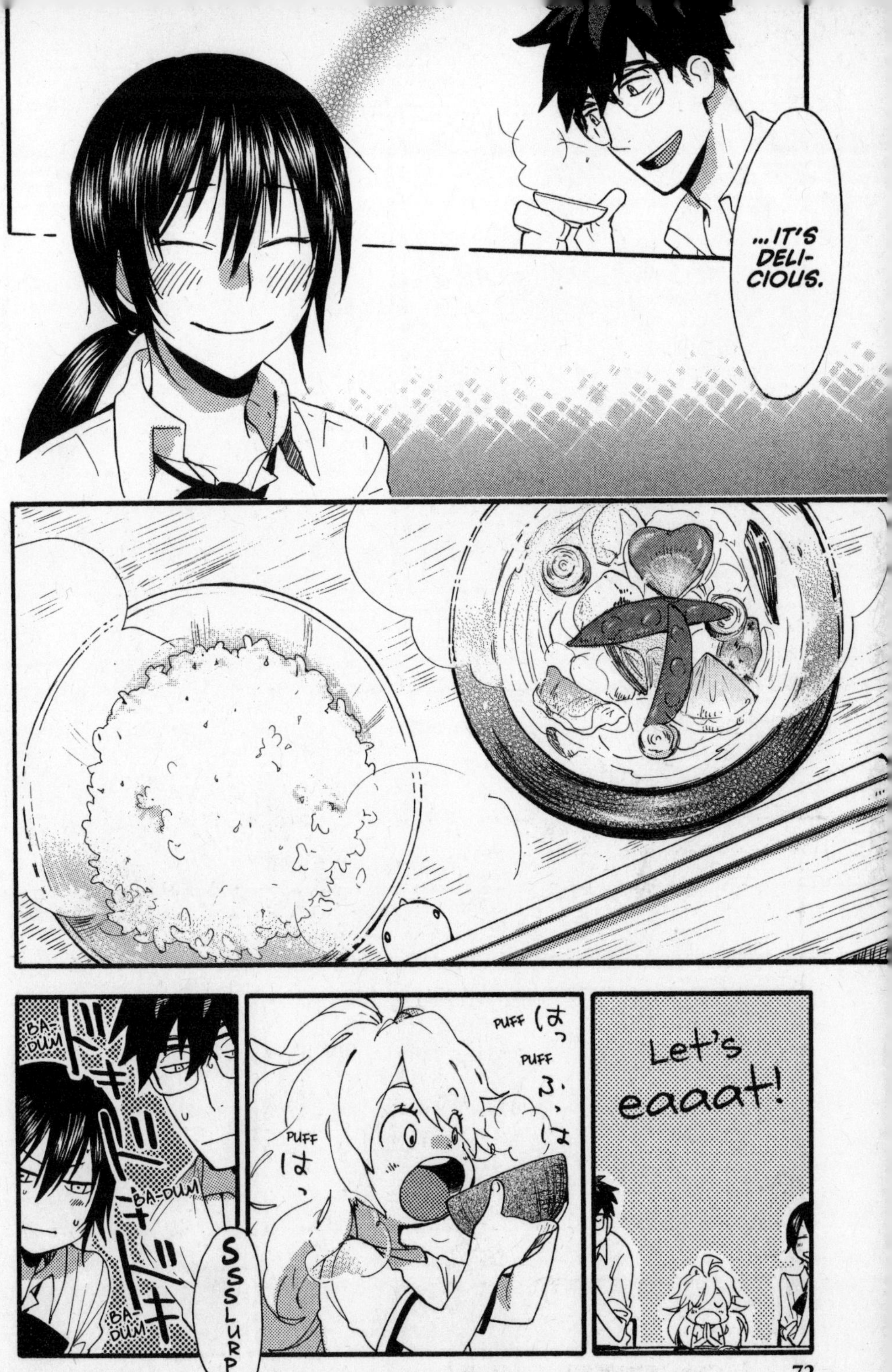
...IT'S DELICIOUS.
Let's eaaat!
PUFF はっ
PUFF ふ、は
PUFF は、
SSSLURP
BA-DUM
BA-DUM
BA-DUM

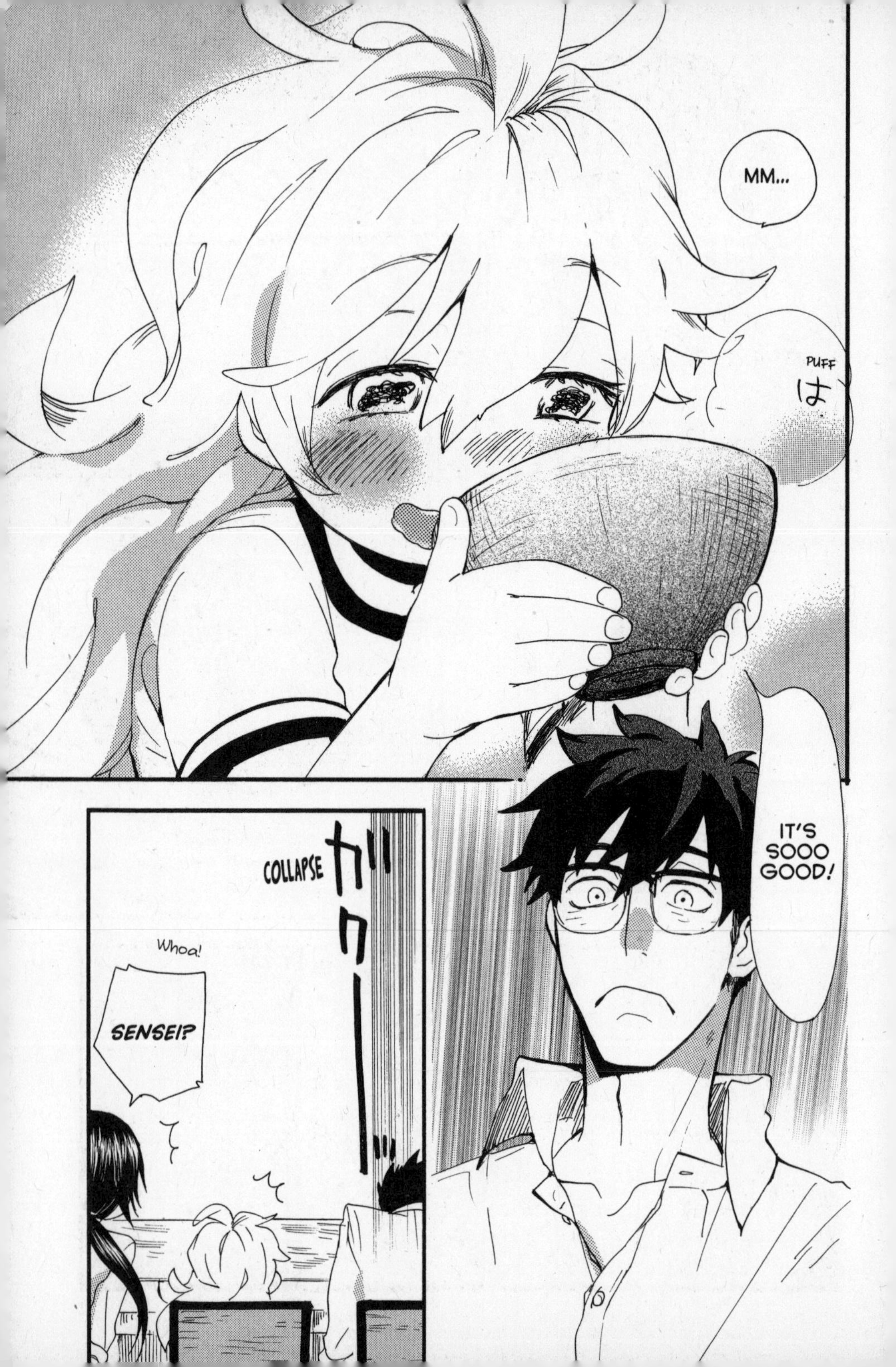
MM...
PUFF
は
IT'S SOOO GOOD!
COLLAPSE
ガクー
Whoa!
SENSEI!?

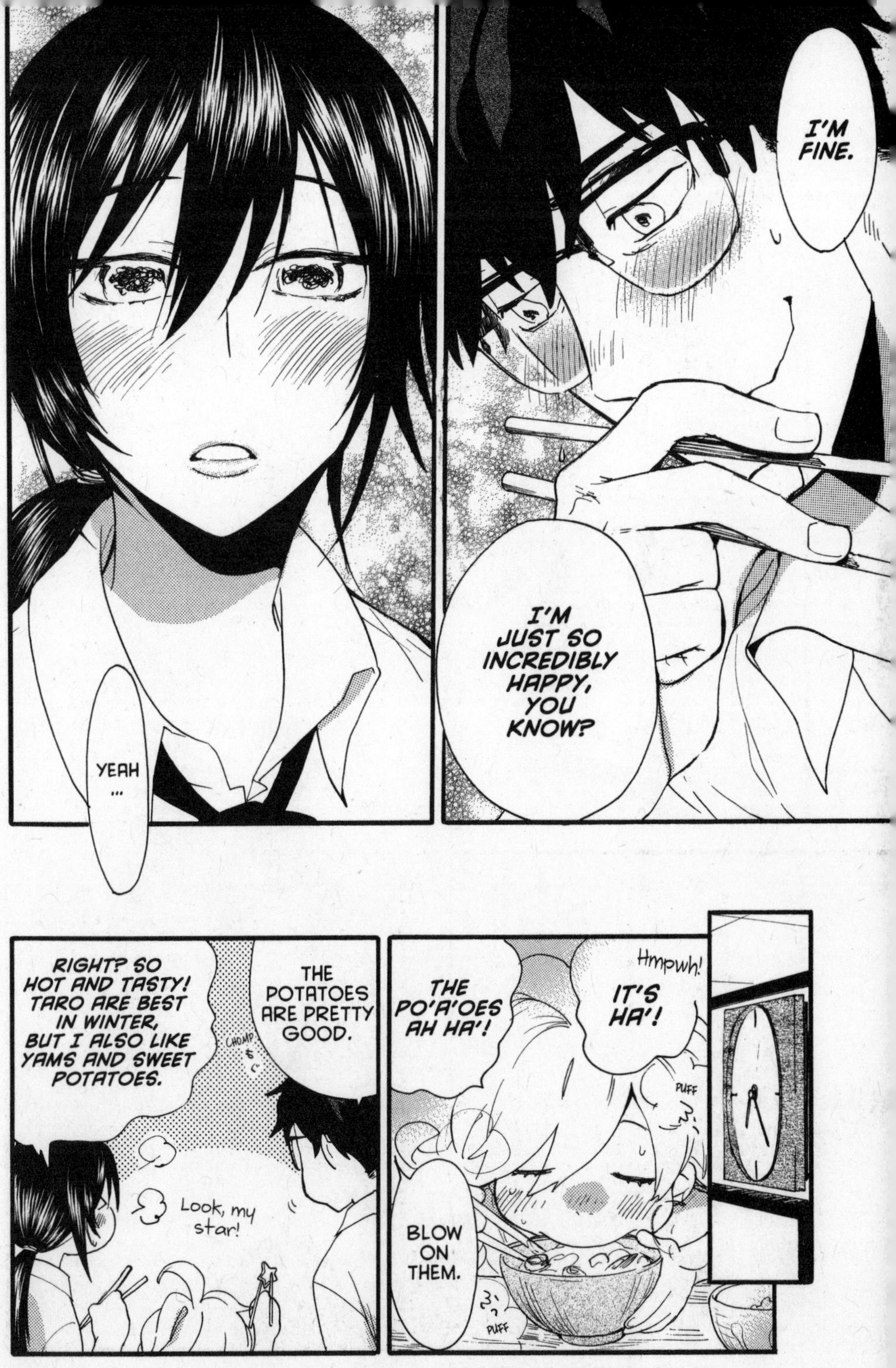
I'M FINE.
I'M JUST SO INCREDIBLY HAPPY, YOU KNOW?
YEAH ...
Hmpwh!
IT'S HA'!
THE PO'A'OES AH HA'!
PUFF
BLOW ON THEM.
PUFF
THE POTATOES ARE PRETTY GOOD.
CHOMP
RIGHT? SO HOT AND TASTY! TARO ARE BEST IN WINTER, BUT I ALSO LIKE YAMS AND SWEET POTATOES.
Look, my star!

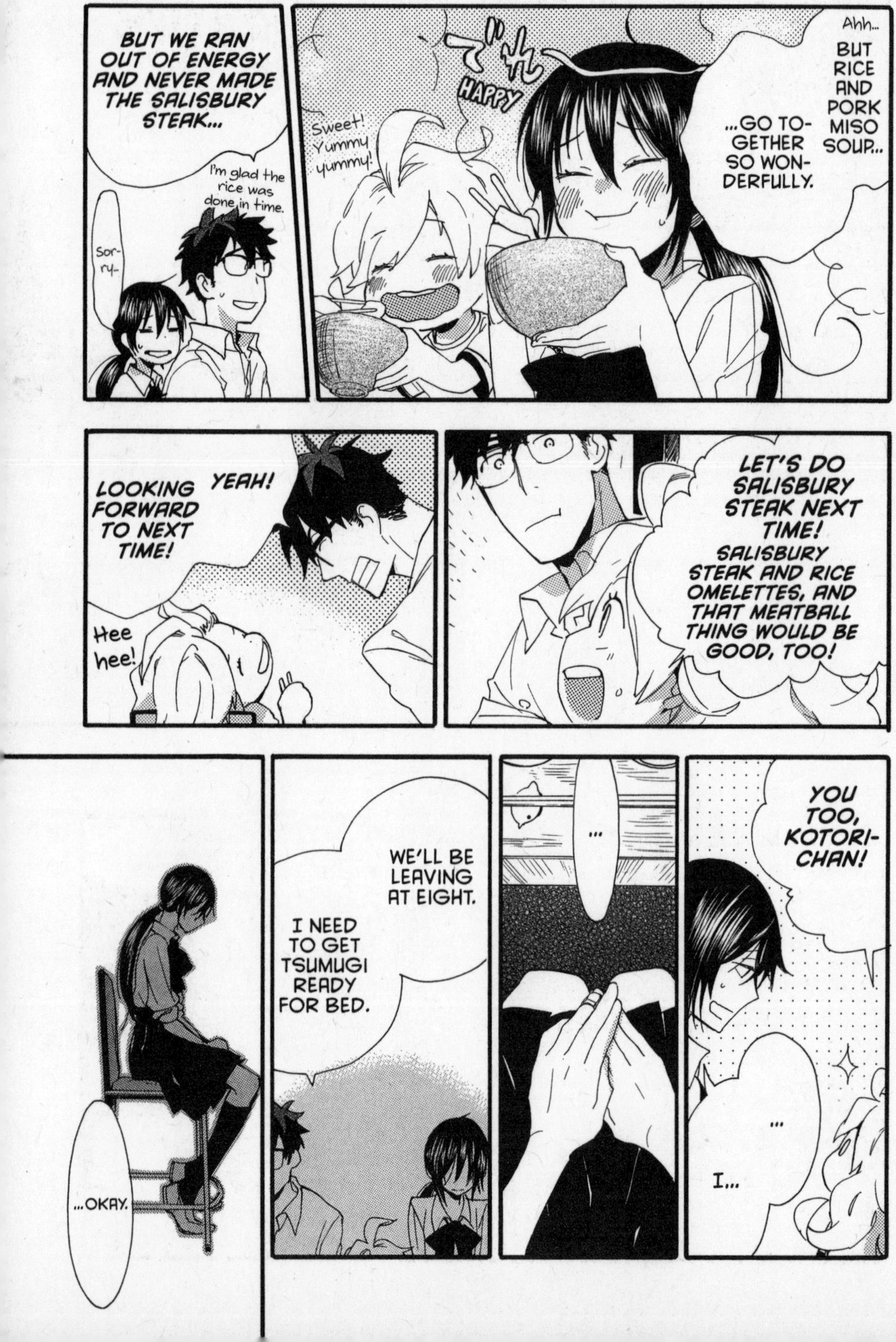
Ahh...
BUT RICE AND PORK MISO SOUP...
...GO TOGETHER SO WONDERFULLY.
でれ
HAPPY
Sweet! Yummy yummy!
BUT WE RAN OUT OF ENERGY AND NEVER MADE THE SALISBURY STEAK...
I'm glad the rice was done in time.
Sorry...
LET'S DO SALISBURY STEAK NEXT TIME!
SALISBURY STEAK AND RICE OMELETTES, AND THAT MEATBALL THING WOULD BE GOOD, TOO!
YEAH!
LOOKING FORWARD TO NEXT TIME!
Hee hee!
YOU TOO, KOTORI-CHAN!
...
I...
...
WE'LL BE LEAVING AT EIGHT.
I NEED TO GET TSUMUGI READY FOR BED.
...OKAY.

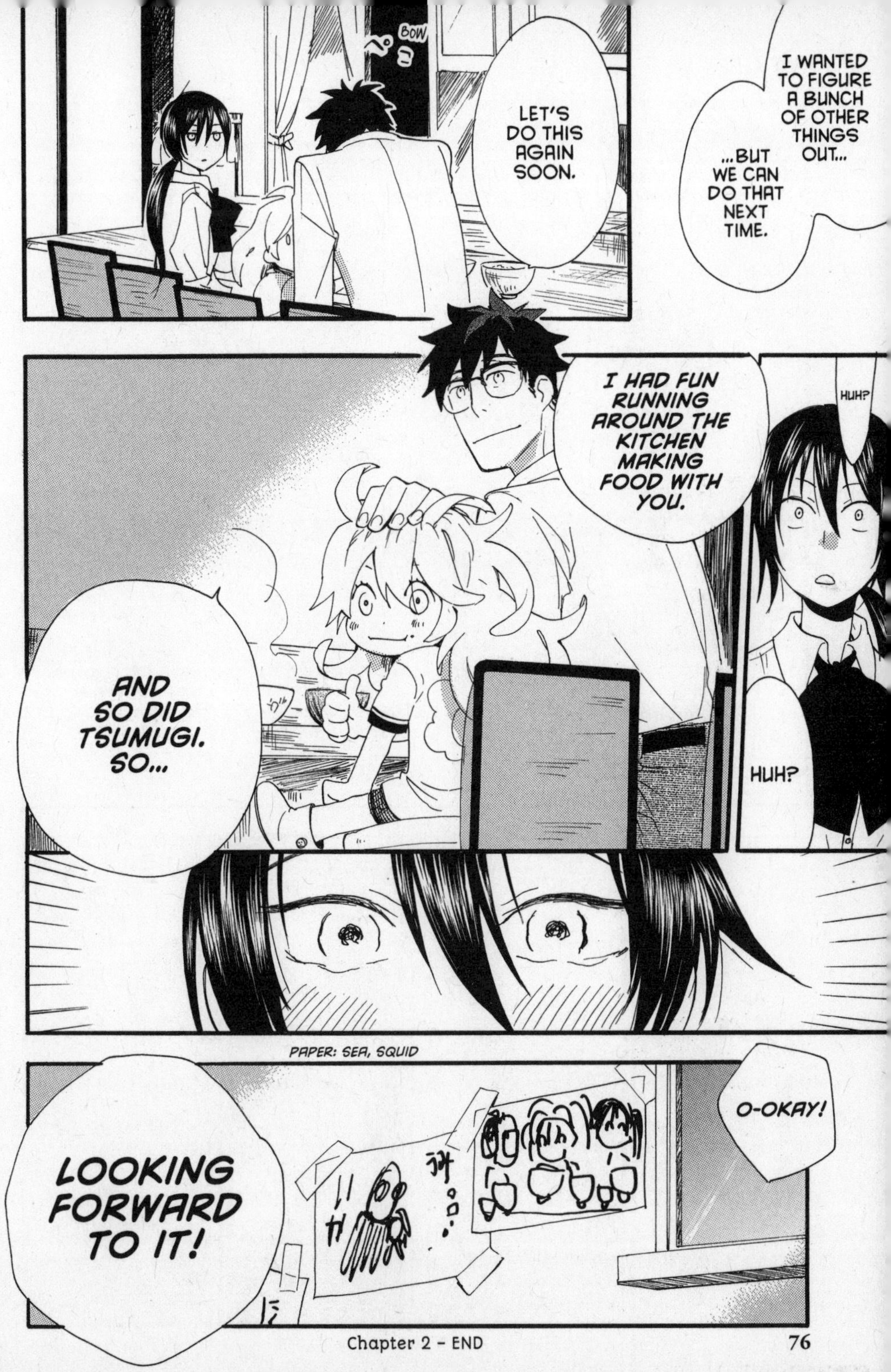
I WANTED TO FIGURE A BUNCH OF OTHER THINGS OUT... ...BUT WE CAN DO THAT NEXT TIME.
LET'S DO THIS AGAIN SOON.
BOW
HUH?
HUH?
I HAD FUN RUNNING AROUND THE KITCHEN MAKING FOOD WITH YOU.
AND SO DID TSUMUGI. SO...
PAPER: SEA, SQUID
O-OKAY!
LOOKING FORWARD TO IT!

Chapter 2 - END

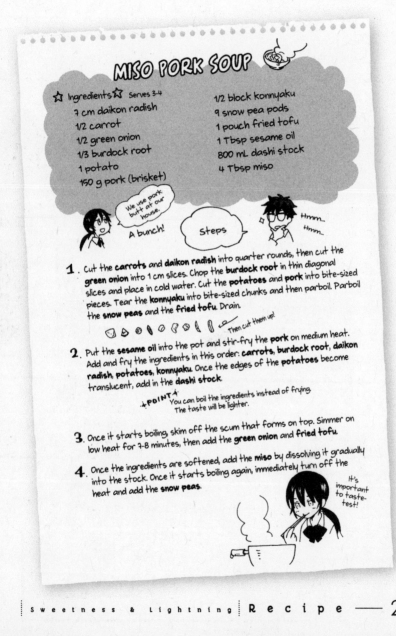

MISO PORK SOUP

☆ Ingredients ☆ Serves 3-4

- 7 cm daikon radish
- 1/2 carrot
- 1/2 green onion
- 1/3 burdock root
- 1 potato
- 150 g pork (brisket)
- 1/2 block konnyaku
- 9 snow pea pods
- 1 pouch fried tofu
- 1 Tbsp sesame oil
- 800 mL dashi stock
- 4 Tbsp miso

Hmm...
Hmm...
Steps
We use pork butt at our house.
A bunch!

1. Cut the **carrots** and **daikon radish** into quarter rounds, then cut the **green onion** into 1 cm slices. Chop the **burdock root** in thin diagonal slices and place in cold water. Cut the **potatoes** and **pork** into bite-sized pieces. Tear the **konnyaku** into bite-sized chunks and then parboil. Parboil the **snow peas** and the **fried tofu**. Drain.

Then cut them up!

2. Put the **sesame oil** into the pot and stir-fry the **pork** on medium heat. Add and fry the ingredients in this order: **carrots, burdock root, daikon radish, potatoes, konnyaku.** Once the edges of the **potatoes** become translucent, add in the **dashi stock**.

   ✦POINT✦ You can boil the ingredients instead of frying. The taste will be lighter.

3. Once it starts boiling, skim off the scum that forms on top. Simmer on low heat for 7-8 minutes, then add the **green onion** and **fried tofu**.

4. Once the ingredients are softened, add the **miso** by dissolving it gradually into the stock. Once it starts boiling again, immediately turn off the heat and add the **snow peas**.

It's important to taste-test!

CONVERSION NOTES:
7 CM DAIKON = 3 IN., 150 G PORK = ABOUT 5 1/4 OZ, 800 ML DASHI = ABOUT 3 1/3 CUPS

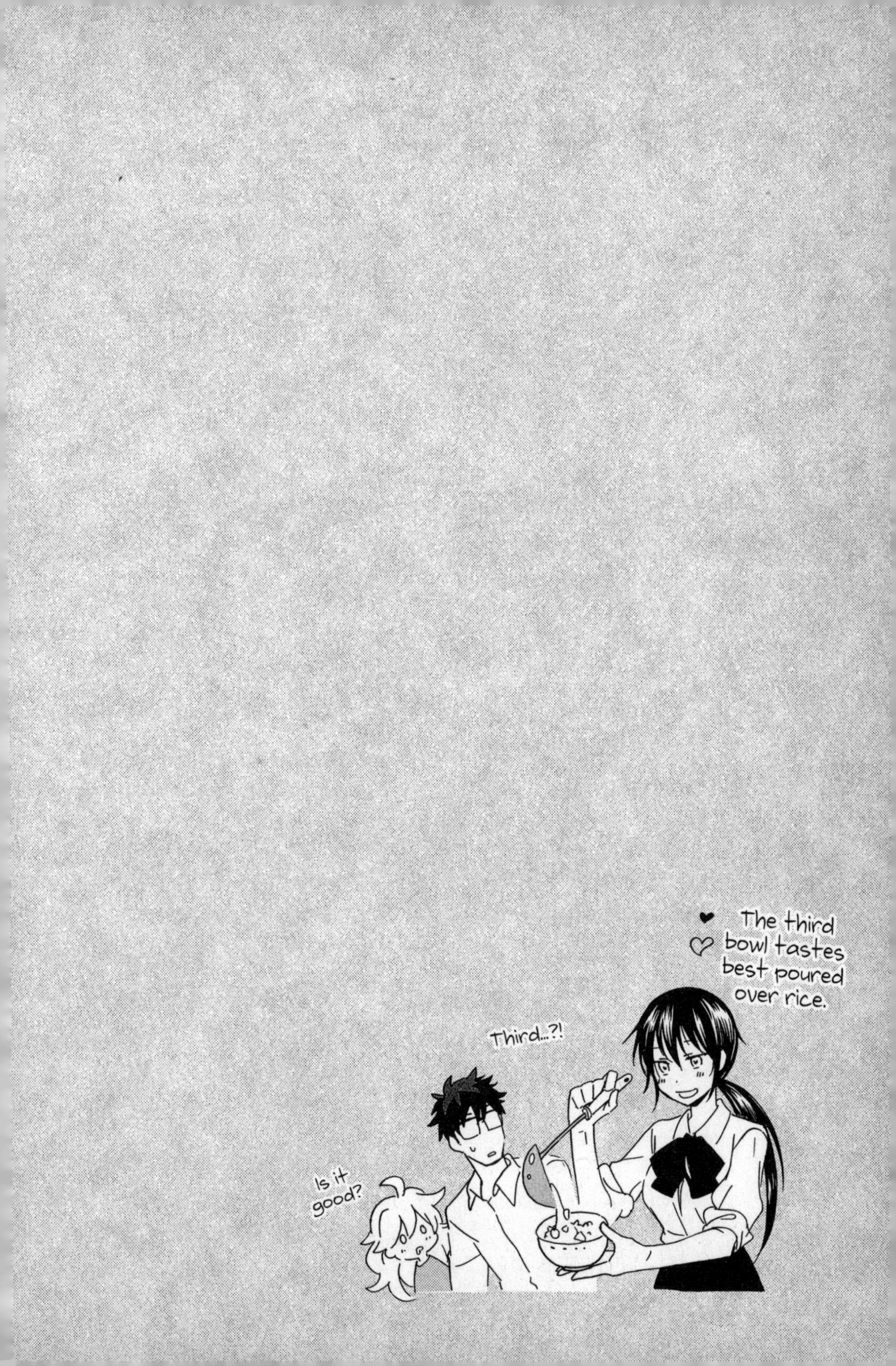
The third bowl tastes best poured over rice.
Third...?!
Is it good?

Chapter 3 Tsumugi and the Long-Awaited Salisbury Steak

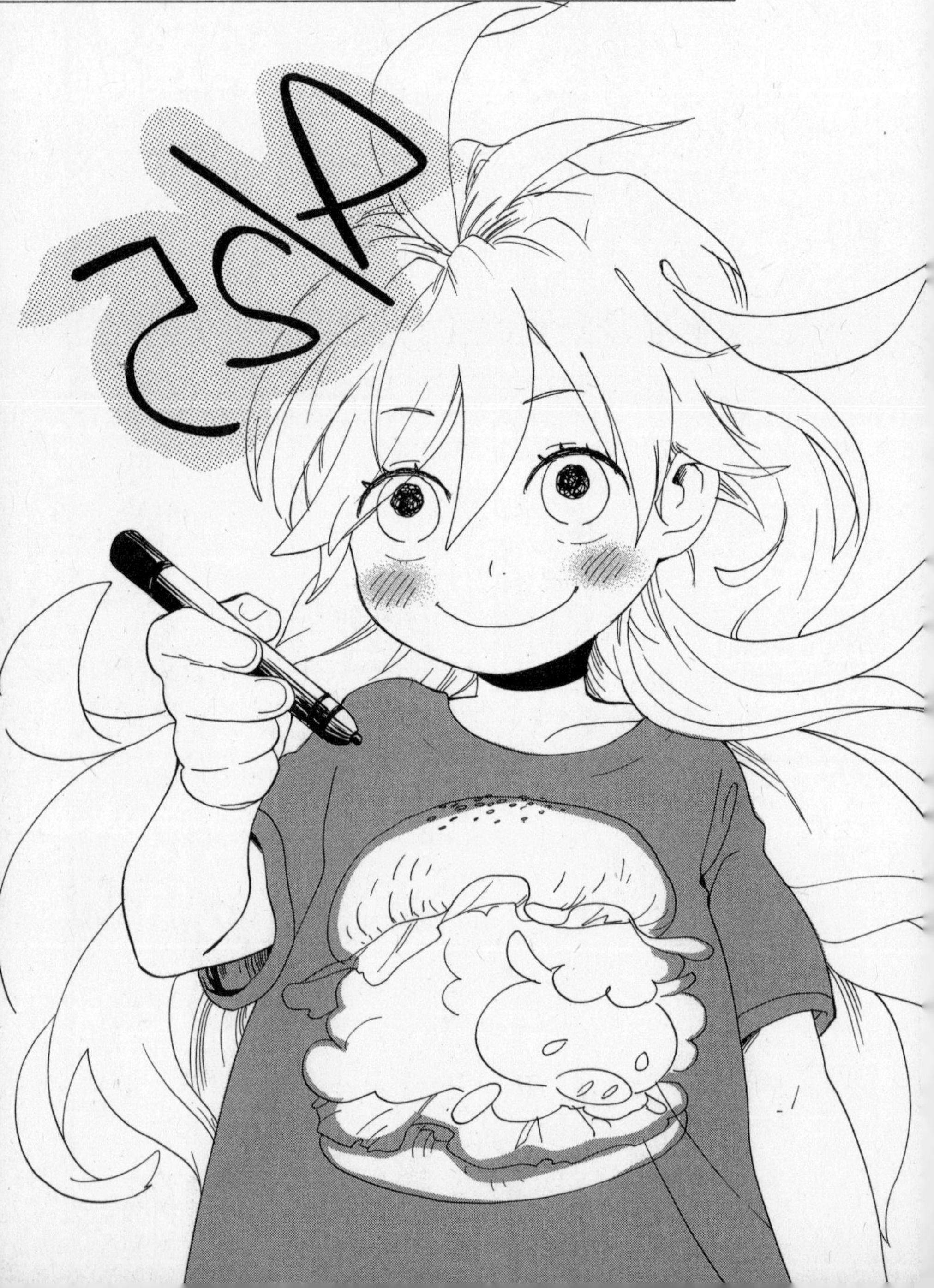

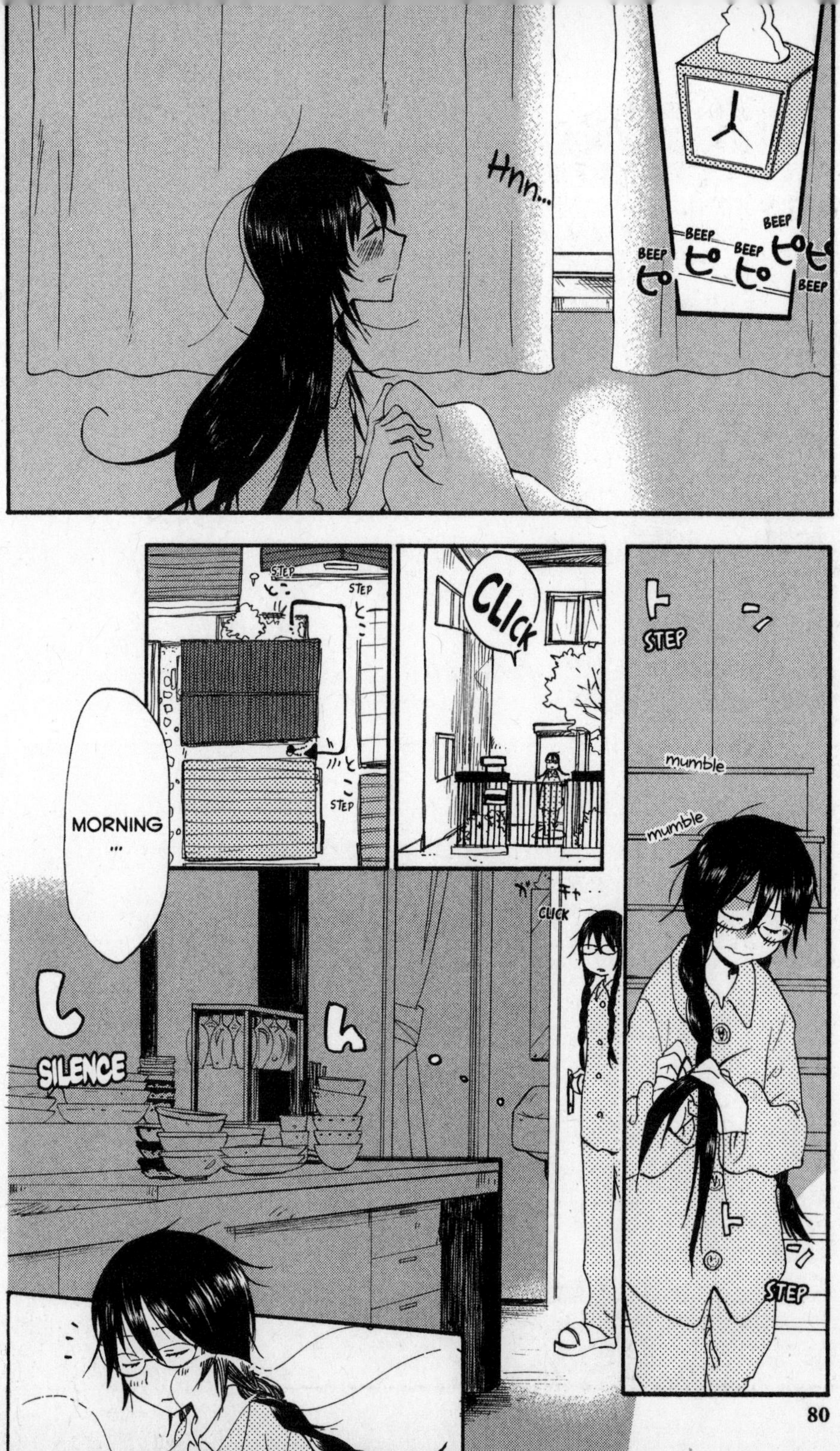

Hnn...
BEEP
ピ
BEEP
ピ
BEEP
ピ
BEEP
ピピ
ト
ン
STEP
mumble
mumble
ト
ン
STEP
CLICK
STEP
とこ
STEP
とこ
とこ
STEP
MORNING ...
しん
SILENCE
ガチャ...
CLICK

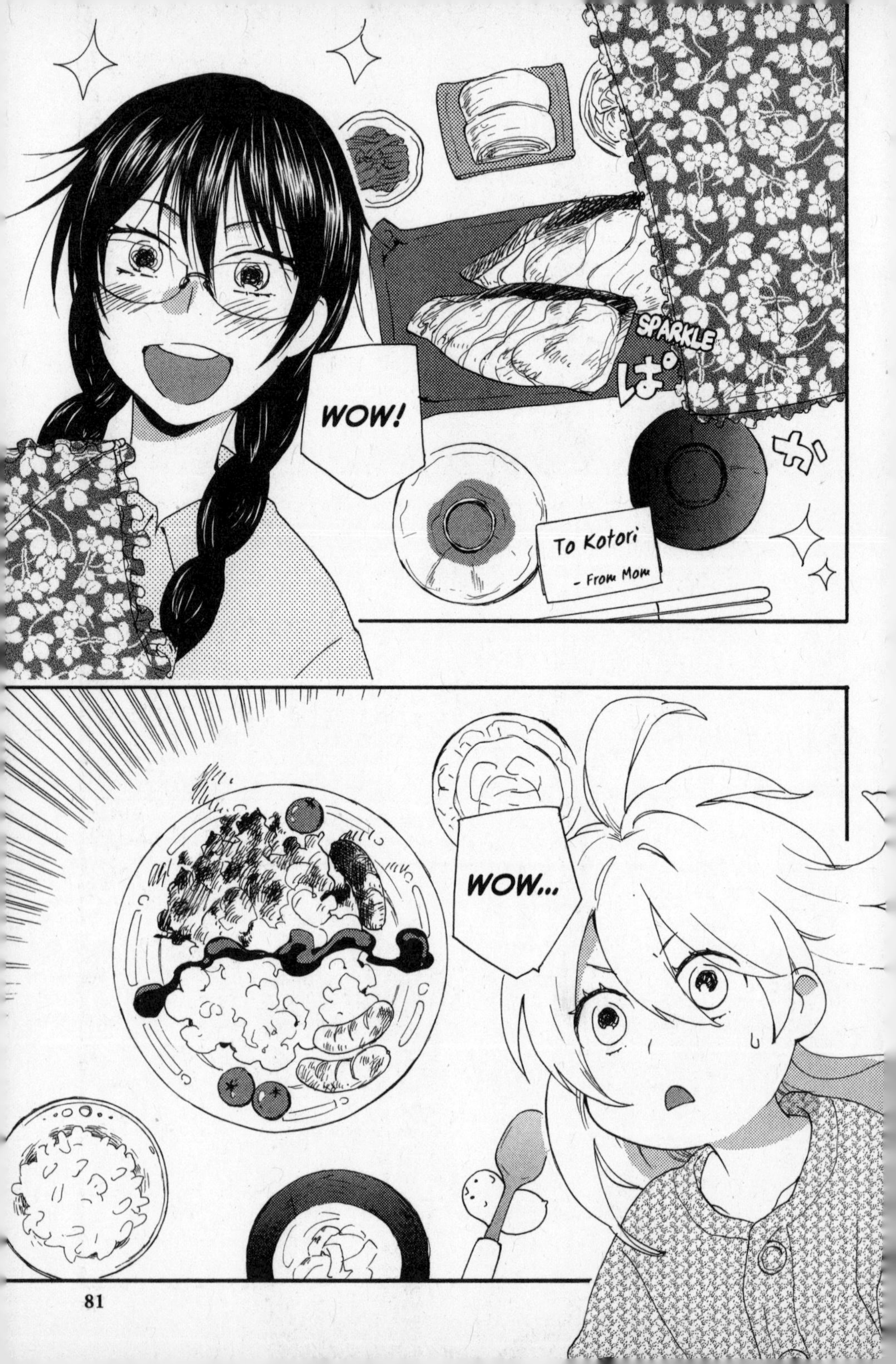
SPARKLE
WOW!
To Kotori
- From Mom
WOW...

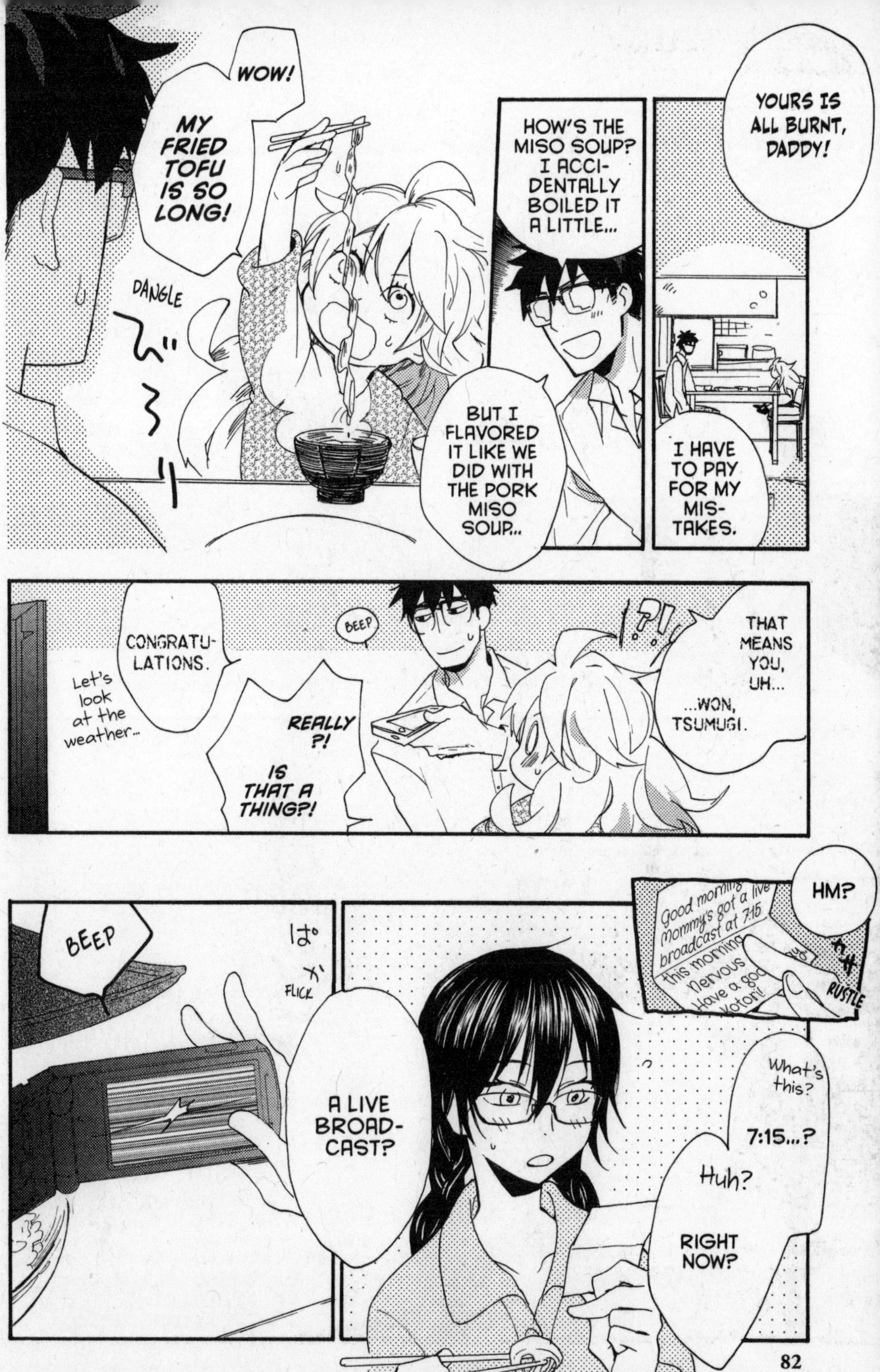
YOURS IS ALL BURNT, DADDY!
I HAVE TO PAY FOR MY MIS-TAKES.
HOW'S THE MISO SOUP? I ACCI-DENTALLY BOILED IT A LITTLE...
BUT I FLAVORED IT LIKE WE DID WITH THE PORK MISO SOUP...
WOW!
MY FRIED TOFU IS SO LONG!
DANGLE
THAT MEANS YOU, UH...
...WON, TSUMUGI.
!?!
BEEP
REALLY?!
IS THAT A THING?!
CONGRATU-LATIONS.
Let's look at the weather...
HM?
Good morning
Mommy's got a live
broadcast at 7:15
this morning
Nervous
Kotori!
RUSTLE
What's this?
7:15...?
Huh?
RIGHT NOW?
A LIVE BROAD-CAST?
BEEP
FLICK

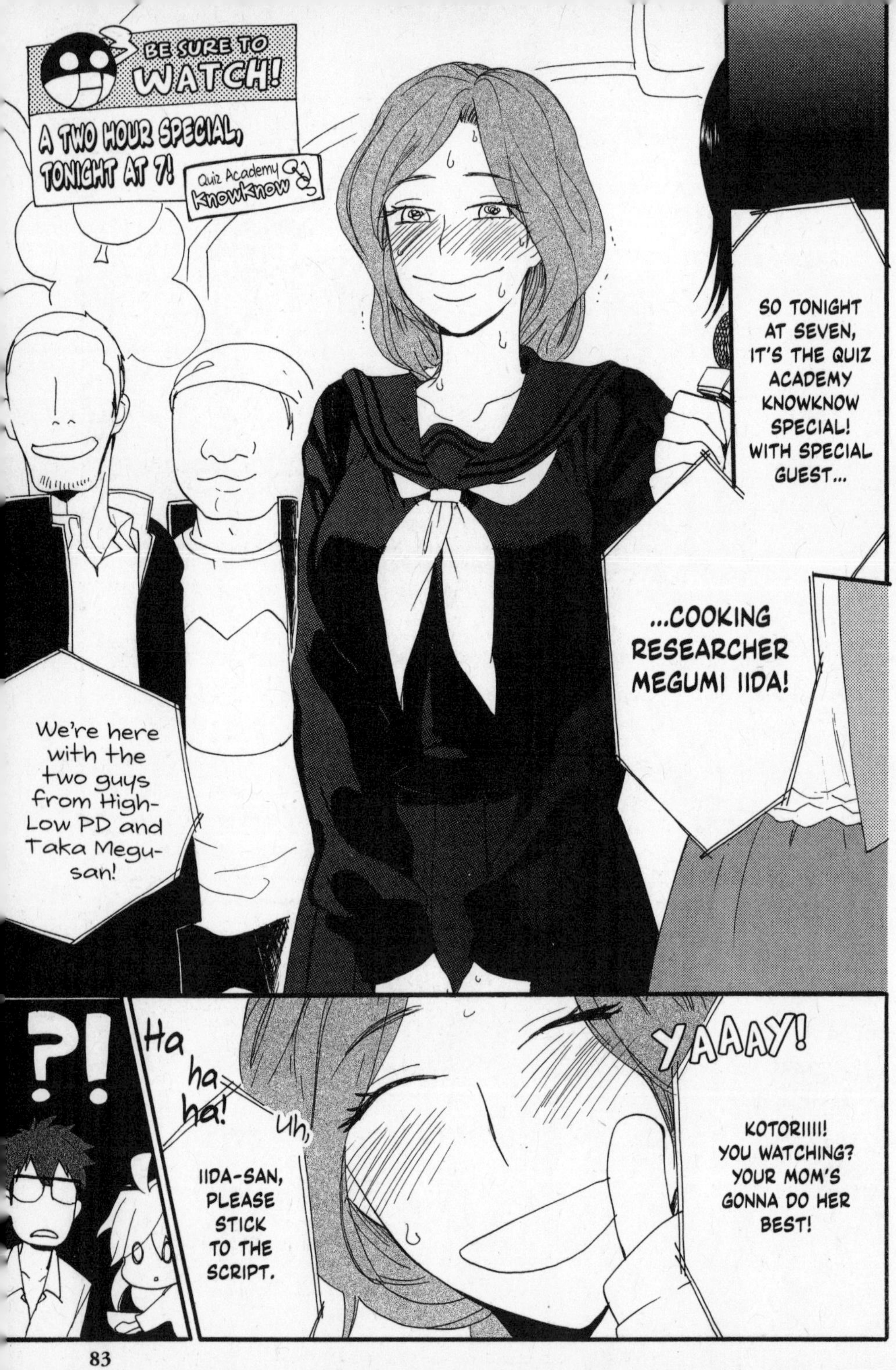
BE SURE TO WATCH!
A TWO HOUR SPECIAL, TONIGHT AT 7!
Quiz Academy KnowKnow
SO TONIGHT AT SEVEN, IT'S THE QUIZ ACADEMY KNOWKNOW SPECIAL! WITH SPECIAL GUEST...
...COOKING RESEARCHER MEGUMI IIDA!
We're here with the two guys from High-Low PD and Taka Megu-san!
YAAAY!
KOTORIIII! YOU WATCHING? YOUR MOM'S GONNA DO HER BEST!
Ha ha ha!
Uh,
IIDA-SAN, PLEASE STICK TO THE SCRIPT.
?!

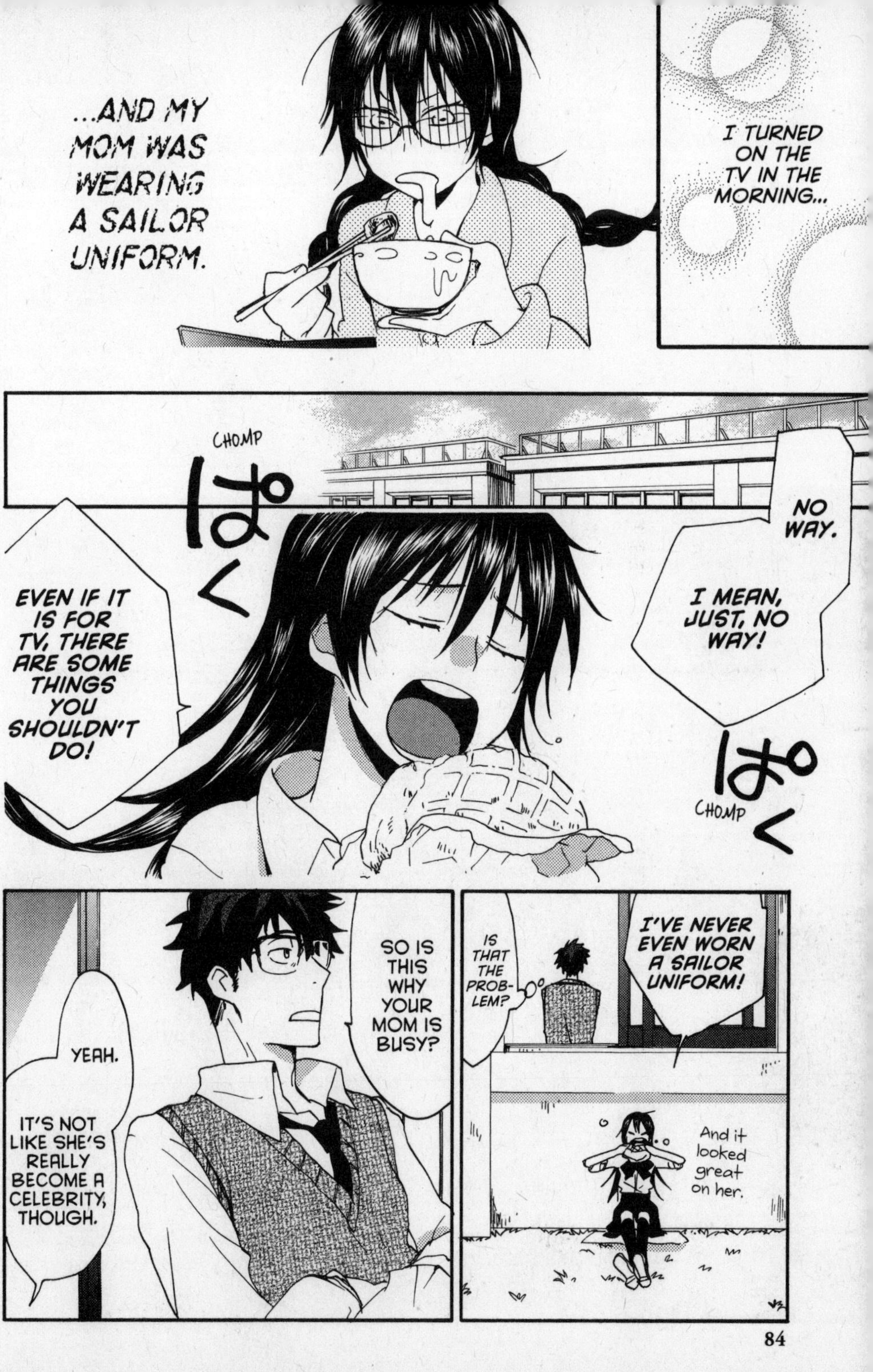
I TURNED ON THE TV IN THE MORNING...
...AND MY MOM WAS WEARING A SAILOR UNIFORM.
NO WAY.
I MEAN, JUST, NO WAY!
ぱく
CHOMP
ぱく
CHOMP
EVEN IF IT IS FOR TV, THERE ARE SOME THINGS YOU SHOULDN'T DO!
I'VE NEVER EVEN WORN A SAILOR UNIFORM!
IS THAT THE PROB-LEM?
And it looked great on her.
SO IS THIS WHY YOUR MOM IS BUSY?
YEAH.
IT'S NOT LIKE SHE'S REALLY BECOME A CELEBRITY, THOUGH.

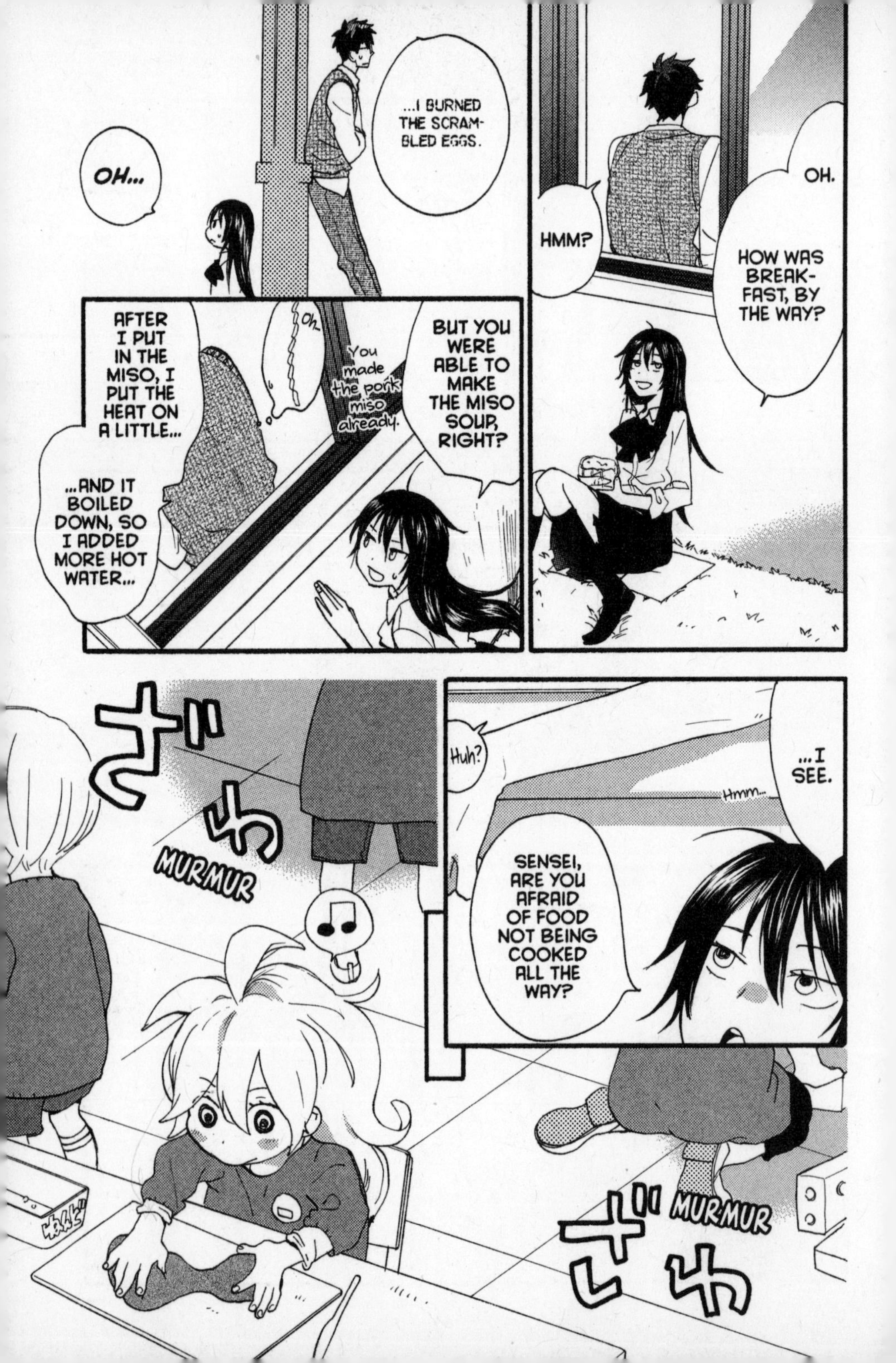
OH.
HOW WAS BREAK-FAST, BY THE WAY?
HMM?
...I BURNED THE SCRAM-BLED EGGS.
OH...
BUT YOU WERE ABLE TO MAKE THE MISO SOUP, RIGHT?
Oh...
You made the pork miso already.
AFTER I PUT IN THE MISO, I PUT THE HEAT ON A LITTLE...
...AND IT BOILED DOWN, SO I ADDED MORE HOT WATER...
...I SEE.
Hmm...
Huh?
SENSEI, ARE YOU AFRAID OF FOOD NOT BEING COOKED ALL THE WAY?
ざわ
MURMUR
ざわ
MURMUR

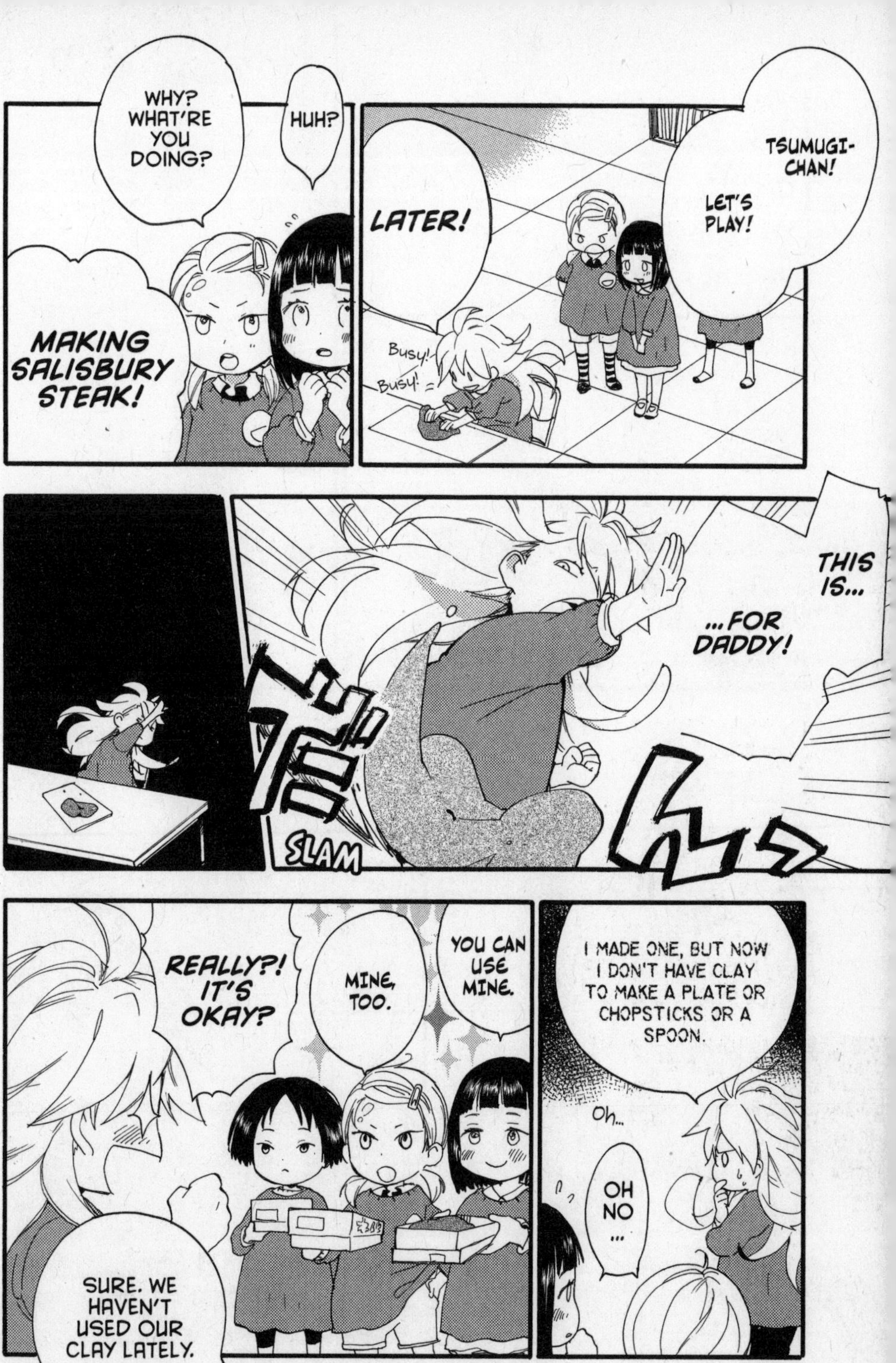
TSUMUGI-CHAN!
LET'S PLAY!
LATER!
Busy! Busy!
HUH?
WHY? WHAT'RE YOU DOING?
MAKING SALISBURY STEAK!
THIS IS...
...FOR DADDY!
SLAM
I MADE ONE, BUT NOW I DON'T HAVE CLAY TO MAKE A PLATE OR CHOPSTICKS OR A SPOON.
Oh...
OH NO ...
YOU CAN USE MINE.
MINE, TOO.
REALLY?! IT'S OKAY?
SURE. WE HAVEN'T USED OUR CLAY LATELY.

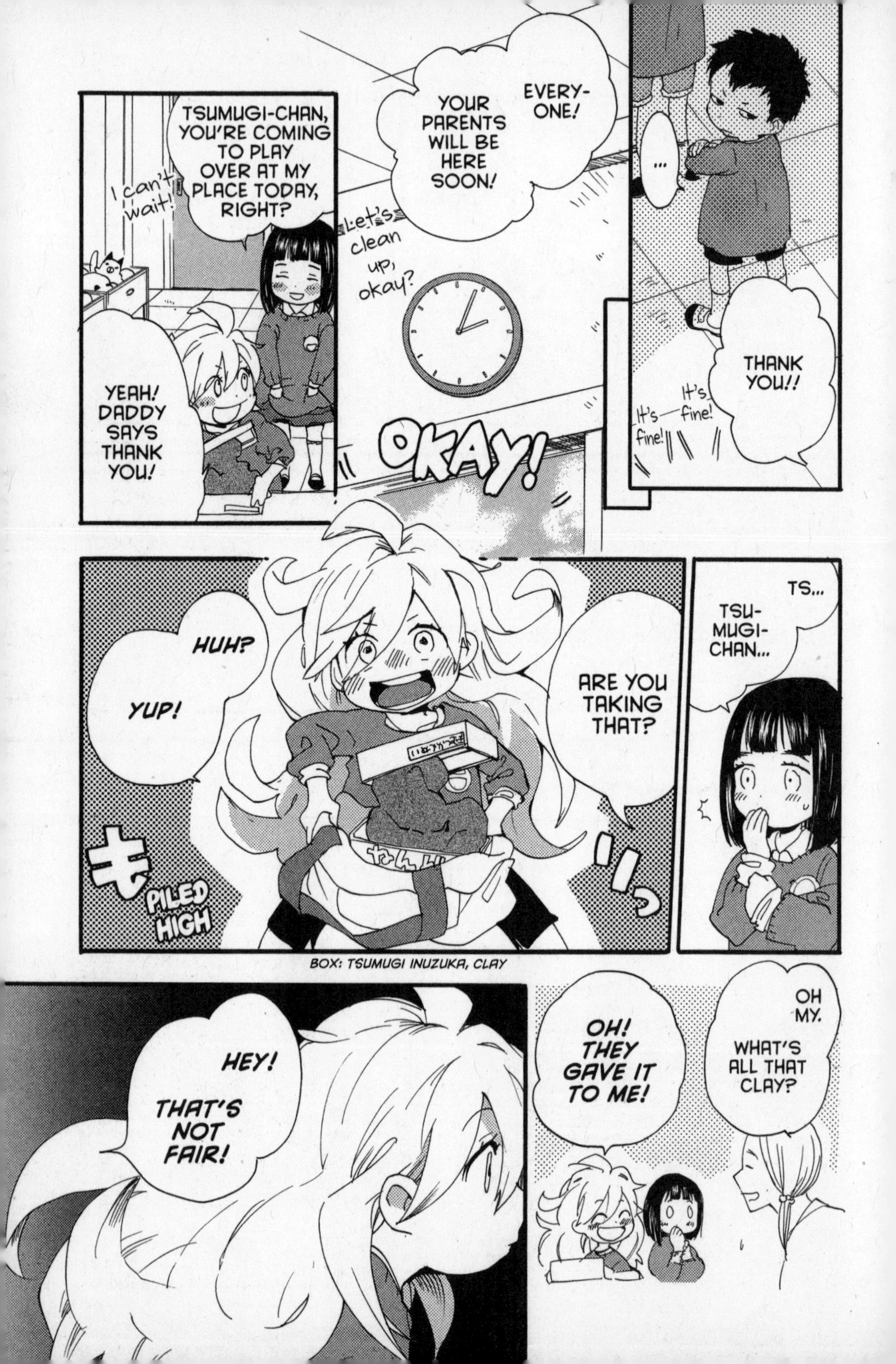
...
THANK YOU!!
It's fine! It's fine!
EVERY-ONE! YOUR PARENTS WILL BE HERE SOON!
Let's clean up, okay?
OKAY!
TSUMUGI-CHAN, YOU'RE COMING TO PLAY OVER AT MY PLACE TODAY, RIGHT?
I can't wait!
YEAH! DADDY SAYS THANK YOU!
TS... TSUMUGI-CHAN...
ARE YOU TAKING THAT?
HUH?
YUP!
PILED HIGH
BOX: TSUMUGI INUZUKA, CLAY
OH MY. WHAT'S ALL THAT CLAY?
OH! THEY GAVE IT TO ME!
HEY! THAT'S NOT FAIR!

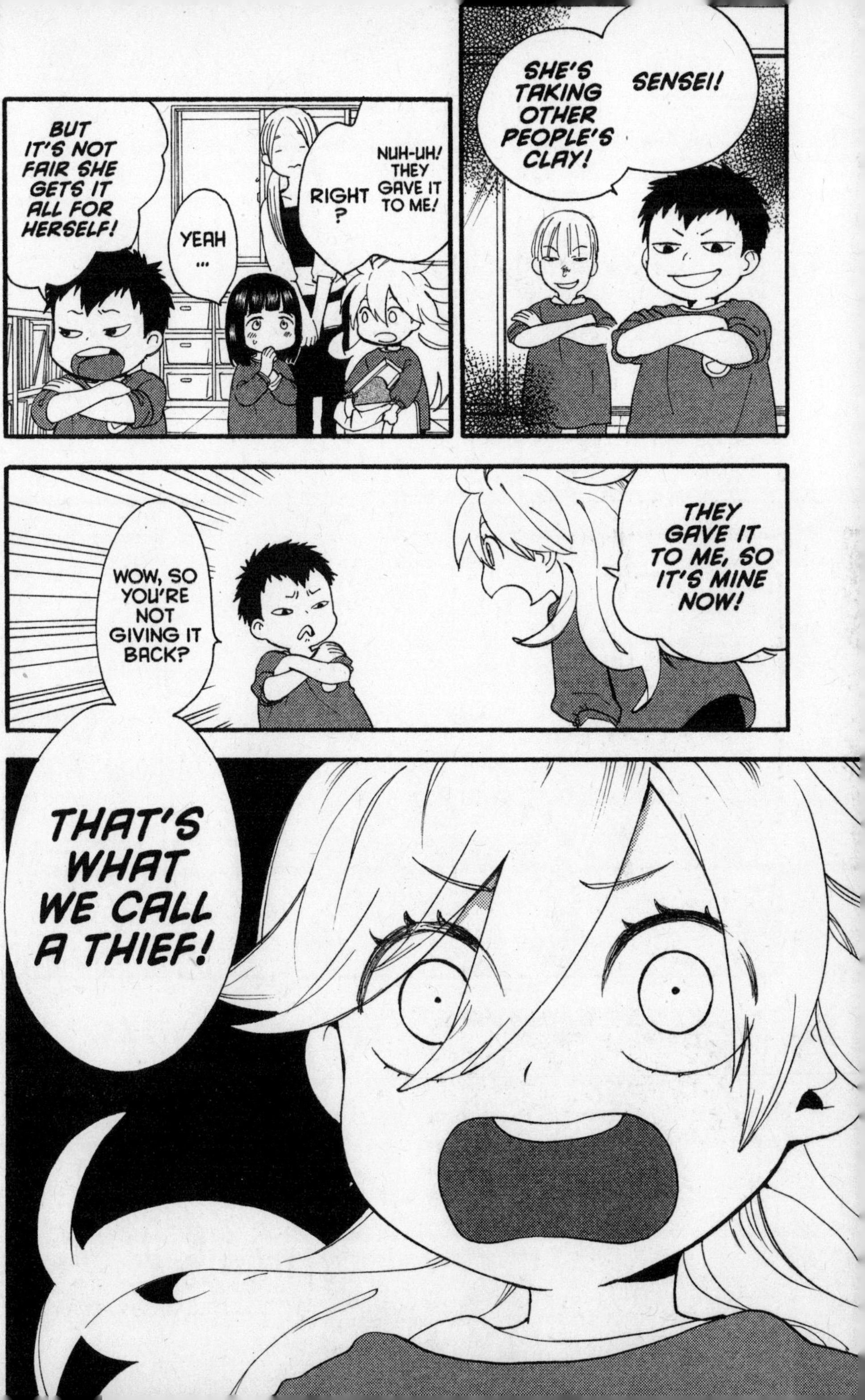
SENSEI!
SHE'S TAKING OTHER PEOPLE'S CLAY!
NUH-UH! THEY GAVE IT TO ME!
RIGHT?
YEAH ...
BUT IT'S NOT FAIR SHE GETS IT ALL FOR HERSELF!
THEY GAVE IT TO ME, SO IT'S MINE NOW!
WOW, SO YOU'RE NOT GIVING IT BACK?
THAT'S WHAT WE CALL A THIEF!

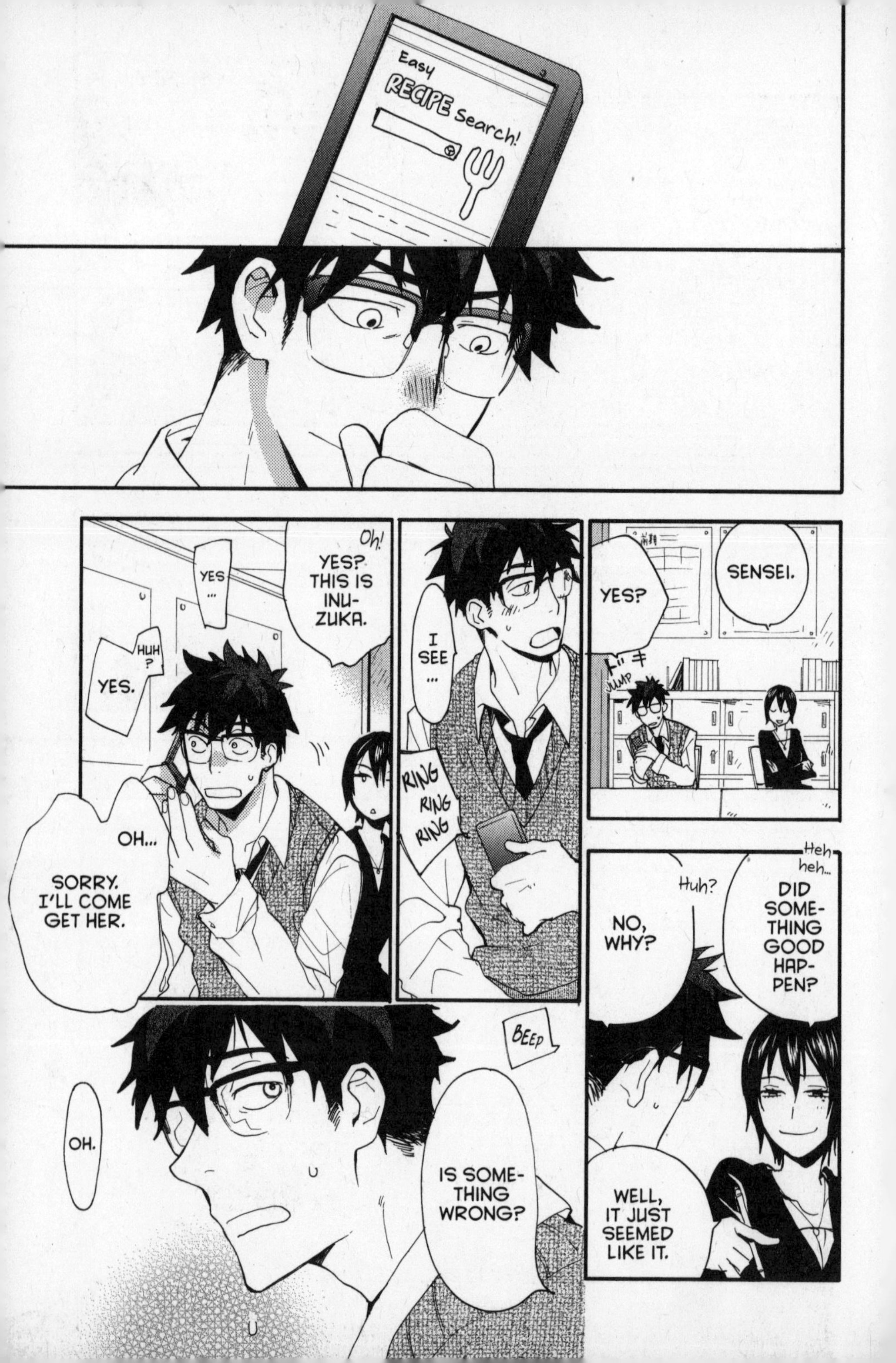

Easy
RECIPE Search!
SENSEI.
YES?
ドキ JUMP
Oh!
YES? THIS IS INUZUKA.
I SEE...
RING RING RING
YES...
HUH?
YES.
OH...
SORRY. I'LL COME GET HER.
Heh heh...
DID SOMETHING GOOD HAPPEN?
Huh?
NO, WHY?
WELL, IT JUST SEEMED LIKE IT.
BEEP
IS SOMETHING WRONG?
OH.

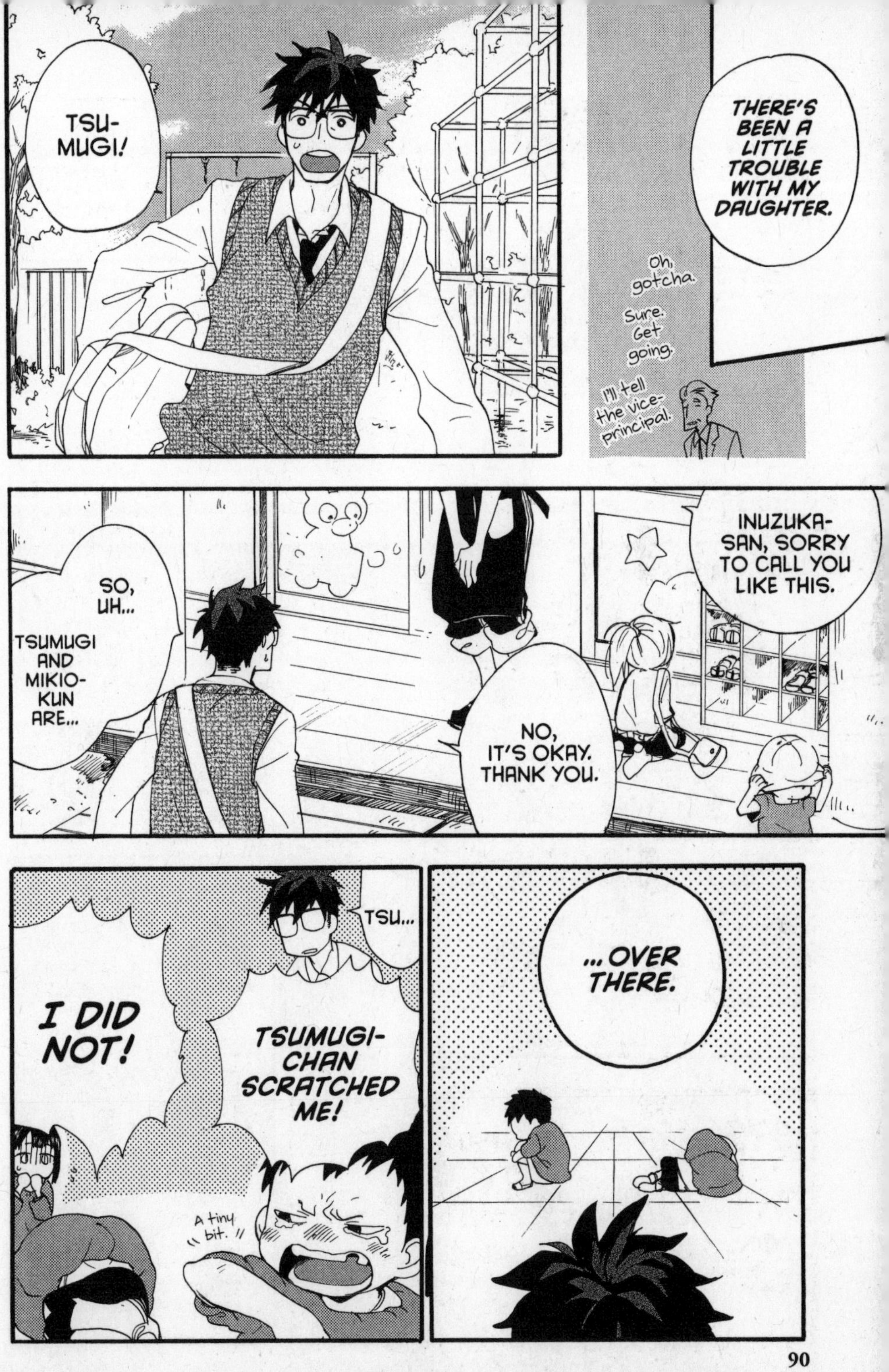
THERE'S BEEN A LITTLE TROUBLE WITH MY DAUGHTER.
Oh, gotcha.
Sure. Get going.
I'll tell the vice-principal.
TSU-MUGI!
INUZUKA-SAN, SORRY TO CALL YOU LIKE THIS.
NO, IT'S OKAY. THANK YOU.
SO, UH...
TSUMUGI AND MIKIO-KUN ARE...
...OVER THERE.
TSU...
TSUMUGI-CHAN SCRATCHED ME!
I DID NOT!
A tiny bit.

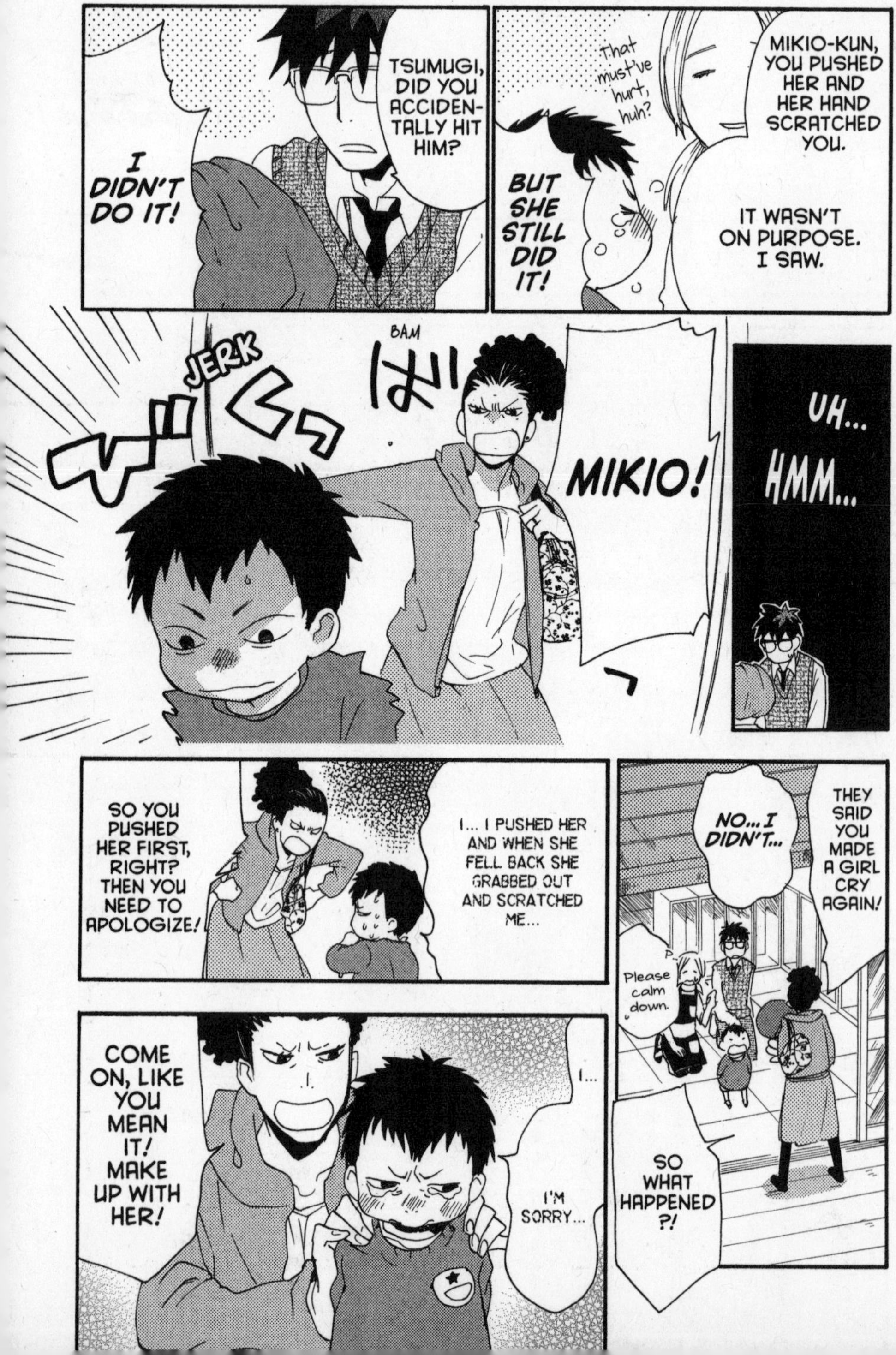
MIKIO-KUN, YOU PUSHED HER AND HER HAND SCRATCHED YOU.
That must've hurt, huh?
IT WASN'T ON PURPOSE. I SAW.
BUT SHE STILL DID IT!
TSUMUGI, DID YOU ACCIDEN-TALLY HIT HIM?
I DIDN'T DO IT!
UH... HMM...
MIKIO!
BAM
JERK
THEY SAID YOU MADE A GIRL CRY AGAIN!
NO... I DIDN'T...
Please calm down.
SO WHAT HAPPENED?!
I... I PUSHED HER AND WHEN SHE FELL BACK SHE GRABBED OUT AND SCRATCHED ME...
SO YOU PUSHED HER FIRST, RIGHT? THEN YOU NEED TO APOLOGIZE!
I...
I'M SORRY...
COME ON, LIKE YOU MEAN IT! MAKE UP WITH HER!

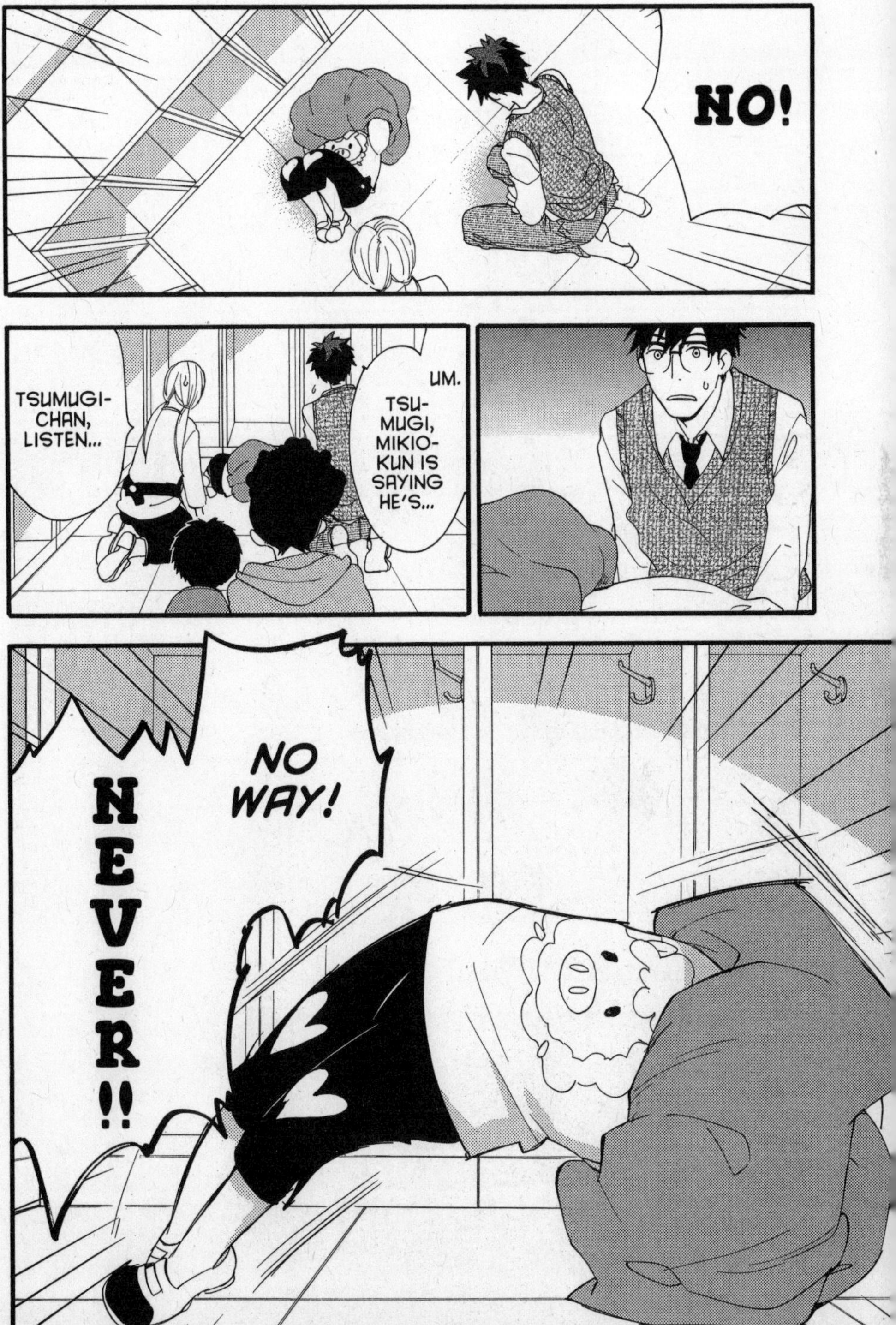
NO!
UM.
TSUMUGI, MIKIO-KUN IS SAYING HE'S...
TSUMUGI-CHAN, LISTEN...
NO WAY!
NEVER!!

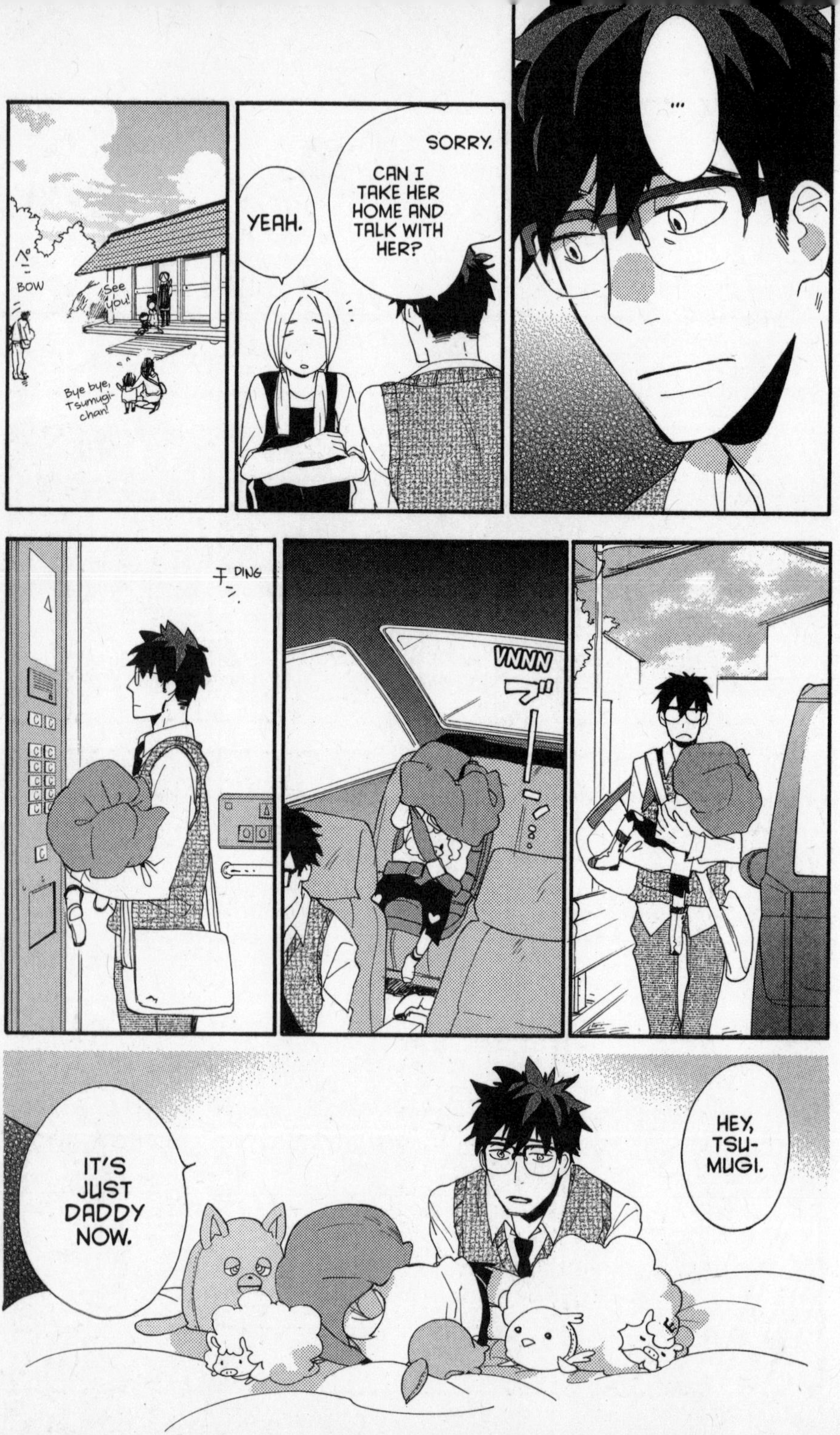
...
SORRY.
CAN I TAKE HER HOME AND TALK WITH HER?
YEAH.
BOW
See you!
Bye bye, Tsumugi-chan!
VNNN
DING
HEY, TSUMUGI.
IT'S JUST DADDY NOW.

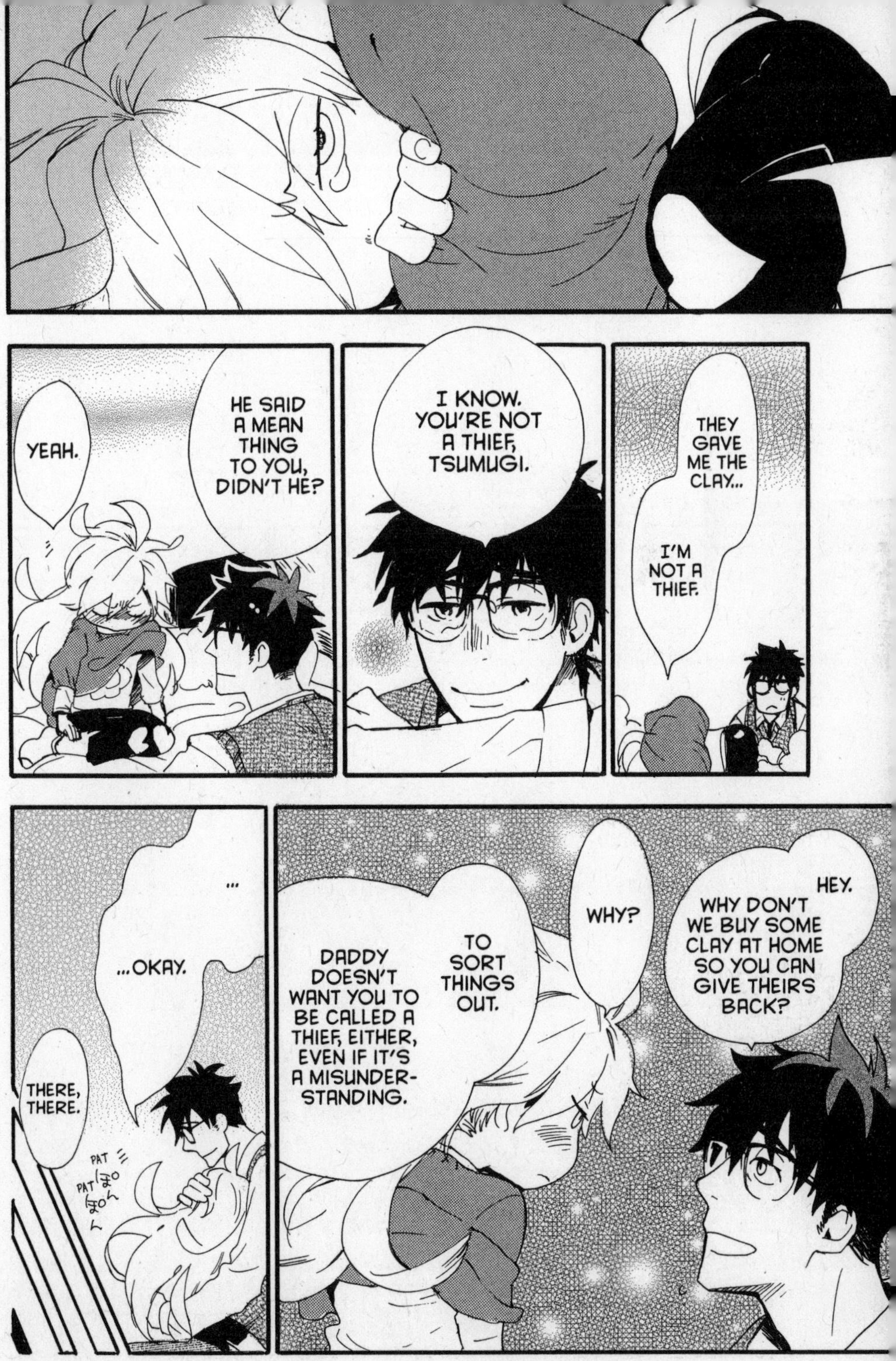
THEY GAVE ME THE CLAY...
I'M NOT A THIEF.
I KNOW. YOU'RE NOT A THIEF, TSUMUGI.
HE SAID A MEAN THING TO YOU, DIDN'T HE?
YEAH.
HEY. WHY DON'T WE BUY SOME CLAY AT HOME SO YOU CAN GIVE THEIRS BACK?
WHY?
TO SORT THINGS OUT.
DADDY DOESN'T WANT YOU TO BE CALLED A THIEF, EITHER, EVEN IF IT'S A MISUNDERSTANDING.
...
...OKAY.
THERE, THERE.
PAT PAT

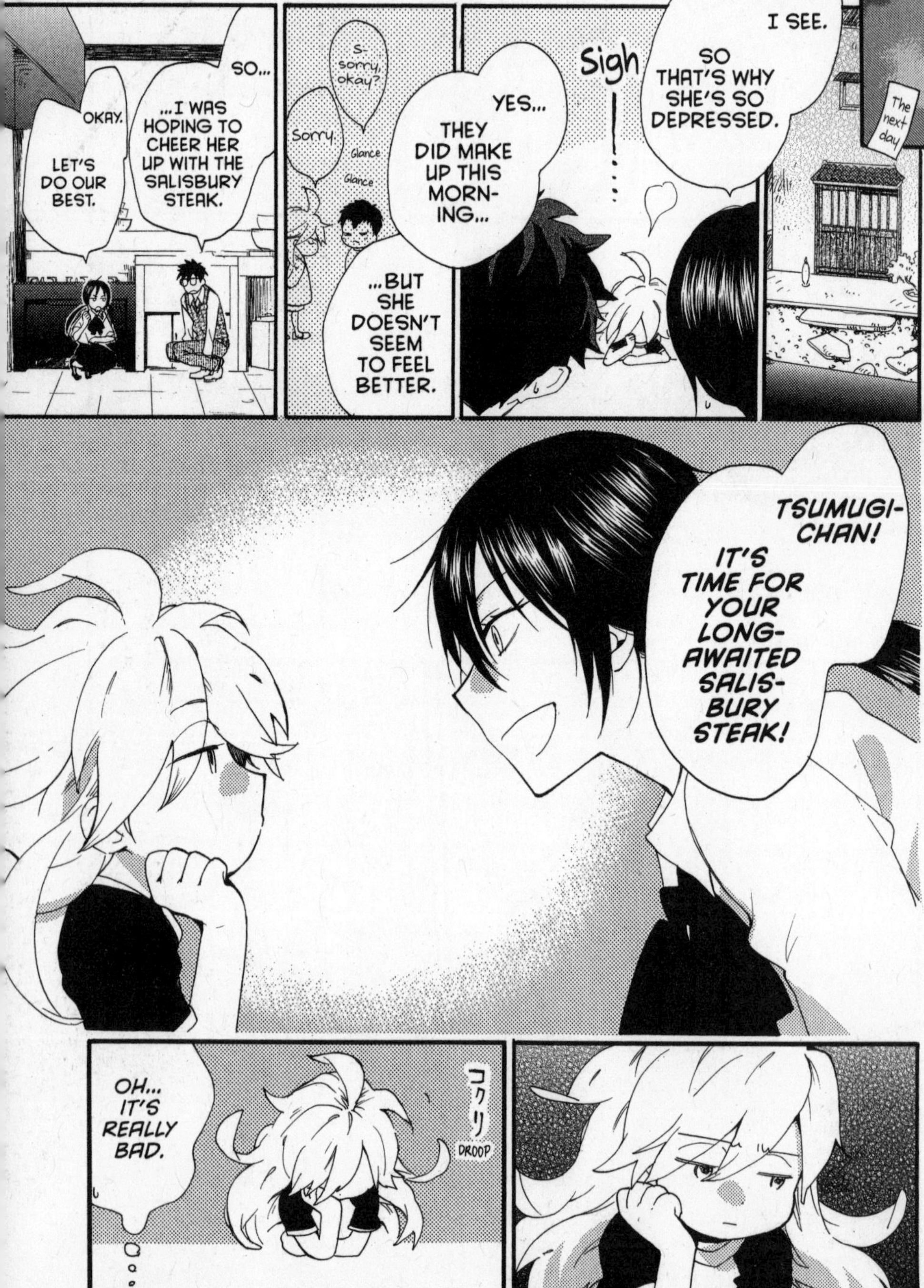

The next day
I SEE.
SO THAT'S WHY SHE'S SO DEPRESSED.
Sigh
YES... THEY DID MAKE UP THIS MORNING...
...BUT SHE DOESN'T SEEM TO FEEL BETTER.
S-sorry, okay?
Sorry.
Glance
Glance
SO...
...I WAS HOPING TO CHEER HER UP WITH THE SALISBURY STEAK.
OKAY.
LET'S DO OUR BEST.
TSUMUGI-CHAN! IT'S TIME FOR YOUR LONG-AWAITED SALISBURY STEAK!
コクリ
DROOP
OH... IT'S REALLY BAD.

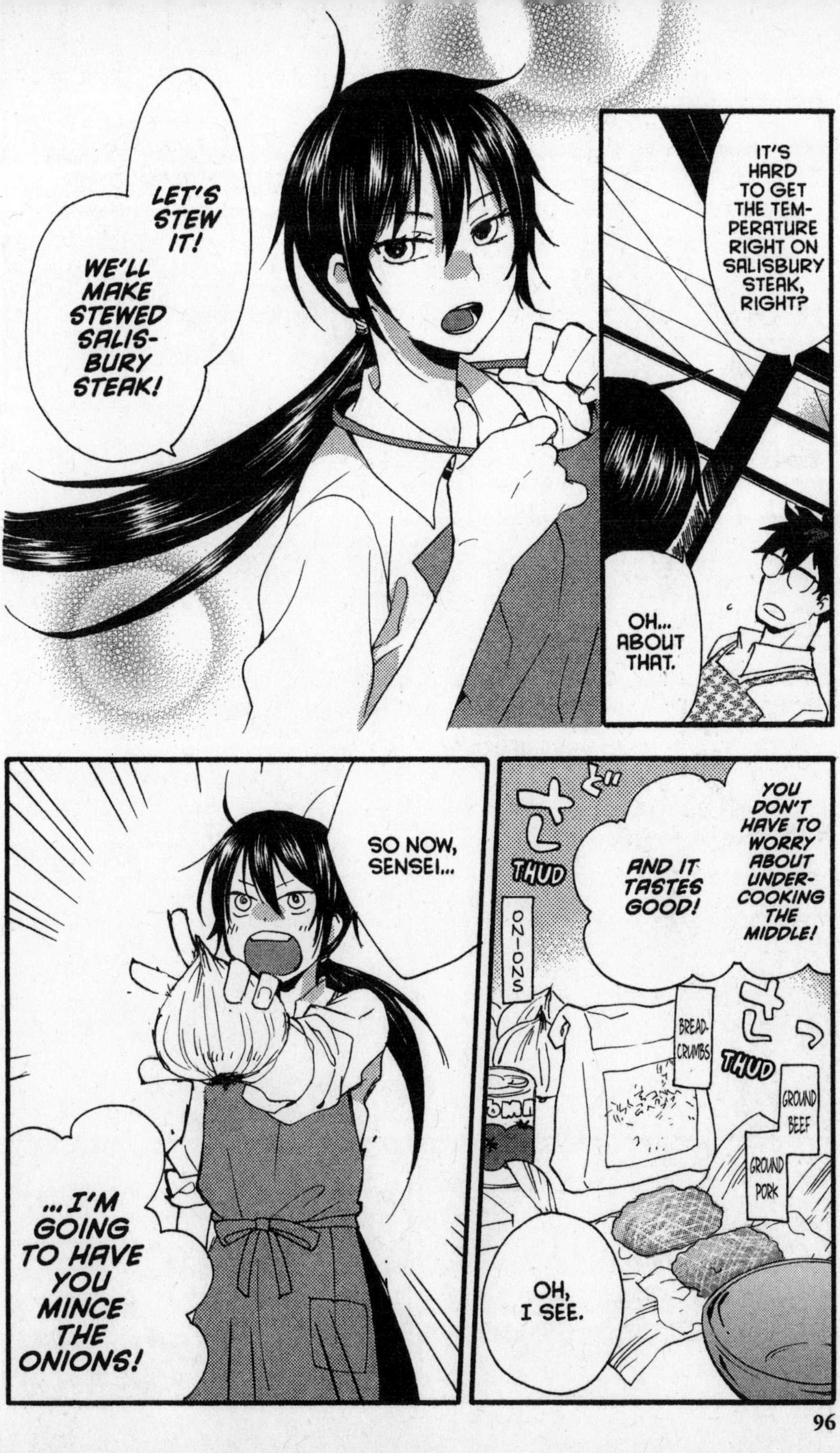
IT'S HARD TO GET THE TEMPERATURE RIGHT ON SALISBURY STEAK, RIGHT?
OH... ABOUT THAT.
LET'S STEW IT!
WE'LL MAKE STEWED SALISBURY STEAK!
YOU DON'T HAVE TO WORRY ABOUT UNDERCOOKING THE MIDDLE!
AND IT TASTES GOOD!
THUD
ONIONS
BREADCRUMBS
THUD
GROUND BEEF
GROUND PORK
OH, I SEE.
SO NOW, SENSEI...
...I'M GOING TO HAVE YOU MINCE THE ONIONS!

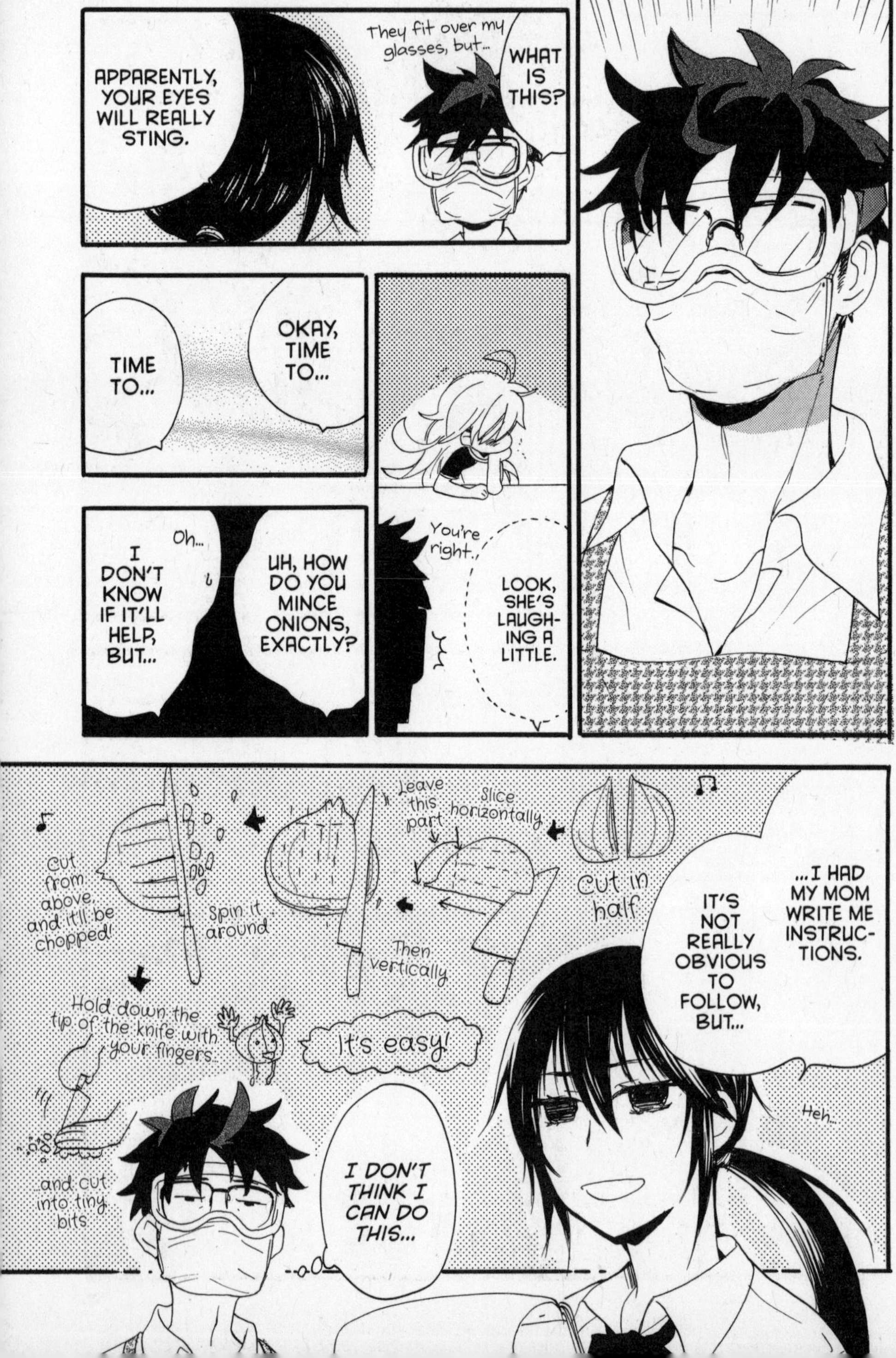

They fit over my glasses, but...
WHAT IS THIS?
APPARENTLY, YOUR EYES WILL REALLY STING.
OKAY, TIME TO...
TIME TO...
You're right..
LOOK, SHE'S LAUGHING A LITTLE.
UH, HOW DO YOU MINCE ONIONS, EXACTLY?
Oh...
I DON'T KNOW IF IT'LL HELP, BUT...
...I HAD MY MOM WRITE ME INSTRUCTIONS.
IT'S NOT REALLY OBVIOUS TO FOLLOW, BUT...
Heh...
Cut in half
Slice horizontally
Leave this part
Then vertically
Spin it around
Cut from above, and it'll be chopped!
Hold down the tip of the knife with your fingers...
...and cut into tiny bits
It's easy!
I DON'T THINK I CAN DO THIS...

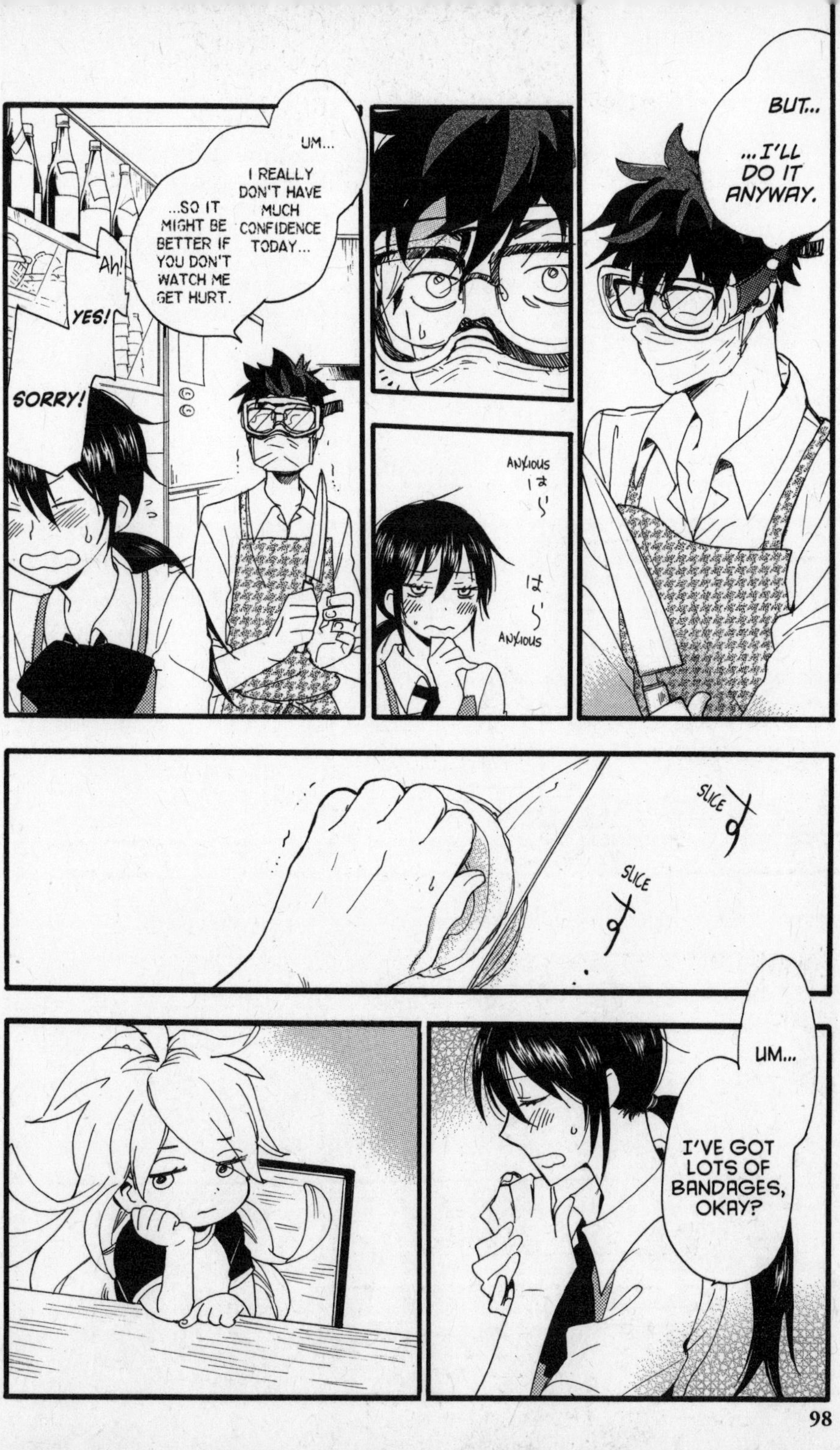
BUT...
...I'LL DO IT ANYWAY.
ANXIOUS はら
はら ANXIOUS
UM...
I REALLY DON'T HAVE MUCH CONFIDENCE TODAY...
...SO IT MIGHT BE BETTER IF YOU DON'T WATCH ME GET HURT.
Ah!
YES!
SORRY!
SLICE す
SLICE す
UM...
I'VE GOT LOTS OF BANDAGES, OKAY?

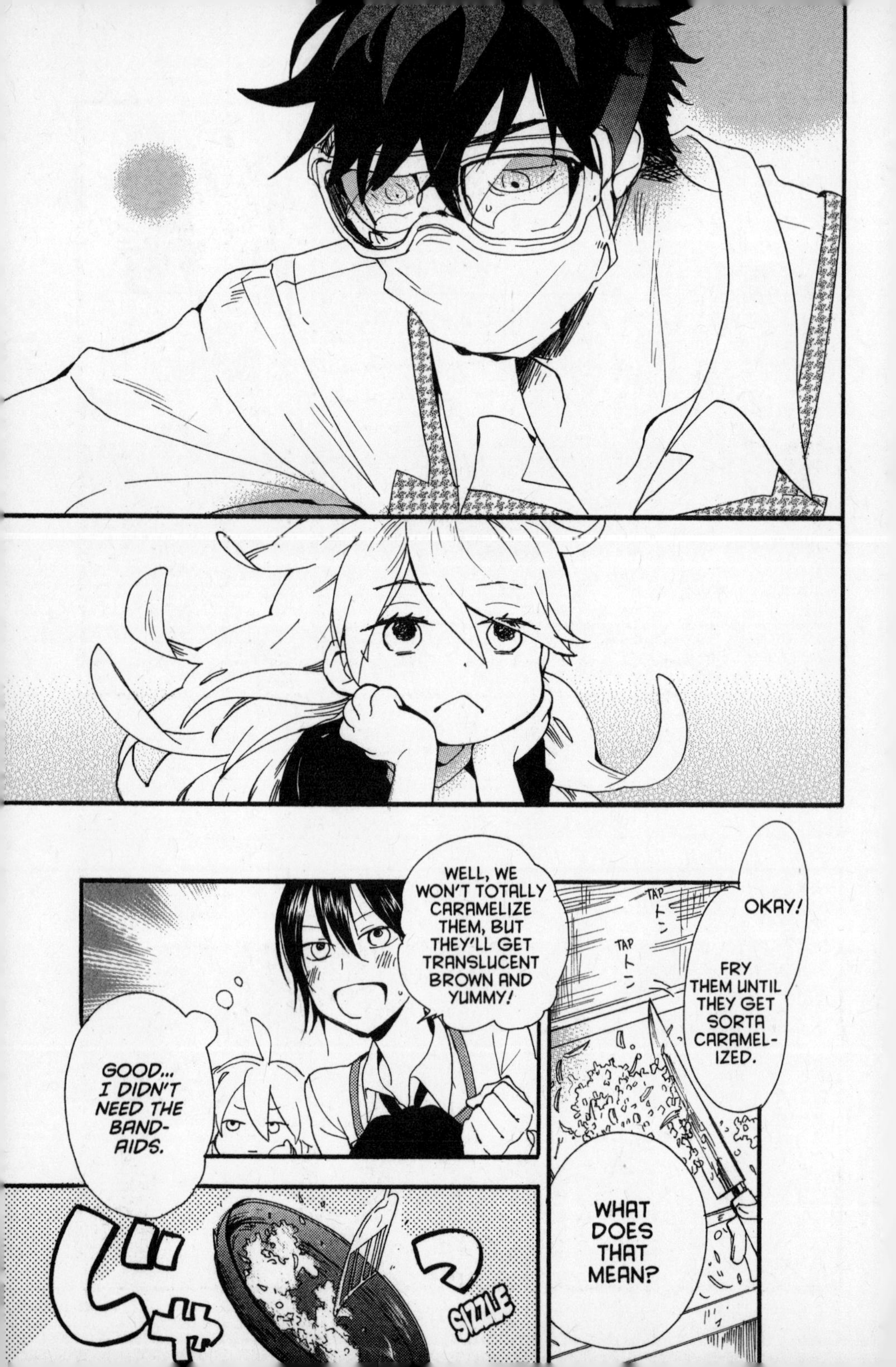
OKAY!
FRY THEM UNTIL THEY GET SORTA CARAMEL-IZED.
TAP
TAP
WHAT DOES THAT MEAN?
WELL, WE WON'T TOTALLY CARAMELIZE THEM, BUT THEY'LL GET TRANSLUCENT BROWN AND YUMMY!
GOOD... I DIDN'T NEED THE BAND-AIDS.
SIZZLE

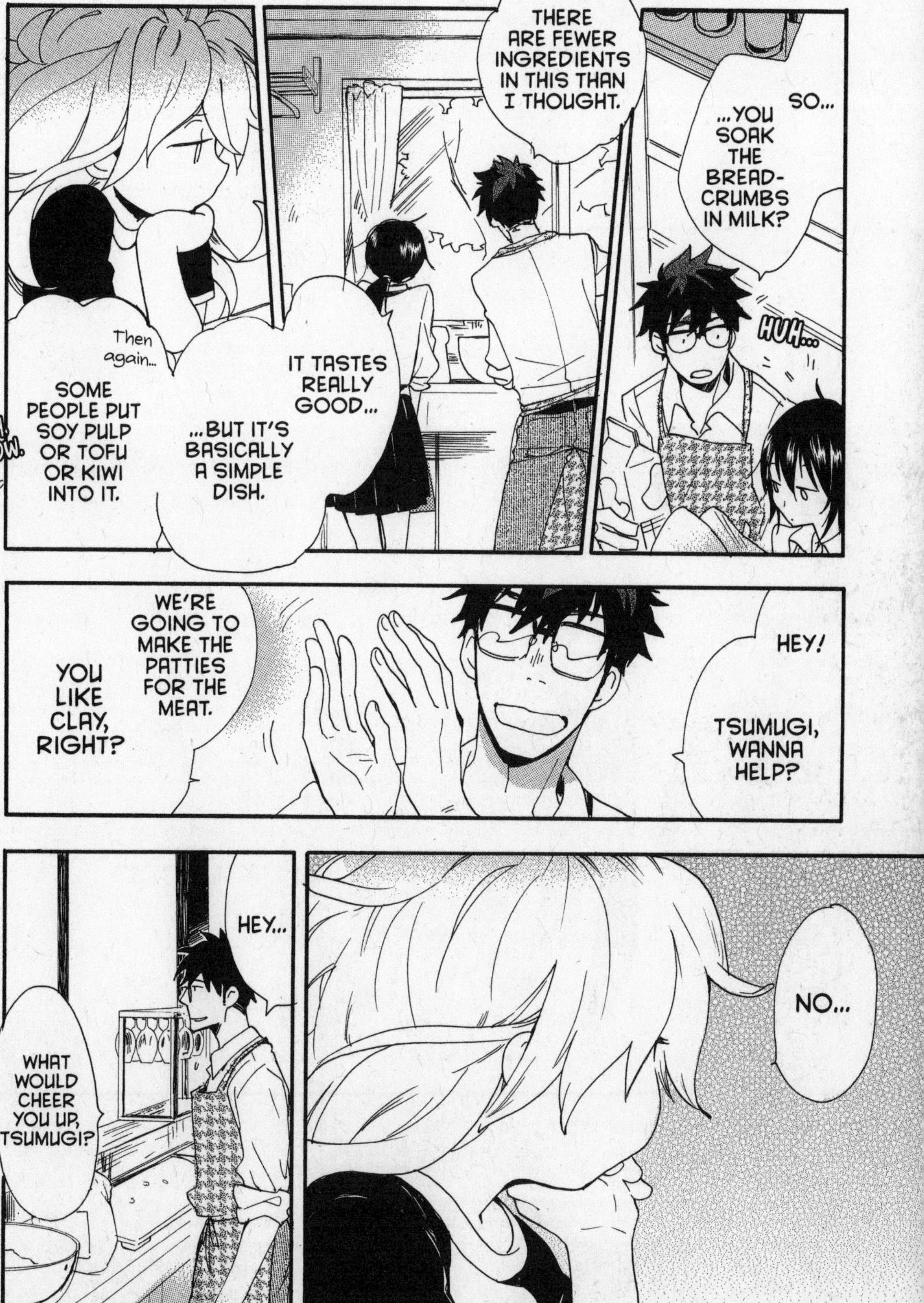
SO...
...YOU SOAK THE BREAD-CRUMBS IN MILK?
HUH...
THERE ARE FEWER INGREDIENTS IN THIS THAN I THOUGHT.
IT TASTES REALLY GOOD...
...BUT IT'S BASICALLY A SIMPLE DISH.
Then again...
SOME PEOPLE PUT SOY PULP OR TOFU OR KIWI INTO IT.
OH. WOW.
HEY!
TSUMUGI, WANNA HELP?
WE'RE GOING TO MAKE THE PATTIES FOR THE MEAT.
YOU LIKE CLAY, RIGHT?
NO...
HEY...
WHAT WOULD CHEER YOU UP, TSUMUGI?

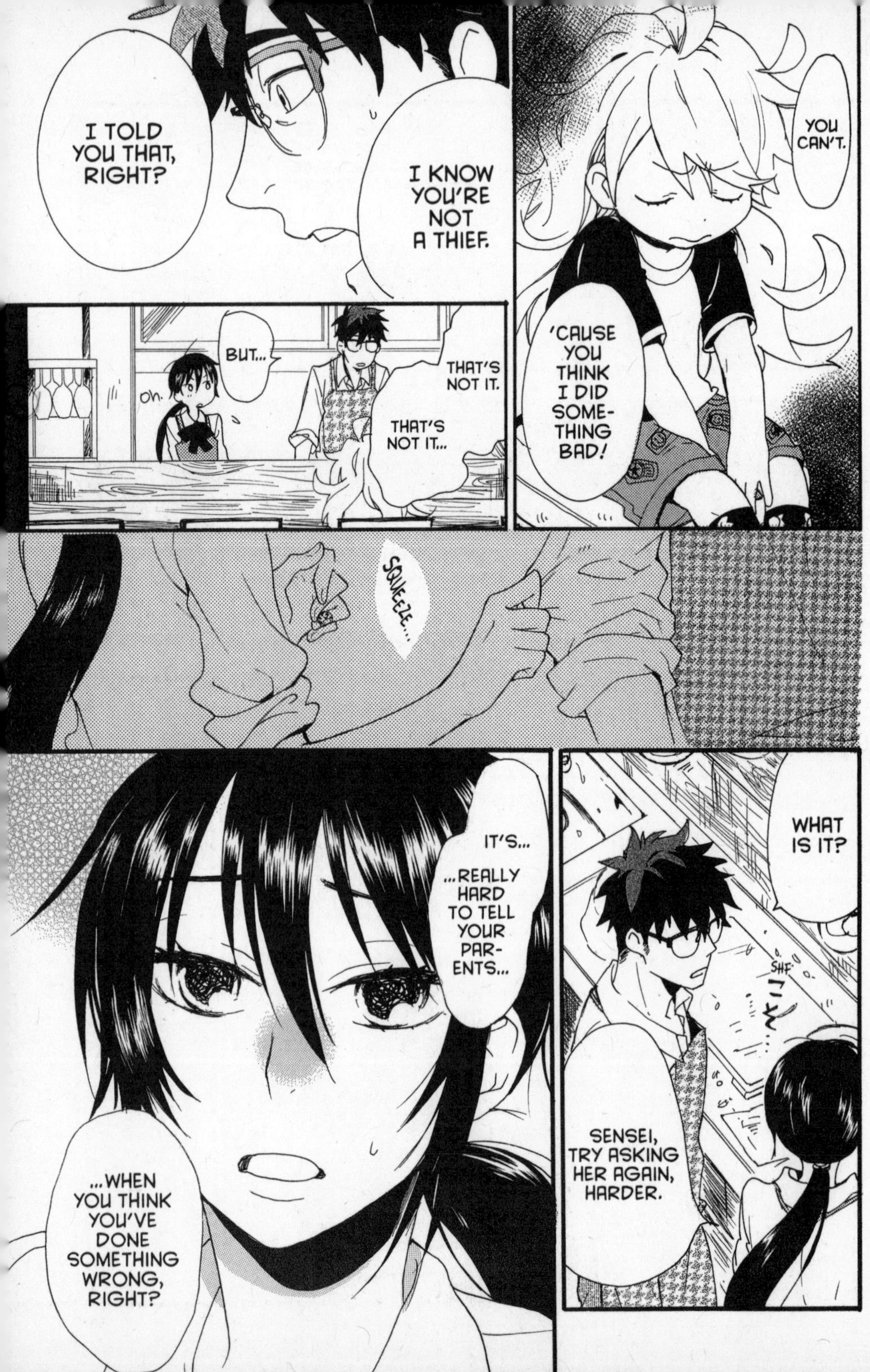
YOU CAN'T.
'CAUSE YOU THINK I DID SOMETHING BAD!
I KNOW YOU'RE NOT A THIEF.
I TOLD YOU THAT, RIGHT?
THAT'S NOT IT.
THAT'S NOT IT...
BUT...
Oh.
SQUEEZE...
WHAT IS IT?
SHF
SENSEI, TRY ASKING HER AGAIN, HARDER.
IT'S...
...REALLY HARD TO TELL YOUR PARENTS...
...WHEN YOU THINK YOU'VE DONE SOMETHING WRONG, RIGHT?

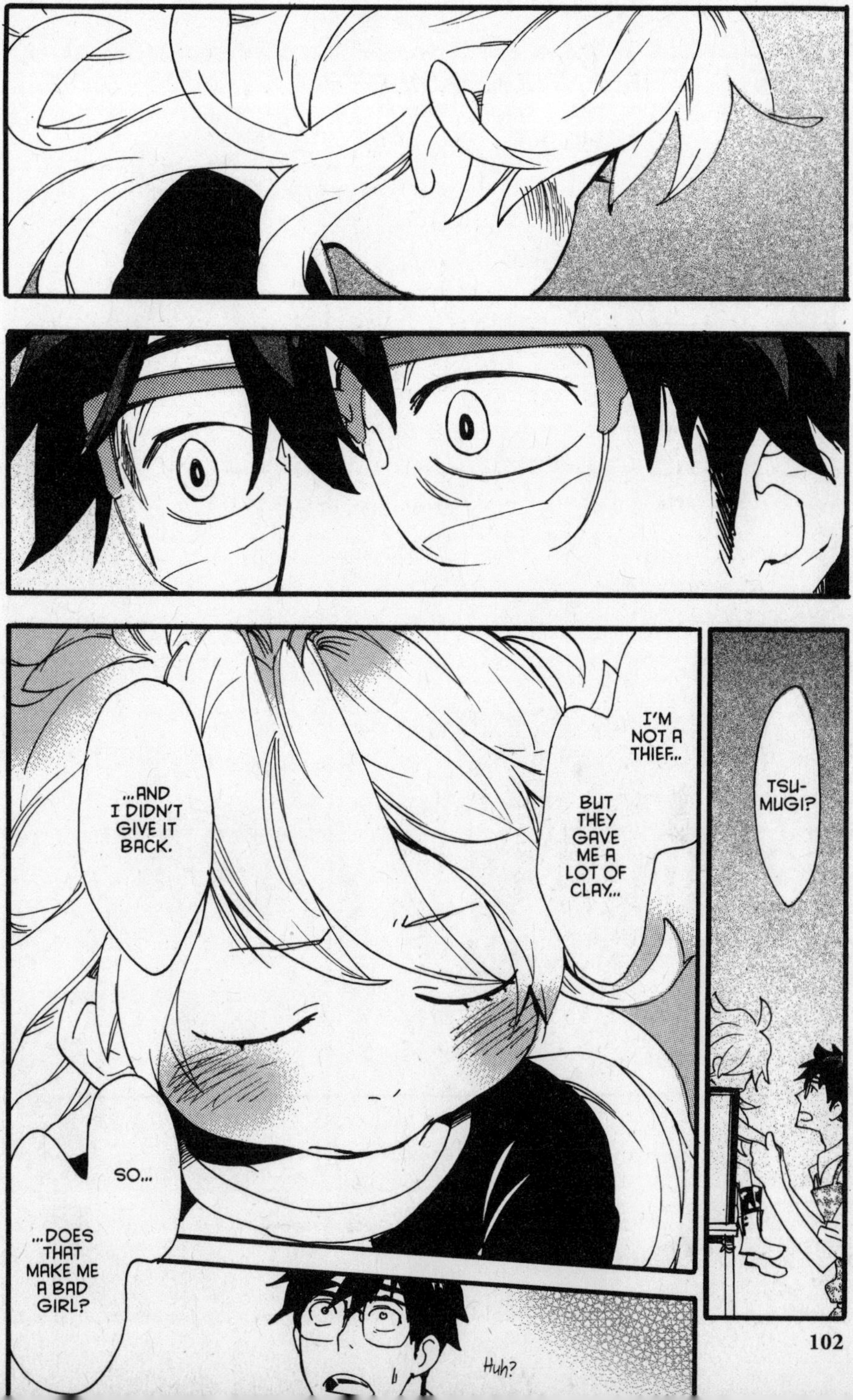
TSU-MUGI?
I'M NOT A THIEF...
BUT THEY GAVE ME A LOT OF CLAY...
...AND I DIDN'T GIVE IT BACK.
SO...
...DOES THAT MAKE ME A BAD GIRL?
Huh?

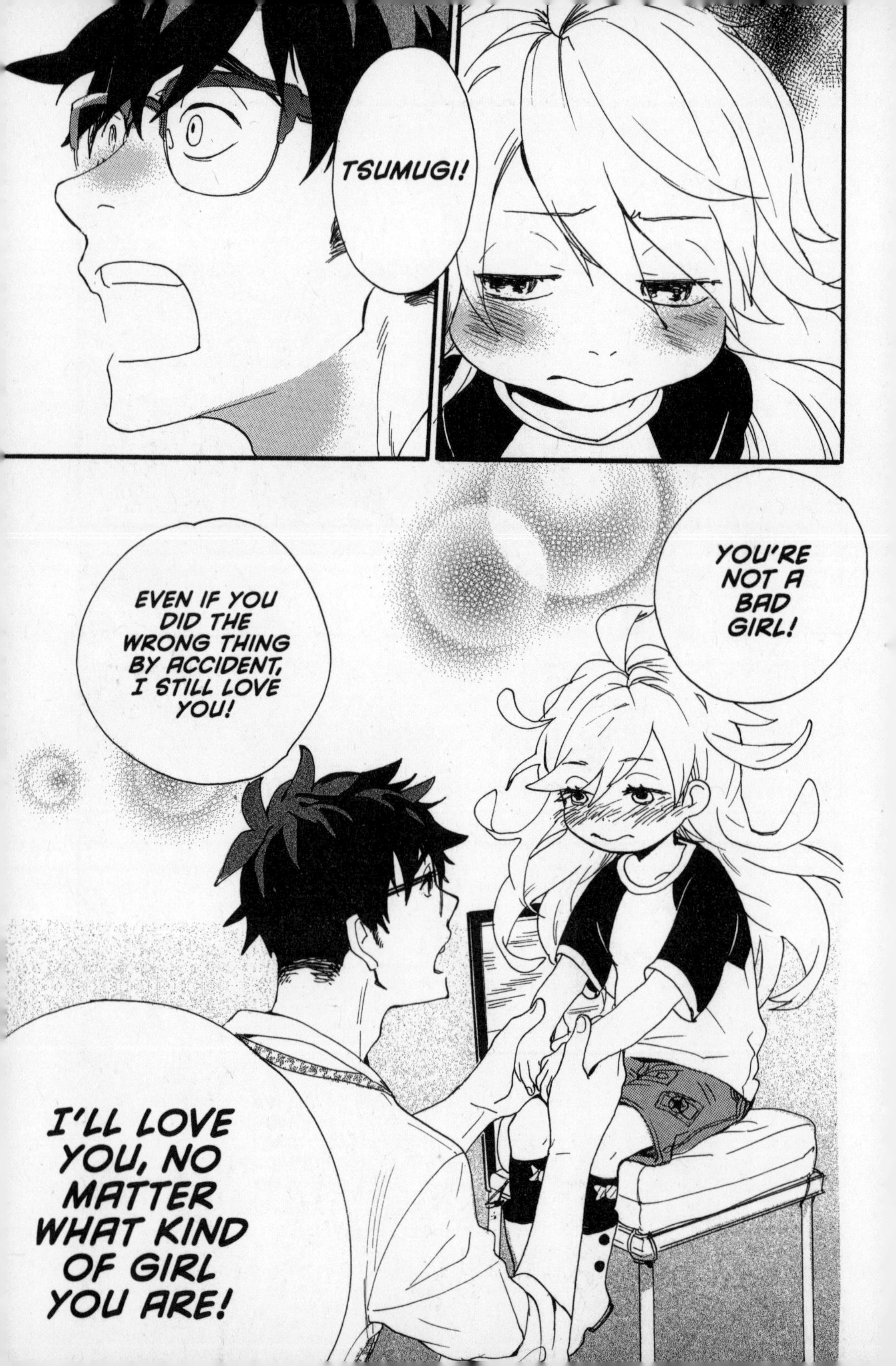
TSUMUGI!
YOU'RE NOT A BAD GIRL!
EVEN IF YOU DID THE WRONG THING BY ACCIDENT, I STILL LOVE YOU!
I'LL LOVE YOU, NO MATTER WHAT KIND OF GIRL YOU ARE!

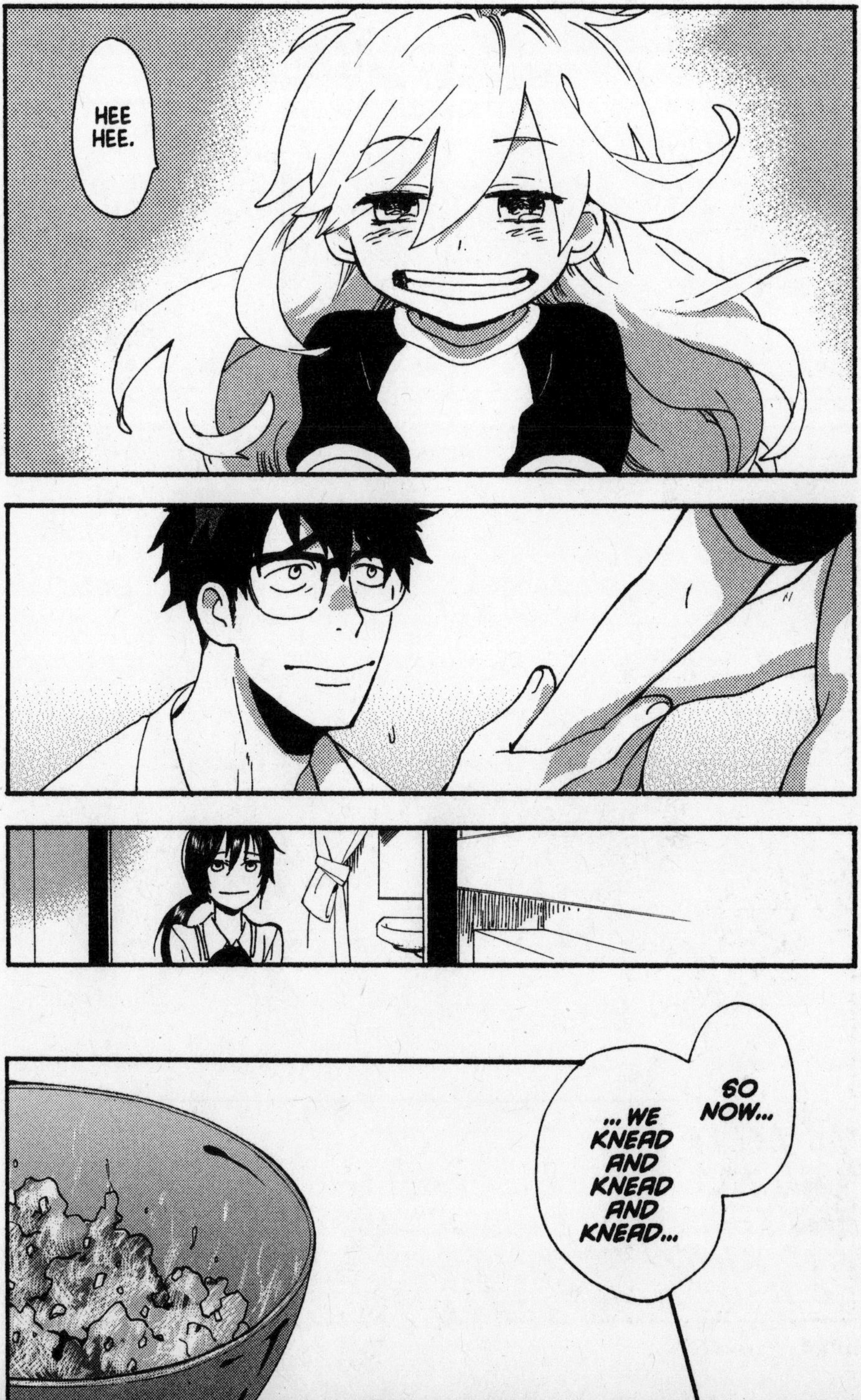
HEE HEE.
SO NOW...
...WE KNEAD AND KNEAD AND KNEAD...

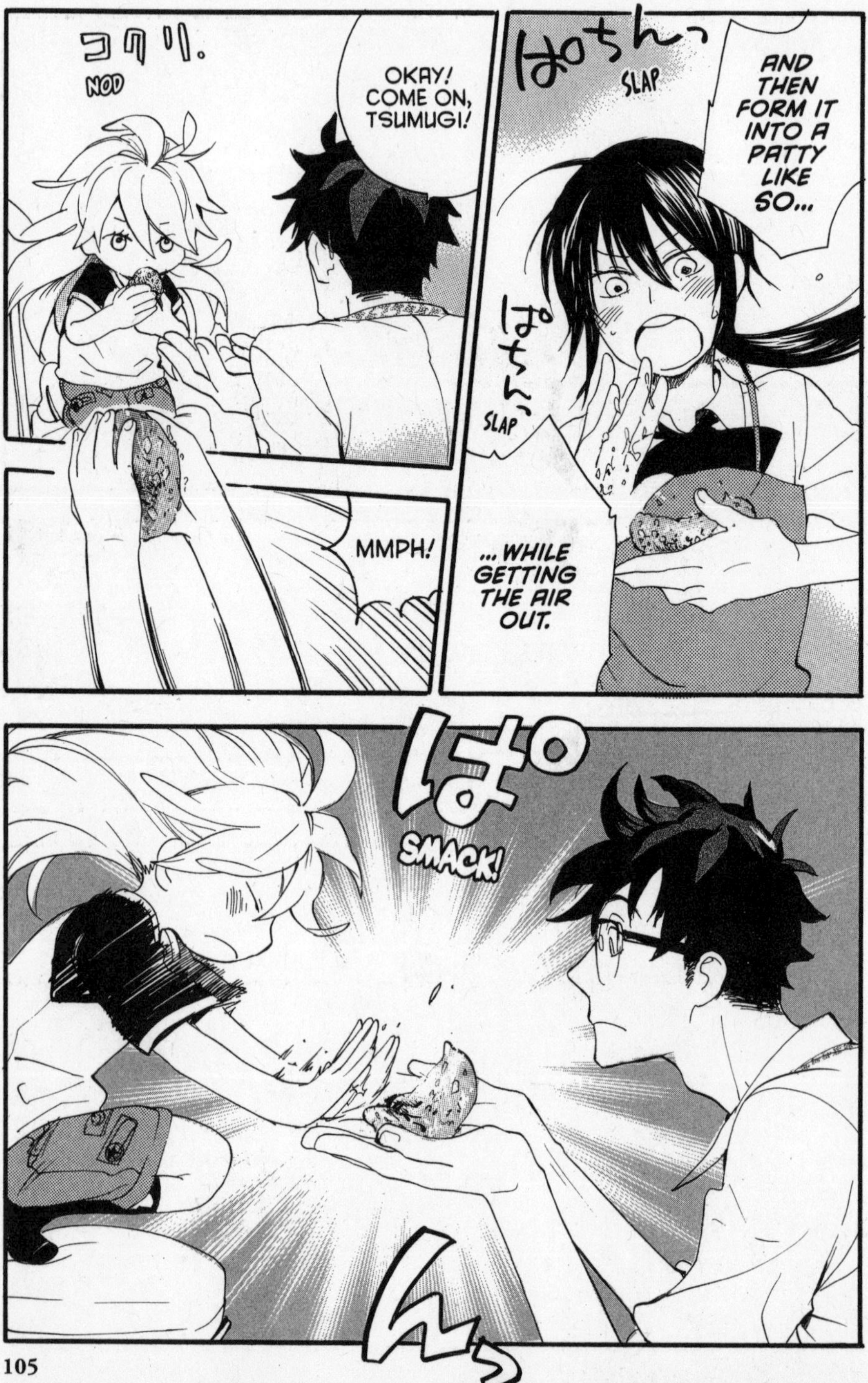
ぱちんっ
SLAP
AND THEN FORM IT INTO A PATTY LIKE SO...
ぱちんっ
SLAP
...WHILE GETTING THE AIR OUT.
OKAY! COME ON, TSUMUGI!
コクリ。
NOD
MMPH!
ぱ
SMACK!
んっ

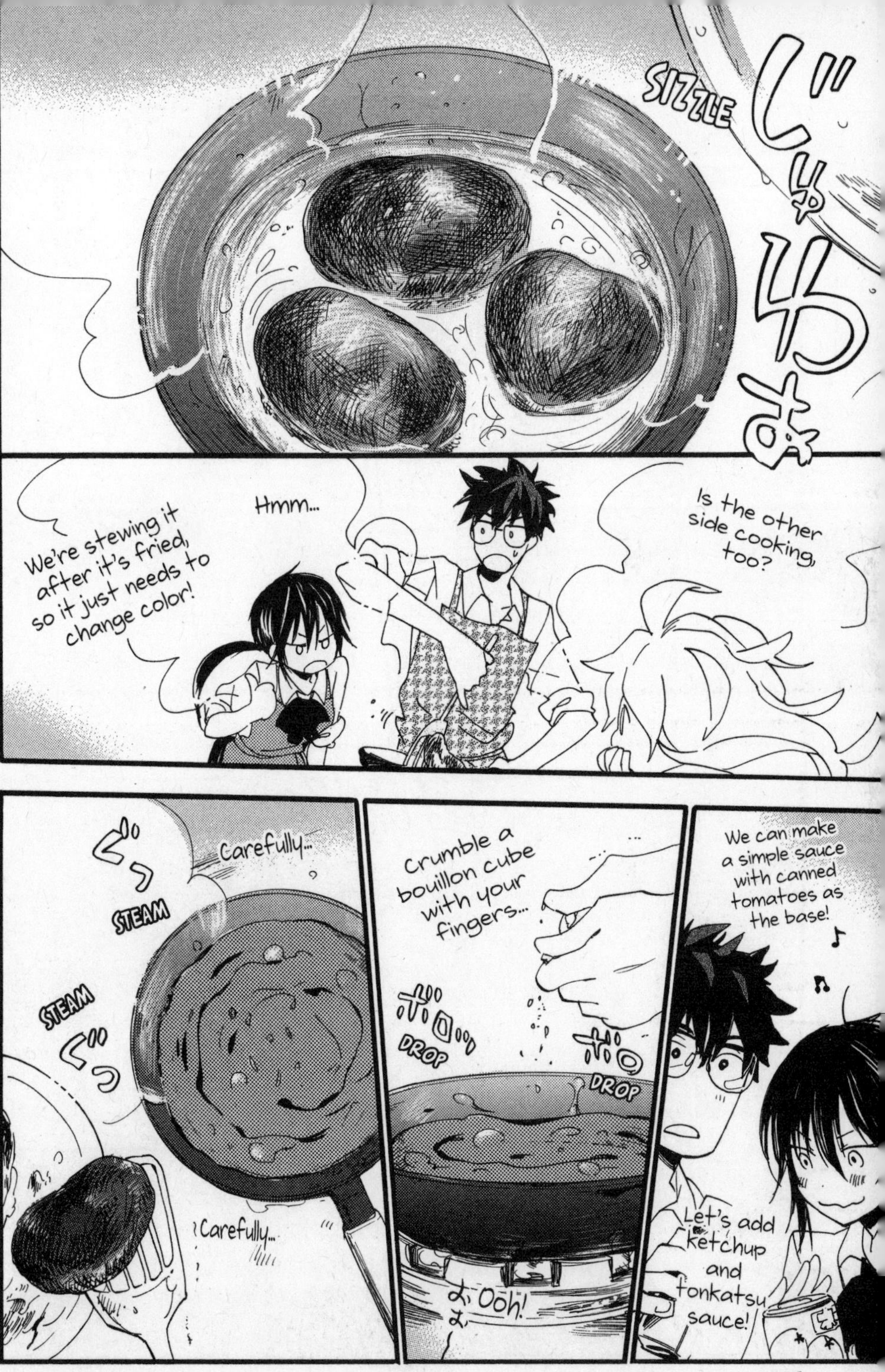
SIZZLE
Is the other side cooking, too?
Hmm...
We're stewing it after it's fried, so it just needs to change color!
We can make a simple sauce with canned tomatoes as the base!
Let's add ketchup and tonkatsu sauce!
...
Crumble a bouillon cube with your fingers...
DROP
DROP
O, Ooh!
Carefully...
STEAM
STEAM
Carefully...

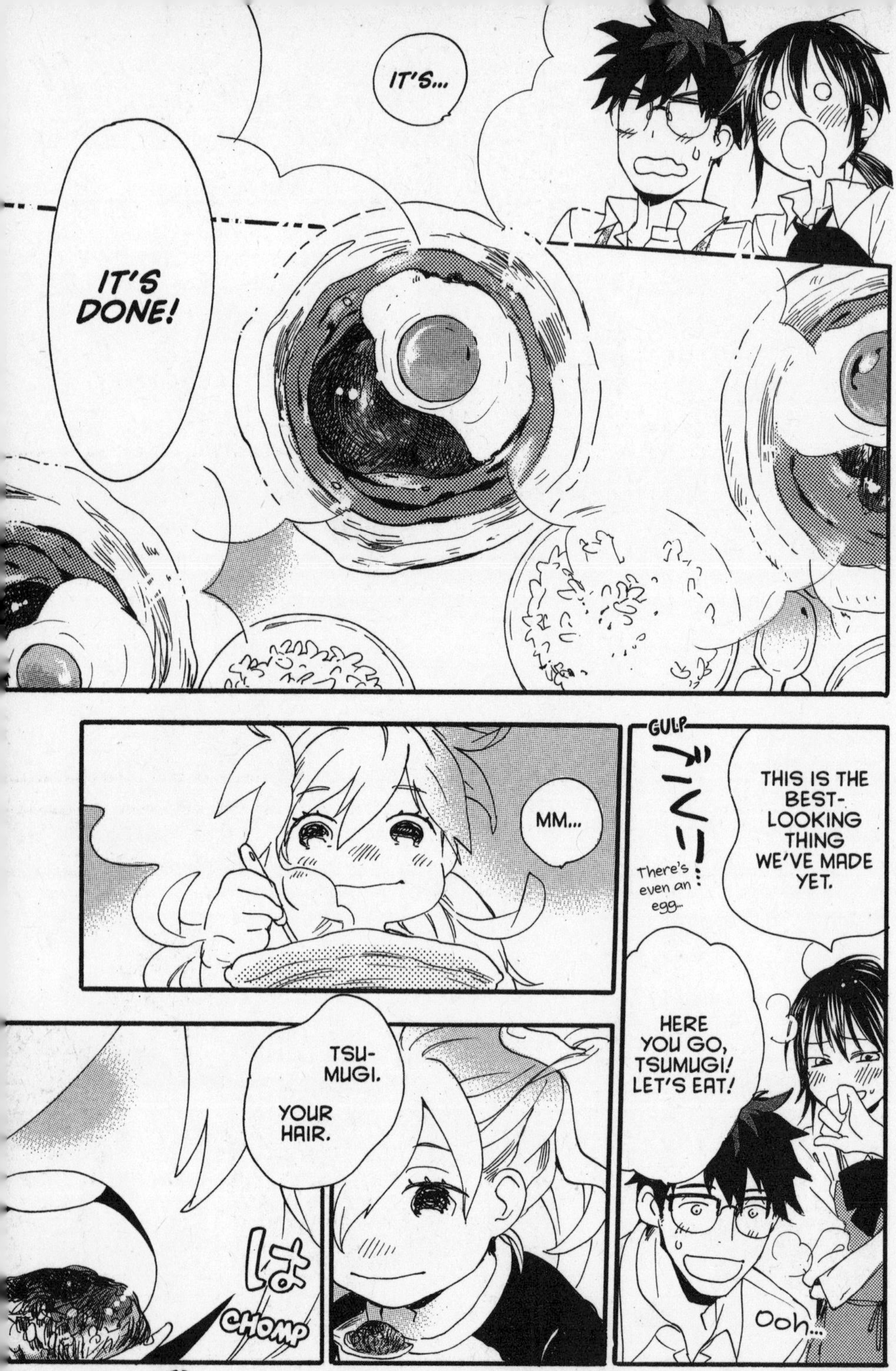
IT'S...
IT'S DONE!
GULP
There's even an egg...
THIS IS THE BEST-LOOKING THING WE'VE MADE YET.
HERE YOU GO, TSUMUGI! LET'S EAT!
Ooh...
MM...
TSU-MUGI.
YOUR HAIR.
CHOMP

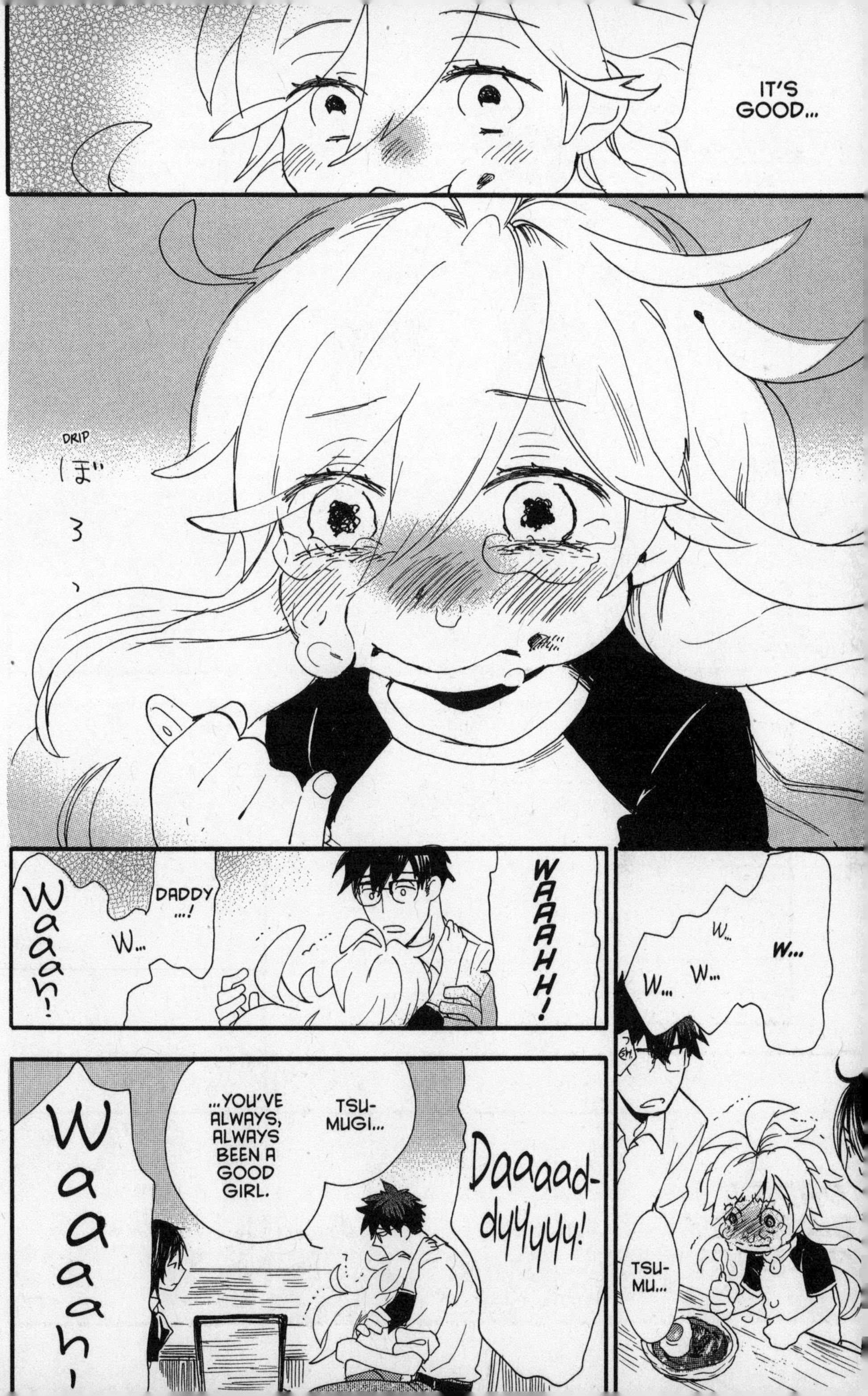

IT'S GOOD...
DRIP
ぽろ、
W...
W...
W...
W...
TSU-MU...
WAAAAHH!
DADDY ...!
W...
Waaan!
Daaaaddyyyyy!
TSU-MUGI...
...YOU'VE ALWAYS, ALWAYS BEEN A GOOD GIRL.
Waaaaah,

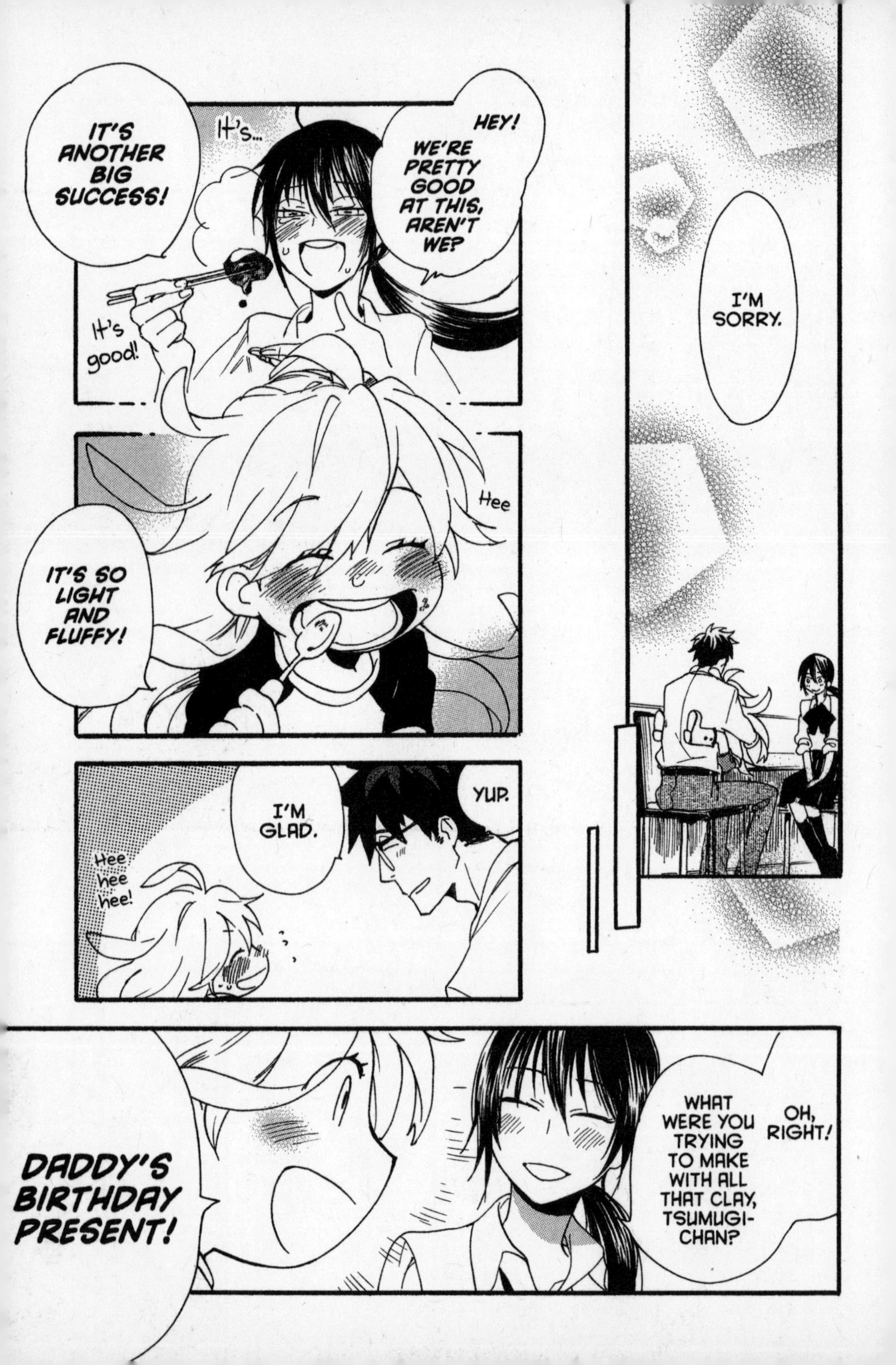
I'M SORRY.
HEY! WE'RE PRETTY GOOD AT THIS, AREN'T WE?
It's...
IT'S ANOTHER BIG SUCCESS!
It's good!
Hee
IT'S SO LIGHT AND FLUFFY!
YUP.
I'M GLAD.
Hee hee hee!
OH, RIGHT!
WHAT WERE YOU TRYING TO MAKE WITH ALL THAT CLAY, TSUMUGI-CHAN?
DADDY'S BIRTHDAY PRESENT!

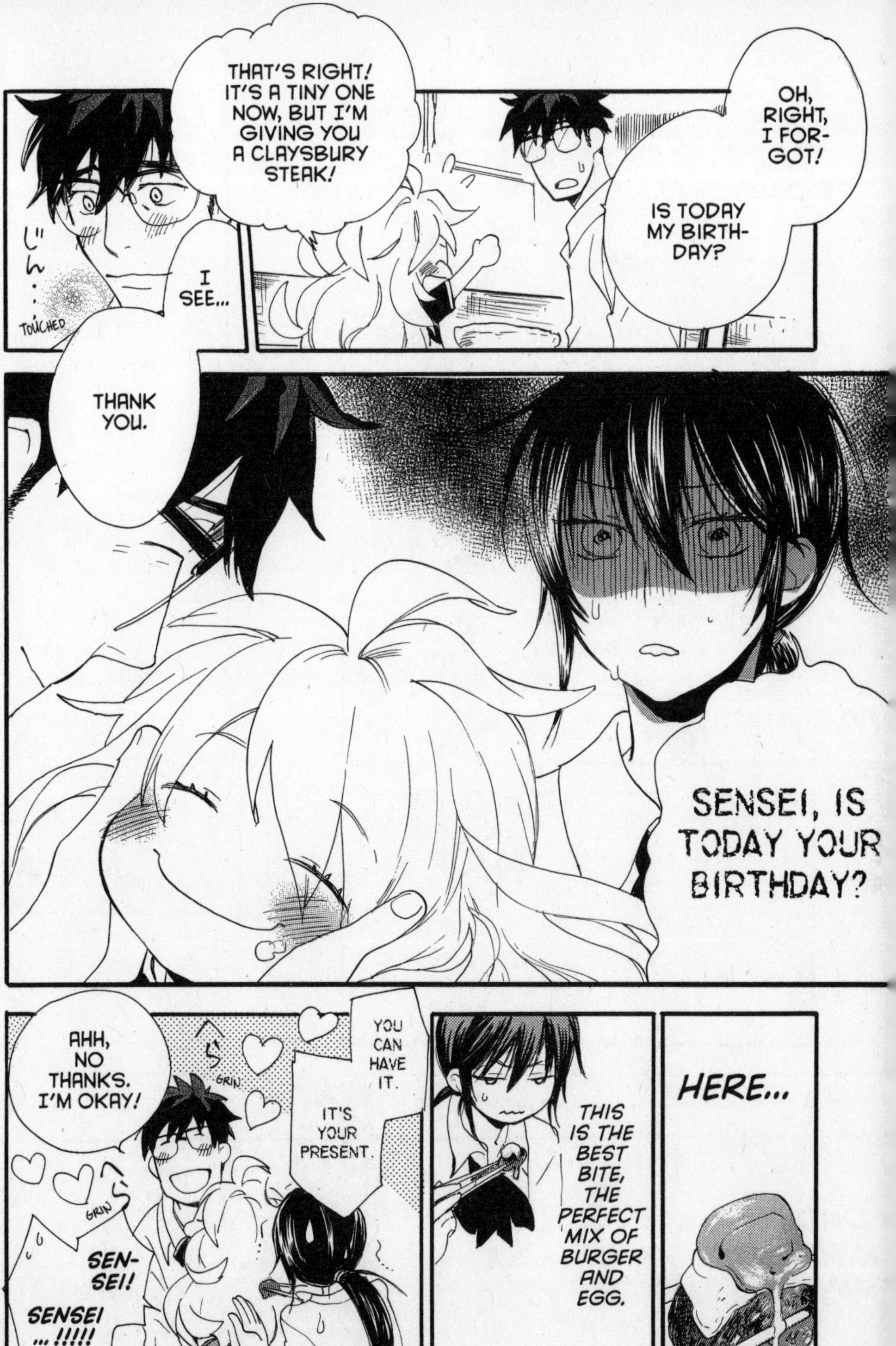
OH, RIGHT, I FORGOT!
IS TODAY MY BIRTHDAY?
THAT'S RIGHT! IT'S A TINY ONE NOW, BUT I'M GIVING YOU A CLAYSBURY STEAK!
I SEE...
じん・・・
TOUCHED
THANK YOU.
SENSEI, IS TODAY YOUR BIRTHDAY?
HERE...
THIS IS THE BEST BITE, THE PERFECT MIX OF BURGER AND EGG.
YOU CAN HAVE IT.
IT'S YOUR PRESENT.
AHH, NO THANKS. I'M OKAY!
GRIN
GRIN
SEN-SEI!
SENSEI...!!!!!

Chapter 3 - END

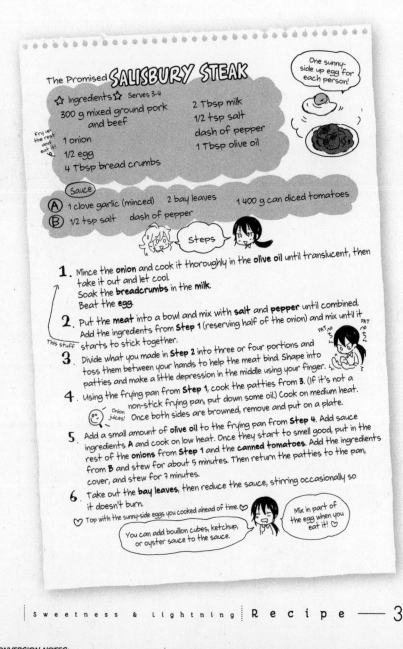

The Promised **SALISBURY STEAK**

One sunny-side up egg for each person!

☆ Ingredients ☆ Serves 3-4

300 g mixed ground pork and beef

1 onion
1/2 egg
4 Tbsp bread crumbs

2 Tbsp milk
1/2 tsp salt
dash of pepper
1 Tbsp olive oil

Fry up the rest and eat it!

Sauce

Ⓐ 1 clove garlic (minced)   2 bay leaves   1 400 g can diced tomatoes
Ⓑ 1/2 tsp salt   dash of pepper

Steps

1. Mince the **onion** and cook it thoroughly in the **olive oil** until translucent, then take it out and let cool.
Soak the **breadcrumbs** in the **milk**.
Beat the **egg**.

2. Put the **meat** into a bowl and mix with **salt** and **pepper** until combined. Add the ingredients from **Step 1** (reserving half of the onion) and mix until it starts to stick together.

This stuff

PAT PAT

3. Divide what you made in **Step 2** into three or four portions and toss them between your hands to help the meat bind. Shape into patties and make a little depression in the middle using your finger.

4. Using the frying pan from **Step 1**, cook the patties from **3**. (If it's not a non-stick frying pan, put down some oil.) Cook on medium heat.
Onion juices!   Once both sides are browned, remove and put on a plate.

5. Add a small amount of **olive oil** to the frying pan from **Step 4**. Add sauce ingredients **A** and cook on low heat. Once they start to smell good, put in the rest of the **onions** from **Step 1** and the **canned tomatoes**. Add the ingredients from **B** and stew for about 5 minutes. Then return the patties to the pan, cover, and stew for 7 minutes.

6. Take out the **bay leaves**, then reduce the sauce, stirring occasionally so it doesn't burn.
♡ Top with the sunny-side eggs you cooked ahead of time. ♡

Mix in part of the egg when you eat it! ♡

You can add bouillon cubes, ketchup, or oyster sauce to the sauce.

CONVERSION NOTES:
300 G PORK AND BEEF = ABOUT 10 1/2 OZ, 400G TOMATOES = ABOUT 1 14.5 OZ CAN

Hey...
The meat...
...was so yummy, wasn't it?
Yeah...
Tsumugi...
...let's go to bed...
...okay...?
It was so juicy...
...wasn't it?

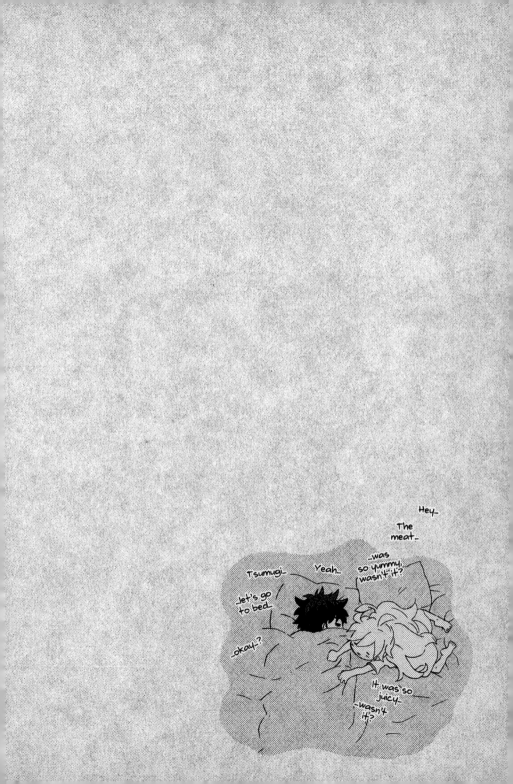

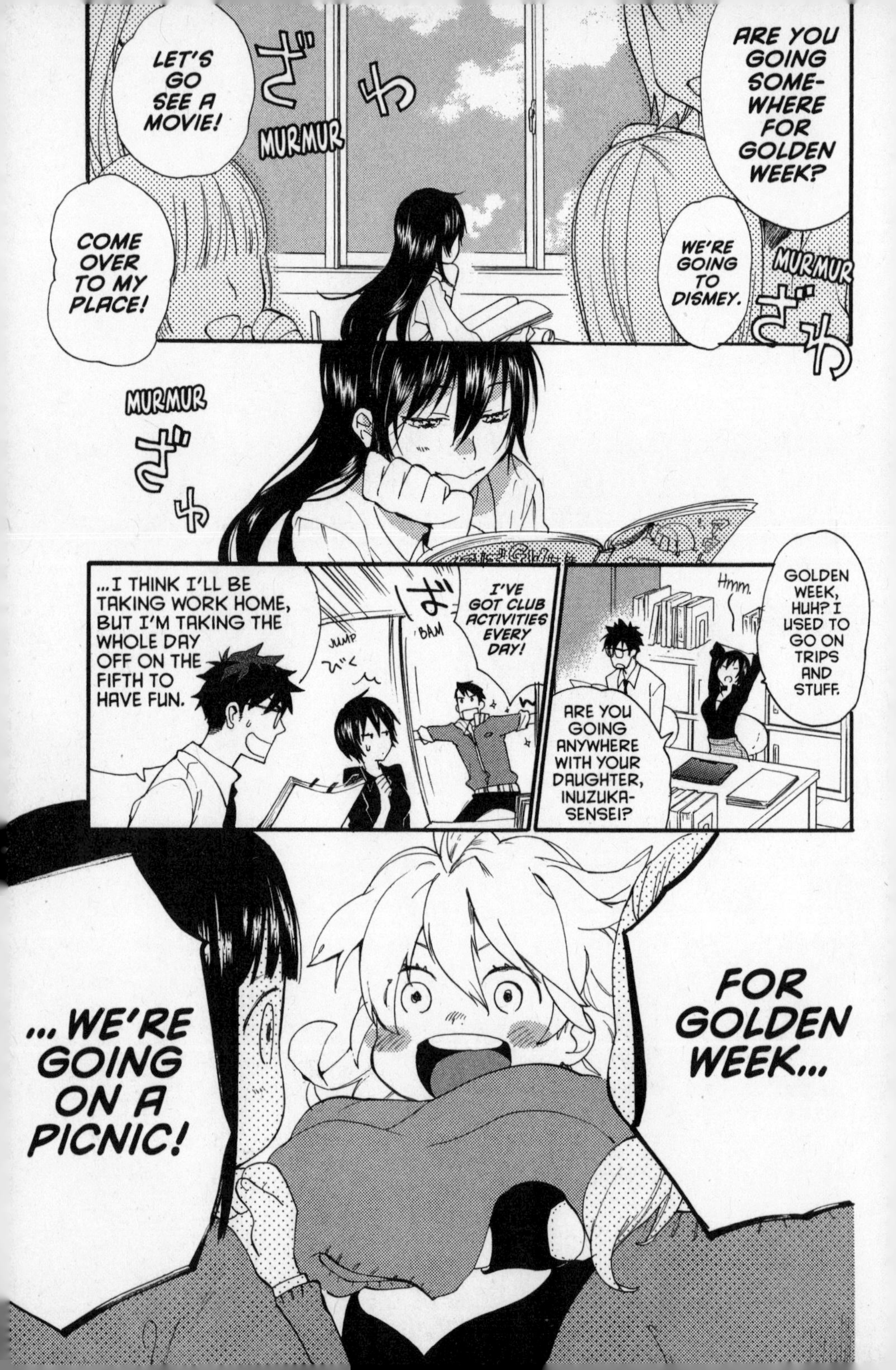
ARE YOU GOING SOMEWHERE FOR GOLDEN WEEK?
WE'RE GOING TO DISMEY.
MURMUR
ざわ
LET'S GO SEE A MOVIE!
ざわ
MURMUR
COME OVER TO MY PLACE!
MURMUR
ざわ
GOLDEN WEEK, HUH? I USED TO GO ON TRIPS AND STUFF.
Hmm.
ARE YOU GOING ANYWHERE WITH YOUR DAUGHTER, INUZUKA-SENSEI?
I'VE GOT CLUB ACTIVITIES EVERY DAY!
ざ
BAM
JUMP
びく
...I THINK I'LL BE TAKING WORK HOME, BUT I'M TAKING THE WHOLE DAY OFF ON THE FIFTH TO HAVE FUN.
FOR GOLDEN WEEK...
...WE'RE GOING ON A PICNIC!

Chapter 4 Golden Week and Packed Lunches

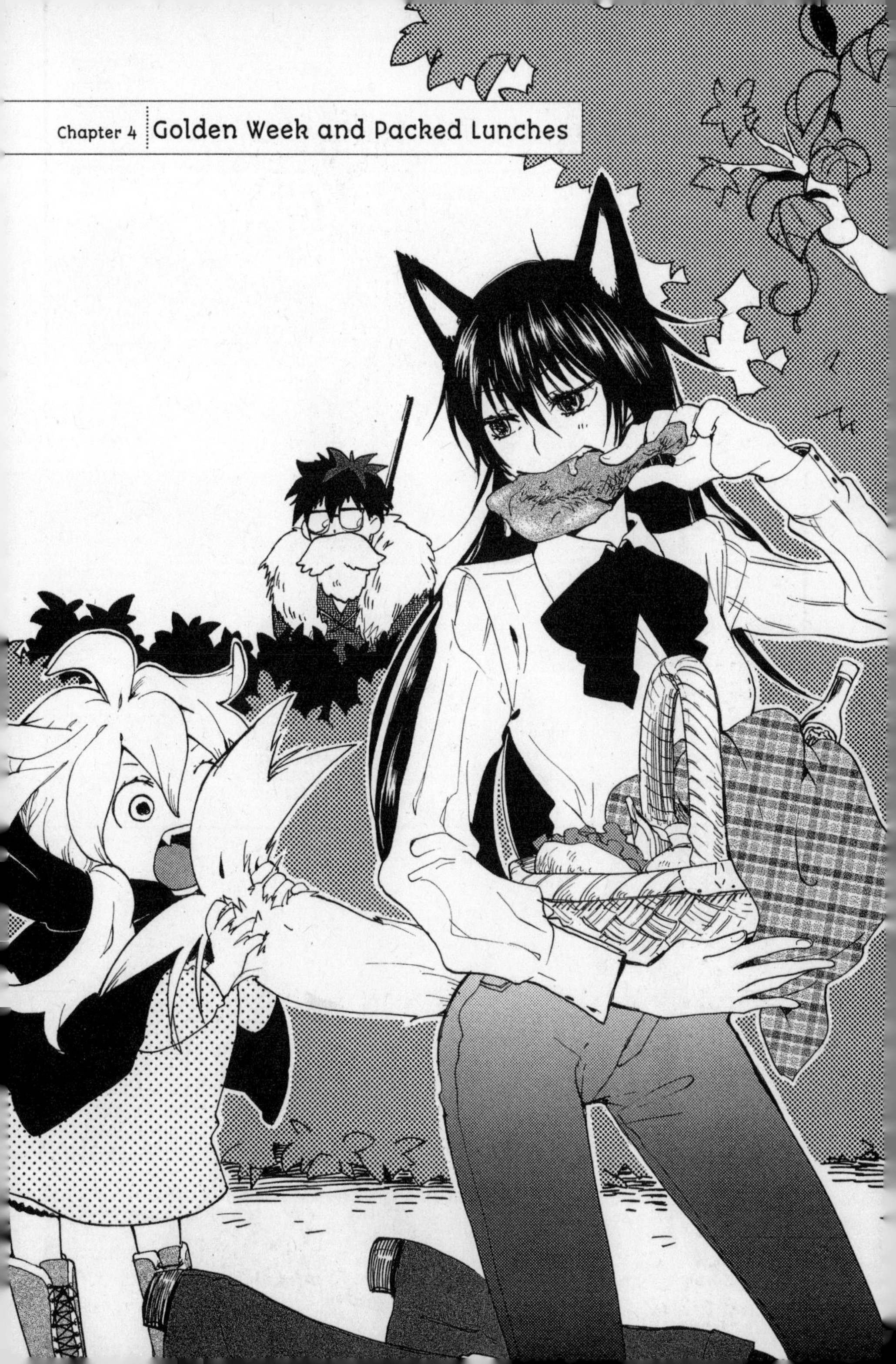

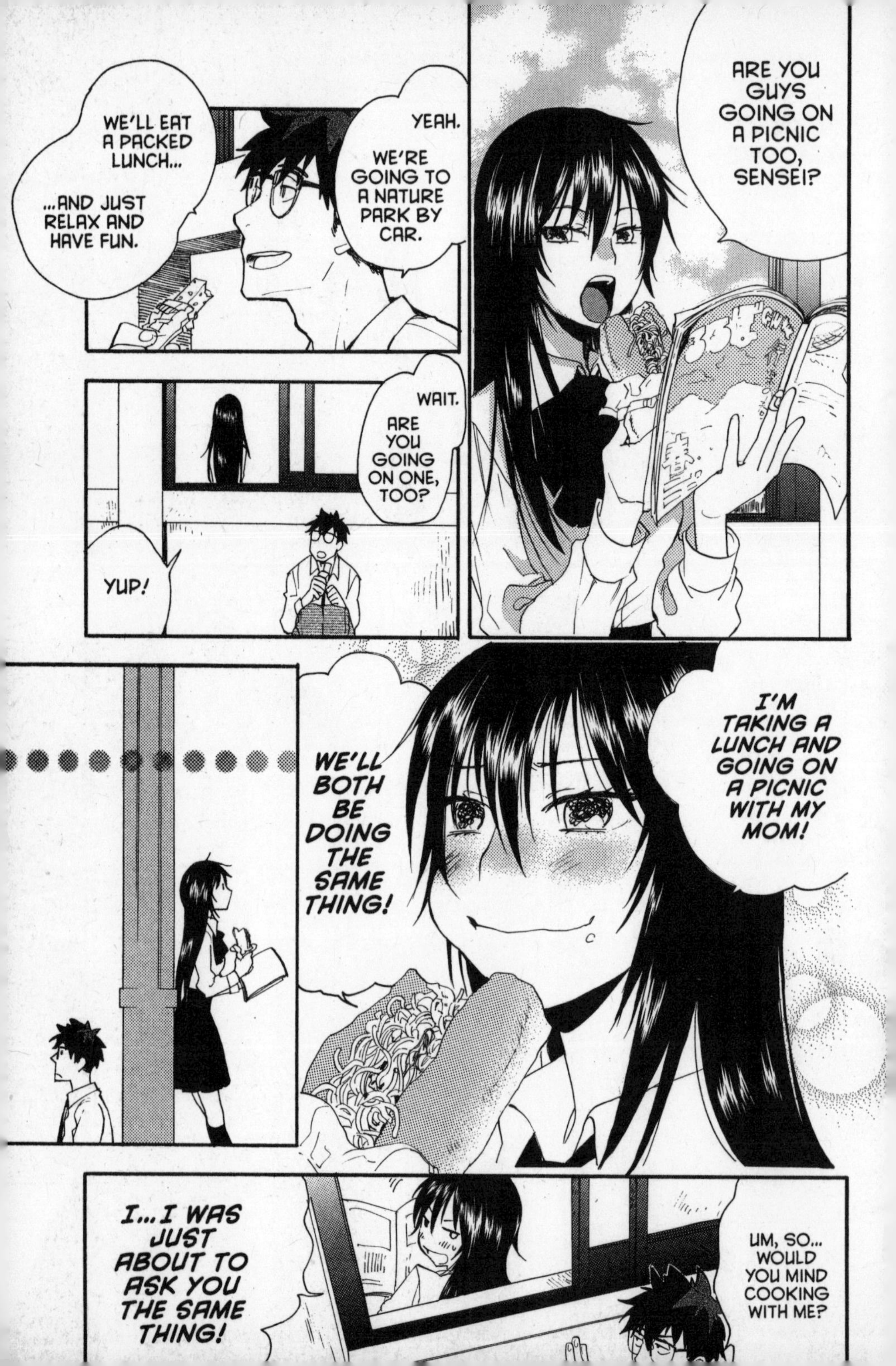
ARE YOU GUYS GOING ON A PICNIC TOO, SENSEI?
YEAH.
WE'RE GOING TO A NATURE PARK BY CAR.
WE'LL EAT A PACKED LUNCH...
...AND JUST RELAX AND HAVE FUN.
WAIT. ARE YOU GOING ON ONE, TOO?
YUP!
I'M TAKING A LUNCH AND GOING ON A PICNIC WITH MY MOM!
WE'LL BOTH BE DOING THE SAME THING!
UM, SO... WOULD YOU MIND COOKING WITH ME?
I...I WAS JUST ABOUT TO ASK YOU THE SAME THING!

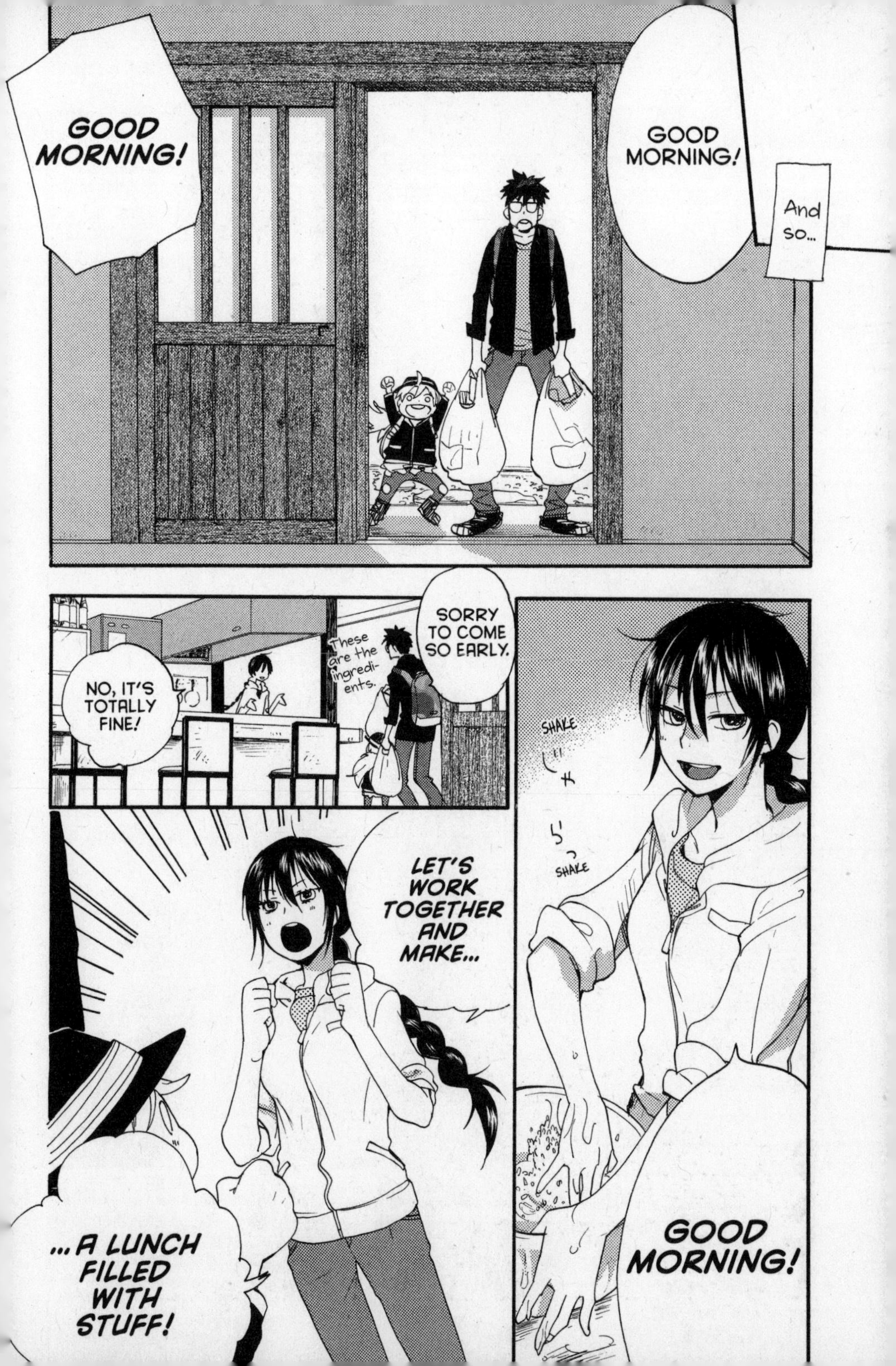
And so...
GOOD MORNING!
GOOD MORNING!
SHAKE
SHAKE
GOOD MORNING!
SORRY TO COME SO EARLY.
These are the ingredients.
NO, IT'S TOTALLY FINE!
LET'S WORK TOGETHER AND MAKE...
...A LUNCH FILLED WITH STUFF!

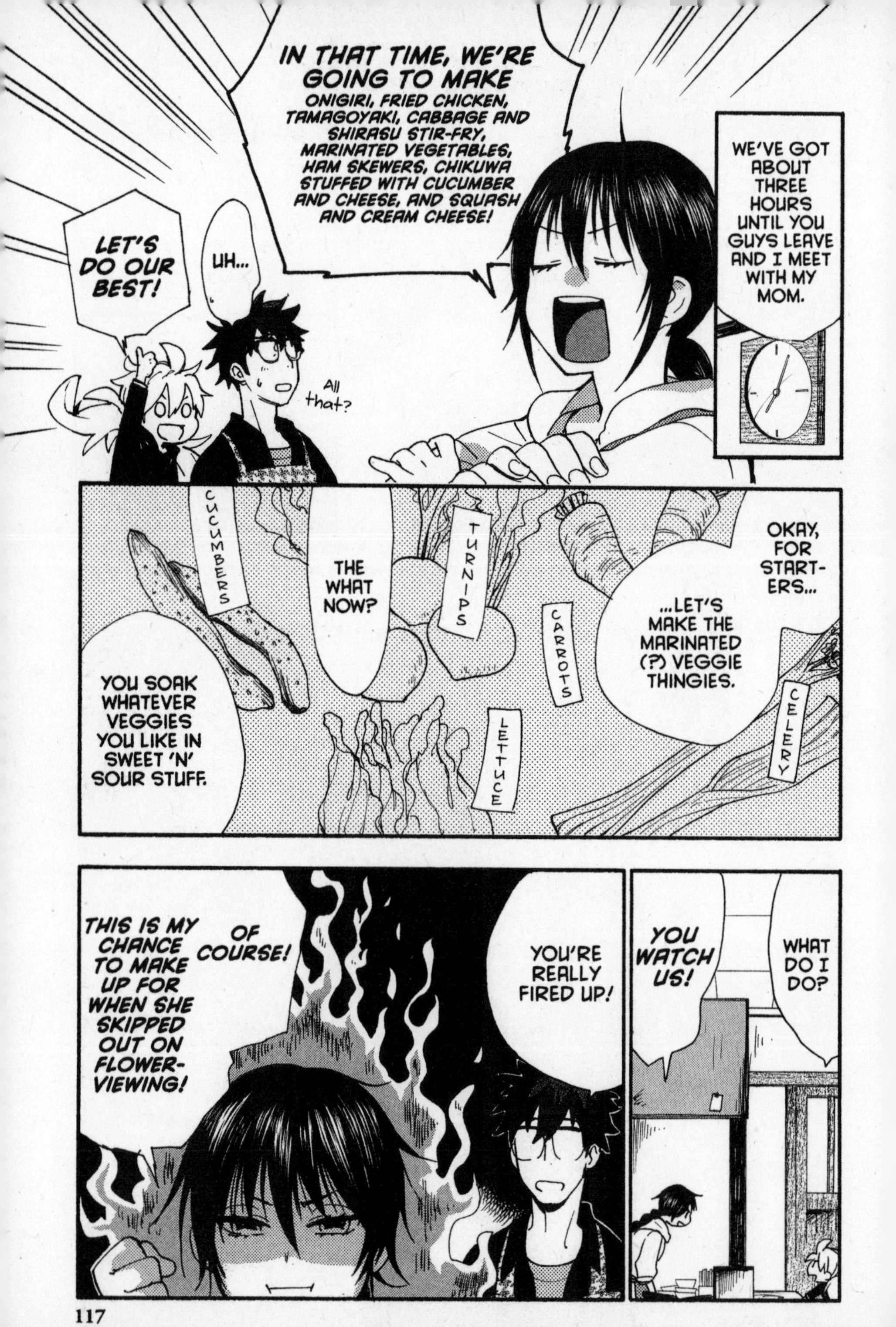
WE'VE GOT ABOUT THREE HOURS UNTIL YOU GUYS LEAVE AND I MEET WITH MY MOM.
IN THAT TIME, WE'RE GOING TO MAKE ONIGIRI, FRIED CHICKEN, TAMAGOYAKI, CABBAGE AND SHIRASU STIR-FRY, MARINATED VEGETABLES, HAM SKEWERS, CHIKUWA STUFFED WITH CUCUMBER AND CHEESE, AND SQUASH AND CREAM CHEESE!
UH...
All that?
LET'S DO OUR BEST!
OKAY, FOR STARTERS...
...LET'S MAKE THE MARINATED (?) VEGGIE THINGIES.
CELERY
CARROTS
TURNIPS
THE WHAT NOW?
CUCUMBERS
LETTUCE
YOU SOAK WHATEVER VEGGIES YOU LIKE IN SWEET 'N' SOUR STUFF.
WHAT DO I DO?
YOU WATCH US!
YOU'RE REALLY FIRED UP!
OF COURSE!
THIS IS MY CHANCE TO MAKE UP FOR WHEN SHE SKIPPED OUT ON FLOWER-VIEWING!

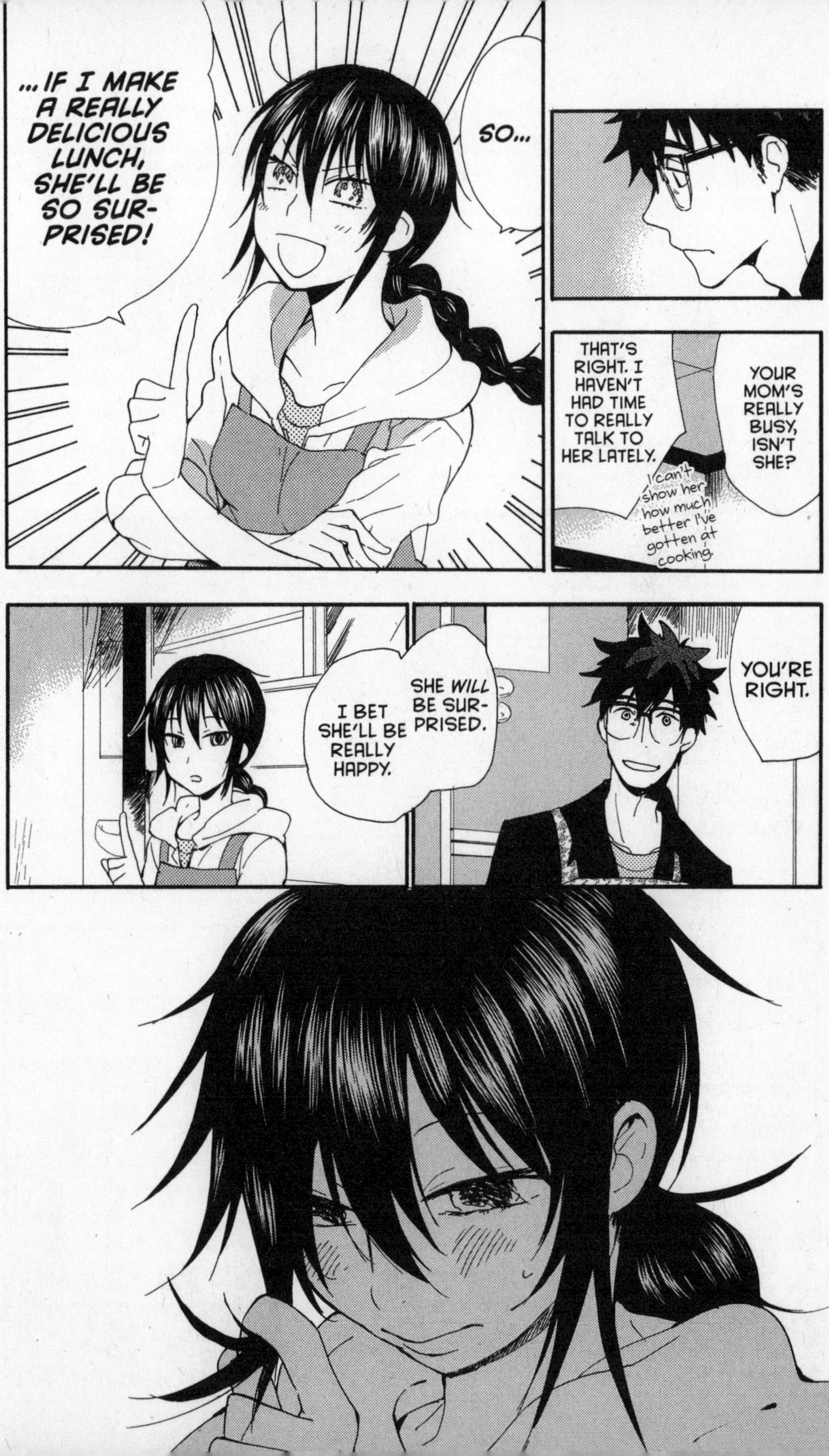
YOUR MOM'S REALLY BUSY, ISN'T SHE?
THAT'S RIGHT. I HAVEN'T HAD TIME TO REALLY TALK TO HER LATELY.
I can't show her how much better I've gotten at cooking.
SO...
...IF I MAKE A REALLY DELICIOUS LUNCH, SHE'LL BE SO SUR-PRISED!
YOU'RE RIGHT.
SHE *WILL* BE SUR-PRISED.
I BET SHE'LL BE REALLY HAPPY.

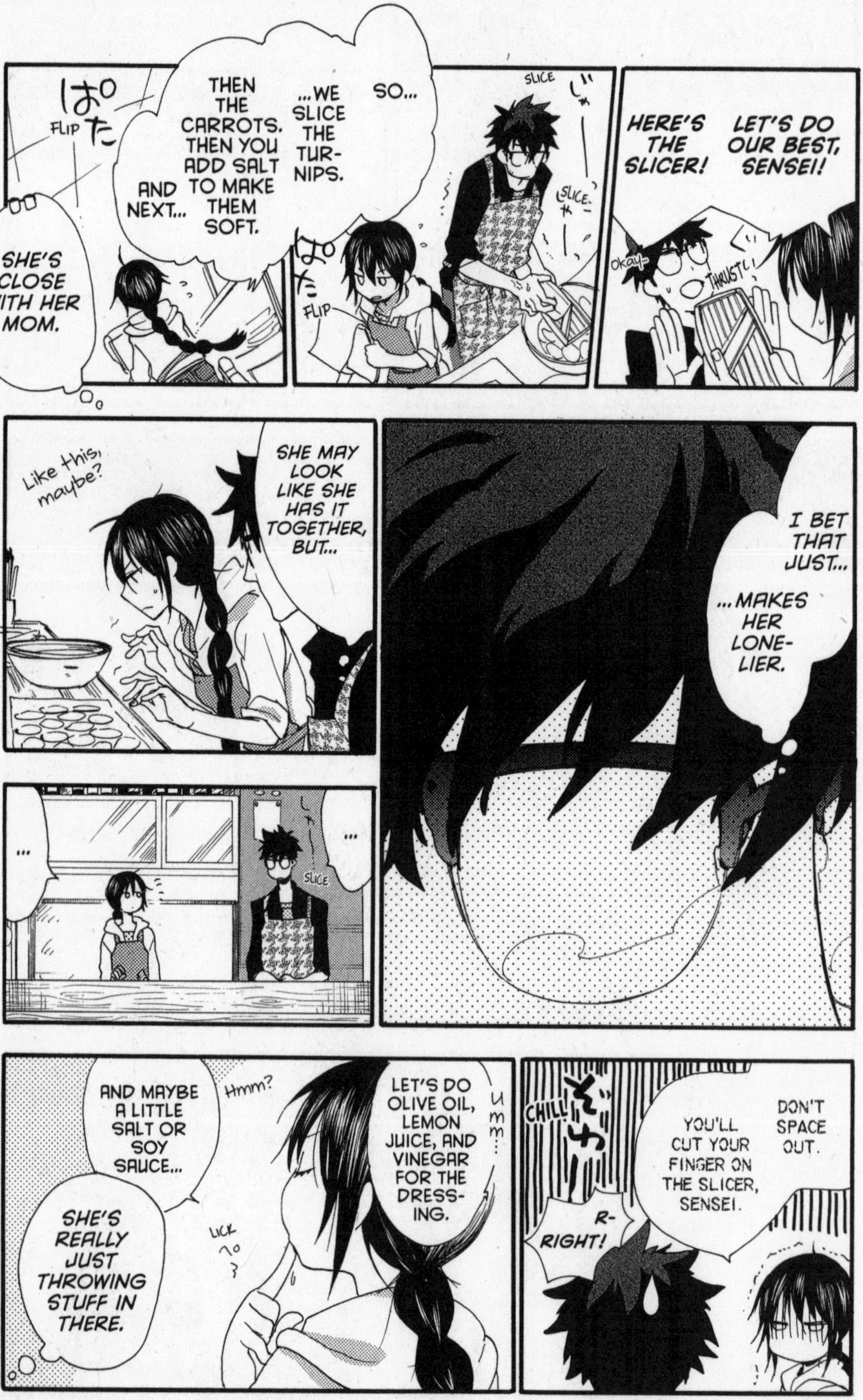
LET'S DO OUR BEST, SENSEI!
HERE'S THE SLICER!
Okay...
THRUST
SLICE
SO...
...WE SLICE THE TURNIPS.
SLICE
FLIP
THEN THE CARROTS. THEN YOU ADD SALT TO MAKE THEM SOFT.
AND NEXT...
FLIP
SHE'S CLOSE WITH HER MOM.
I BET THAT JUST...
...MAKES HER LONELIER.
SHE MAY LOOK LIKE SHE HAS IT TOGETHER, BUT...
Like this, maybe?
...
SLICE
...
DON'T SPACE OUT.
YOU'LL CUT YOUR FINGER ON THE SLICER, SENSEI.
CHILL!
R-RIGHT!
Umm...
LET'S DO OLIVE OIL, LEMON JUICE, AND VINEGAR FOR THE DRESSING.
Hmm?
AND MAYBE A LITTLE SALT OR SOY SAUCE...
LICK
SHE'S REALLY JUST THROWING STUFF IN THERE.

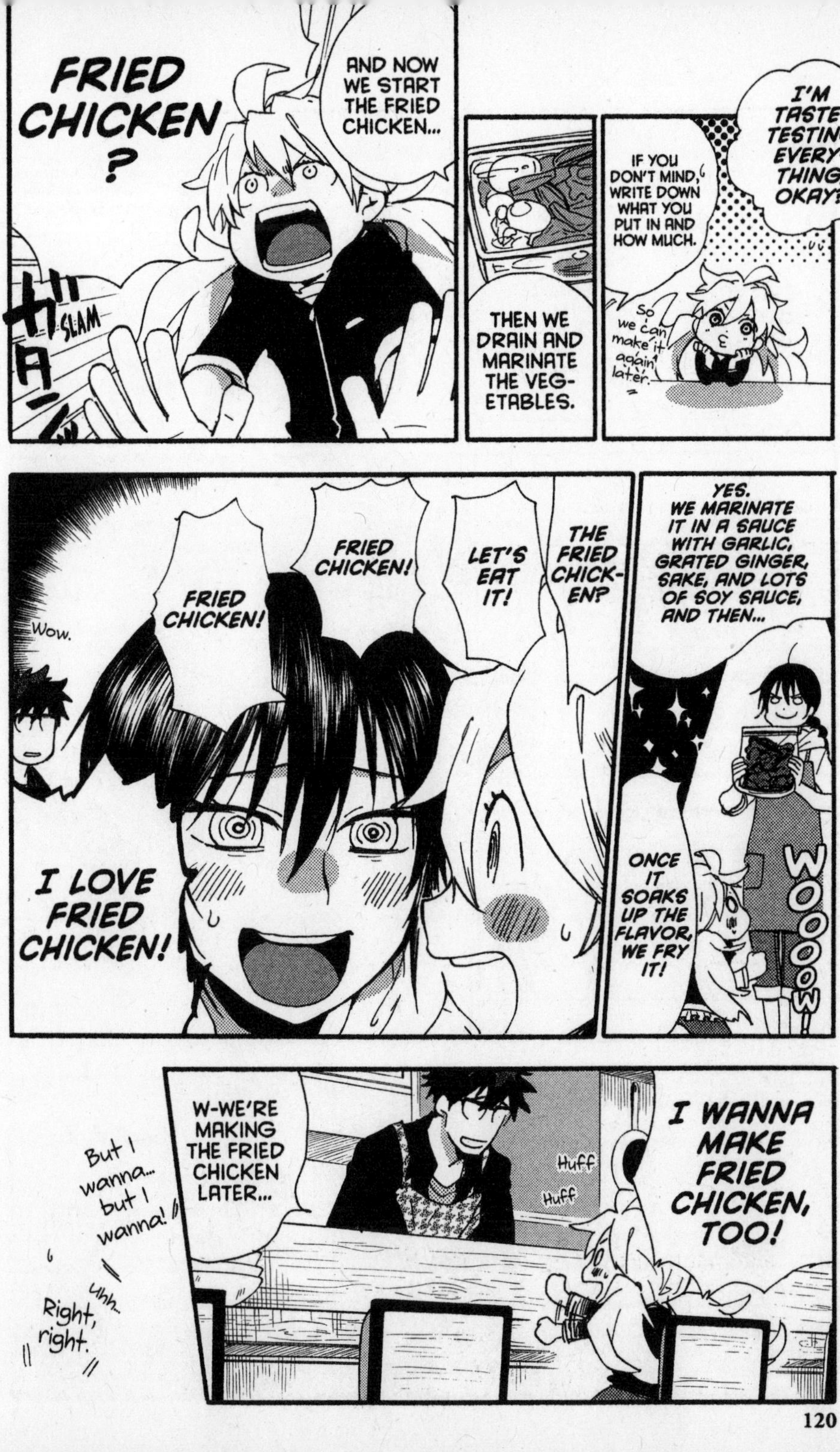
I'M TASTE-TESTING EVERY-THING, OKAY?
IF YOU DON'T MIND, WRITE DOWN WHAT YOU PUT IN AND HOW MUCH.
So we can make it again later.
THEN WE DRAIN AND MARINATE THE VEG-ETABLES.
AND NOW WE START THE FRIED CHICKEN...
FRIED CHICKEN?
SLAM
YES. WE MARINATE IT IN A SAUCE WITH GARLIC, GRATED GINGER, SAKE, AND LOTS OF SOY SAUCE, AND THEN...
WOOOOOW!
ONCE IT SOAKS UP THE FLAVOR, WE FRY IT!
THE FRIED CHICK-EN?
LET'S EAT IT!
FRIED CHICKEN!
FRIED CHICKEN!
Wow.
I LOVE FRIED CHICKEN!
I WANNA MAKE FRIED CHICKEN, TOO!
Huff
Huff
W-WE'RE MAKING THE FRIED CHICKEN LATER...
But I wanna... but I wanna!
Uhh... Right, right.

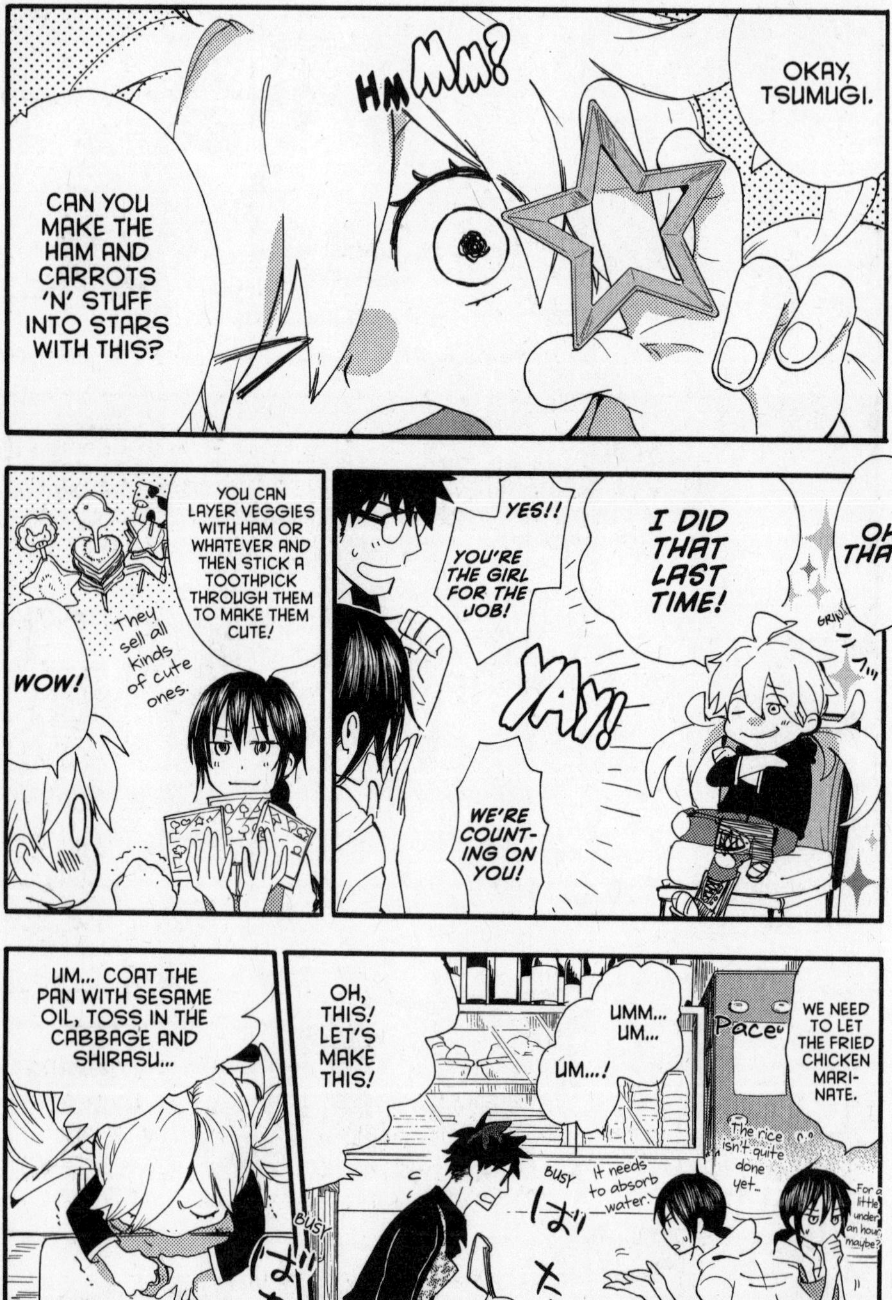
OKAY, TSUMUGI.
HMMM?
CAN YOU MAKE THE HAM AND CARROTS 'N' STUFF INTO STARS WITH THIS?
OH, THAT...
GRIN
I DID THAT LAST TIME!
YES!!
YOU'RE THE GIRL FOR THE JOB!
YAY!
WE'RE COUNTING-ING ON YOU!
YOU CAN LAYER VEGGIES WITH HAM OR WHATEVER AND THEN STICK A TOOTHPICK THROUGH THEM TO MAKE THEM CUTE!
They sell all kinds of cute ones.
WOW!
WE NEED TO LET THE FRIED CHICKEN MARI-NATE.
Pace
UMM... UM...
UM...!
OH, THIS! LET'S MAKE THIS!
The rice isn't quite done yet..
For a little under an hour, maybe?
It needs to absorb water.
Busy
ぱた
Pace
UM... COAT THE PAN WITH SESAME OIL, TOSS IN THE CABBAGE AND SHIRASU...
BUSY
ぱた

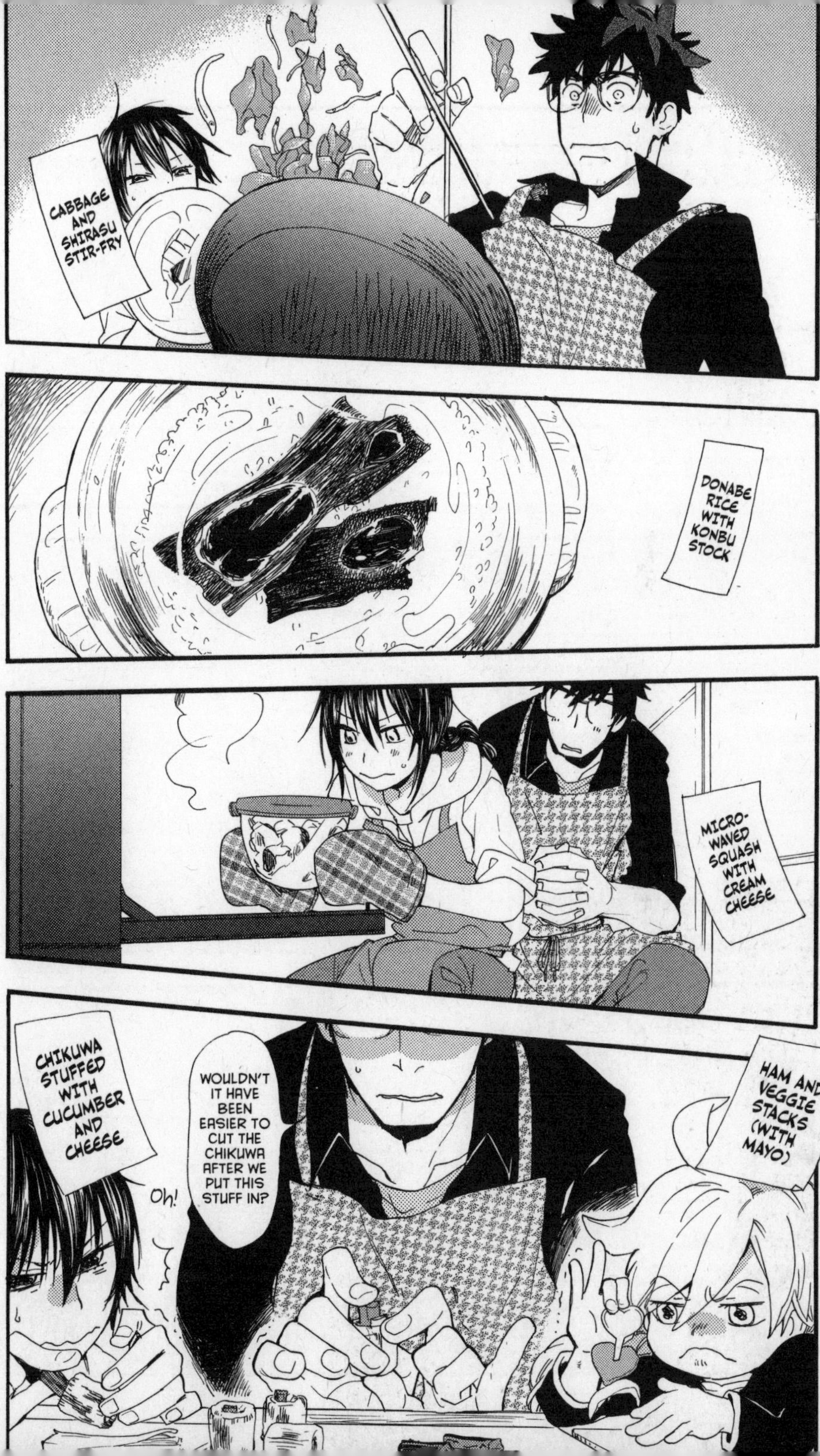
CABBAGE AND SHIRASU STIR-FRY
DONABE RICE WITH KONBU STOCK
MICRO-WAVED SQUASH WITH CREAM CHEESE
HAM AND VEGGIE STACKS (WITH MAYO)
WOULDN'T IT HAVE BEEN EASIER TO CUT THE CHIKUWA AFTER WE PUT THIS STUFF IN?
Oh!
CHIKUWA STUFFED WITH CUCUMBER AND CHEESE

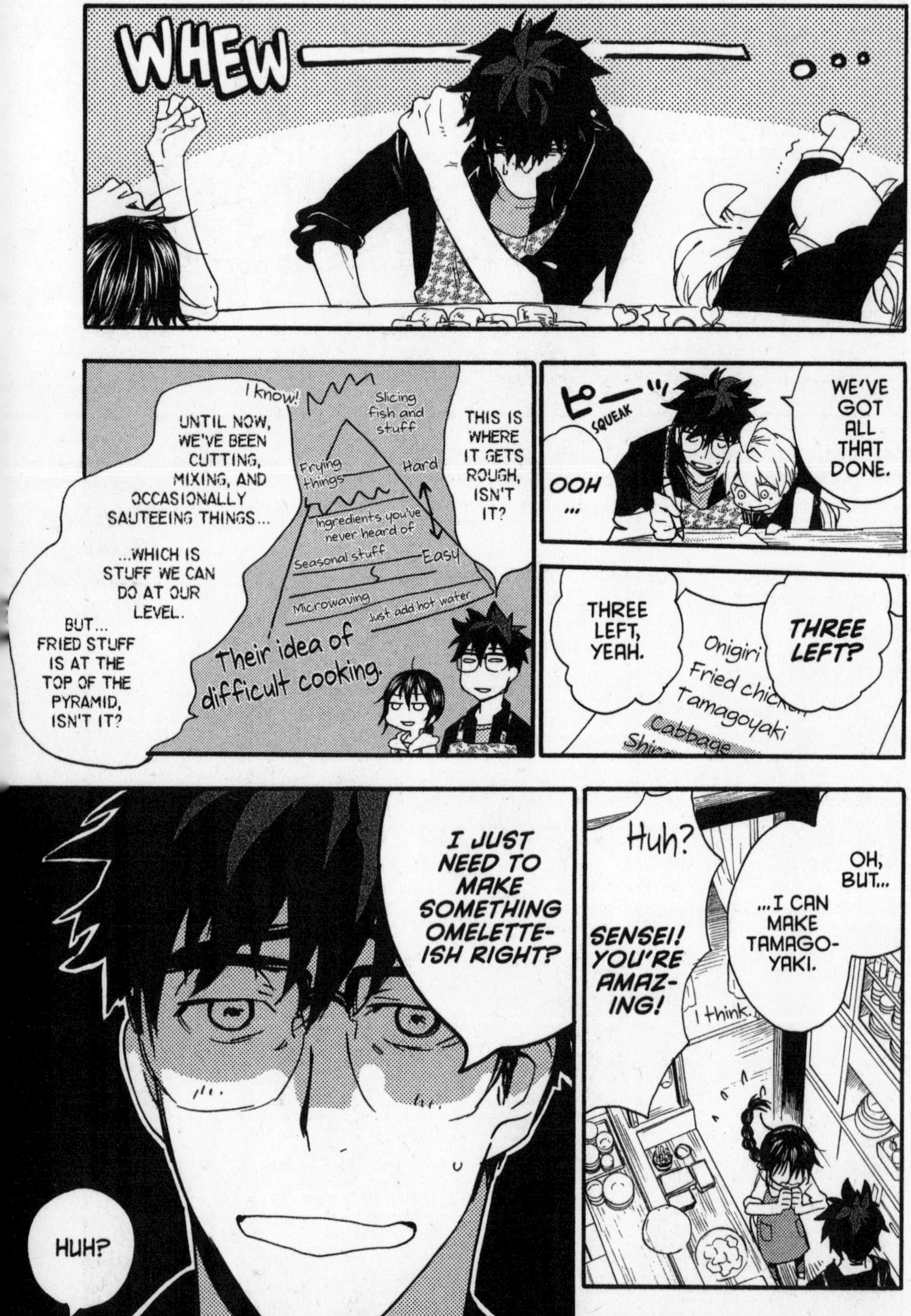
WHEW
WE'VE GOT ALL THAT DONE.
ピー
SQUEAK
OOH ...
THREE LEFT?
THREE LEFT, YEAH.
Onigiri
Tamagoyaki
Cabbage
THIS IS WHERE IT GETS ROUGH, ISN'T IT?
UNTIL NOW, WE'VE BEEN CUTTING, MIXING, AND OCCASIONALLY SAUTEEING THINGS...
...WHICH IS STUFF WE CAN DO AT OUR LEVEL.
BUT... FRIED STUFF IS AT THE TOP OF THE PYRAMID, ISN'T IT?
I know!
Slicing fish and stuff
Frying things
Hard
Ingredients you've never heard of
Seasonal stuff
Easy
Microwaving
Just add hot water
Their idea of difficult cooking.
Huh?
OH, BUT...
...I CAN MAKE TAMAGO-YAKI.
I think.
SENSEI! YOU'RE AMAZ-ING!
I JUST NEED TO MAKE SOMETHING OMELETTE-ISH RIGHT?
HUH?

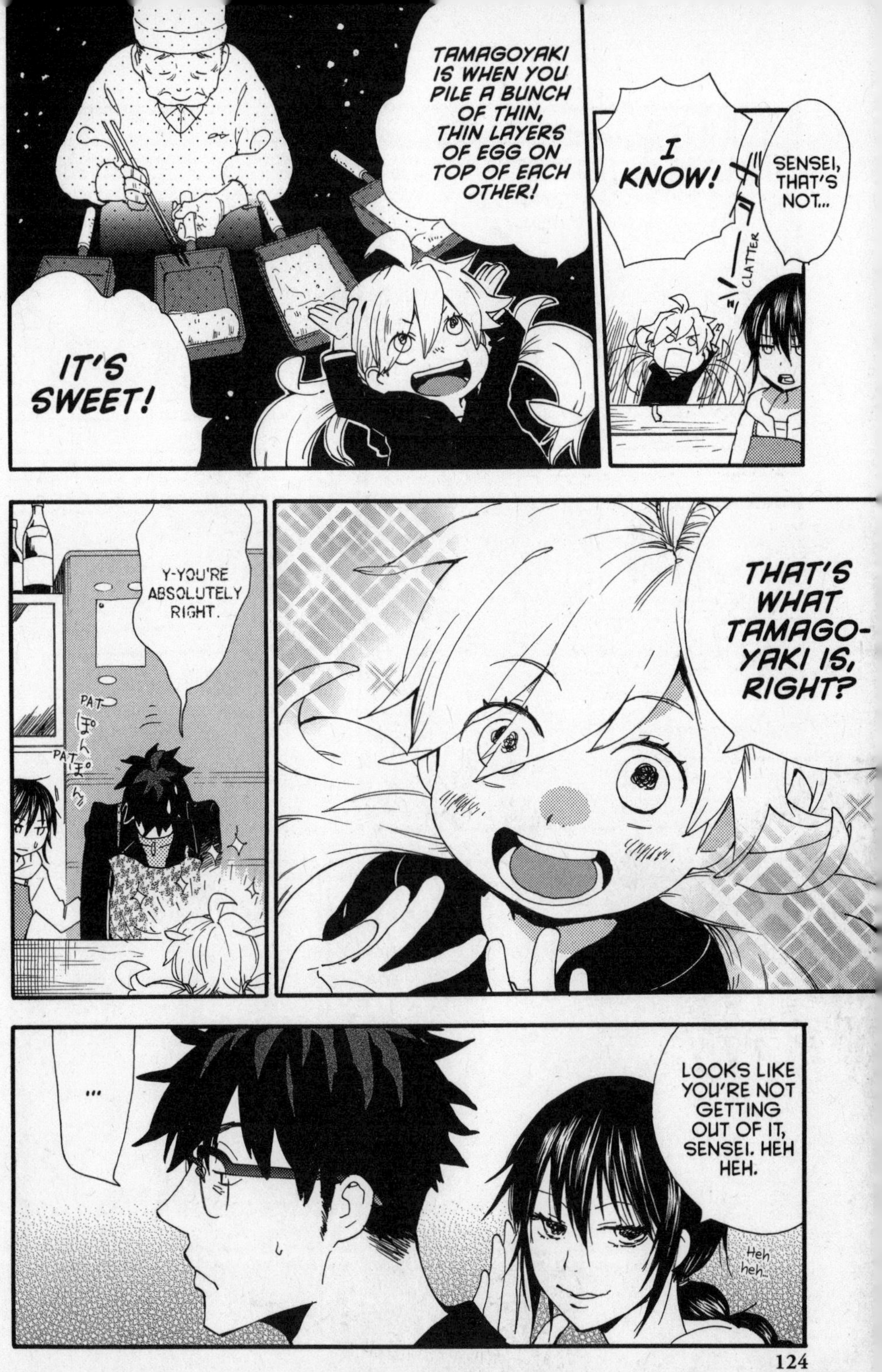

SENSEI, THAT'S NOT...
I KNOW!
CLATTER
TAMAGOYAKI IS WHEN YOU PILE A BUNCH OF THIN, THIN LAYERS OF EGG ON TOP OF EACH OTHER!
IT'S SWEET!
THAT'S WHAT TAMAGO-YAKI IS, RIGHT?
Y-YOU'RE ABSOLUTELY RIGHT.
PAT ぽん
PAT ぽん
LOOKS LIKE YOU'RE NOT GETTING OUT OF IT, SENSEI. HEH HEH.
Heh heh...
...

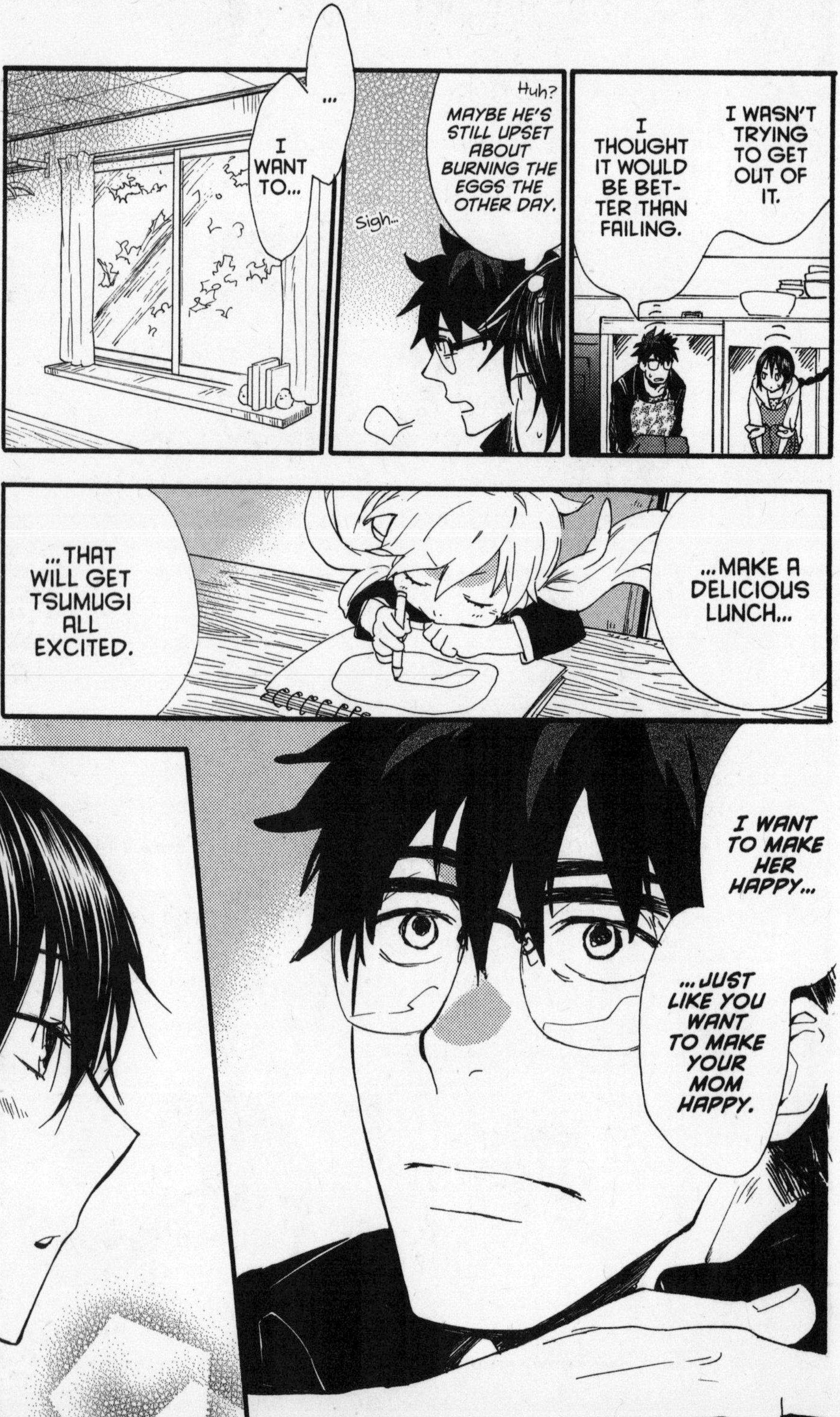
I WASN'T TRYING TO GET OUT OF IT.
I THOUGHT IT WOULD BE BET-TER THAN FAILING.
Huh?
MAYBE HE'S STILL UPSET ABOUT BURNING THE EGGS THE OTHER DAY.
Sigh...
...
I WANT TO...
...MAKE A DELICIOUS LUNCH...
...THAT WILL GET TSUMUGI ALL EXCITED.
I WANT TO MAKE HER HAPPY...
...JUST LIKE YOU WANT TO MAKE YOUR MOM HAPPY.

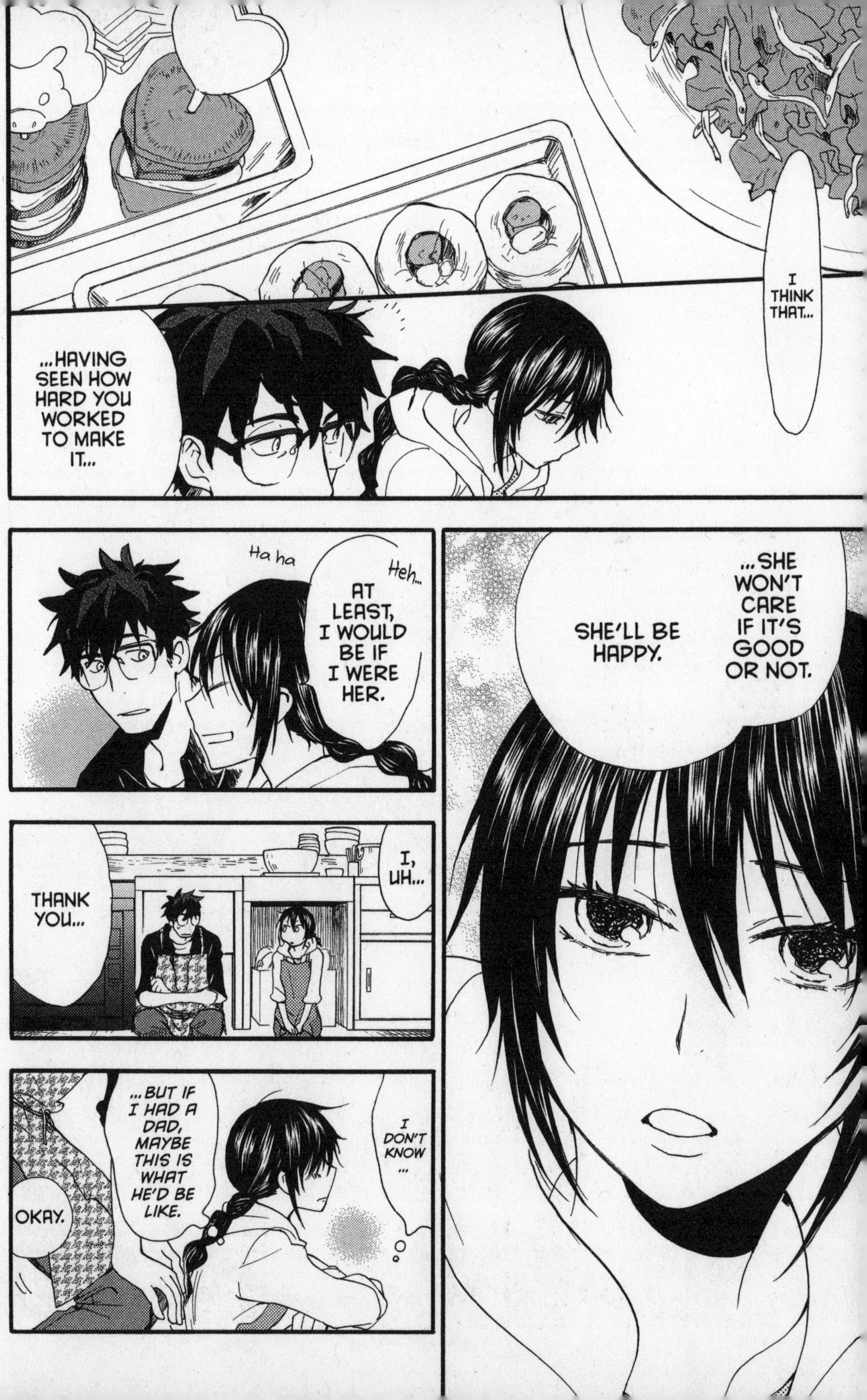

I THINK THAT...
...HAVING SEEN HOW HARD YOU WORKED TO MAKE IT...
...SHE WON'T CARE IF IT'S GOOD OR NOT.
SHE'LL BE HAPPY.
Heh...
AT LEAST, I WOULD BE IF I WERE HER.
Ha ha
I, UH...
THANK YOU...
I DON'T KNOW...
...BUT IF I HAD A DAD, MAYBE THIS IS WHAT HE'D BE LIKE.
OKAY.

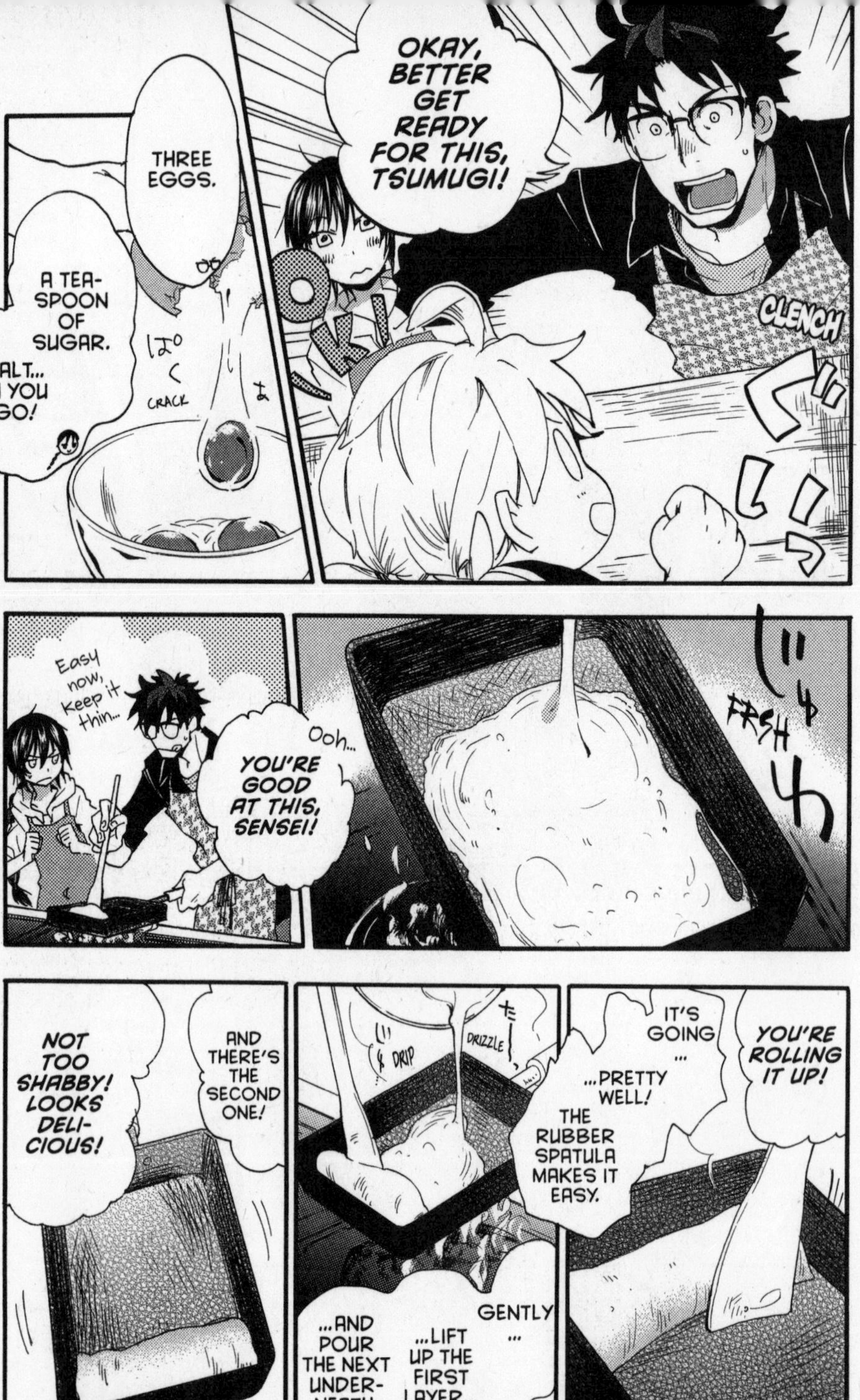
OKAY, BETTER GET READY FOR THIS, TSUMUGI!
CLENCH
THREE EGGS.
A TEA-SPOON OF SUGAR.
SALT... IN YOU GO!
CRACK
FRSH
Easy now, keep it thin...
Ooh...
YOU'RE GOOD AT THIS, SENSEI!
YOU'RE ROLLING IT UP!
IT'S GOING...
...PRETTY WELL!
THE RUBBER SPATULA MAKES IT EASY.
DRIZZLE
DRIP
GENTLY...
...LIFT UP THE FIRST LAYER...
...AND POUR THE NEXT UNDER-NEATH.
AND THERE'S THE SECOND ONE!
NOT TOO SHABBY! LOOKS DELI-CIOUS!

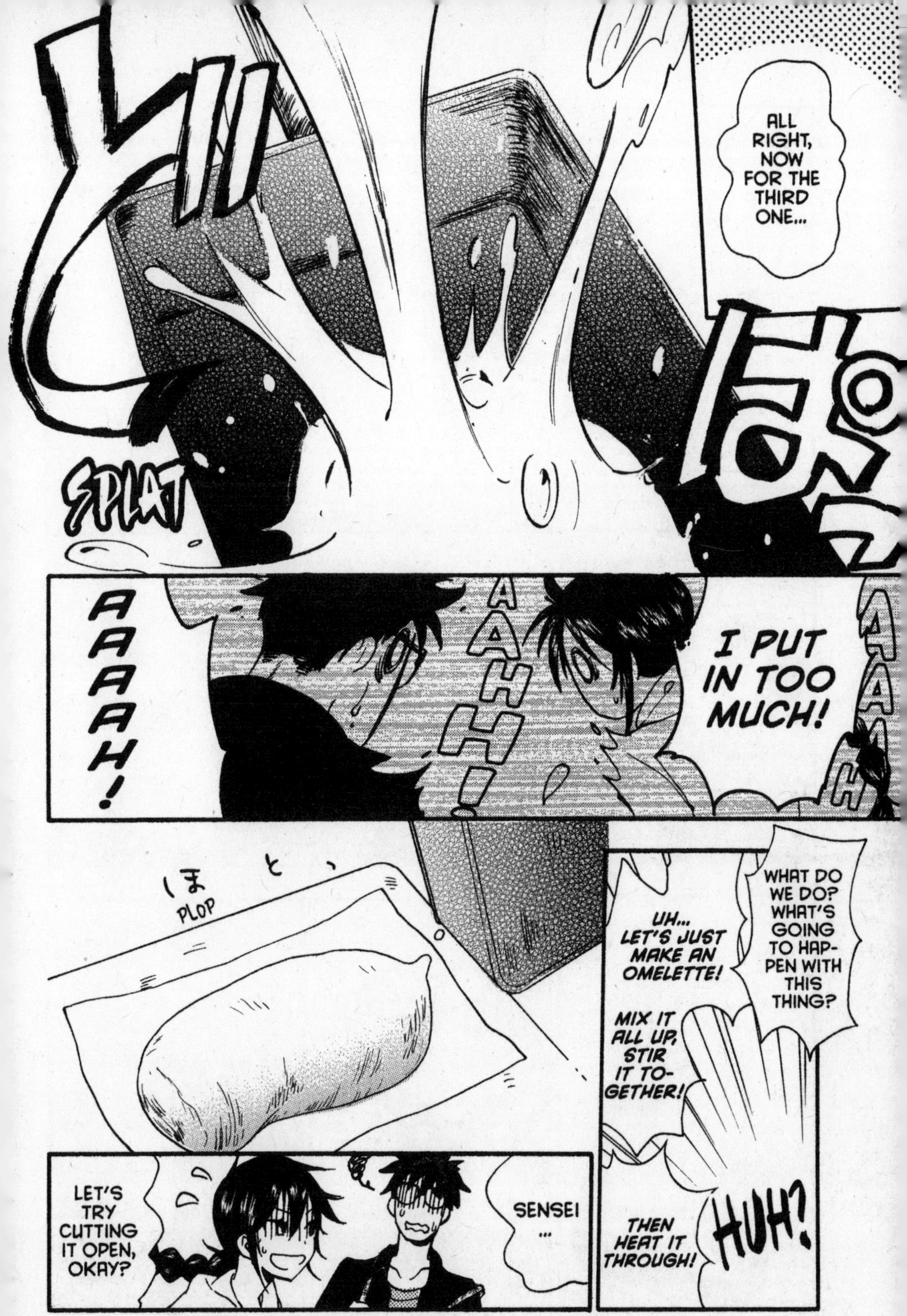
ALL RIGHT, NOW FOR THE THIRD ONE...
SPLAT
AAAAAH!
I PUT IN TOO MUCH!
AAHH!
AAAAAH!
WHAT DO WE DO? WHAT'S GOING TO HAP-PEN WITH THIS THING?
UH... LET'S JUST MAKE AN OMELETTE!
MIX IT ALL UP, STIR IT TO-GETHER!
HUH?
THEN HEAT IT THROUGH!
ほと、
PLOP
SENSEI ...
LET'S TRY CUTTING IT OPEN, OKAY?

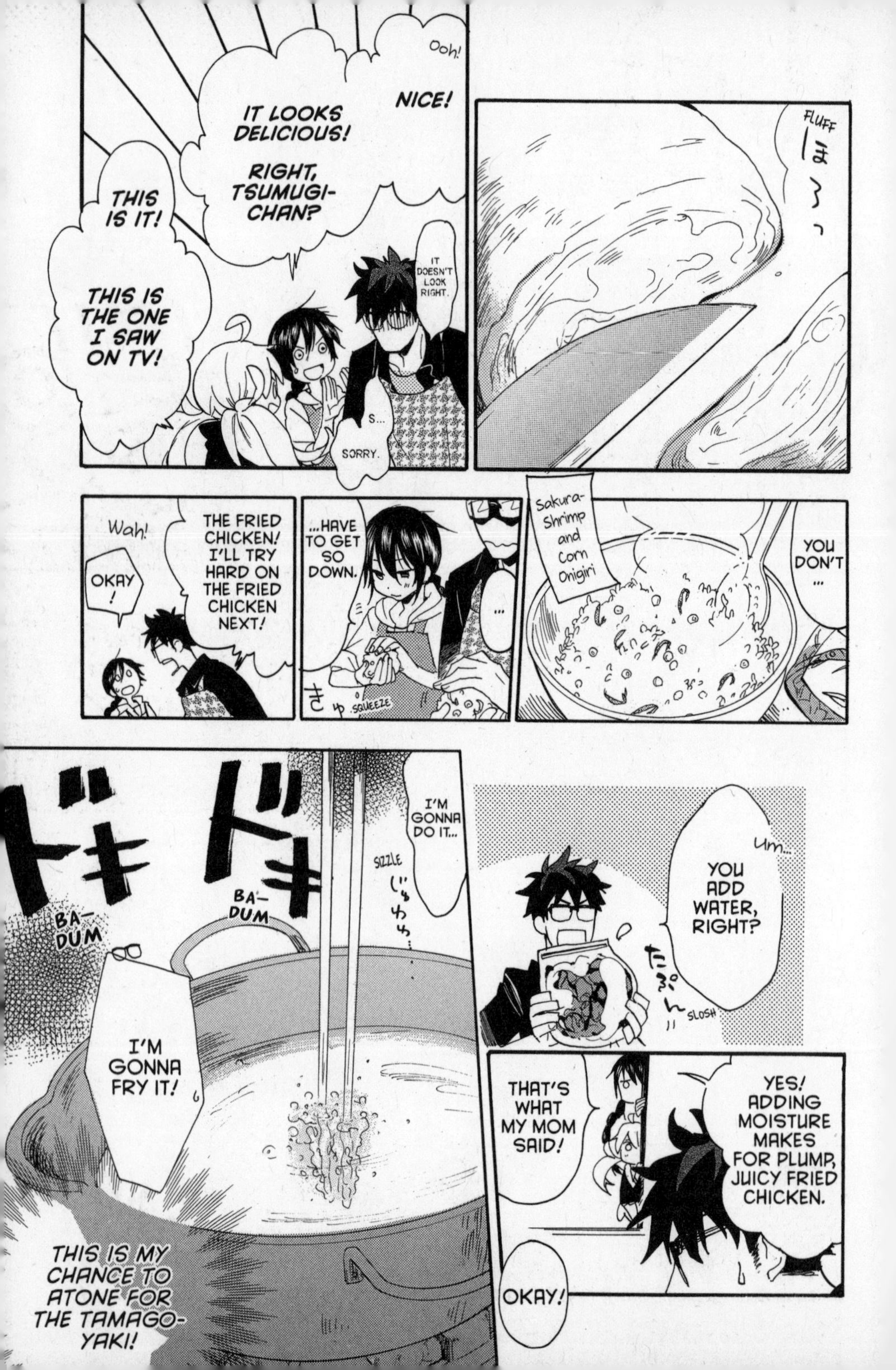
FLUFF
Ooh!
NICE!
IT LOOKS DELICIOUS!
RIGHT, TSUMUGI-CHAN?
THIS IS IT!
THIS IS THE ONE I SAW ON TV!
IT DOESN'T LOOK RIGHT.
S...
SORRY.
YOU DON'T ...
Sakura-Shrimp and Corn Onigiri
...HAVE TO GET SO DOWN.
...
SQUEEZE
THE FRIED CHICKEN! I'LL TRY HARD ON THE FRIED CHICKEN NEXT!
Wah!
OKAY!
Um...
YOU ADD WATER, RIGHT?
SLOSH
YES! ADDING MOISTURE MAKES FOR PLUMP, JUICY FRIED CHICKEN.
THAT'S WHAT MY MOM SAID!
OKAY!
I'M GONNA DO IT...
SIZZLE
BA-DUM
BA-DUM
I'M GONNA FRY IT!
THIS IS MY CHANCE TO ATONE FOR THE TAMAGO-YAKI!

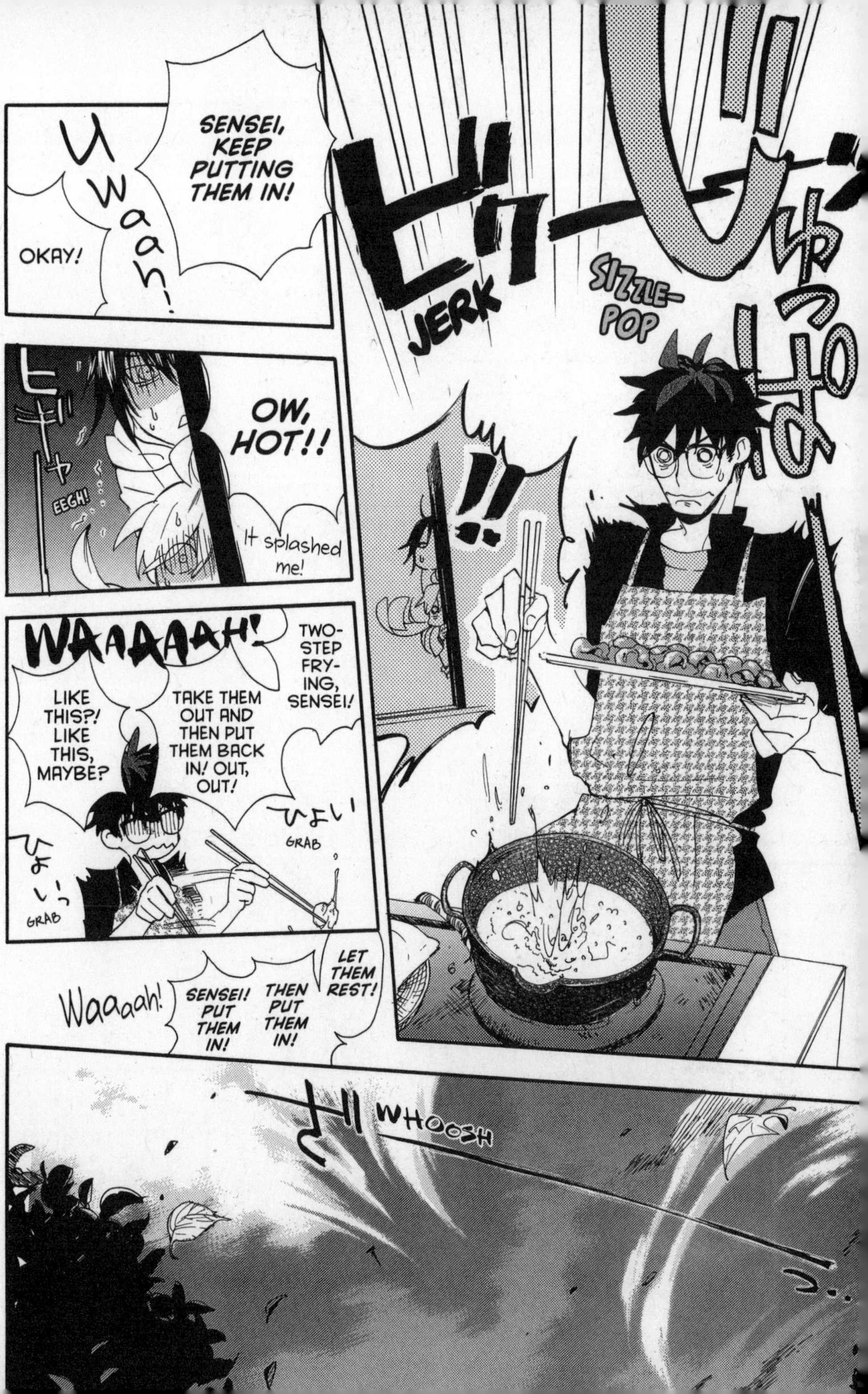
JERK
SIZZLE-POP
SENSEI, KEEP PUTTING THEM IN!
Uwaah!
OKAY!
OW, HOT!!
EEGH!
It splashed me!
WAAAAAH!
TWO-STEP FRY-ING, SENSEI!
LIKE THIS?! LIKE THIS, MAYBE?
TAKE THEM OUT AND THEN PUT THEM BACK IN! OUT, OUT!
GRAB
GRAB
LET THEM REST!
THEN PUT THEM IN!
SENSEI! PUT THEM IN!
Waaaah!
WHOOSH

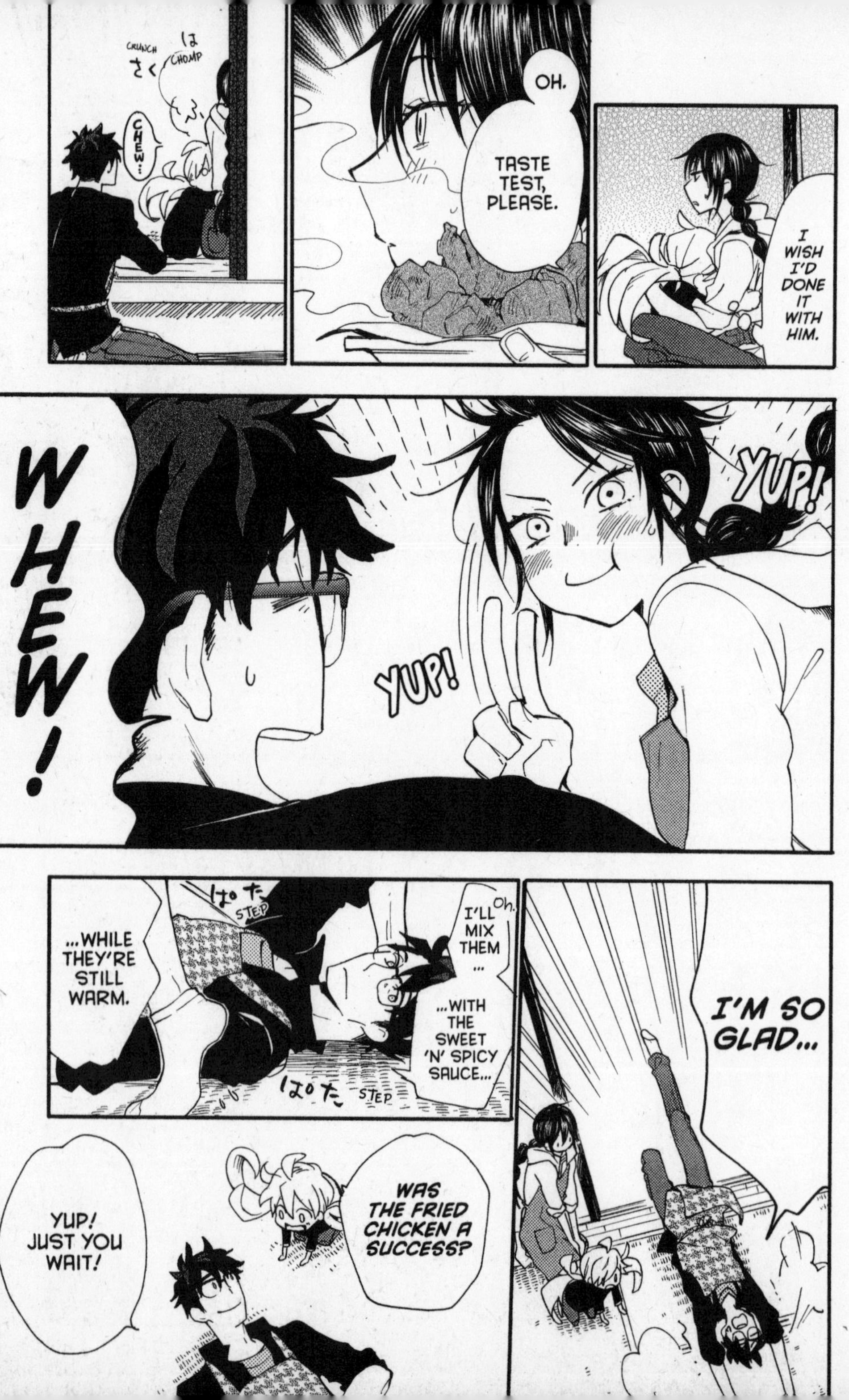
I WISH I'D DONE IT WITH HIM.
OH.
TASTE TEST, PLEASE.
は CHOMP
さく CRUNCH
CHEW...
YUP!
YUP!
WHEW!
I'M SO GLAD...
Oh.
I'LL MIX THEM...
...WITH THE SWEET 'N' SPICY SAUCE...
ぱた STEP
...WHILE THEY'RE STILL WARM.
ぱた STEP
WAS THE FRIED CHICKEN A SUCCESS?
YUP! JUST YOU WAIT!

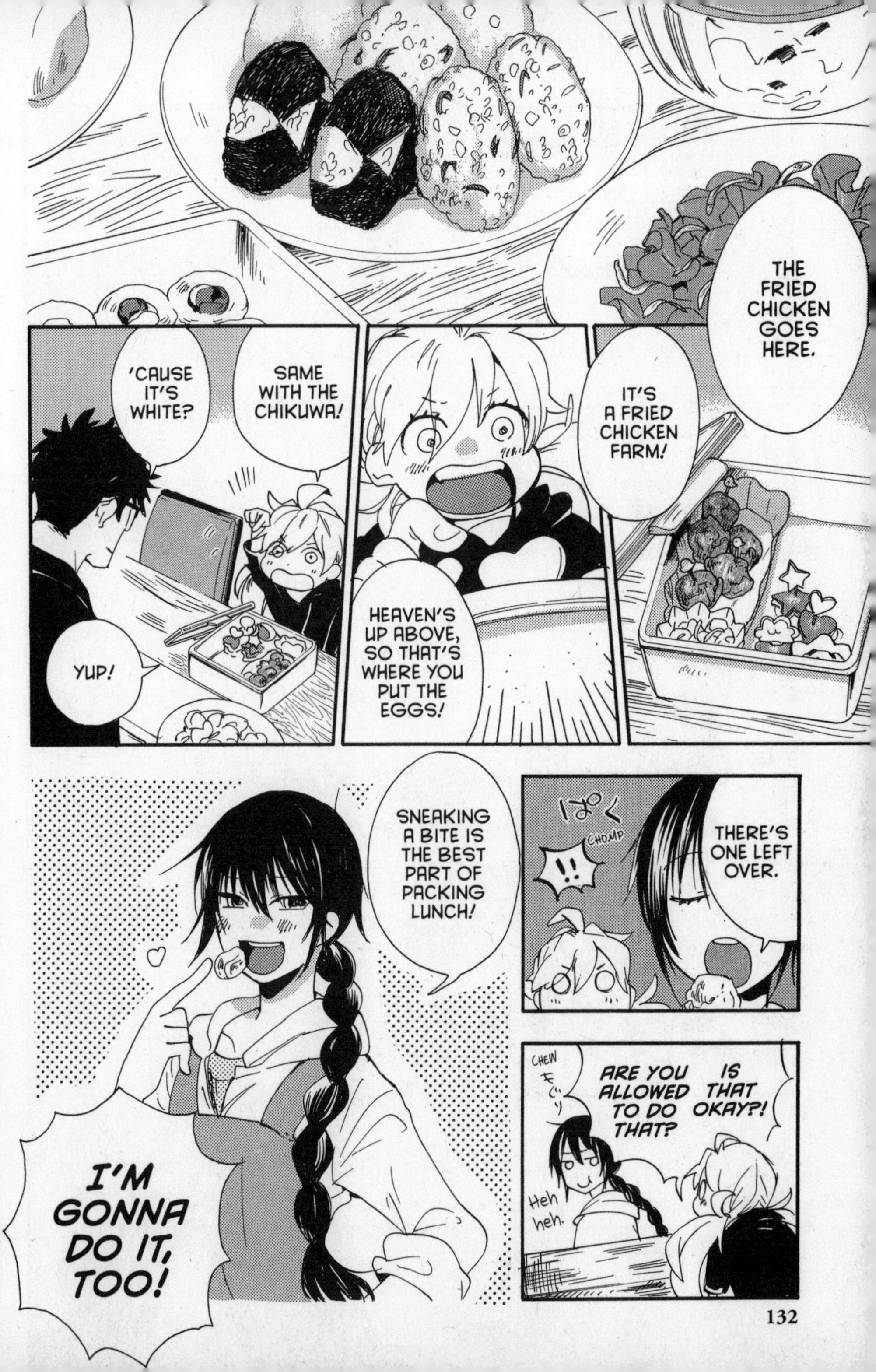
THE FRIED CHICKEN GOES HERE.
IT'S A FRIED CHICKEN FARM!
HEAVEN'S UP ABOVE, SO THAT'S WHERE YOU PUT THE EGGS!
SAME WITH THE CHIKUWA!
'CAUSE IT'S WHITE?
YUP!
THERE'S ONE LEFT OVER.
ぱく
CHOMP
!!
IS THAT OKAY?!
ARE YOU ALLOWED TO DO THAT?
モグ
CHEW
Heh heh.
SNEAKING A BITE IS THE BEST PART OF PACKING LUNCH!
I'M GONNA DO IT, TOO!

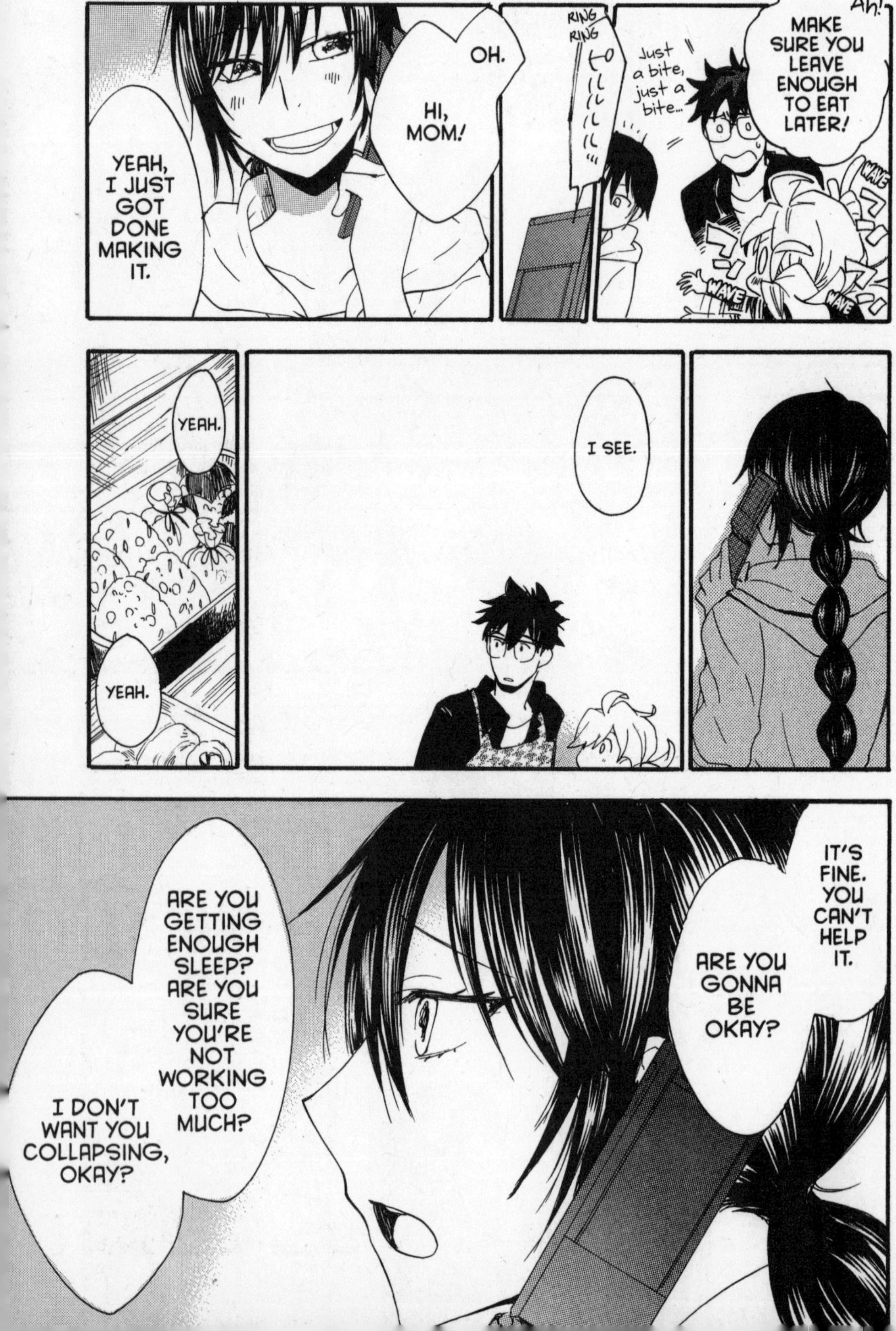
Ah!
MAKE SURE YOU LEAVE ENOUGH TO EAT LATER!
Just a bite, just a bite...
WAVE
WAVE
WAVE
RING RING
OH.
HI, MOM!
YEAH, I JUST GOT DONE MAKING IT.
I SEE.
YEAH.
YEAH.
IT'S FINE. YOU CAN'T HELP IT.
ARE YOU GONNA BE OKAY?
ARE YOU GETTING ENOUGH SLEEP? ARE YOU SURE YOU'RE NOT WORKING TOO MUCH?
I DON'T WANT YOU COLLAPSING, OKAY?

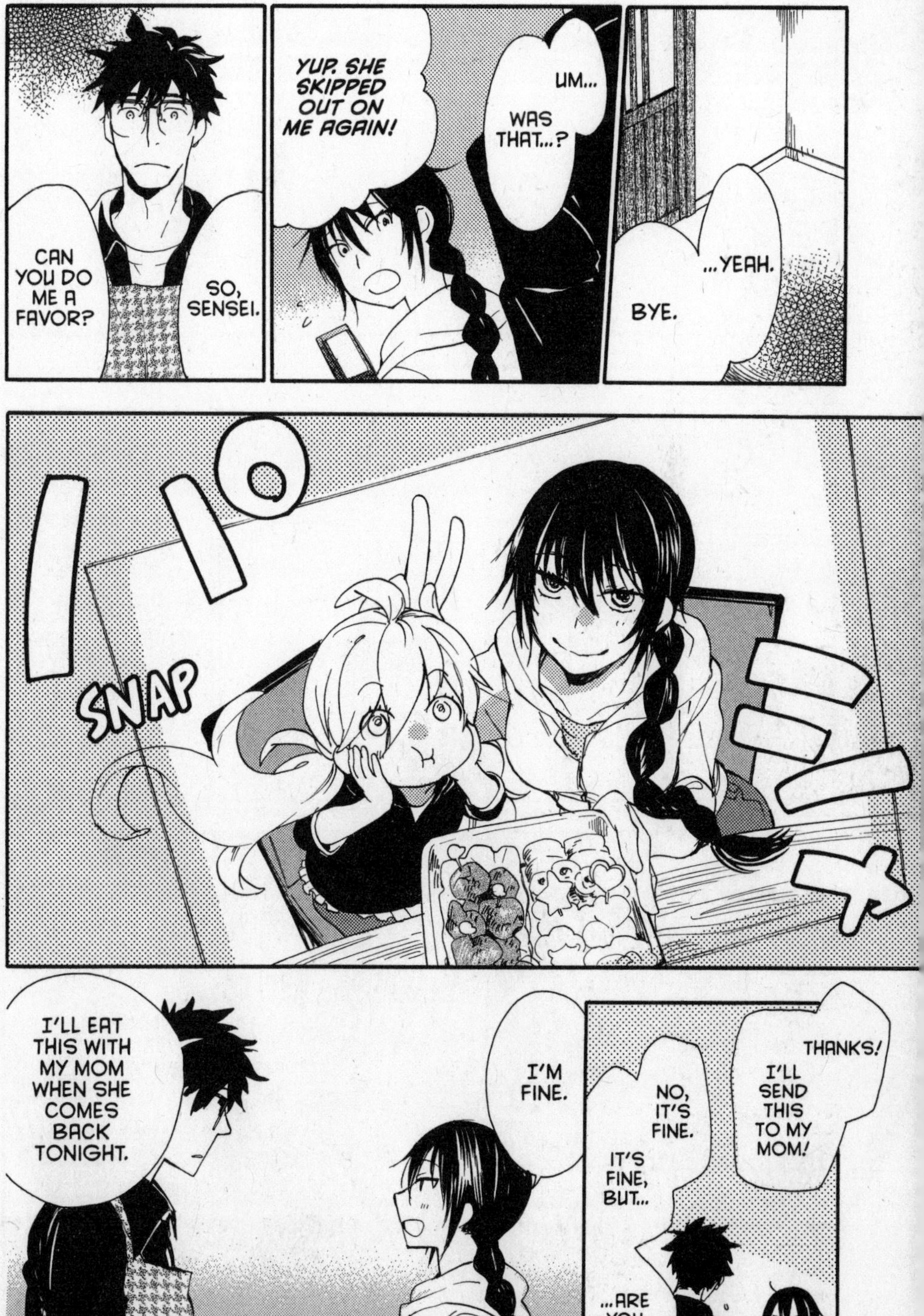
...YEAH.
BYE.
UM... WAS THAT...?
YUP. SHE SKIPPED OUT ON ME AGAIN!
SO, SENSEI.
CAN YOU DO ME A FAVOR?
SNAP
THANKS! I'LL SEND THIS TO MY MOM!
NO, IT'S FINE.
IT'S FINE, BUT...
...ARE YOU OKAY?
I'M FINE.
I'LL EAT THIS WITH MY MOM WHEN SHE COMES BACK TONIGHT.

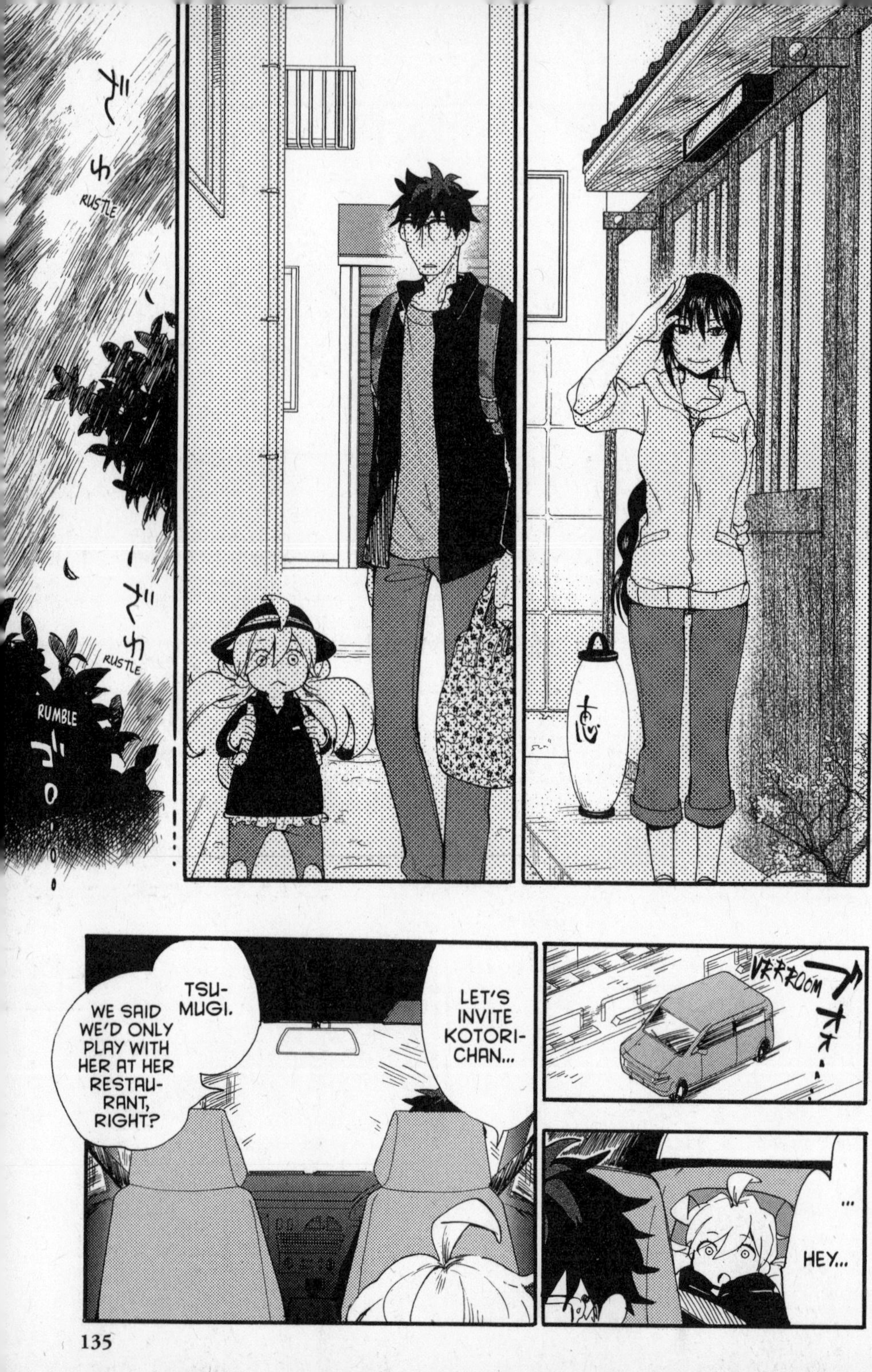

RUSTLE
RUSTLE
RUMBLE
VRRROOM
...
HEY...
LET'S INVITE KOTORI-CHAN...
TSU-MUGI.
WE SAID WE'D ONLY PLAY WITH HER AT HER RESTAU-RANT, RIGHT?

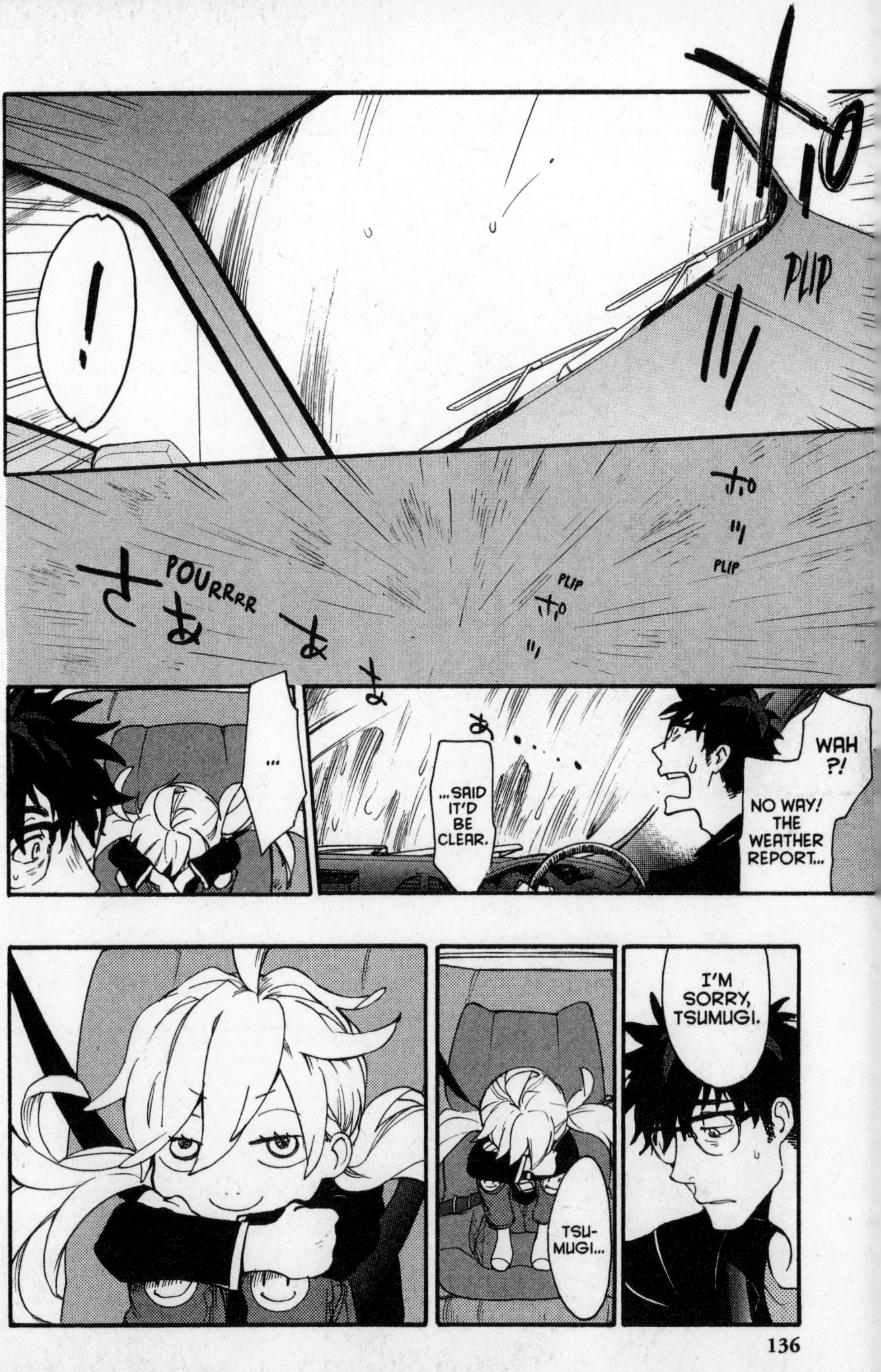
PLIP
!
PLIP
PLIP
POURRRR
WAH ?!
NO WAY! THE WEATHER REPORT...
...SAID IT'D BE CLEAR.
...
I'M SORRY, TSUMUGI.
TSU-MUGI...

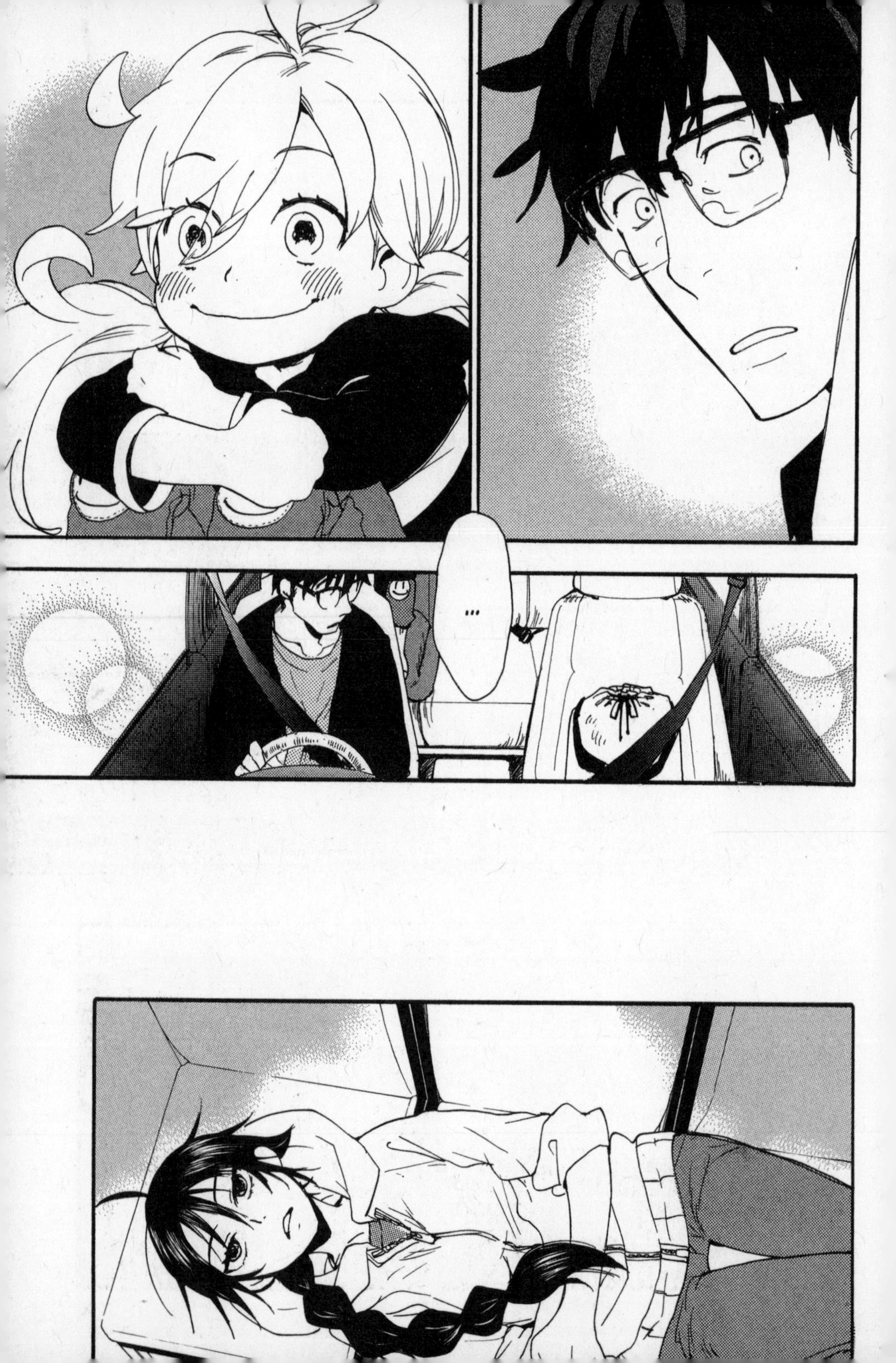
...

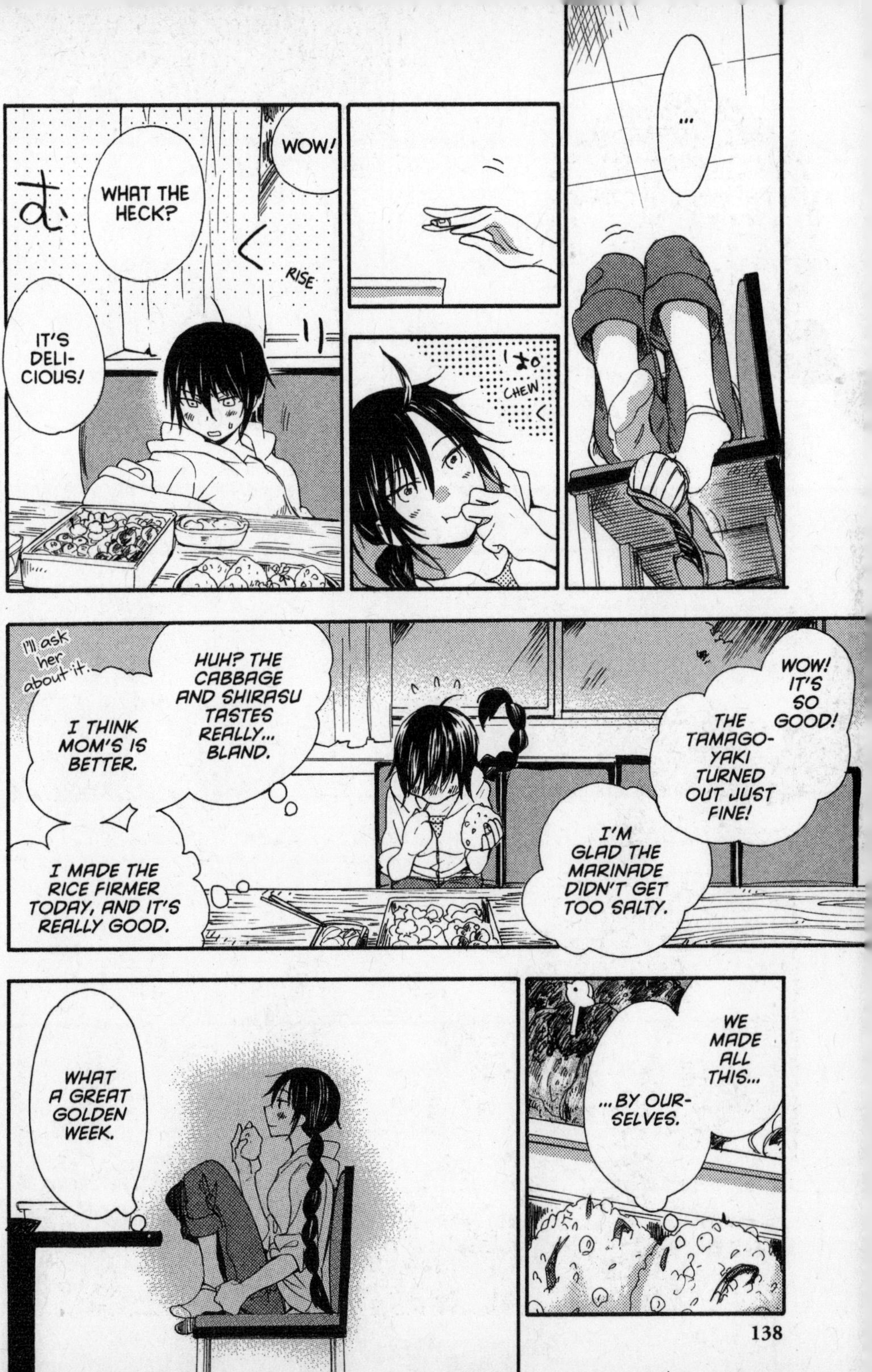
...
CHEW
WOW!
WHAT THE HECK?
RISE
IT'S DELICIOUS!
WOW! IT'S SO GOOD!
THE TAMAGO-YAKI TURNED OUT JUST FINE!
I'M GLAD THE MARINADE DIDN'T GET TOO SALTY.
HUH? THE CABBAGE AND SHIRASU TASTES REALLY... BLAND.
I'll ask her about it.
I THINK MOM'S IS BETTER.
I MADE THE RICE FIRMER TODAY, AND IT'S REALLY GOOD.
WE MADE ALL THIS...
...BY OURSELVES.
WHAT A GREAT GOLDEN WEEK.

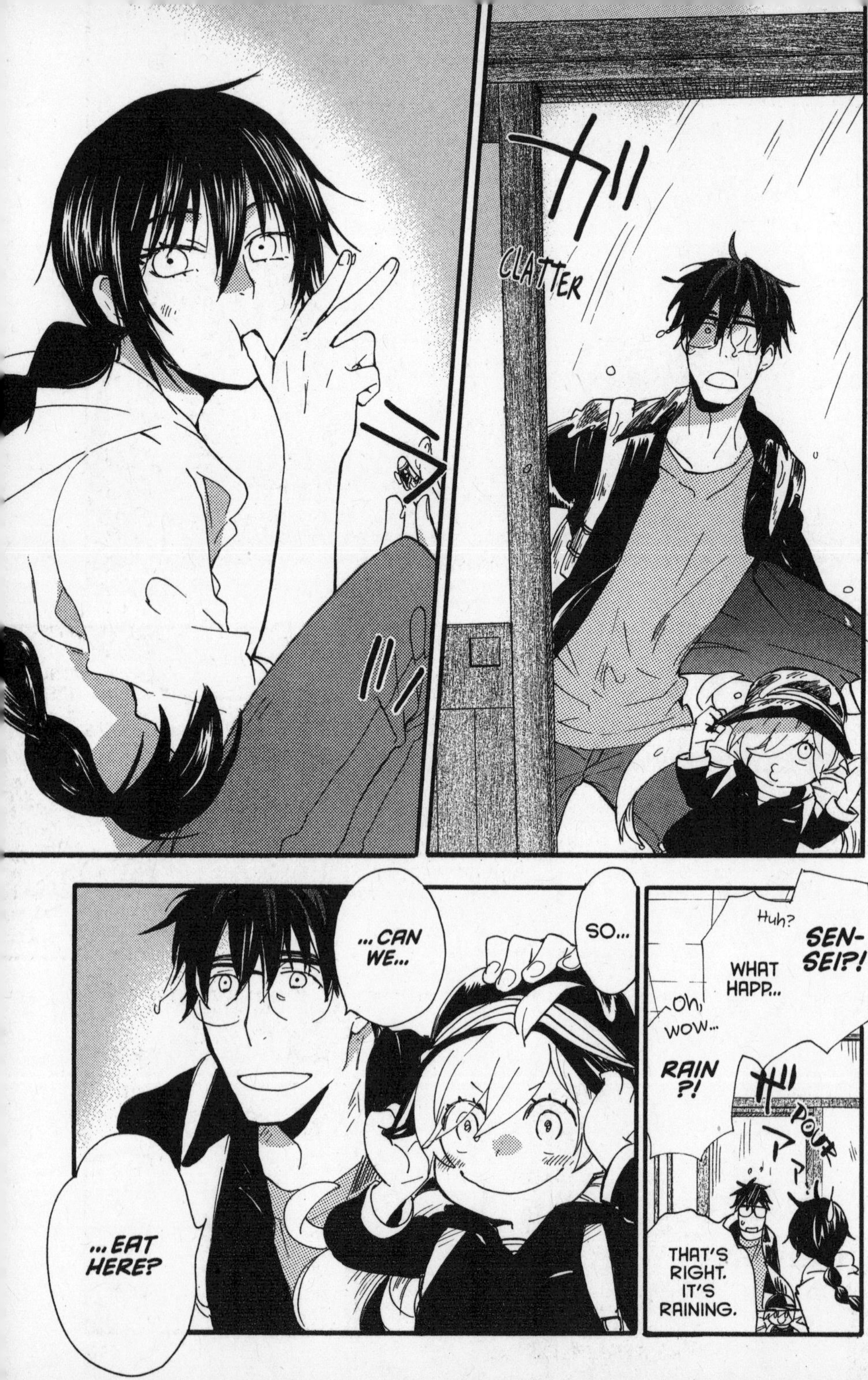
CLATTER
SEN-SEI?!
Huh?
WHAT HAPP...
Oh, WOW...
RAIN?!
POUT
THAT'S RIGHT. IT'S RAINING.
SO...
...CAN WE...
...EAT HERE?

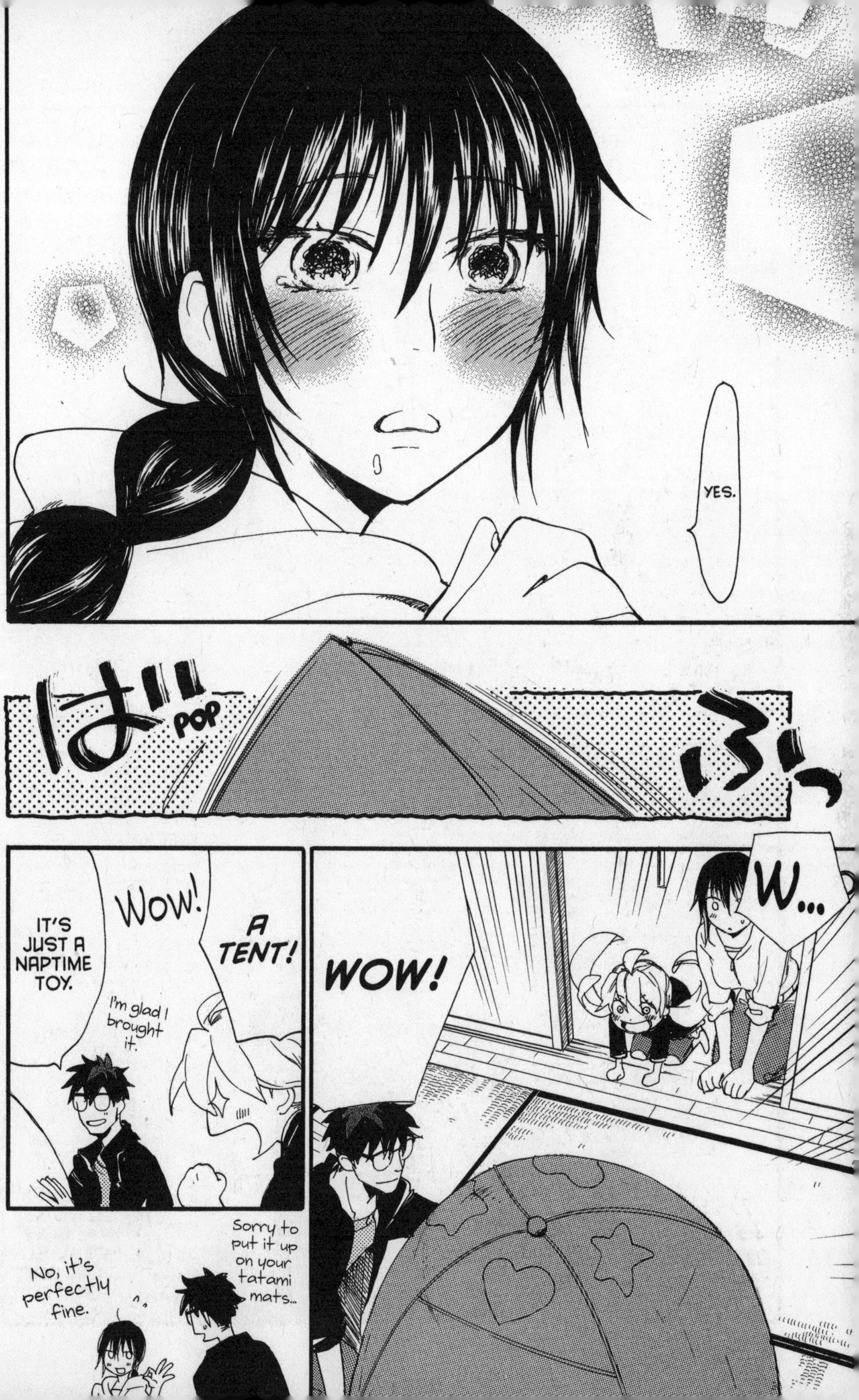
YES.
ふっ
POP
W...
WOW!
A TENT!
Wow!
I'm glad I brought it.
IT'S JUST A NAPTIME TOY.
Sorry to put it up on your tatami mats...
No, it's perfectly fine.

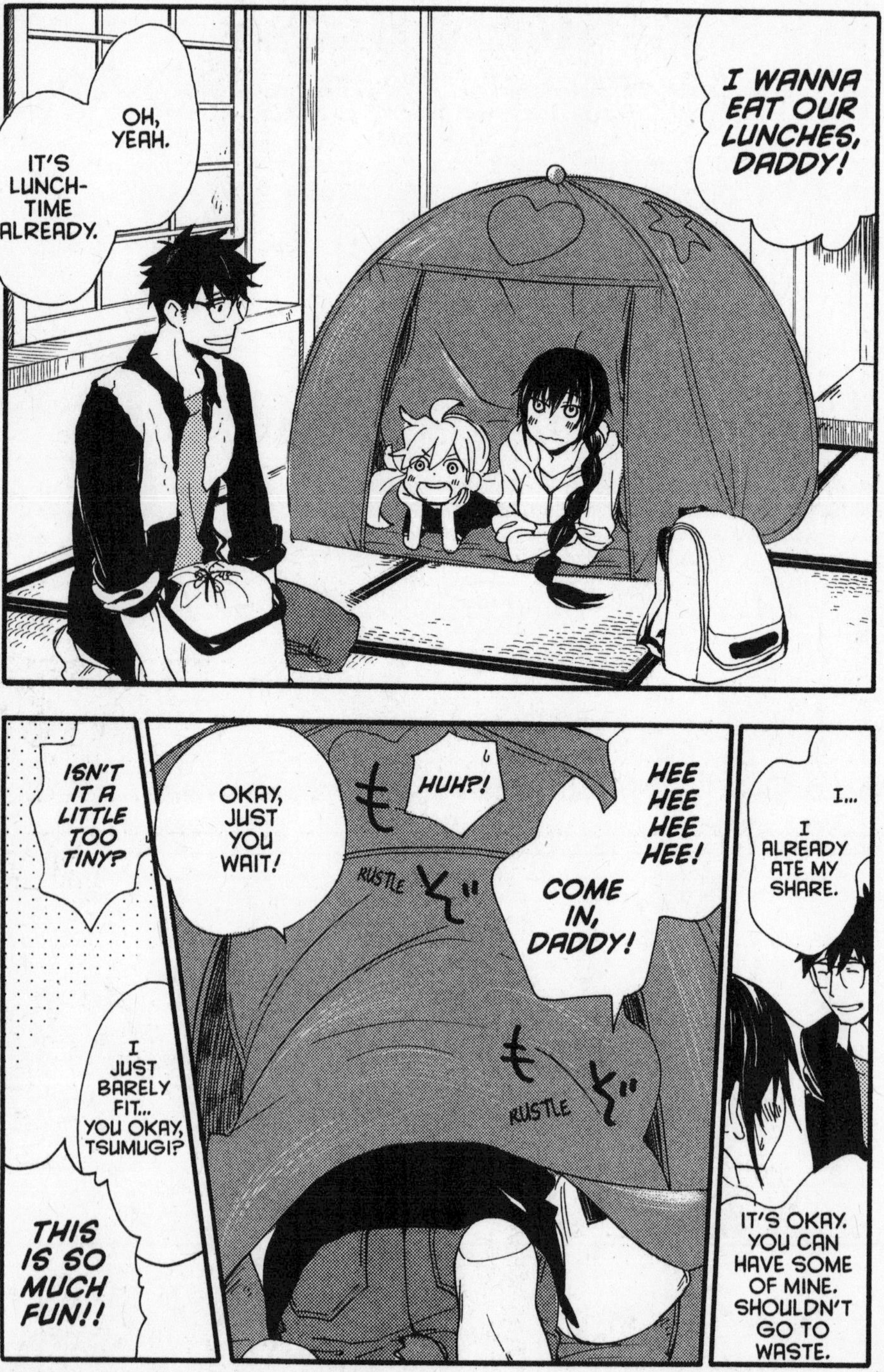
I WANNA EAT OUR LUNCHES, DADDY!
OH, YEAH.
IT'S LUNCH-TIME ALREADY.
I...
I ALREADY ATE MY SHARE.
IT'S OKAY. YOU CAN HAVE SOME OF MINE. SHOULDN'T GO TO WASTE.
HEE HEE HEE HEE!
COME IN, DADDY!
HUH?!
OKAY, JUST YOU WAIT!
RUSTLE
RUSTLE
ISN'T IT A LITTLE TOO TINY?
I JUST BARELY FIT... YOU OKAY, TSUMUGI?
THIS IS SO MUCH FUN!!

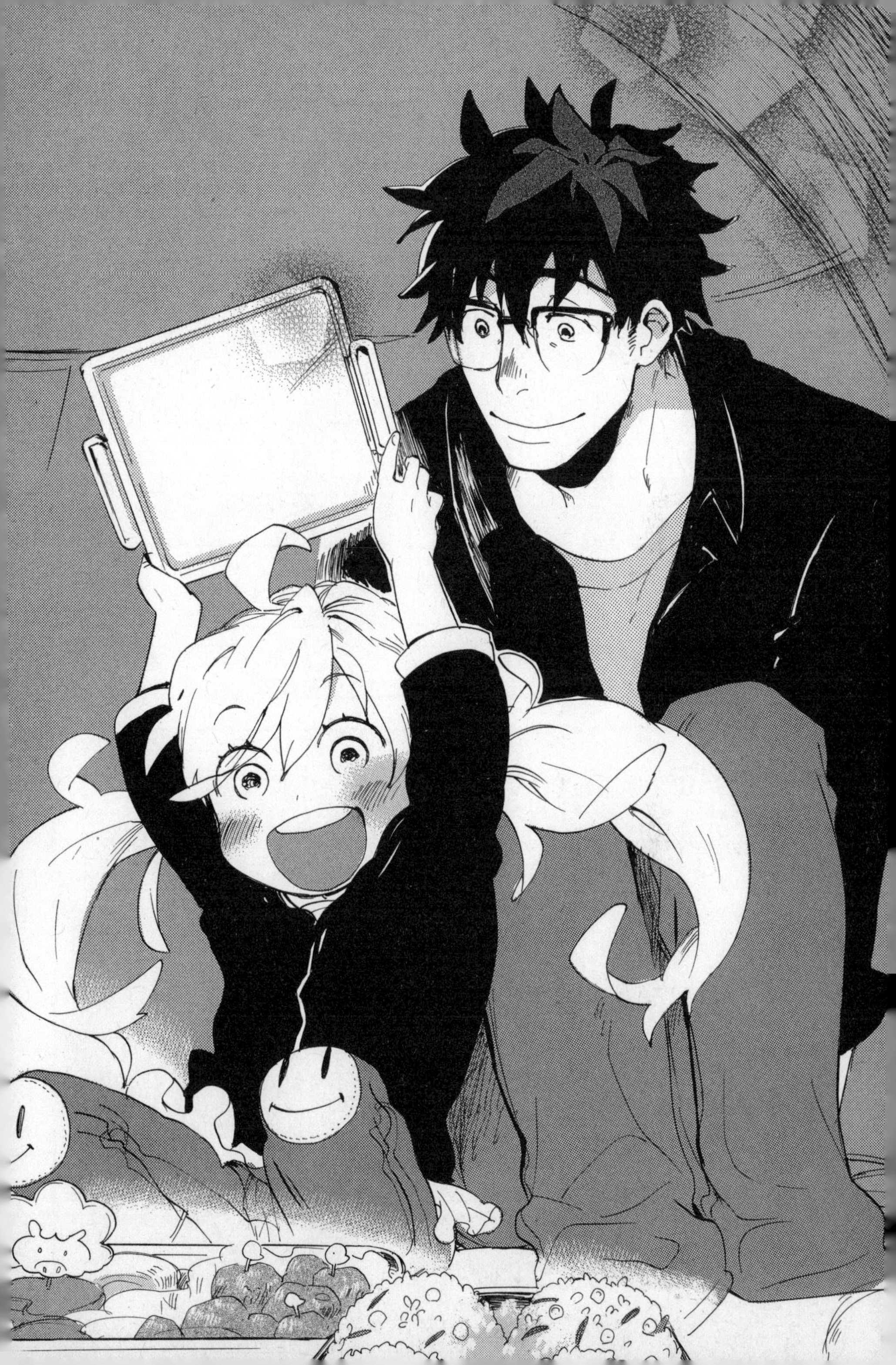

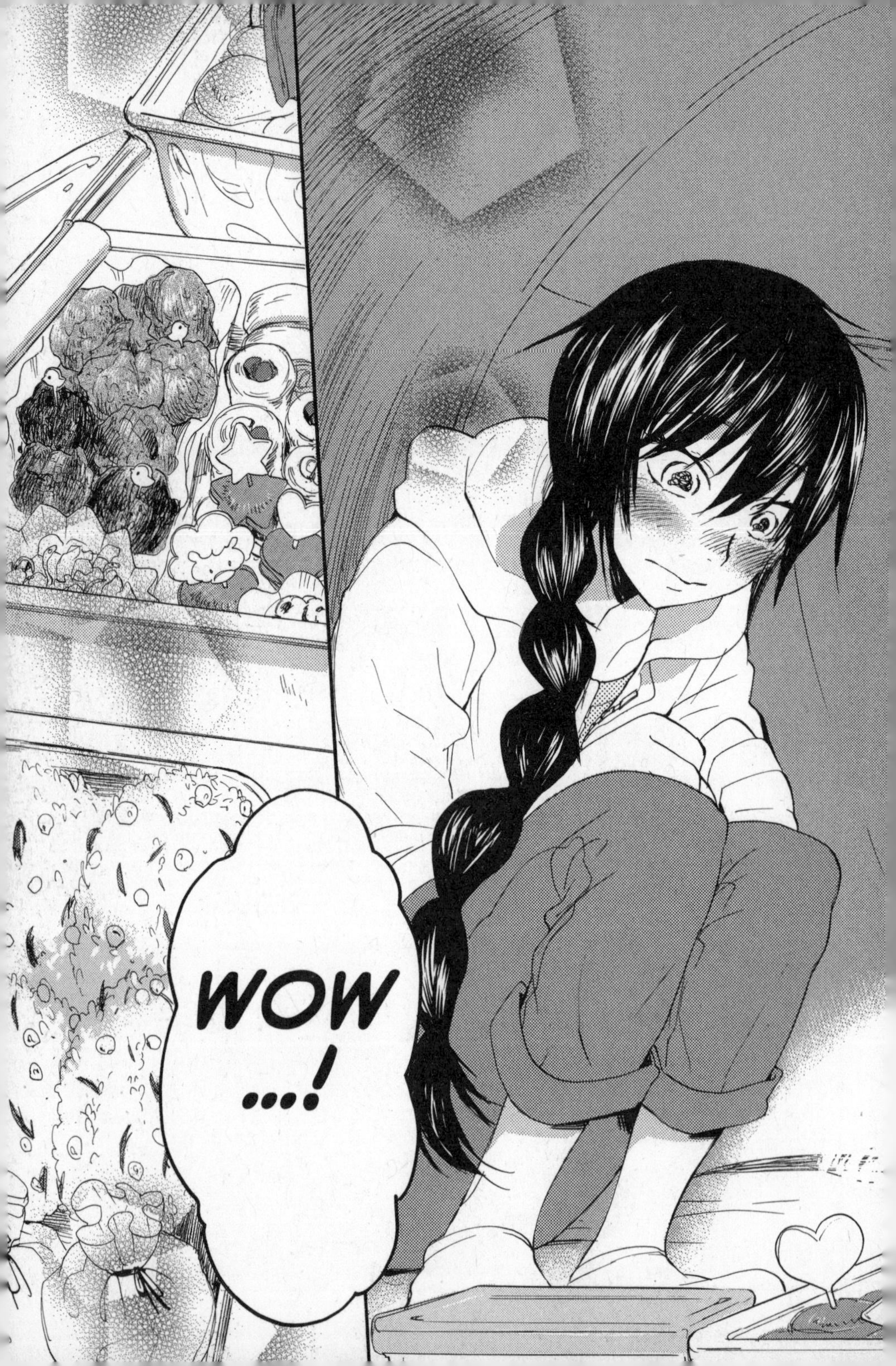
WOW ...!

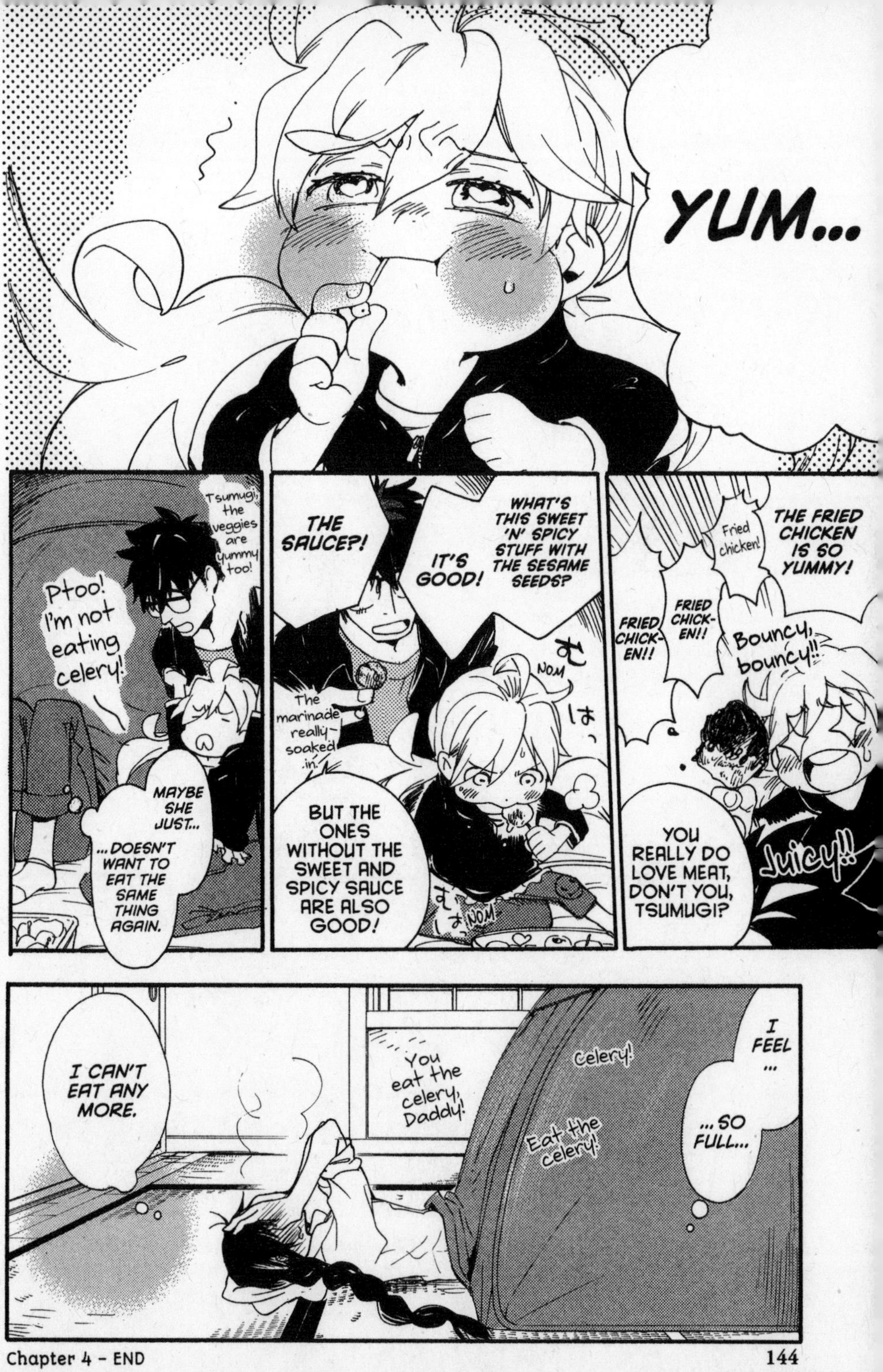
YUM...
THE FRIED CHICKEN IS SO YUMMY!
Fried chicken!
FRIED CHICK-EN!!
FRIED CHICK-EN!!
Bouncy, bouncy!!
YOU REALLY DO LOVE MEAT, DON'T YOU, TSUMUGI?
Juicy!!
WHAT'S THIS SWEET 'N' SPICY STUFF WITH THE SESAME SEEDS?
IT'S GOOD!
THE SAUCE?!
NOM
The marinade really soaked in.
BUT THE ONES WITHOUT THE SWEET AND SPICY SAUCE ARE ALSO GOOD!
NOM
Tsumugi, the veggies are yummy too!
Ptoo! I'm not eating celery!
MAYBE SHE JUST...
...DOESN'T WANT TO EAT THE SAME THING AGAIN.
I FEEL...
...SO FULL...
Celery!
Eat the celery!
You eat the celery, Daddy!
I CAN'T EAT ANY MORE.

Sweet and Spicy

FRIED CHICKEN

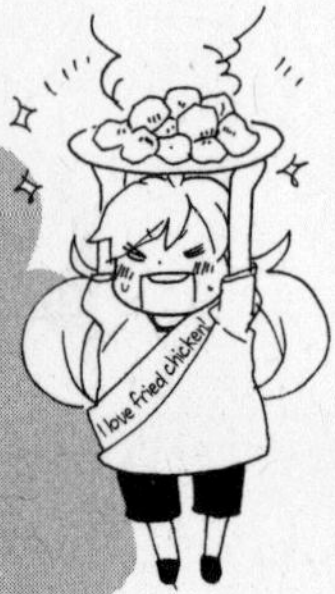
I love fried chicken!

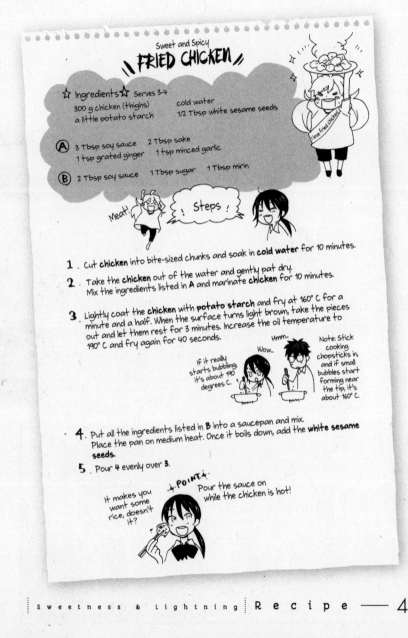

☆ Ingredients ☆ Serves 3-4

300 g chicken (thighs)
a little potato starch
cold water
1/2 Tbsp white sesame seeds

Ⓐ 3 Tbsp soy sauce 2 Tbsp sake
1 tsp grated ginger 1 tsp minced garlic

Ⓑ 2 Tbsp soy sauce 1 Tbsp sugar 1 Tbsp mirin

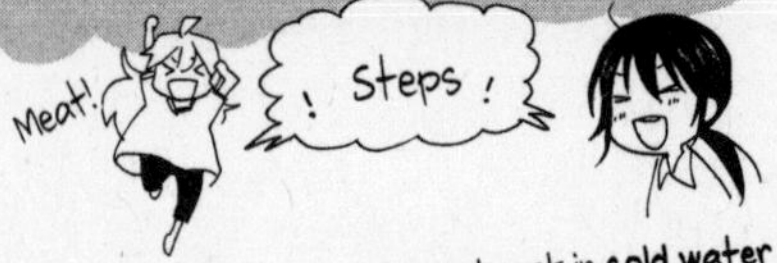
Meat!

! Steps !

1. Cut **chicken** into bite-sized chunks and soak in **cold water** for 10 minutes.
2. Take the **chicken** out of the water and gently pat dry. Mix the ingredients listed in **A** and marinate **chicken** for 10 minutes.
3. Lightly coat the **chicken** with **potato starch** and fry at 160° C for a minute and a half. When the surface turns light brown, take the pieces out and let them rest for 3 minutes. Increase the oil temperature to 190° C and fry again for 40 seconds.

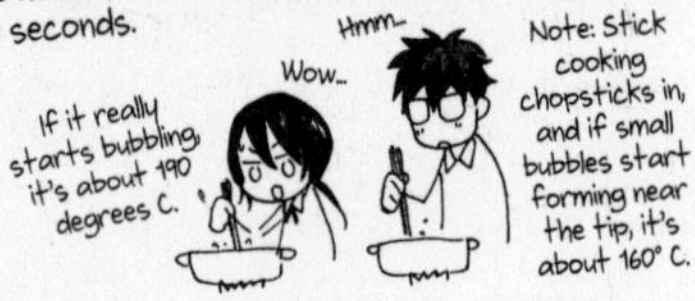
Note: Stick cooking chopsticks in, and if small bubbles start forming near the tip, it's about 160° C.
Hmm...
Wow...
If it really starts bubbling, it's about 190 degrees C.

4. Put all the ingredients listed in **B** into a saucepan and mix. Place the pan on medium heat. Once it boils down, add the **white sesame seeds.**
5. Pour **4** evenly over **3**.

POINT

Pour the sauce on while the chicken is hot!

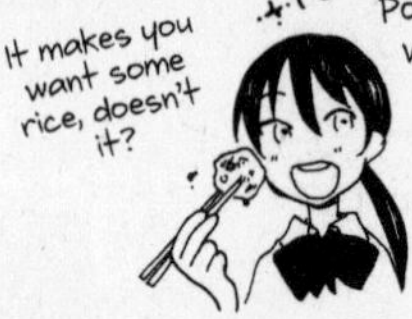
It makes you want some rice, doesn't it?

CONVERSION NOTES:
300 G CHICKEN = ABOUT 10 1/2 OZ, 160° C = 320° F, 190° C = 375° F

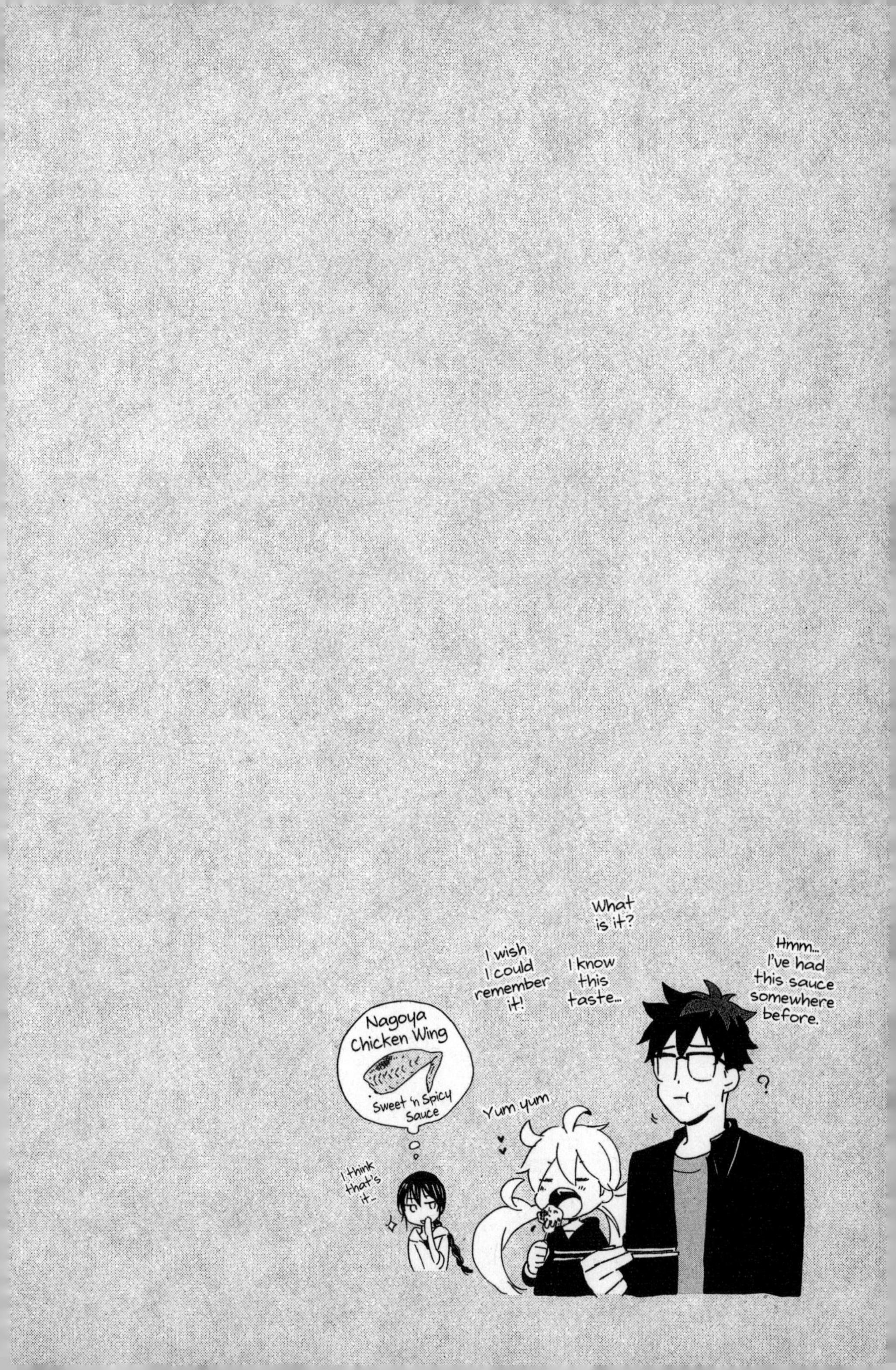
Hmm... I've had this sauce somewhere before.
What is it?
I know this taste...
I wish I could remember it!
Nagoya Chicken Wing
Sweet 'n Spicy Sauce
Yum yum
I think that's it...

Chapter 5 Daddy's Restaurant: "You Got a Cold" Special

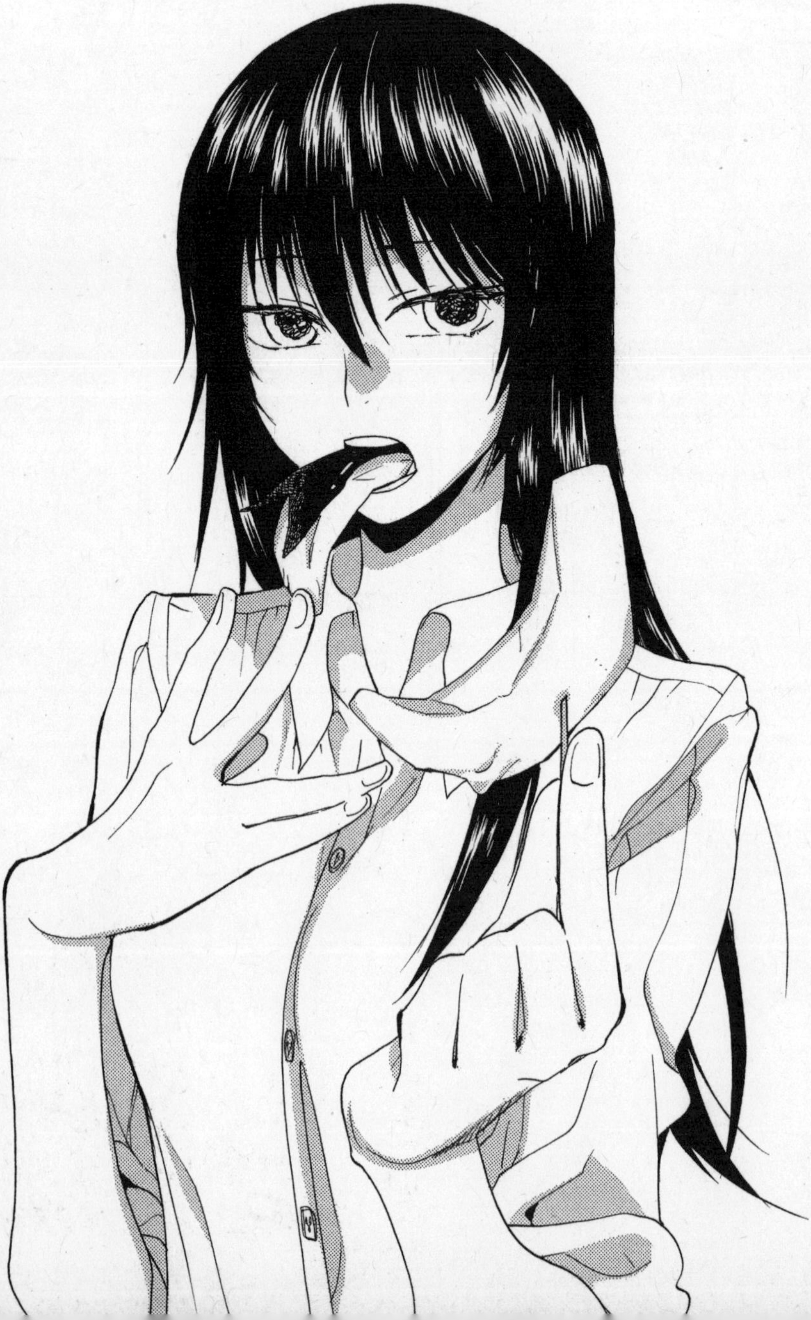

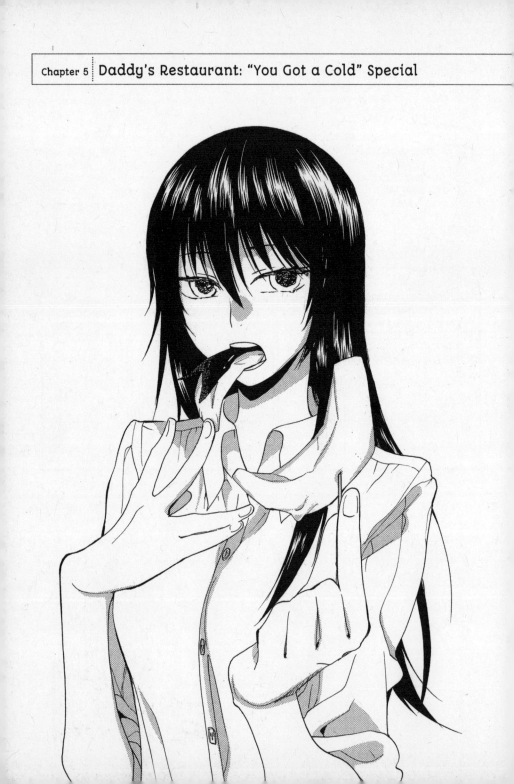

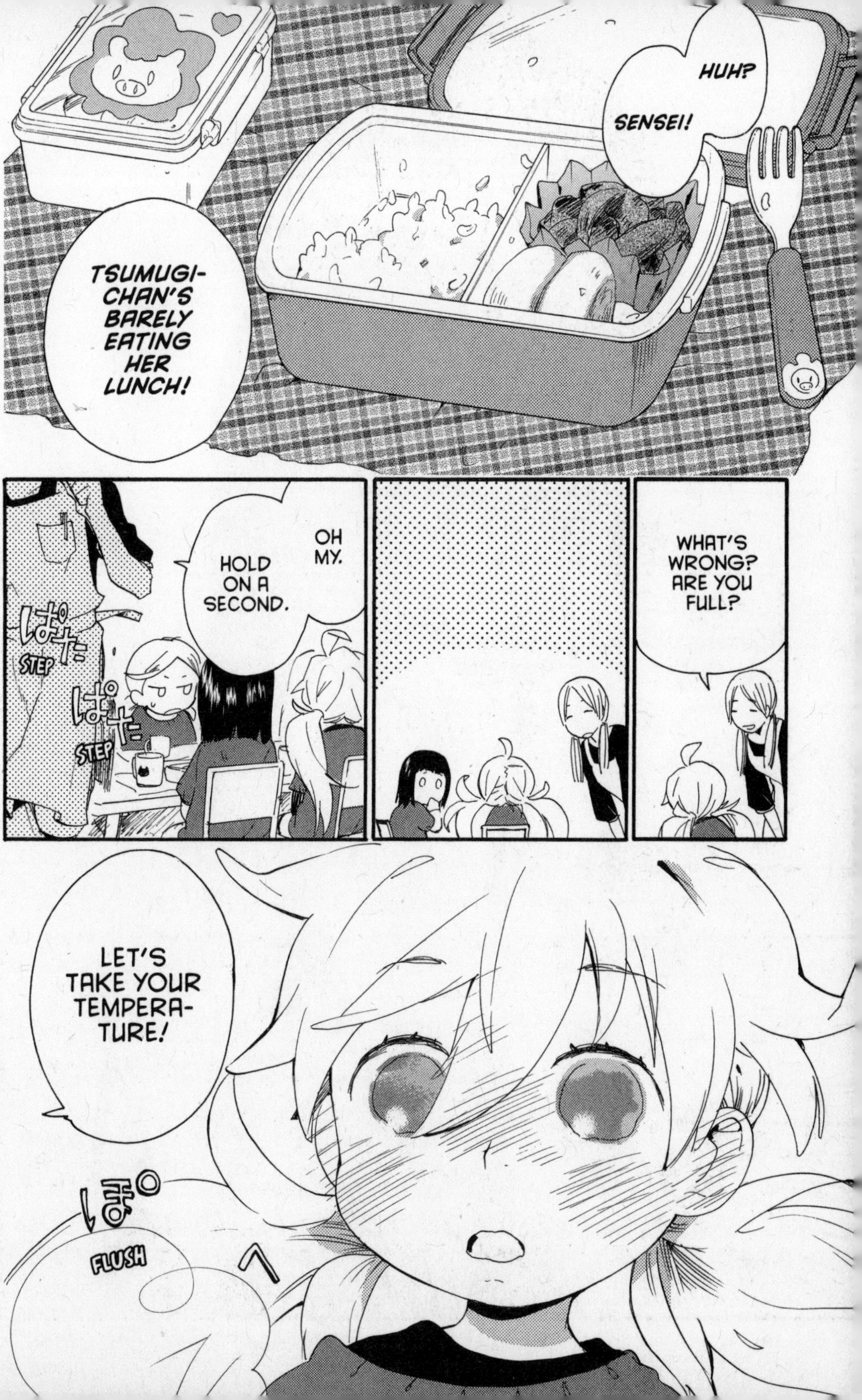
HUH? SENSEI!
TSUMUGI-CHAN'S BARELY EATING HER LUNCH!
WHAT'S WRONG? ARE YOU FULL?
OH MY. HOLD ON A SECOND.
STEP
STEP
LET'S TAKE YOUR TEMPERA-TURE!
FLUSH

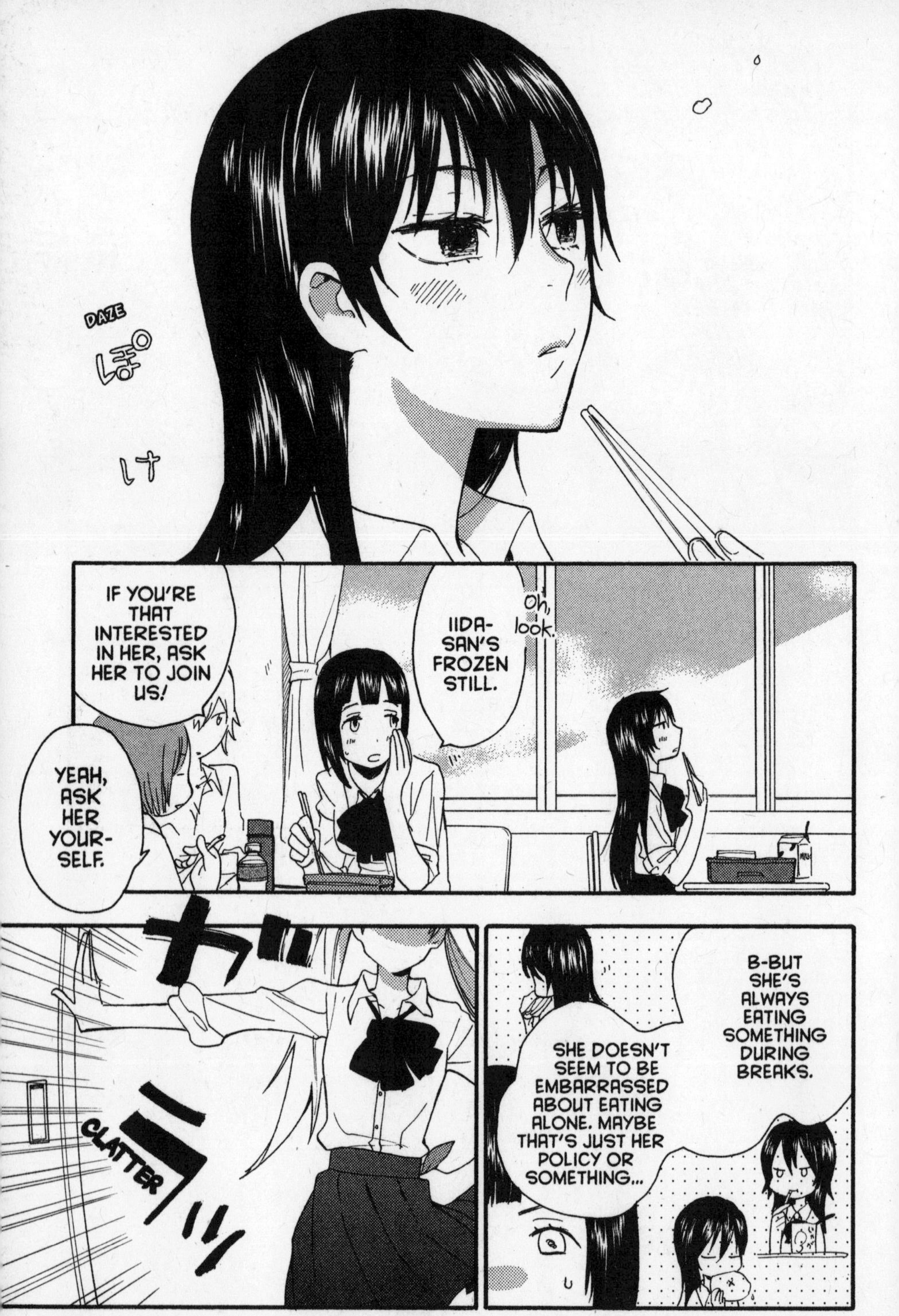
DAZE
Oh, look.
IIDA-SAN'S FROZEN STILL.
IF YOU'RE THAT INTERESTED IN HER, ASK HER TO JOIN US!
YEAH, ASK HER YOURSELF.
B-BUT SHE'S ALWAYS EATING SOMETHING DURING BREAKS.
SHE DOESN'T SEEM TO BE EMBARRASSED ABOUT EATING ALONE. MAYBE THAT'S JUST HER POLICY OR SOMETHING...
CLATTER

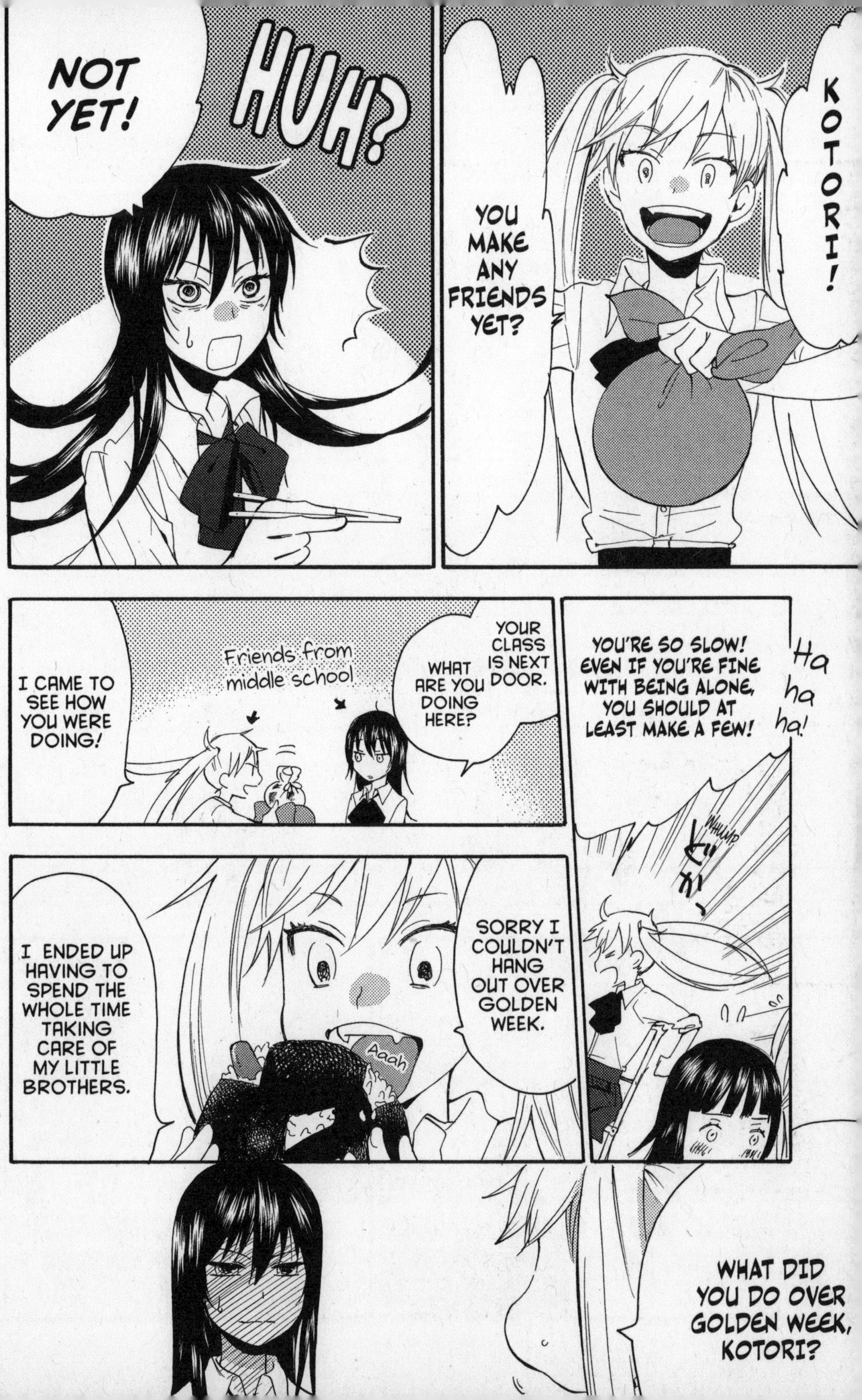
KOTORI!
YOU MAKE ANY FRIENDS YET?
HUH?
NOT YET!
YOU'RE SO SLOW! EVEN IF YOU'RE FINE WITH BEING ALONE, YOU SHOULD AT LEAST MAKE A FEW!
Ha ha ha!
WHUMP
YOUR CLASS IS NEXT DOOR.
WHAT ARE YOU DOING HERE?
Friends from middle school
I CAME TO SEE HOW YOU WERE DOING!
SORRY I COULDN'T HANG OUT OVER GOLDEN WEEK.
Aaah
I ENDED UP HAVING TO SPEND THE WHOLE TIME TAKING CARE OF MY LITTLE BROTHERS.
WHAT DID YOU DO OVER GOLDEN WEEK, KOTORI?

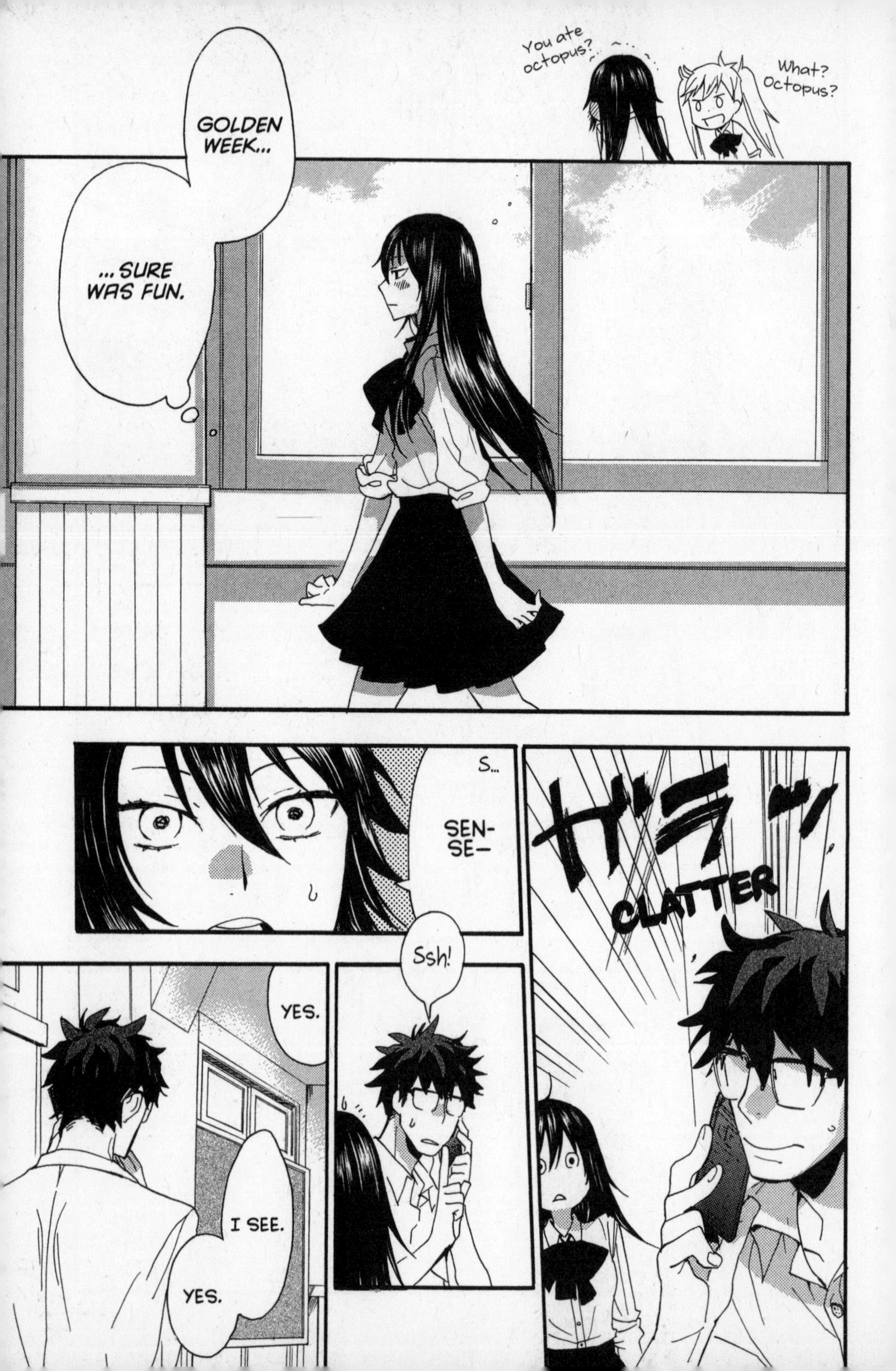
What? Octopus?
You ate octopus?
GOLDEN WEEK...
...SURE WAS FUN.
ガラッ
CLATTER
S...
SEN-SE—
Ssh!
YES.
I SEE.
YES.

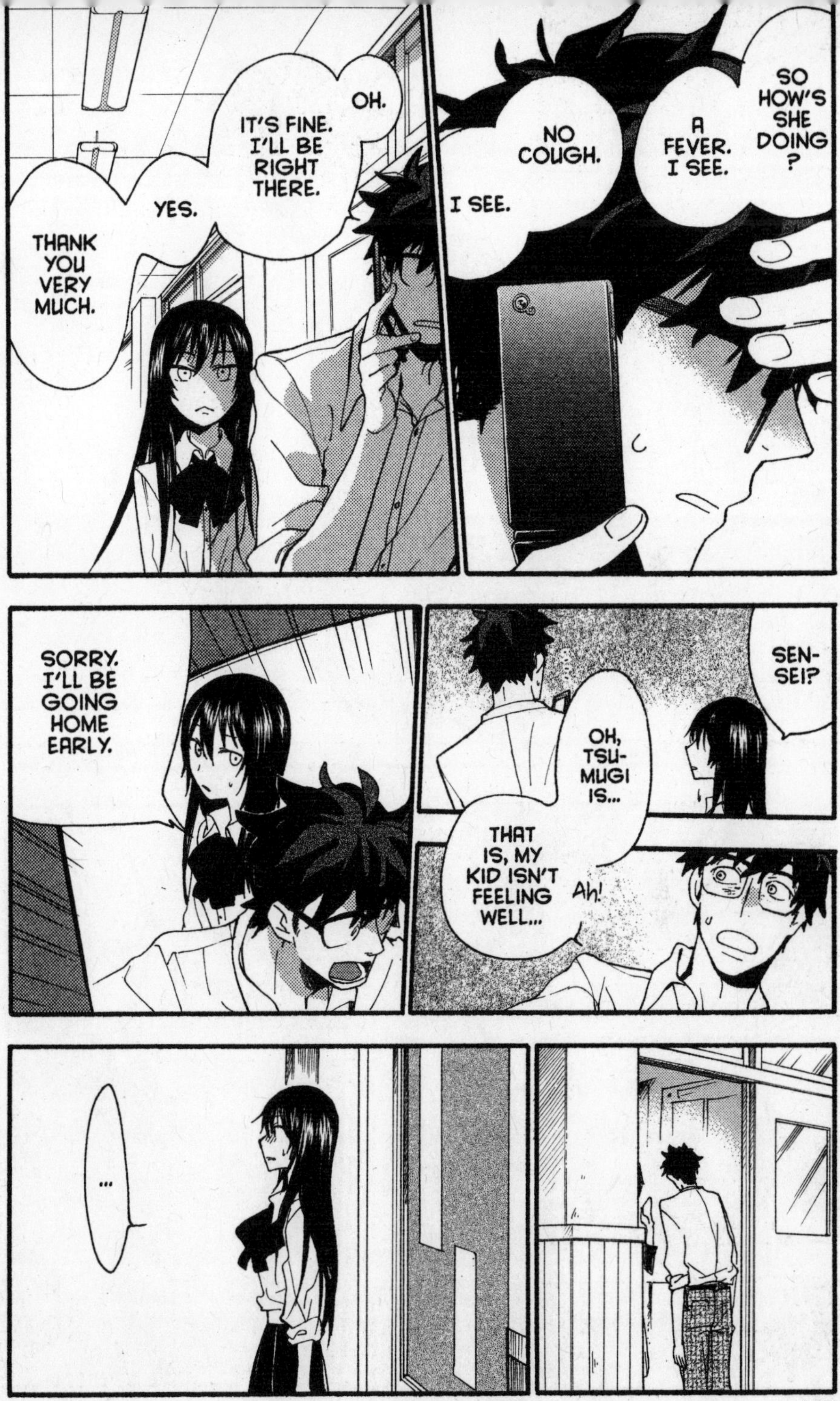
SO HOW'S SHE DOING?
A FEVER. I SEE.
NO COUGH.
I SEE.
OH.
IT'S FINE. I'LL BE RIGHT THERE.
YES.
THANK YOU VERY MUCH.
SEN-SEI?
OH, TSU-MUGI IS...
Ah!
THAT IS, MY KID ISN'T FEELING WELL...
SORRY. I'LL BE GOING HOME EARLY.
...

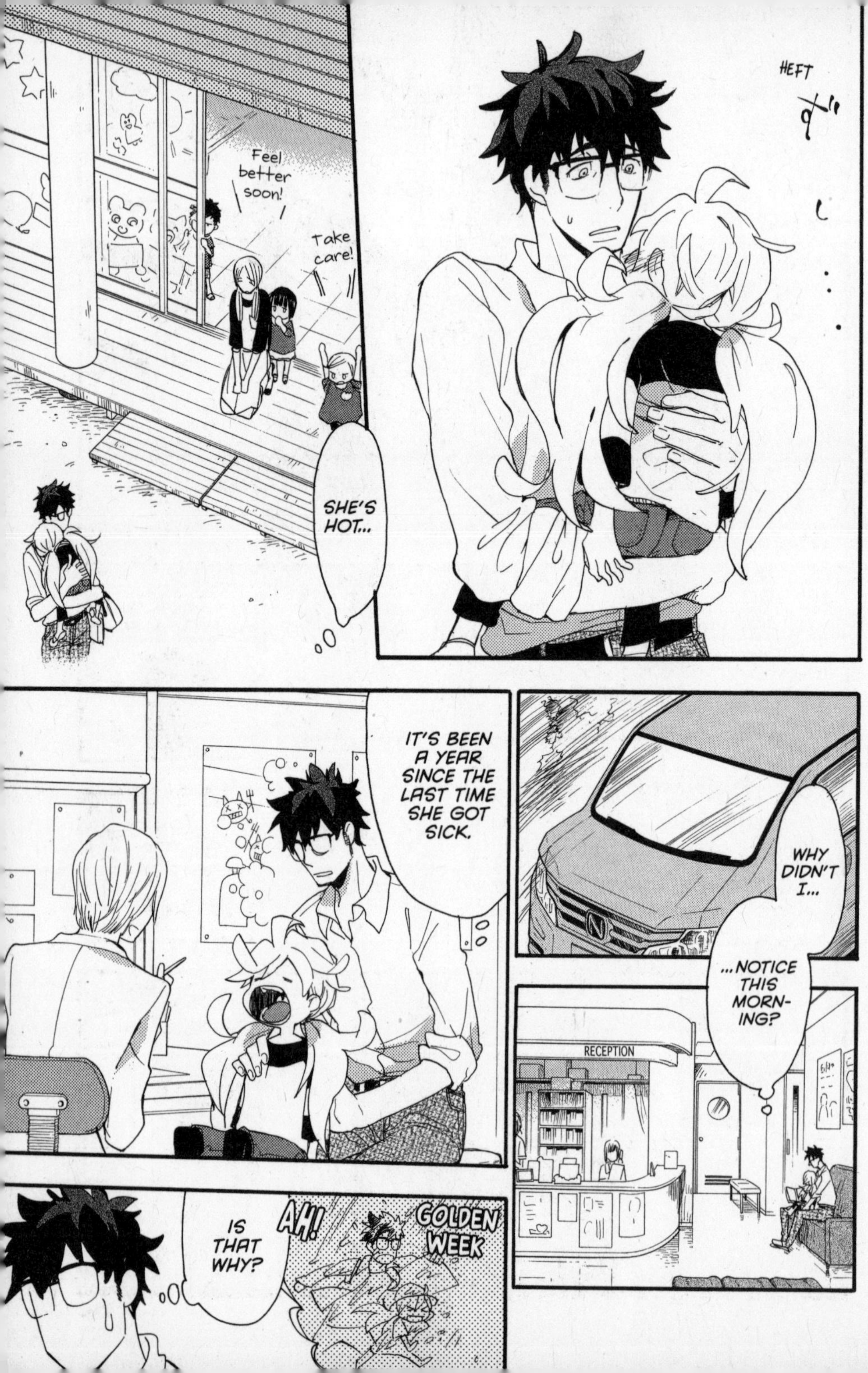
HEFT
Feel better soon!
Take care!
SHE'S HOT...
WHY DIDN'T I...
RECEPTION
...NOTICE THIS MORNING?
IT'S BEEN A YEAR SINCE THE LAST TIME SHE GOT SICK.
GOLDEN WEEK
AH!
IS THAT WHY?

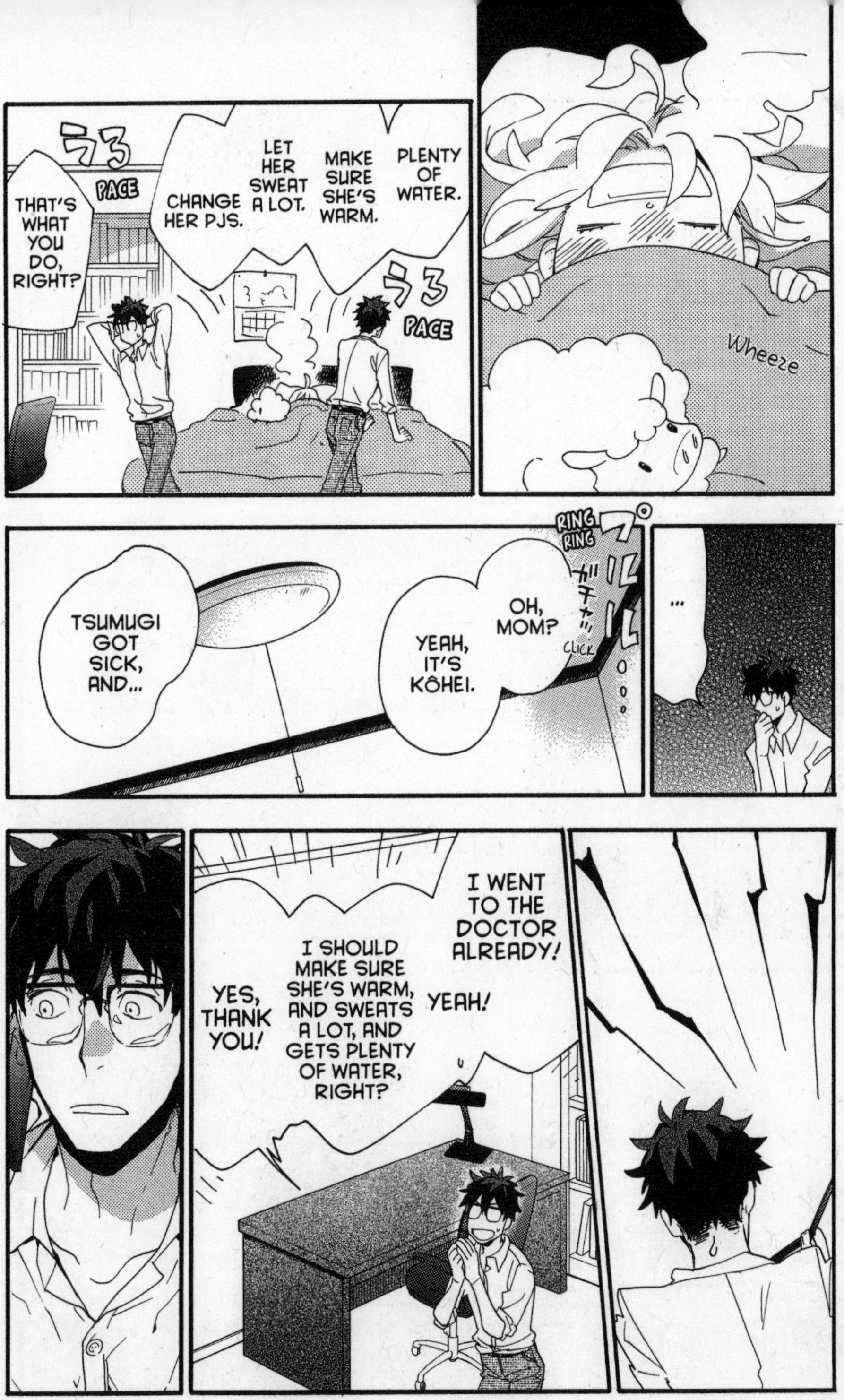
Wheeze
PLENTY OF WATER.
MAKE SURE SHE'S WARM.
LET HER SWEAT A LOT.
CHANGE HER PJS.
PACE
THAT'S WHAT YOU DO, RIGHT?
PACE
...
RING RING
CLICK
OH, MOM?
YEAH, IT'S KÔHEI.
TSUMUGI GOT SICK, AND...
I WENT TO THE DOCTOR ALREADY!
YEAH!
I SHOULD MAKE SURE SHE'S WARM, AND SWEATS A LOT, AND GETS PLENTY OF WATER, RIGHT?
YES, THANK YOU!

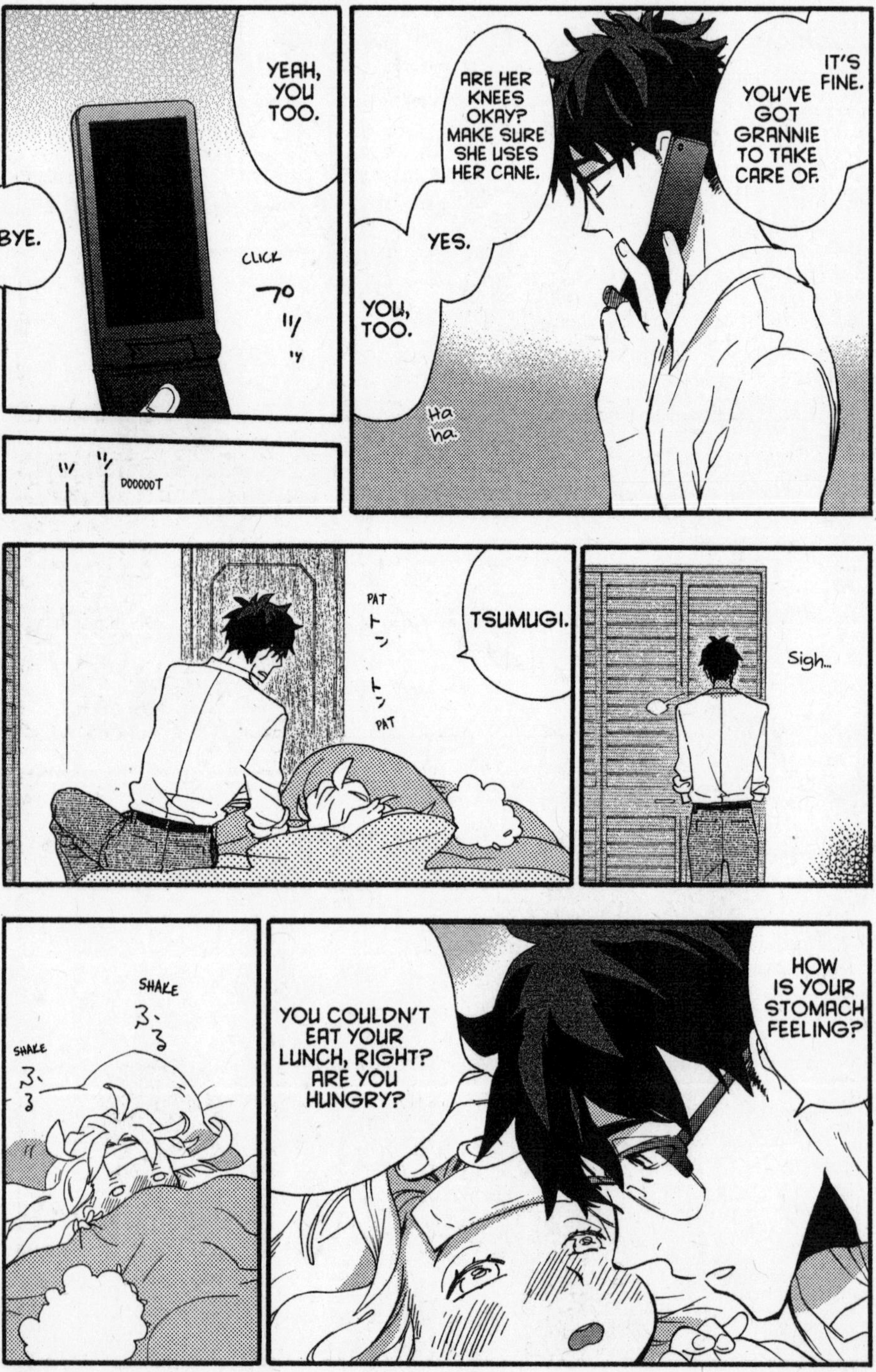
IT'S FINE.
YOU'VE GOT GRANNIE TO TAKE CARE OF.
ARE HER KNEES OKAY? MAKE SURE SHE USES HER CANE.
YES.
YOU, TOO.
Ha ha.
YEAH, YOU TOO.
BYE.
CLICK
DOOOOOT
Sigh...
TSUMUGI.
PAT
PAT
HOW IS YOUR STOMACH FEELING?
YOU COULDN'T EAT YOUR LUNCH, RIGHT? ARE YOU HUNGRY?
SHAKE
SHAKE

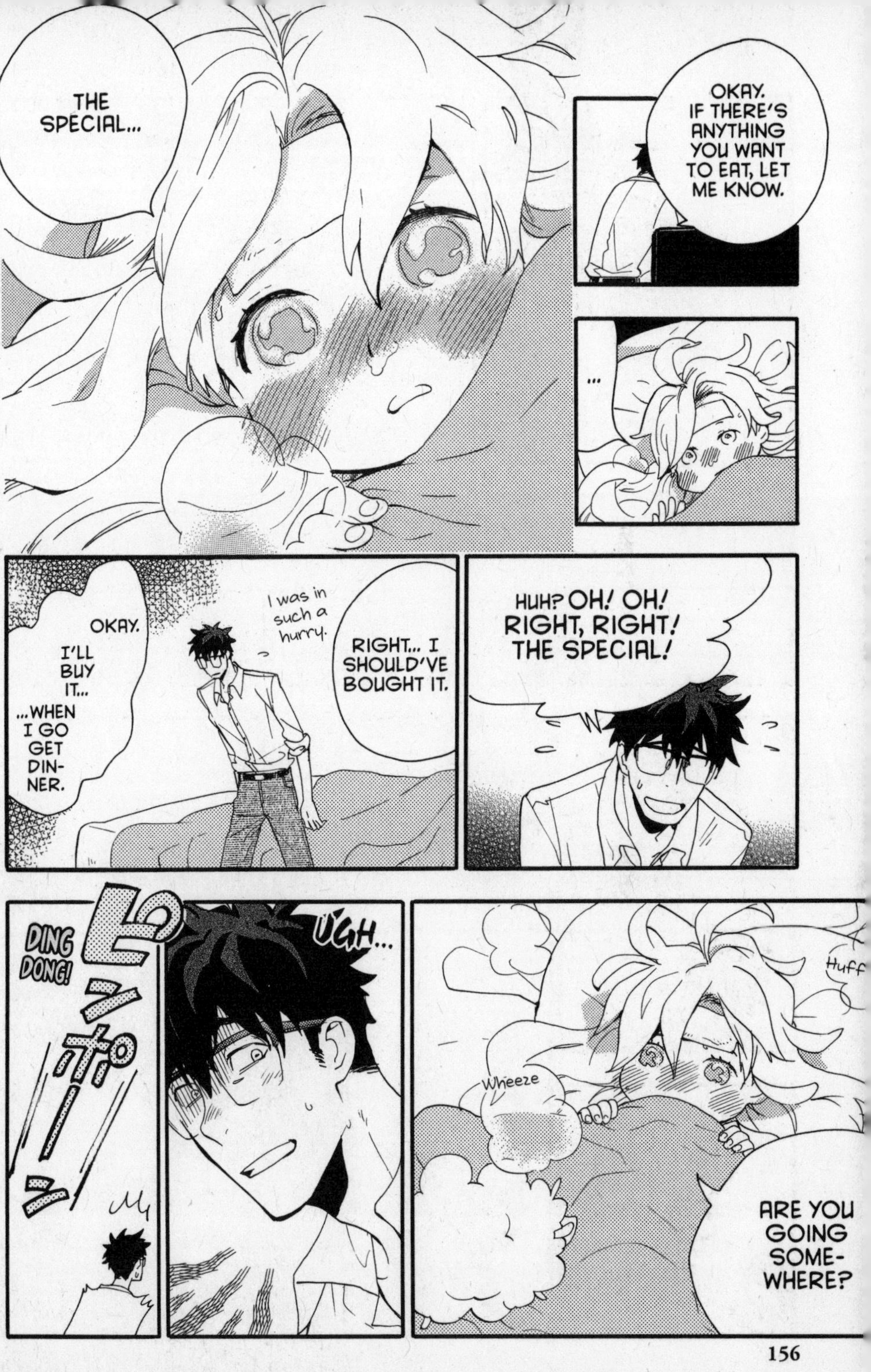
OKAY. IF THERE'S ANYTHING YOU WANT TO EAT, LET ME KNOW.
...
THE SPECIAL...
HUH? OH! OH! RIGHT, RIGHT! THE SPECIAL!
RIGHT... I SHOULD'VE BOUGHT IT.
I was in such a hurry.
OKAY. I'LL BUY IT... ...WHEN I GO GET DINNER.
Huff
Wheeze
ARE YOU GOING SOMEWHERE?
ÜGH...
DING DONG!

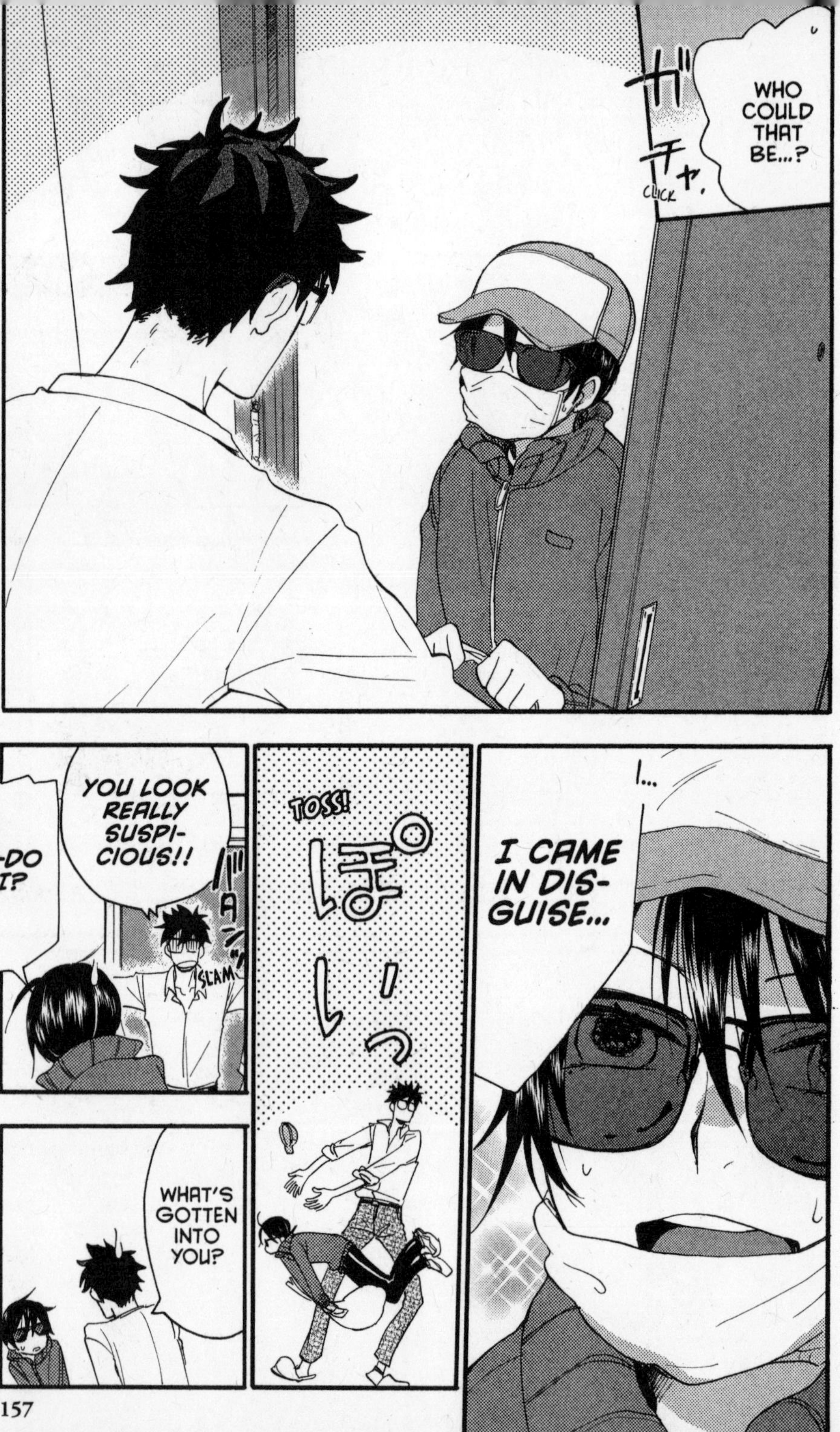
ガチャ
CLICK
WHO COULD THAT BE...?
I...
I CAME IN DISGUISE...
TOSS!
ぽいっ
YOU LOOK REALLY SUSPICIOUS!!
D-DO I?
バーン
SLAM
WHAT'S GOTTEN INTO YOU?

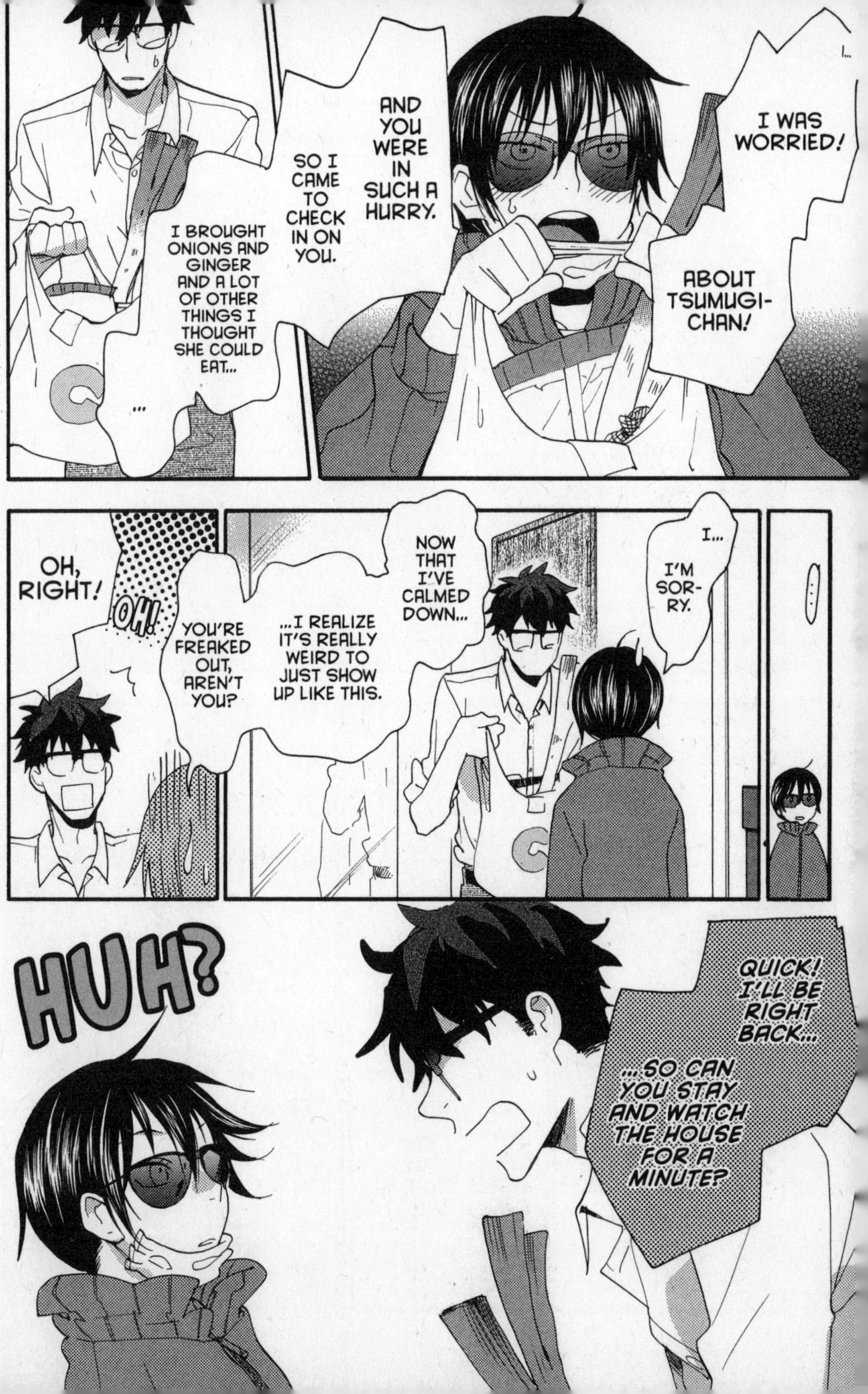
I...
I WAS WORRIED!
ABOUT TSUMUGI-CHAN!
AND YOU WERE IN SUCH A HURRY.
SO I CAME TO CHECK IN ON YOU.
I BROUGHT ONIONS AND GINGER AND A LOT OF OTHER THINGS I THOUGHT SHE COULD EAT...
...
...
I... I'M SORRY.
NOW THAT I'VE CALMED DOWN...
...I REALIZE IT'S REALLY WEIRD TO JUST SHOW UP LIKE THIS.
YOU'RE FREAKED OUT, AREN'T YOU?
OH!
OH, RIGHT!
QUICK! I'LL BE RIGHT BACK...
...SO CAN YOU STAY AND WATCH THE HOUSE FOR A MINUTE?
HUH?

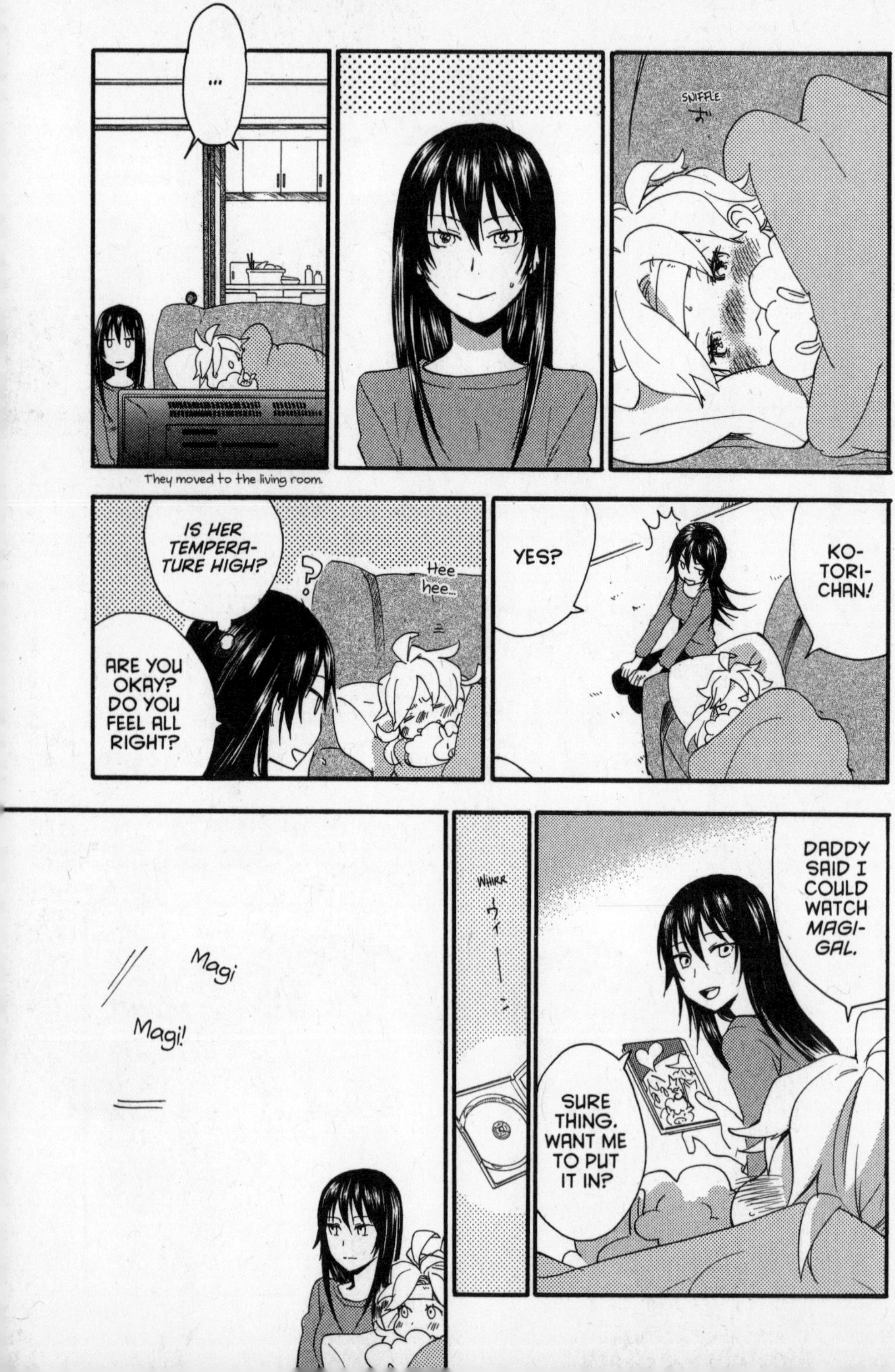

SNIFFLE
...
They moved to the living room.
KO-TORI-CHAN!
YES?
IS HER TEMPERA-TURE HIGH?
ARE YOU OKAY? DO YOU FEEL ALL RIGHT?
Hee hee...
DADDY SAID I COULD WATCH MAGI-GAL.
SURE THING. WANT ME TO PUT IT IN?
WHIRR
Magi Magi!

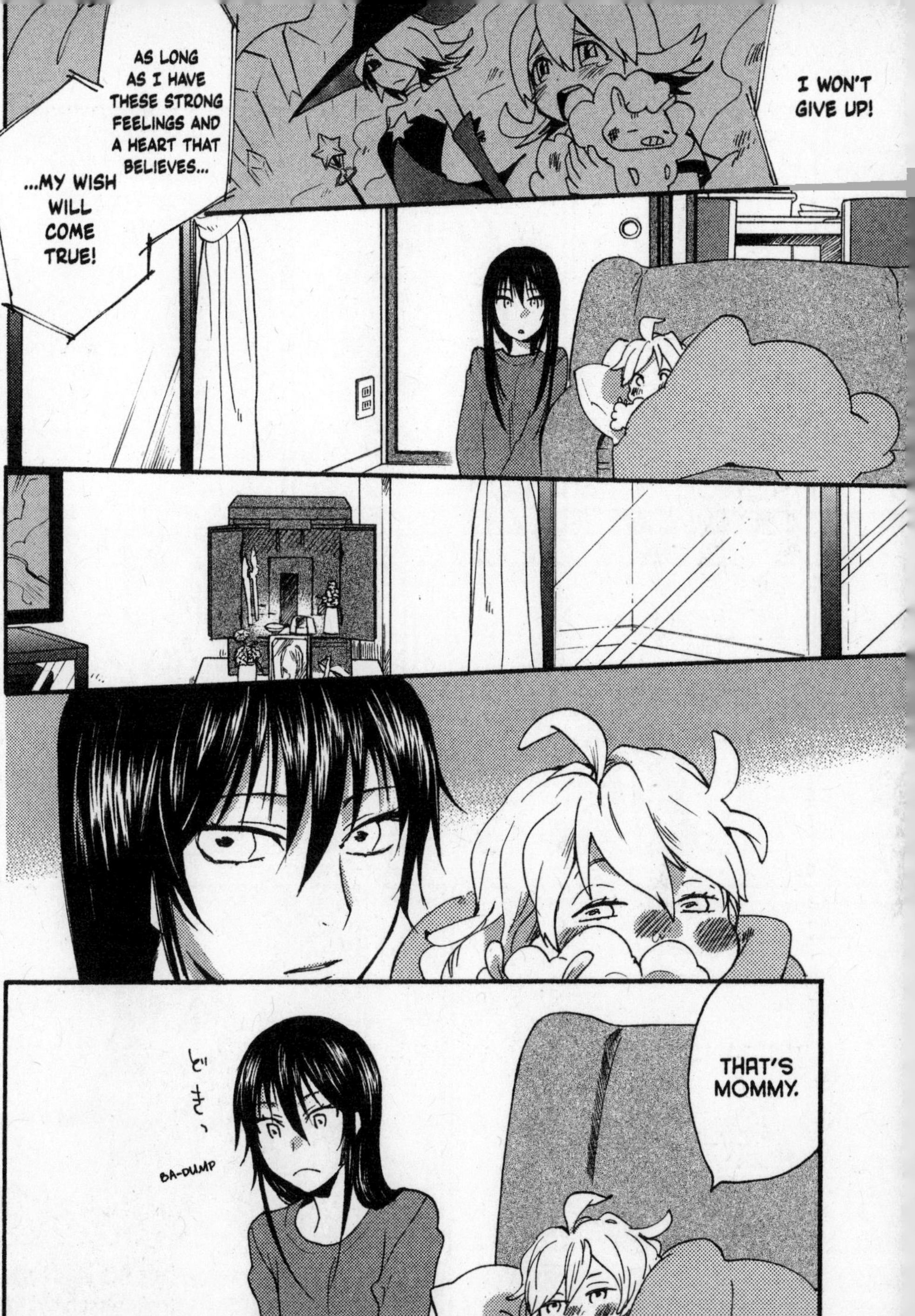
I WON'T GIVE UP!
AS LONG AS I HAVE THESE STRONG FEELINGS AND A HEART THAT BELIEVES...
...MY WISH WILL COME TRUE!
THAT'S MOMMY.
どき、
BA-DUMP

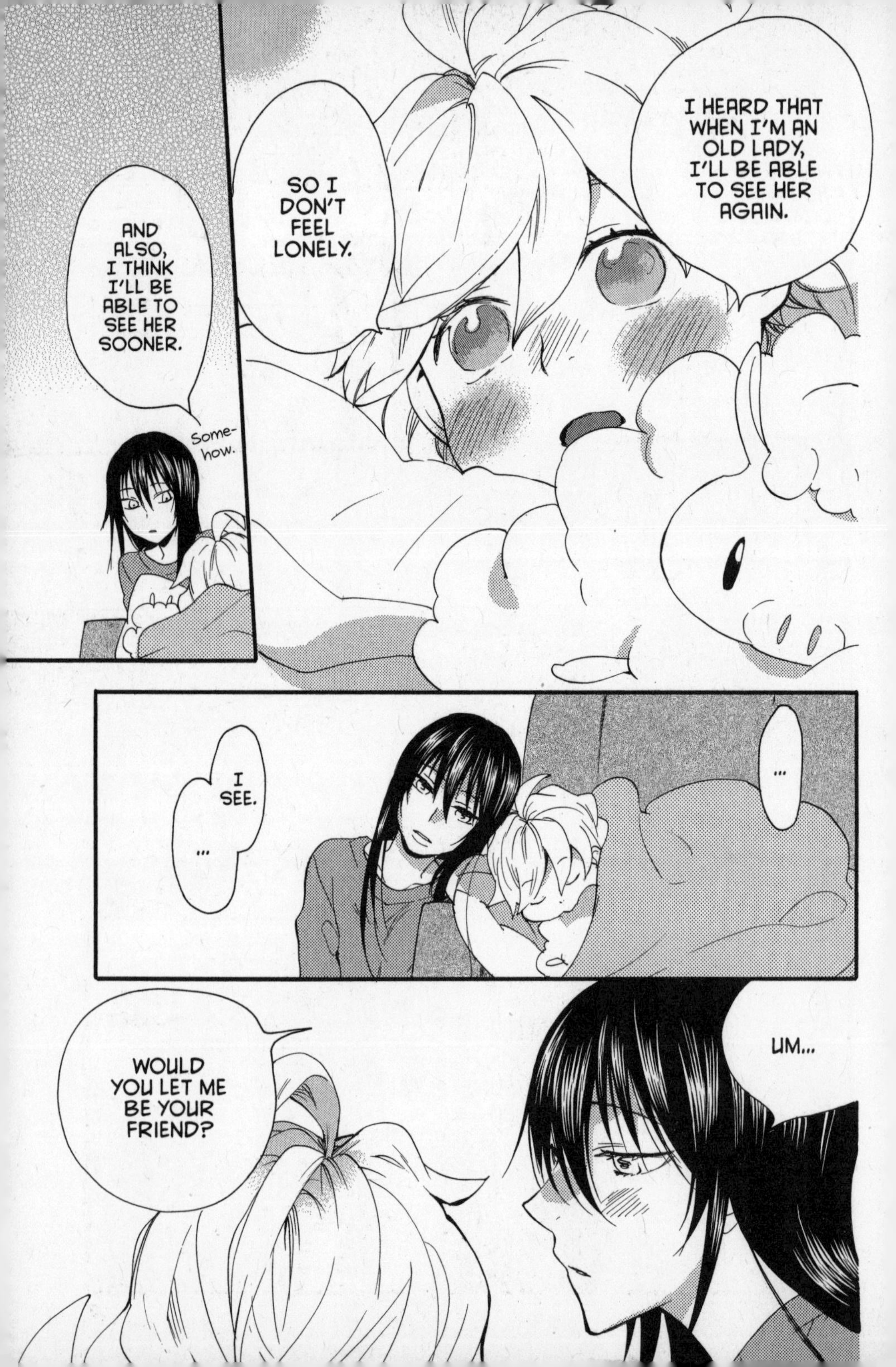
I HEARD THAT WHEN I'M AN OLD LADY, I'LL BE ABLE TO SEE HER AGAIN.
SO I DON'T FEEL LONELY.
AND ALSO, I THINK I'LL BE ABLE TO SEE HER SOONER.
Some-how.
...
I SEE.
...
UM...
WOULD YOU LET ME BE YOUR FRIEND?

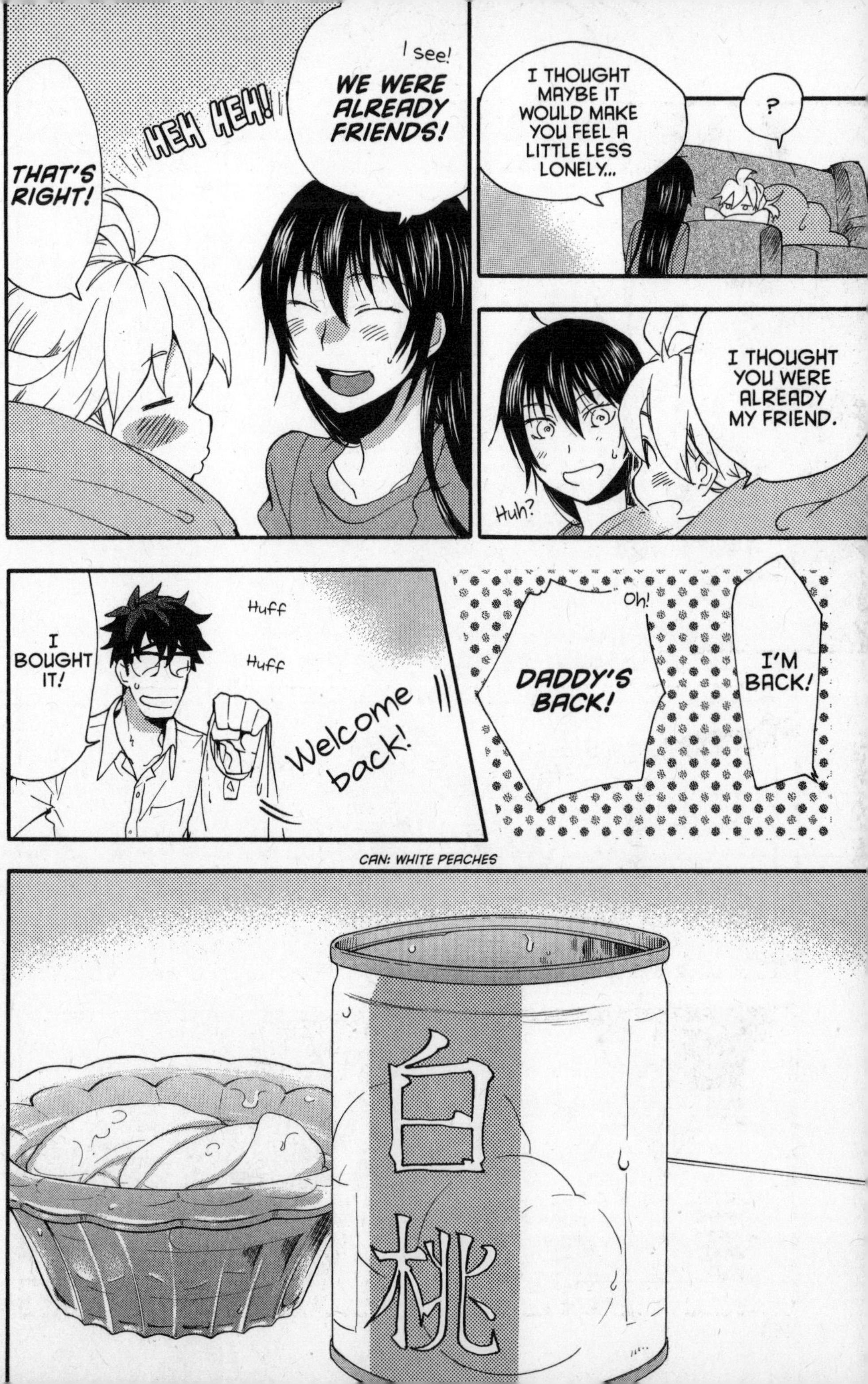
?
I THOUGHT MAYBE IT WOULD MAKE YOU FEEL A LITTLE LESS LONELY...
I THOUGHT YOU WERE ALREADY MY FRIEND.
Huh?
I see! WE WERE ALREADY FRIENDS!
HEH HEH!
THAT'S RIGHT!
I'M BACK!
Oh! DADDY'S BACK!
Welcome back!
Huff
Huff
I BOUGHT IT!
CAN: WHITE PEACHES
白桃

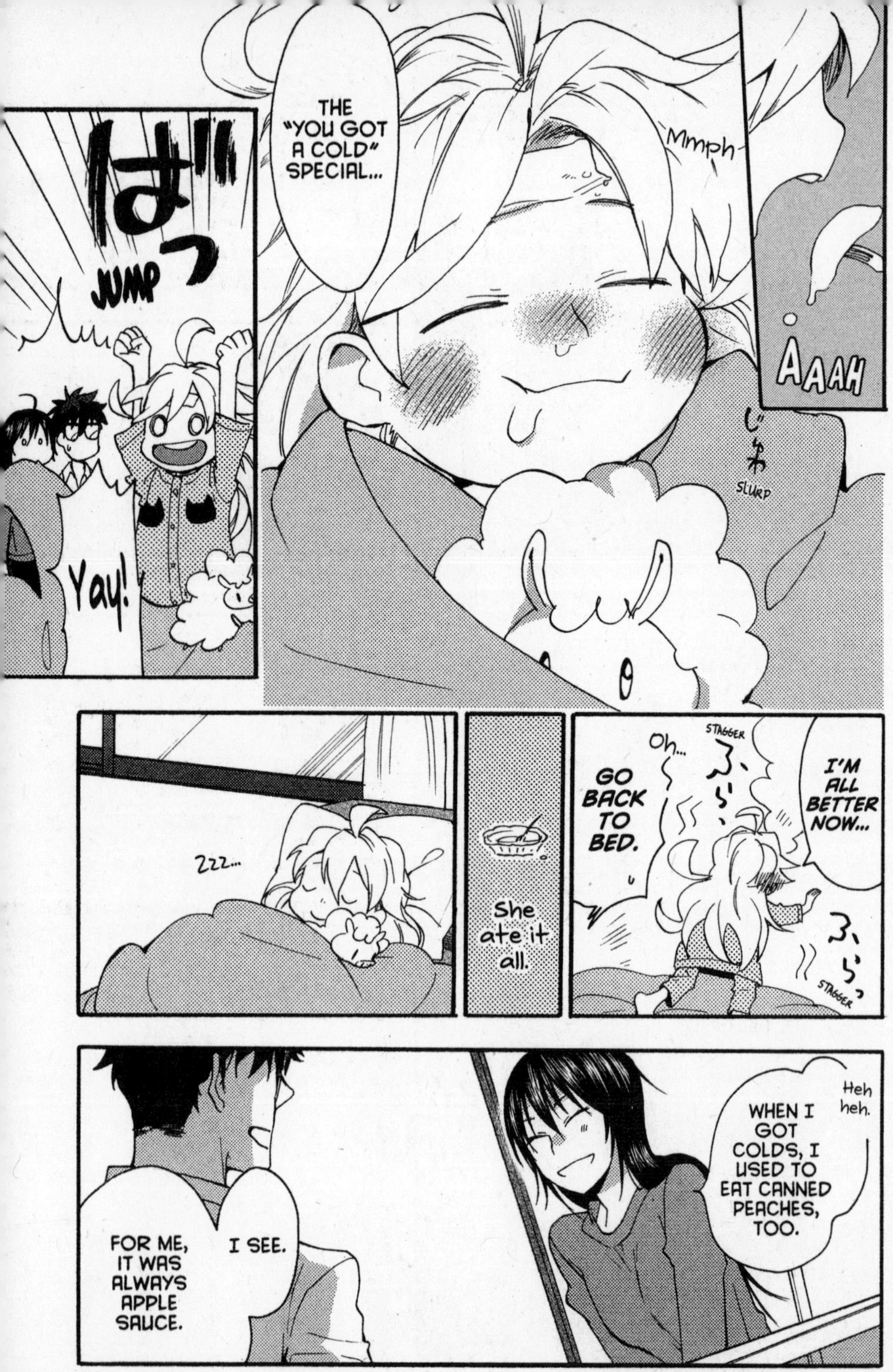

AAAH
THE "YOU GOT A COLD" SPECIAL...
Mmph
じゅわ
SLURP
ばっ
JUMP
Yay!
I'M ALL BETTER NOW...
ふら
STAGGER
Oh...
GO BACK TO BED.
ふらっ
STAGGER
She ate it all.
Zzz...
Heh heh.
WHEN I GOT COLDS, I USED TO EAT CANNED PEACHES, TOO.
I SEE.
FOR ME, IT WAS ALWAYS APPLE SAUCE.

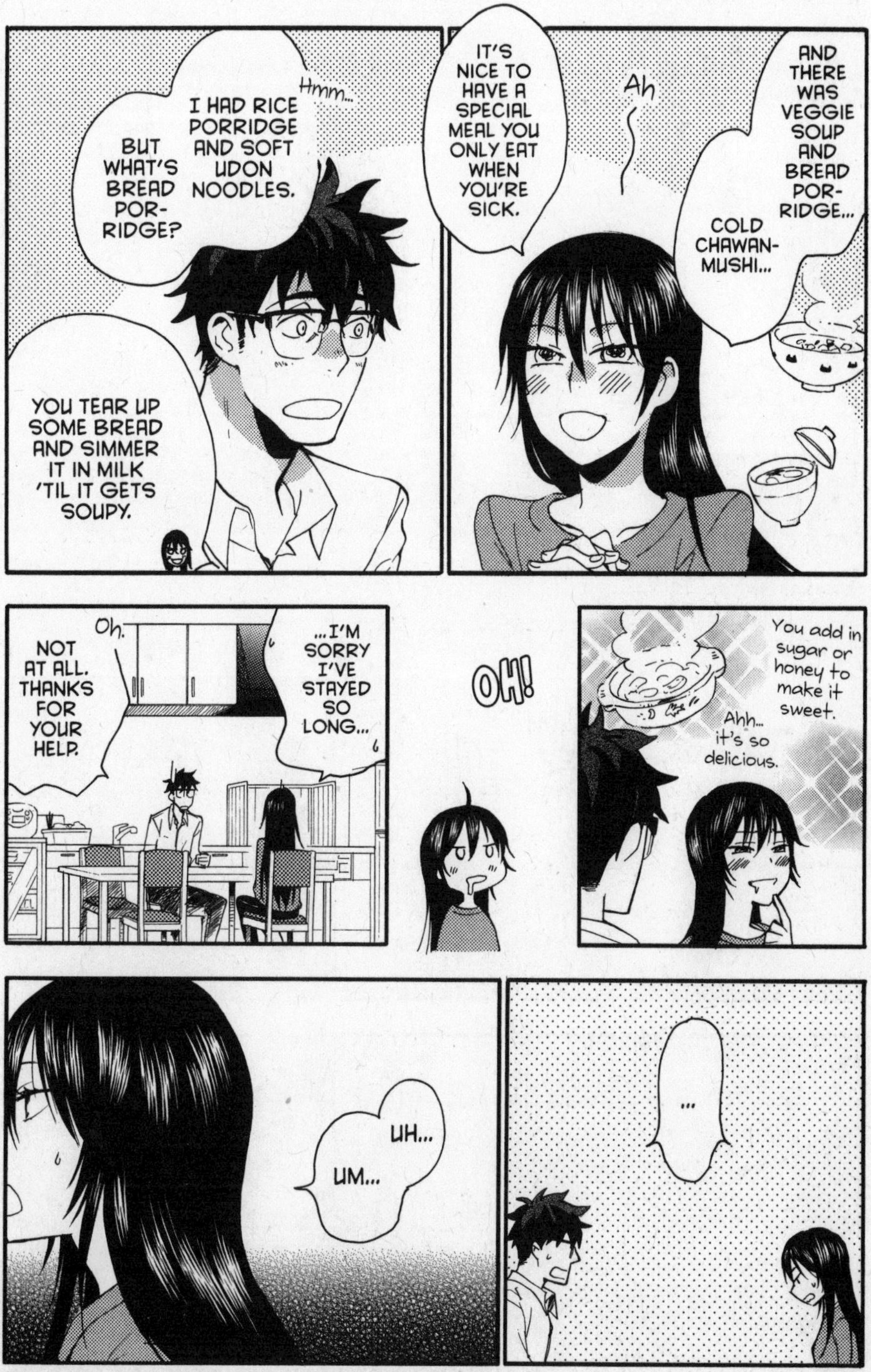
AND THERE WAS VEGGIE SOUP AND BREAD PORRIDGE...
COLD CHAWAN-MUSHI...
Ah
IT'S NICE TO HAVE A SPECIAL MEAL YOU ONLY EAT WHEN YOU'RE SICK.
Hmm...
I HAD RICE PORRIDGE AND SOFT UDON NOODLES.
BUT WHAT'S BREAD POR-RIDGE?
YOU TEAR UP SOME BREAD AND SIMMER IT IN MILK 'TIL IT GETS SOUPY.
You add in sugar or honey to make it sweet.
Ahh... it's so delicious.
OH!
...I'M SORRY I'VE STAYED SO LONG...
Oh.
NOT AT ALL. THANKS FOR YOUR HELP.
...
UH...
UM...

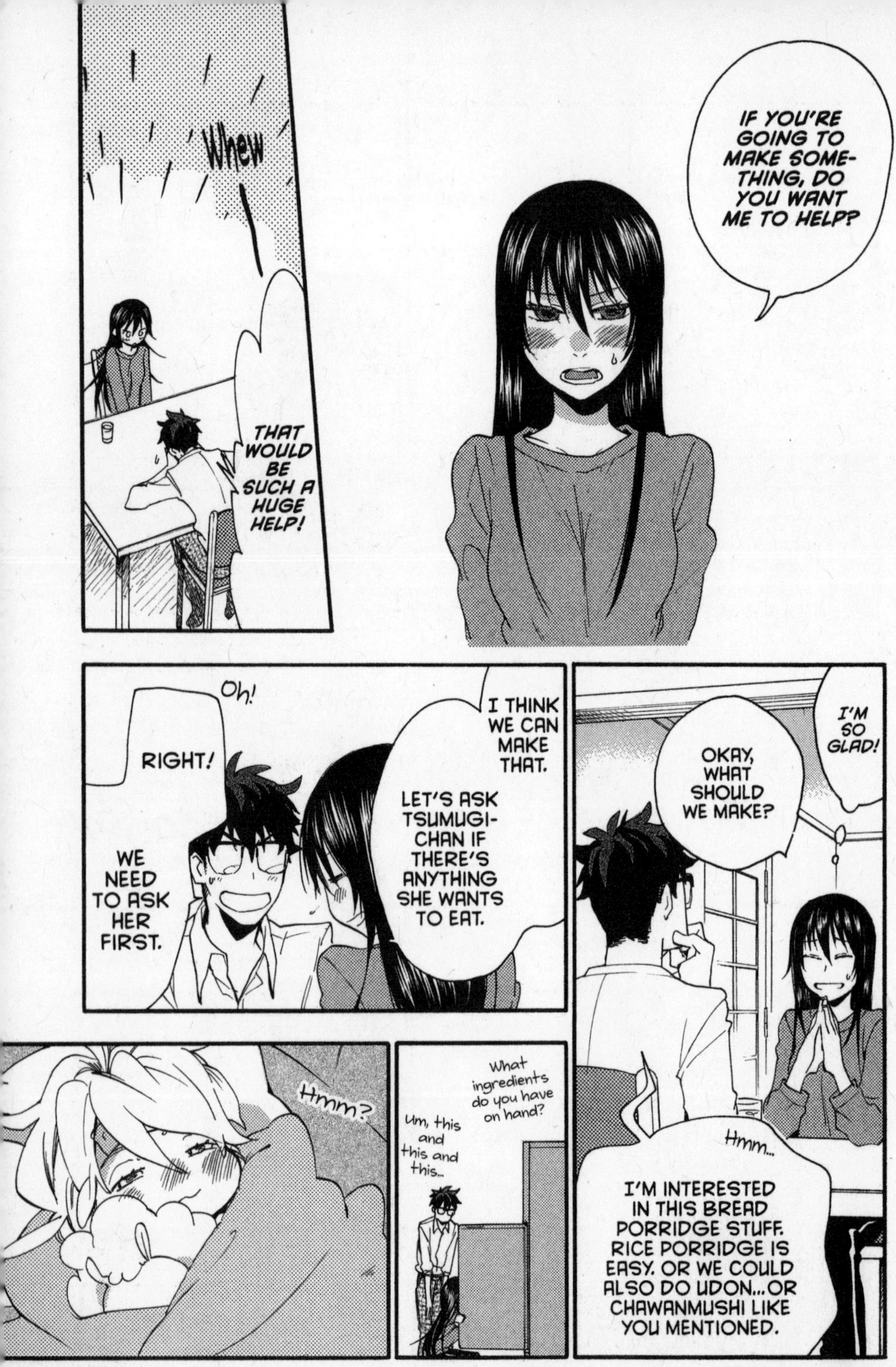
IF YOU'RE GOING TO MAKE SOME-THING, DO YOU WANT ME TO HELP?
Whew
THAT WOULD BE SUCH A HUGE HELP!
I'M SO GLAD!
OKAY, WHAT SHOULD WE MAKE?
Hmm...
I'M INTERESTED IN THIS BREAD PORRIDGE STUFF. RICE PORRIDGE IS EASY. OR WE COULD ALSO DO UDON...OR CHAWANMUSHI LIKE YOU MENTIONED.
I THINK WE CAN MAKE THAT.
LET'S ASK TSUMUGI-CHAN IF THERE'S ANYTHING SHE WANTS TO EAT.
Oh!
RIGHT!
WE NEED TO ASK HER FIRST.
What ingredients do you have on hand?
Um, this and this and this...
Hmm?

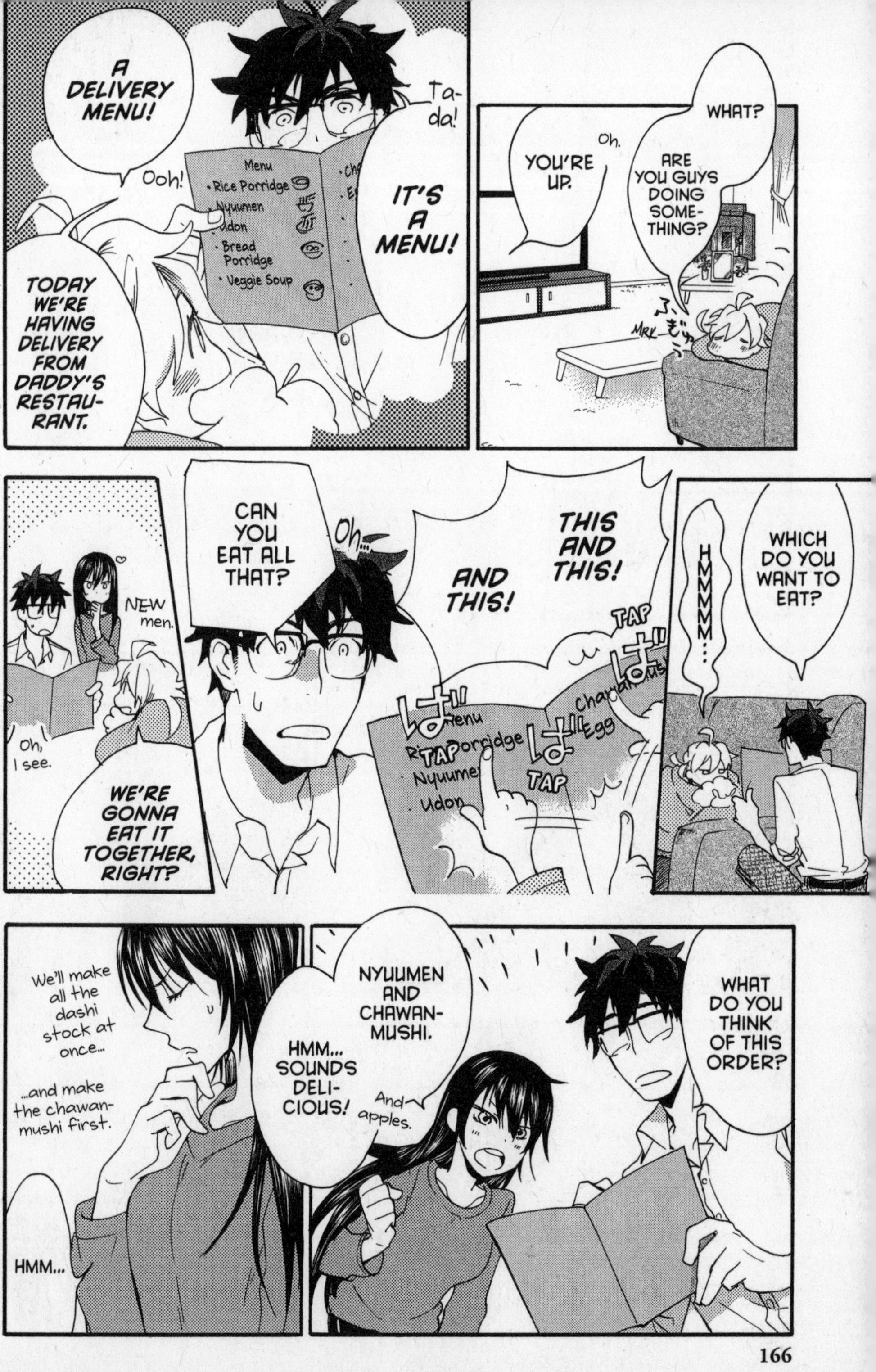
WHAT?
ARE YOU GUYS DOING SOMETHING?
Oh.
YOU'RE UP.
MRK
A DELIVERY MENU!
Ta-da!
IT'S A MENU!
Menu
• Rice Porridge
• Nyuumen
• Udon
• Bread Porridge
• Veggie Soup
Ooh!
TODAY WE'RE HAVING DELIVERY FROM DADDY'S RESTAURANT.
WHICH DO YOU WANT TO EAT?
HMMMMM...
THIS AND THIS!
AND THIS!
TAP
TAP
TAP
CAN YOU EAT ALL THAT?
Oh...
NEW men.
Oh, I see.
WE'RE GONNA EAT IT TOGETHER, RIGHT?
WHAT DO YOU THINK OF THIS ORDER?
NYUUMEN AND CHAWAN-MUSHI.
HMM... SOUNDS DELICIOUS!
And apples.
We'll make all the dashi stock at once...
...and make the chawan-mushi first.
HMM...

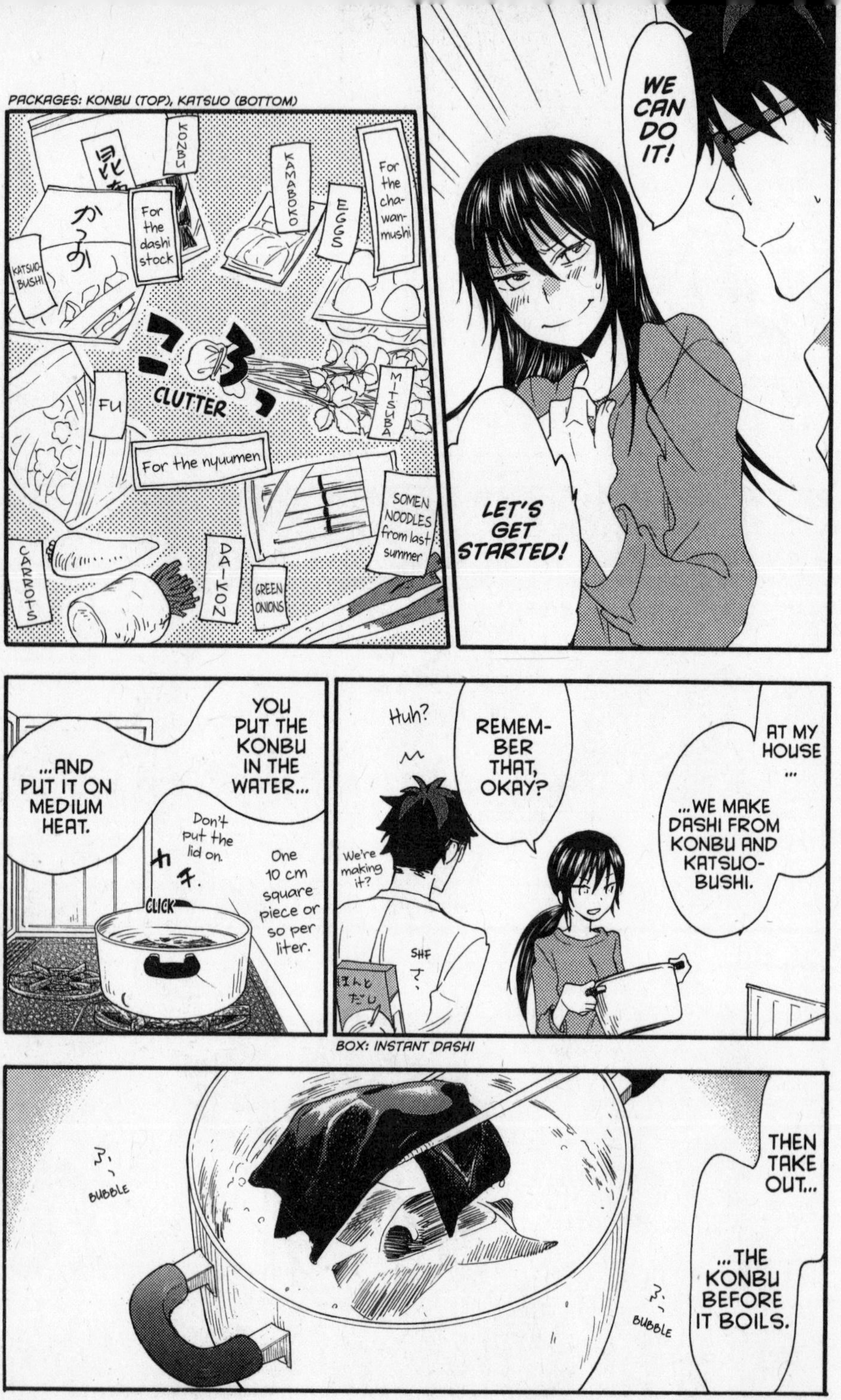
WE CAN DO IT!
LET'S GET STARTED!
PACKAGES: KONBU (TOP), KATSUO (BOTTOM)
KONBU
For the dashi stock
KATSUO-BUSHI
KAMABOKO
EGGS
For the cha-wan-mushi
CLUTTER
MITSUBA
FU
For the nyuumen
SOMEN NOODLES from last summer
CARROTS
DAIKON
GREEN ONIONS
AT MY HOUSE...
...WE MAKE DASHI FROM KONBU AND KATSUO-BUSHI.
REMEMBER THAT, OKAY?
Huh?
We're making it?
SHF
BOX: INSTANT DASHI
YOU PUT THE KONBU IN THE WATER...
One 10 cm square piece or so per liter.
Don't put the lid on.
...AND PUT IT ON MEDIUM HEAT.
CLICK
THEN TAKE OUT...
...THE KONBU BEFORE IT BOILS.
BUBBLE
BUBBLE

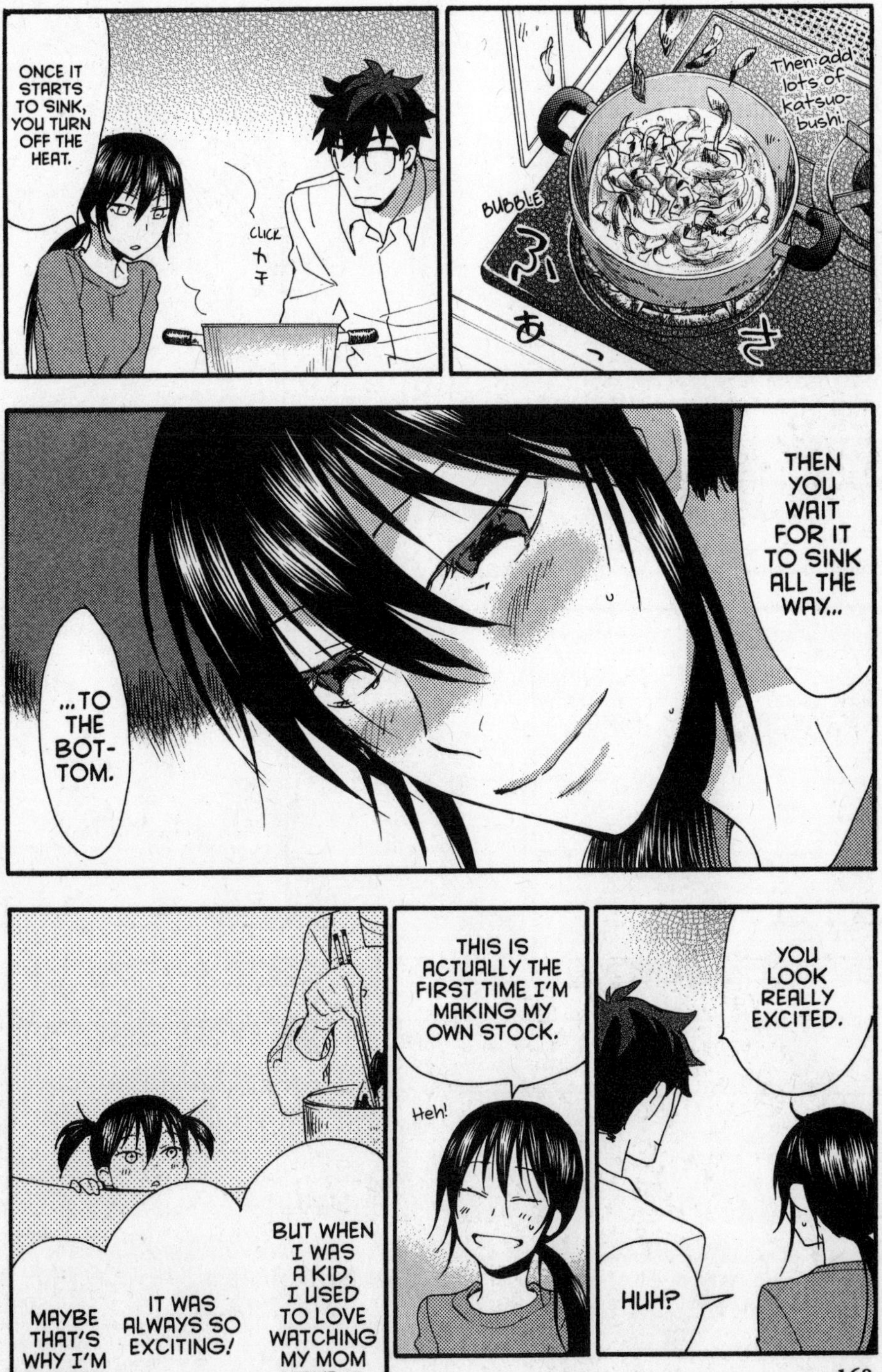
Then add lots of katsuo-bushi.
BUBBLE
ONCE IT STARTS TO SINK, YOU TURN OFF THE HEAT.
CLICK
カチ
THEN YOU WAIT FOR IT TO SINK ALL THE WAY...
...TO THE BOT-TOM.
YOU LOOK REALLY EXCITED.
HUH?
THIS IS ACTUALLY THE FIRST TIME I'M MAKING MY OWN STOCK.
Heh!
BUT WHEN I WAS A KID, I USED TO LOVE WATCHING MY MOM MAKE IT.
IT WAS ALWAYS SO EXCITING!
MAYBE THAT'S WHY I'M EXCITED NOW.

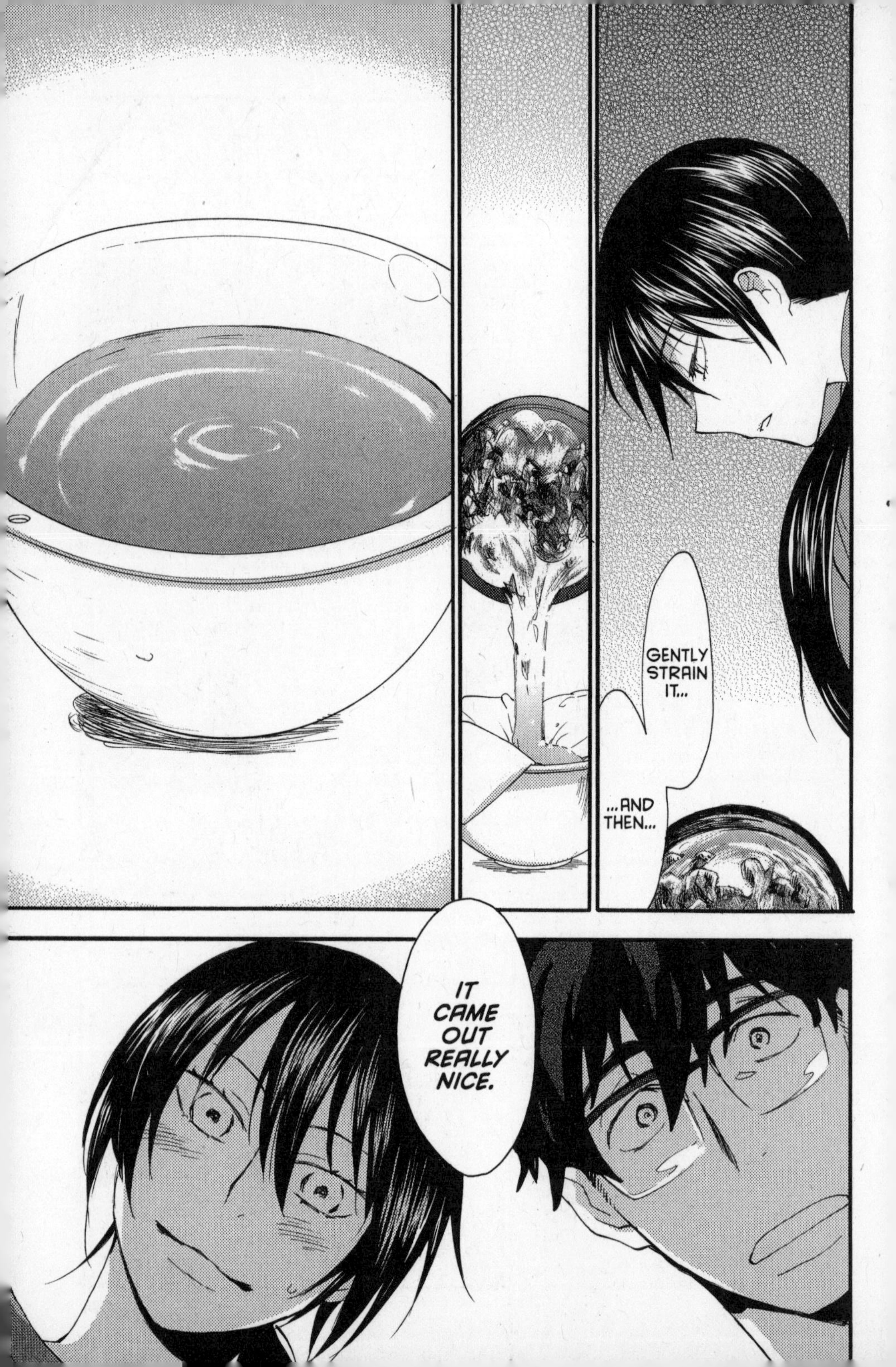
GENTLY STRAIN IT...
...AND THEN...
IT CAME OUT REALLY NICE.

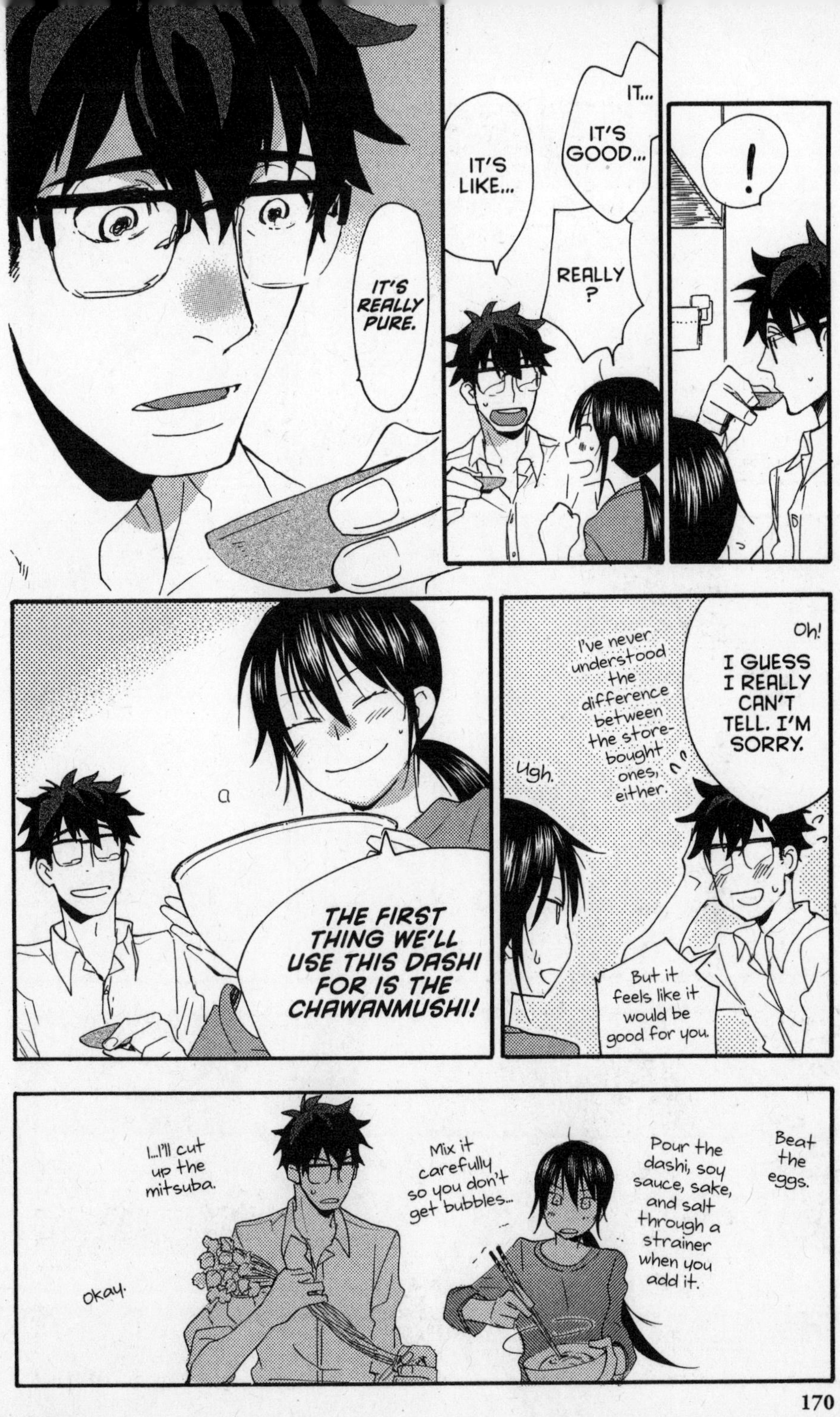

!
IT...
IT'S GOOD...
IT'S LIKE...
REALLY?
IT'S REALLY PURE.
Oh!
I GUESS I REALLY CAN'T TELL. I'M SORRY.
I've never understood the difference between the store-bought ones, either.
Ugh.
But it feels like it would be good for you.
THE FIRST THING WE'LL USE THIS DASHI FOR IS THE CHAWANMUSHI!
Beat the eggs.
Pour the dashi, soy sauce, sake, and salt through a strainer when you add it.
Mix it carefully so you don't get bubbles...
I...I'll cut up the mitsuba.
Okay.

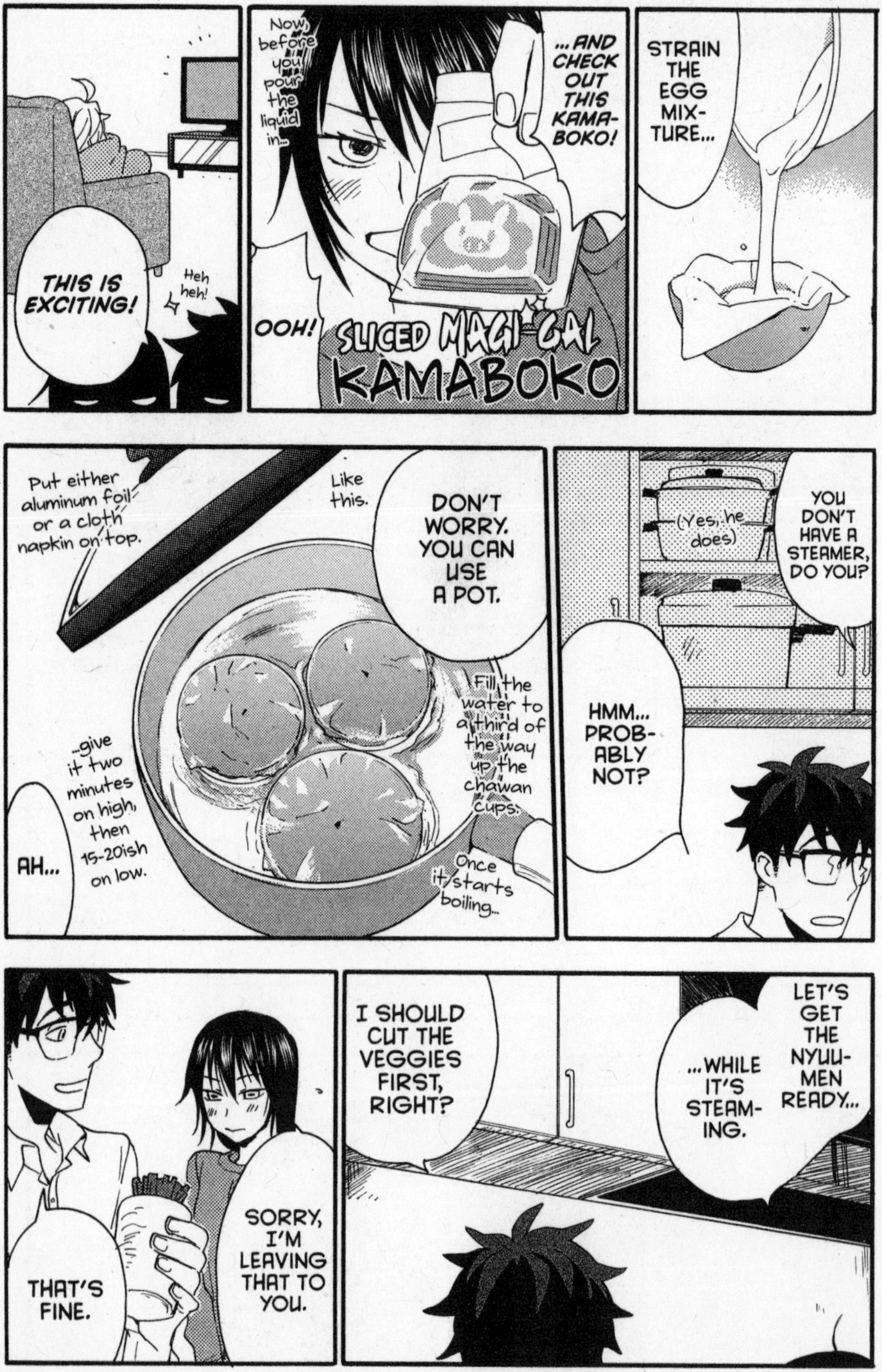
STRAIN THE EGG MIXTURE...
...AND CHECK OUT THIS KAMABOKO!
Now, before you pour the liquid in...
SLICED MAGI-GAL KAMABOKO
OOH!
THIS IS EXCITING!
Heh heh!
YOU DON'T HAVE A STEAMER, DO YOU?
(Yes, he does)
HMM... PROBABLY NOT?
DON'T WORRY. YOU CAN USE A POT.
Like this.
Put either aluminum foil or a cloth napkin on top.
Fill the water to a third of the way up the chawan cups.
Once it starts boiling...
...give it two minutes on high, then 15-20ish on low.
AH...
LET'S GET THE NYUUMEN READY...
...WHILE IT'S STEAMING.
I SHOULD CUT THE VEGGIES FIRST, RIGHT?
SORRY, I'M LEAVING THAT TO YOU.
THAT'S FINE.

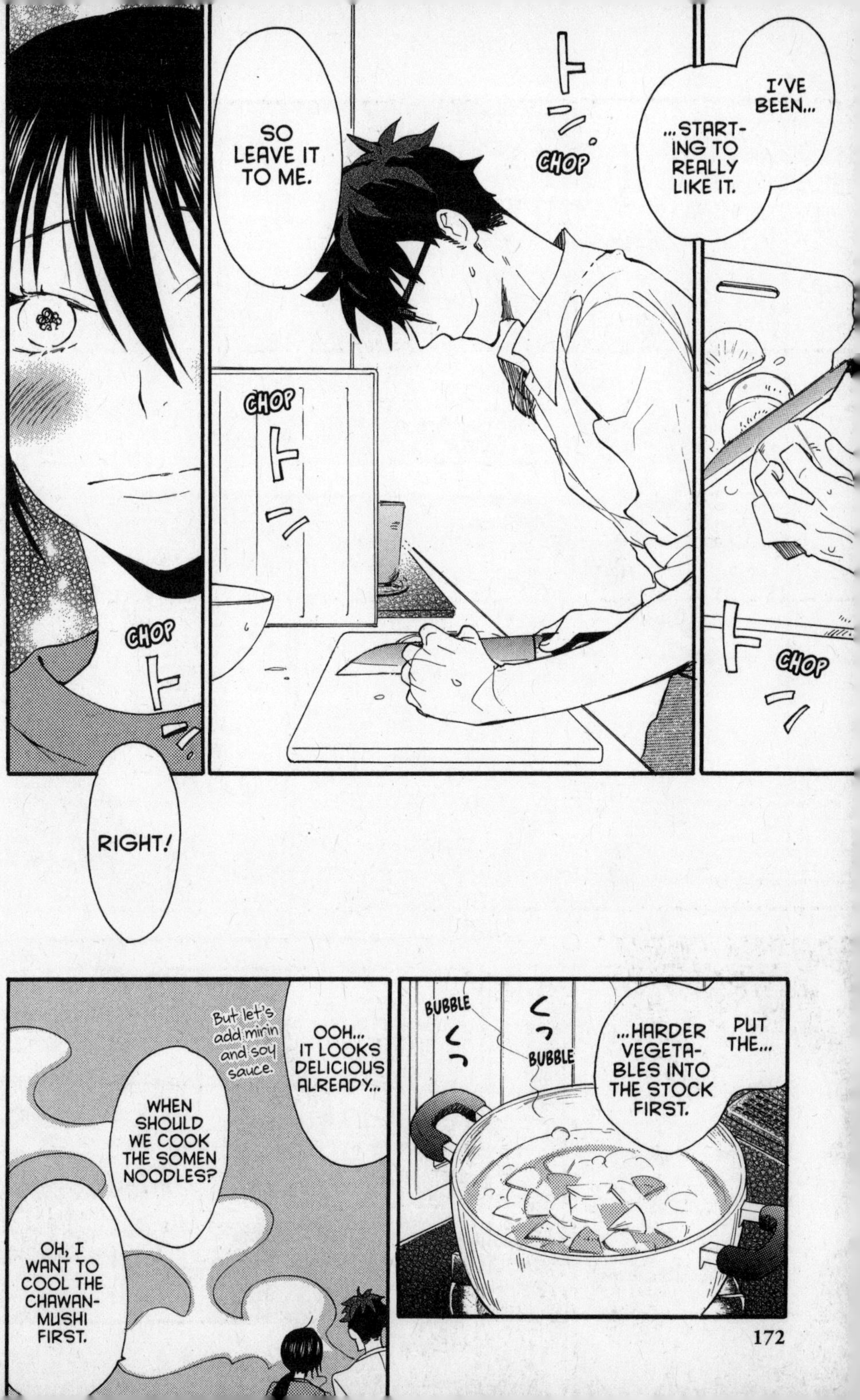
I'VE BEEN...
...START-ING TO REALLY LIKE IT.
CHOP
CHOP
SO LEAVE IT TO ME.
CHOP
CHOP
RIGHT!
PUT THE...
...HARDER VEGETA-BLES INTO THE STOCK FIRST.
BUBBLE
BUBBLE
OOH... IT LOOKS DELICIOUS ALREADY...
But let's add mirin and soy sauce.
WHEN SHOULD WE COOK THE SOMEN NOODLES?
OH, I WANT TO COOL THE CHAWAN-MUSHI FIRST.

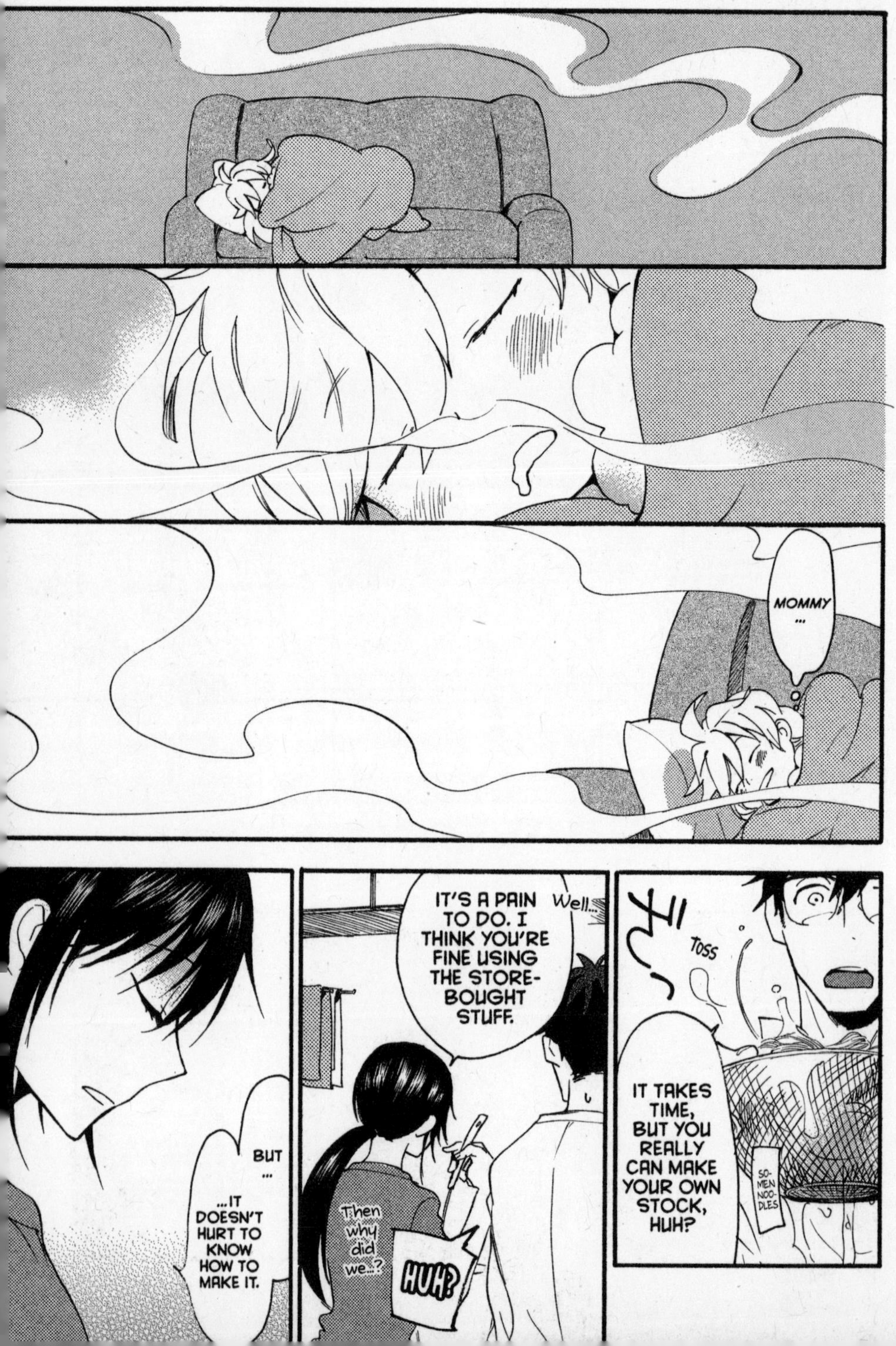
MOMMY ...
TOSS
IT TAKES TIME, BUT YOU REALLY CAN MAKE YOUR OWN STOCK, HUH?
SOMEN NOODLES
Well...
IT'S A PAIN TO DO. I THINK YOU'RE FINE USING THE STORE-BOUGHT STUFF.
Then why did we...?
HUH?
BUT ...
...IT DOESN'T HURT TO KNOW HOW TO MAKE IT.

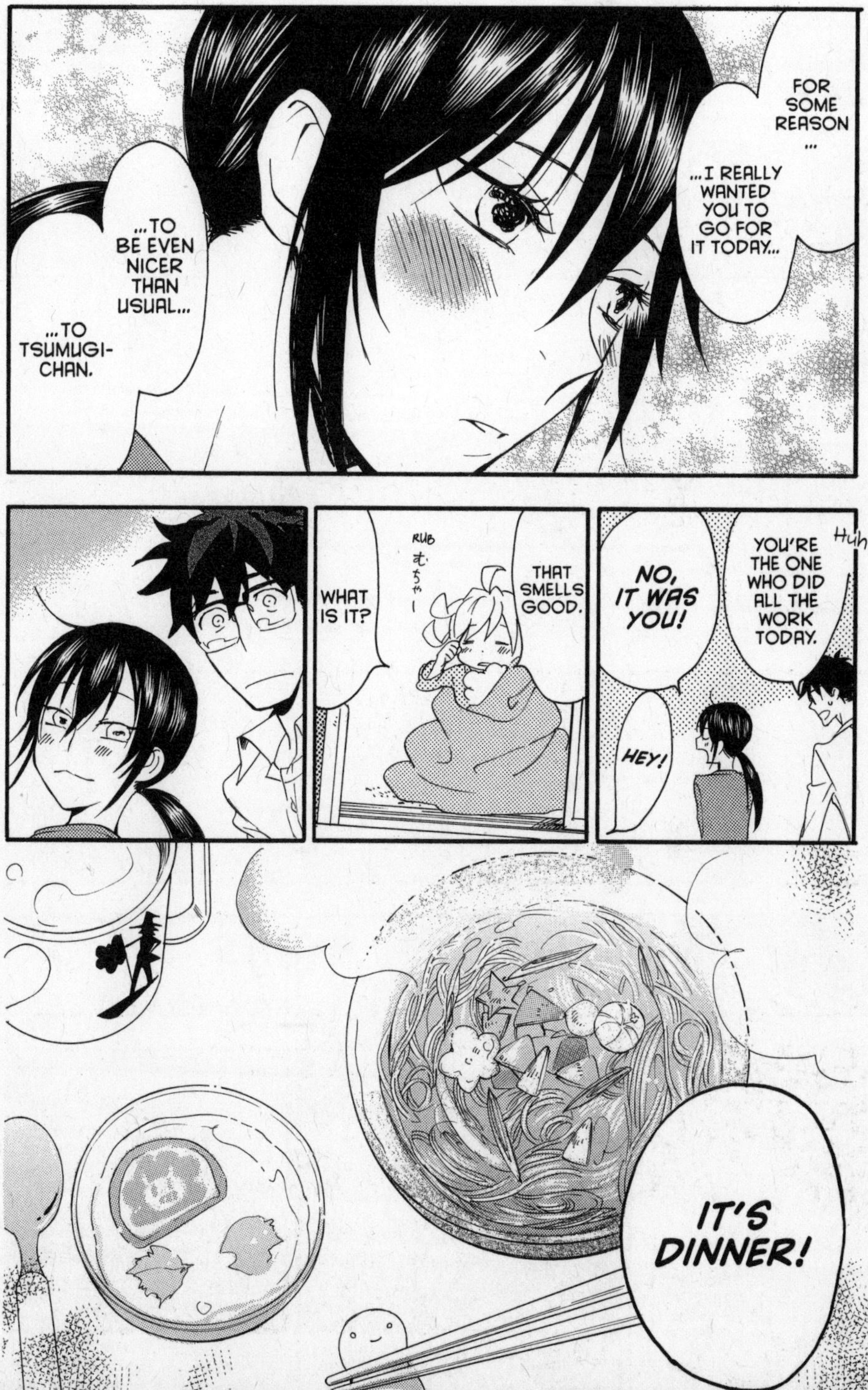
FOR SOME REASON ...
...I REALLY WANTED YOU TO GO FOR IT TODAY...
...TO BE EVEN NICER THAN USUAL...
...TO TSUMUGI-CHAN.
Huh?
YOU'RE THE ONE WHO DID ALL THE WORK TODAY.
NO, IT WAS YOU!
HEY!
THAT SMELLS GOOD.
RUB
むちゃ
WHAT IS IT?
IT'S DINNER!

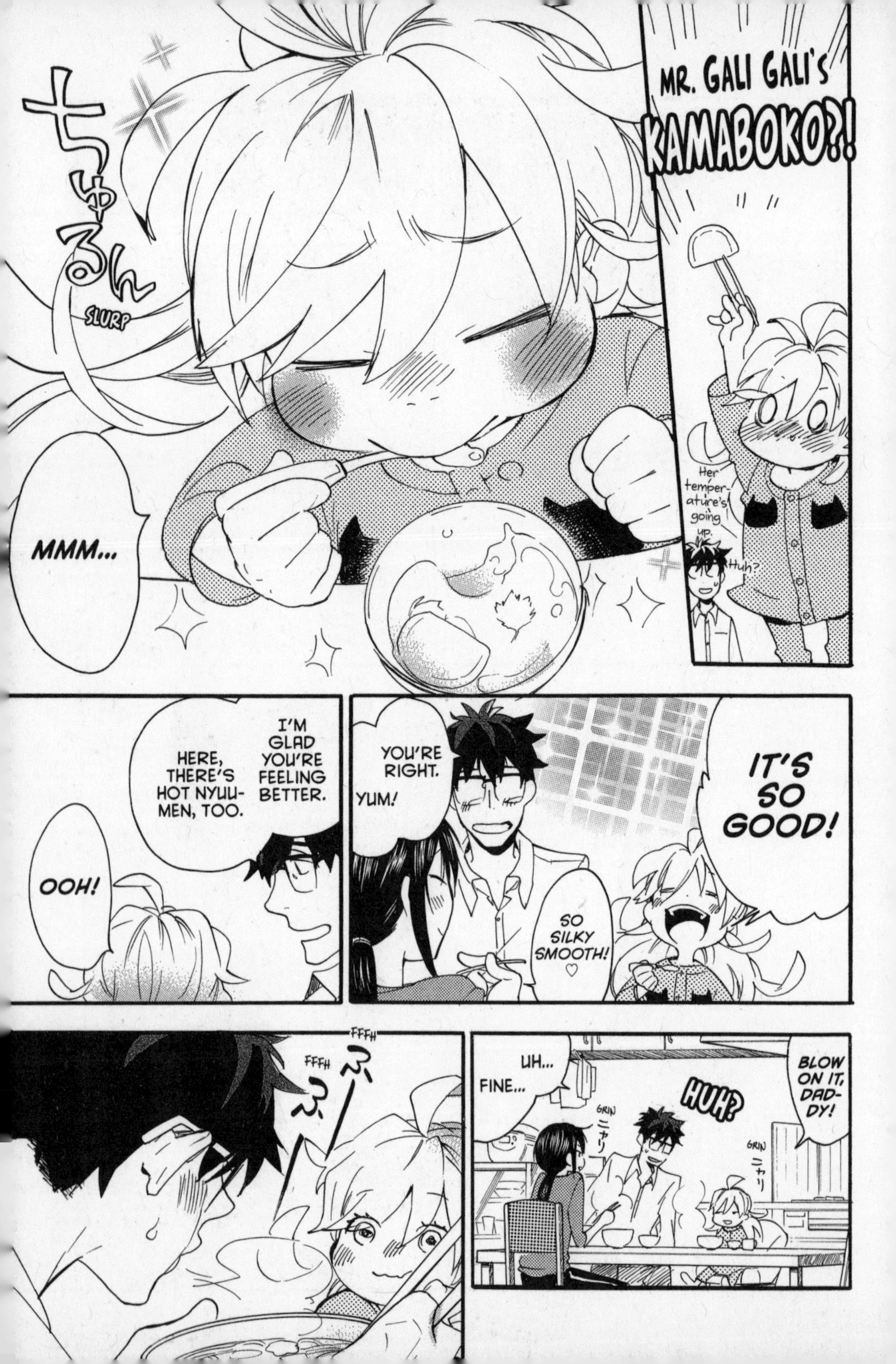
MR. GALI GALI's
KAMABOKO?!
Her temper-ature's going up.
Huh?
ちゅるん
SLURP
MMM...
IT'S SO GOOD!
SO SILKY SMOOTH! ♡
YOU'RE RIGHT.
YUM!
I'M GLAD YOU'RE FEELING BETTER.
HERE, THERE'S HOT NYUU-MEN, TOO.
OOH!
BLOW ON IT, DAD-DY!
HUH?
UH...
FINE...
GRIN
ニヤリ
GRIN
ニヤリ
ふ
FFFH
ふ
FFFH

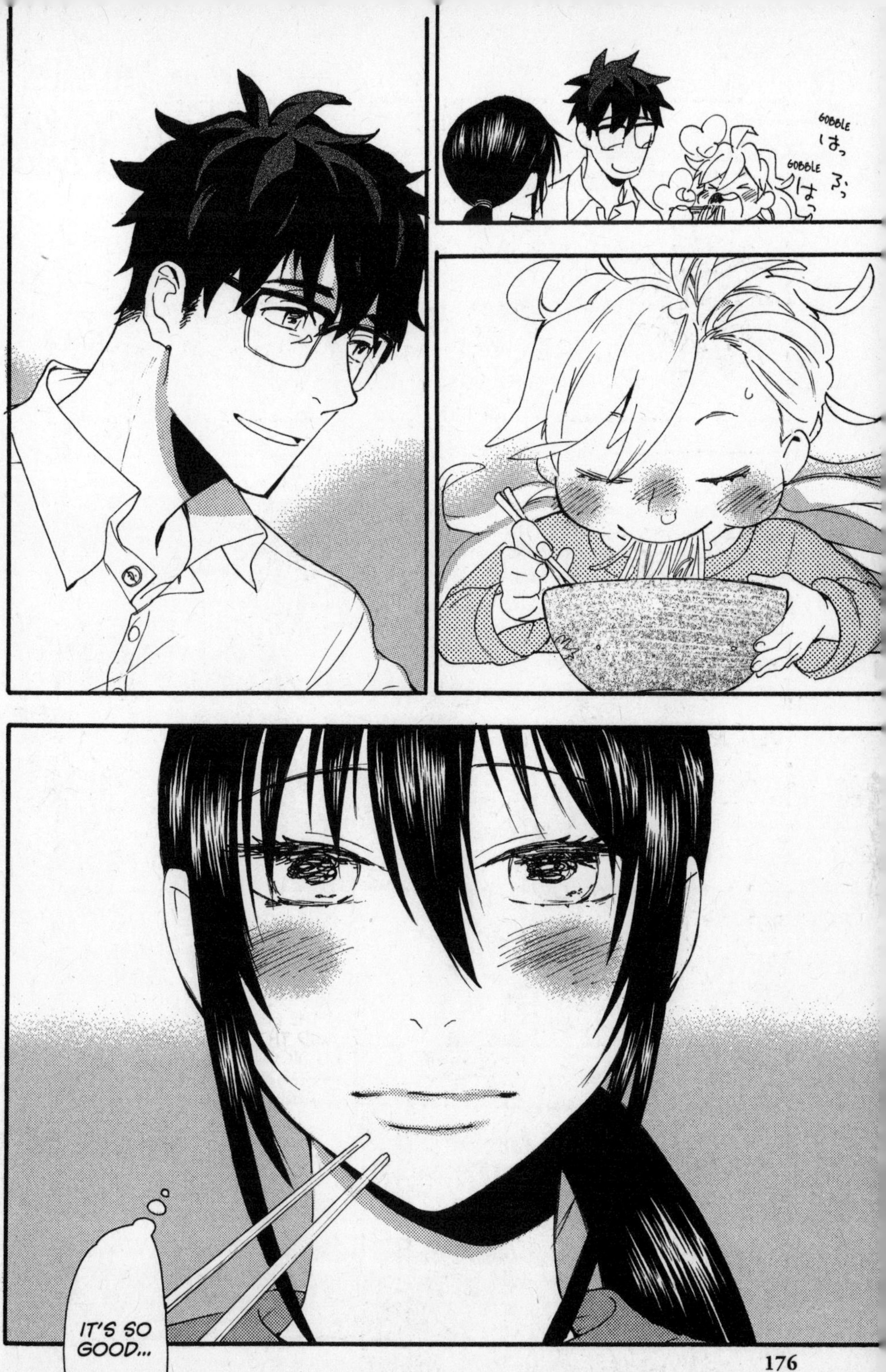
GOBBLE
はっ
GOBBLE
はふっ
IT'S SO GOOD...

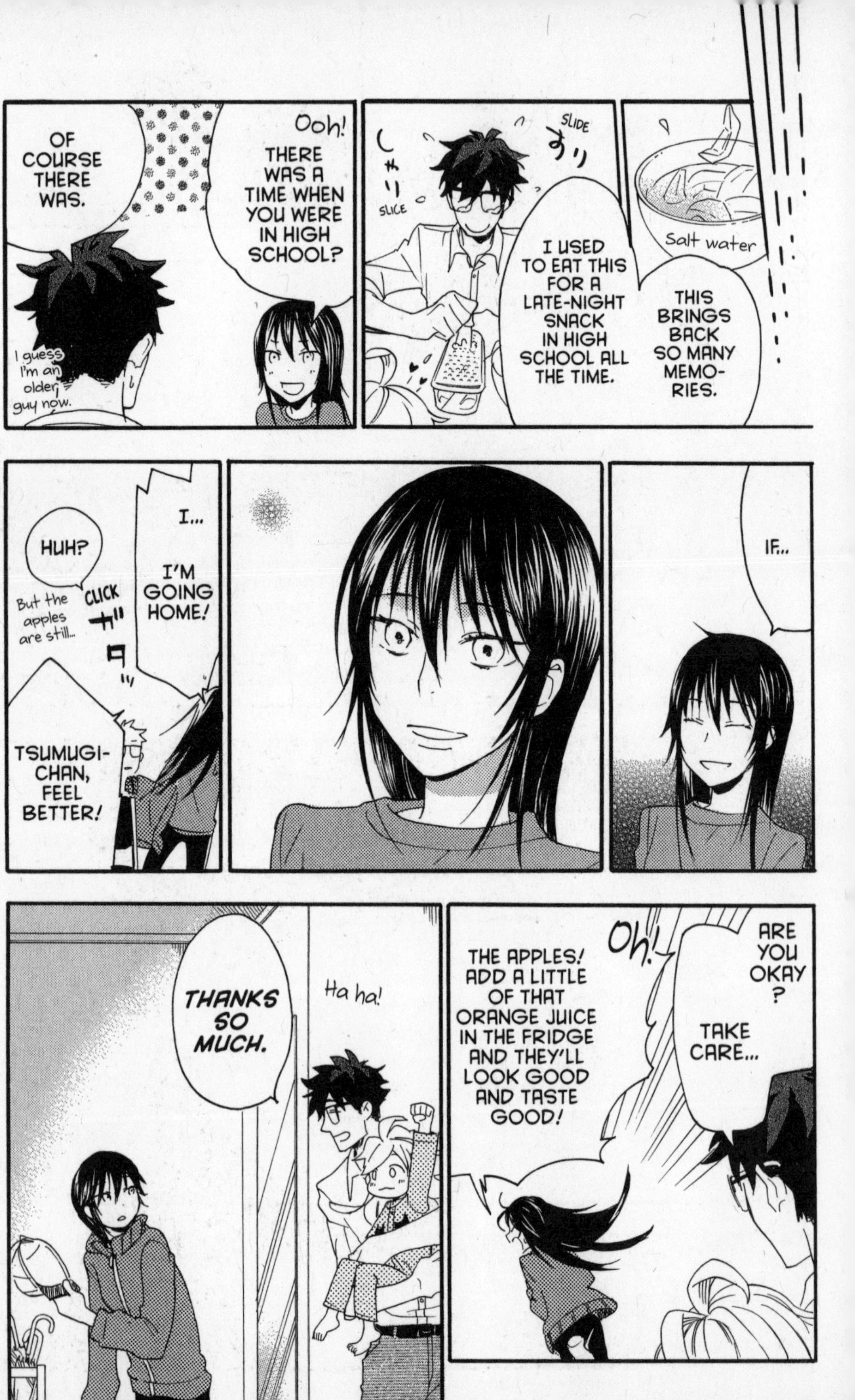
Salt water
SLIDE
SLICE
I USED TO EAT THIS FOR A LATE-NIGHT SNACK IN HIGH SCHOOL ALL THE TIME.
THIS BRINGS BACK SO MANY MEMORIES.
Ooh!
THERE WAS A TIME WHEN YOU WERE IN HIGH SCHOOL?
OF COURSE THERE WAS.
I guess I'm an older guy now.
IF...
I...
I'M GOING HOME!
HUH?
CLICK
But the apples are still...
TSUMUGI-CHAN, FEEL BETTER!
ARE YOU OKAY?
TAKE CARE...
Oh!
THE APPLES! ADD A LITTLE OF THAT ORANGE JUICE IN THE FRIDGE AND THEY'LL LOOK GOOD AND TASTE GOOD!
Ha ha!
THANKS SO MUCH.

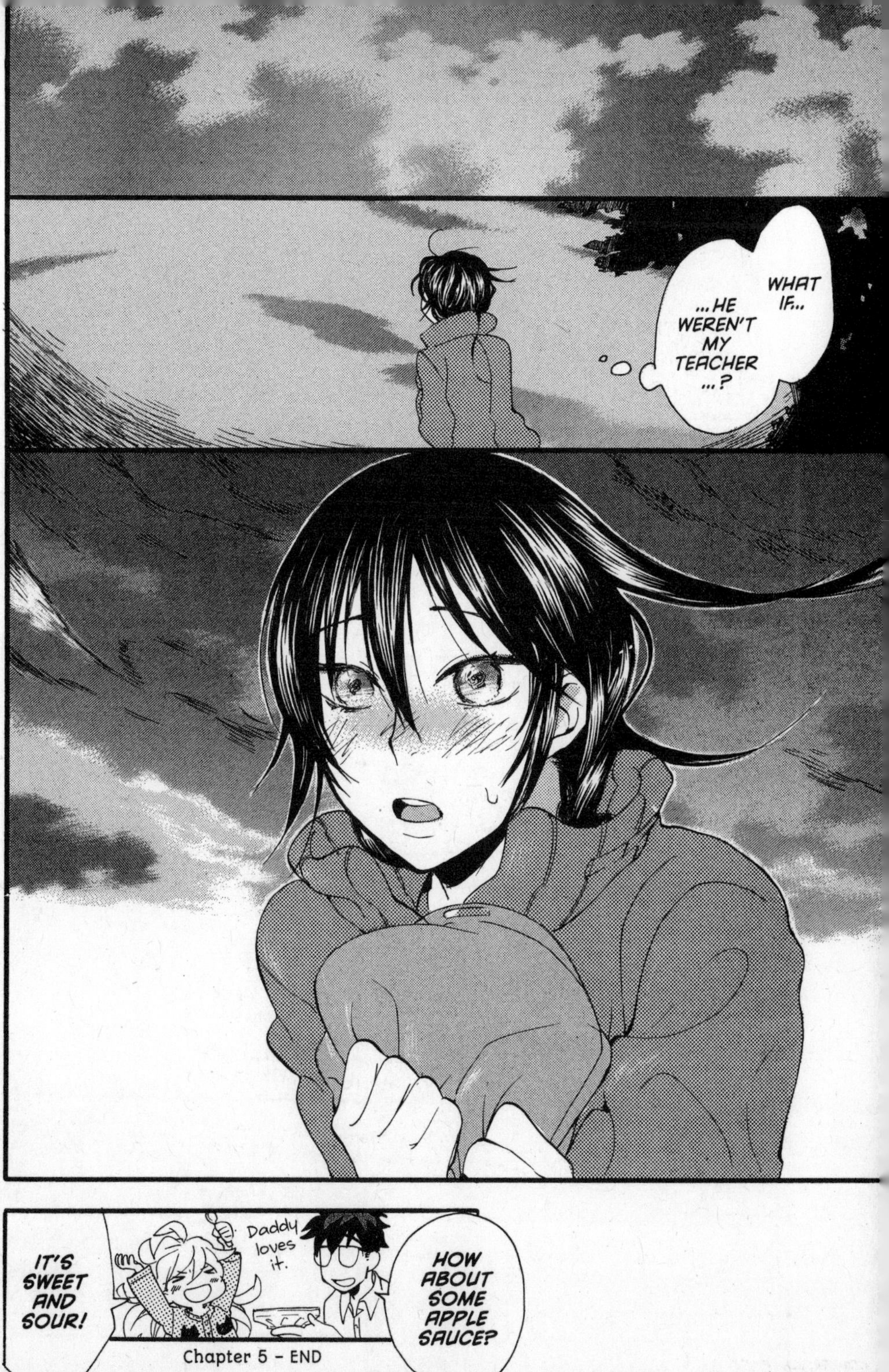
WHAT IF... ...HE WEREN'T MY TEACHER...?
HOW ABOUT SOME APPLE SAUCE?
Daddy loves it.
IT'S SWEET AND SOUR!
Chapter 5 - END

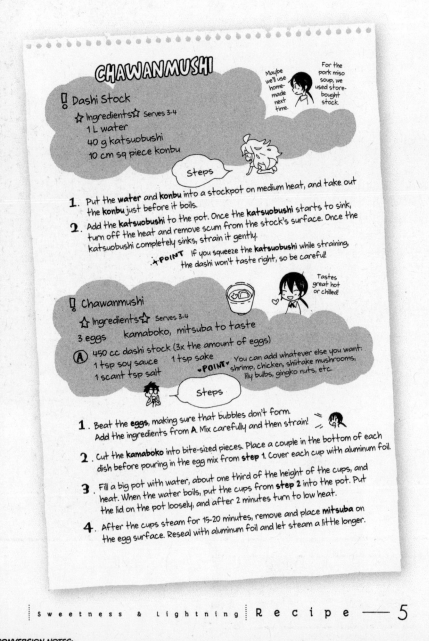

CHAWANMUSHI

Maybe we'll use home-made next time.

For the pork miso soup, we used store-bought stock.

Dashi Stock

☆ Ingredients ☆ Serves 3-4

1 L water
40 g katsuobushi
10 cm sq piece konbu

Steps

1. Put the **water** and **konbu** into a stockpot on medium heat, and take out the **konbu** just before it boils.

2. Add the **katsuobushi** to the pot. Once the **katsuobushi** starts to sink, turn off the heat and remove scum from the stock's surface. Once the katsuobushi completely sinks, strain it gently.

   ◆POINT▸ If you squeeze the **katsuobushi** while straining, the dashi won't taste right, so be careful!

Tastes great hot or chilled!

Chawanmushi

☆ Ingredients ☆ Serves 3-4

3 eggs   kamaboko, mitsuba to taste

Ⓐ 450 cc dashi stock (3x the amount of eggs)
1 tsp soy sauce   1 tsp sake
1 scant tsp salt   ◆POINT▸ You can add whatever else you want: shrimp, chicken, shiitake mushrooms, lily bulbs, gingko nuts, etc.

Steps

1. Beat the **eggs**, making sure that bubbles don't form. Add the ingredients from A. Mix carefully and then strain!

2. Cut the **kamaboko** into bite-sized pieces. Place a couple in the bottom of each dish before pouring in the egg mix from **step 1**. Cover each cup with aluminum foil.

3. Fill a big pot with water, about one third of the height of the cups, and heat. When the water boils, put the cups from **step 2** into the pot. Put the lid on the pot loosely, and after 2 minutes turn to low heat.

4. After the cups steam for 15-20 minutes, remove and place **mitsuba** on the egg surface. Reseal with aluminum foil and let steam a little longer.

CONVERSION NOTES:
1 L WATER = ABOUT 4 1/4 CUPS, 40 G KATSUOBUSHI = ABOUT 1.5 OZ, 10 CM KONBU = 4 IN., 450 CC DASHI = 2 CUPS

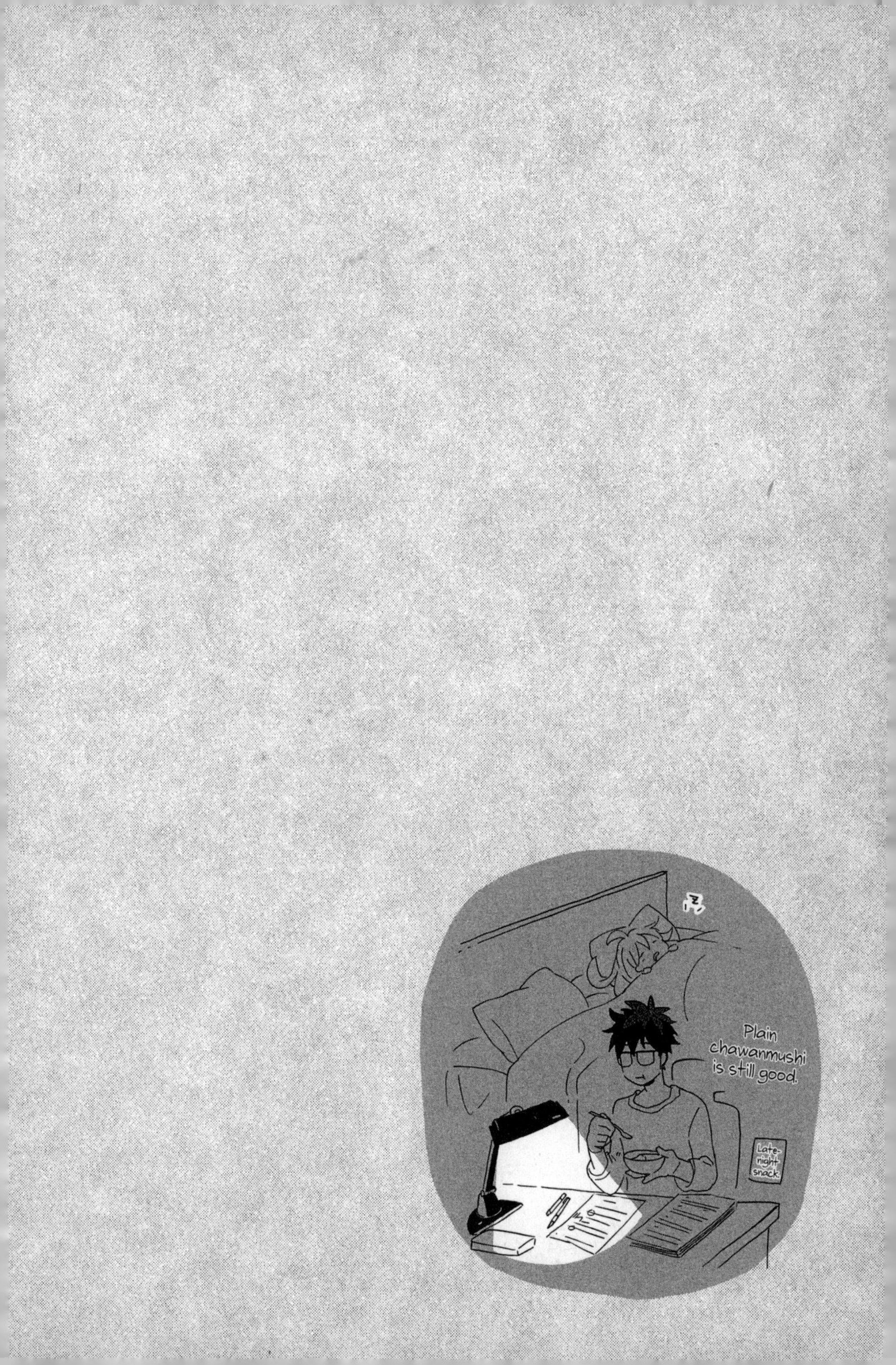
Plain chawanmushi is still good.
Late-night snack.

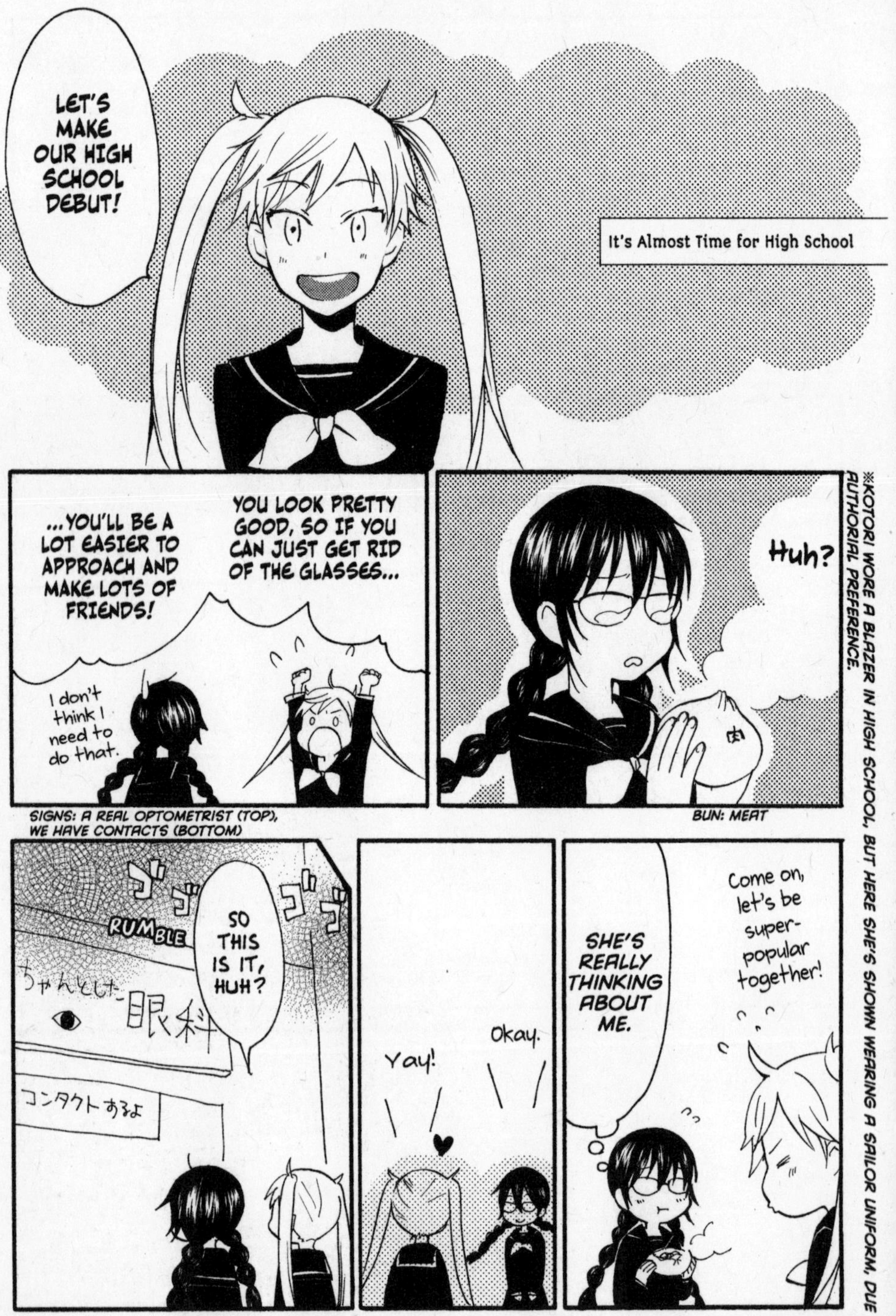
It's Almost Time for High School
LET'S MAKE OUR HIGH SCHOOL DEBUT!
Huh?
BUN: MEAT
YOU LOOK PRETTY GOOD, SO IF YOU CAN JUST GET RID OF THE GLASSES...
...YOU'LL BE A LOT EASIER TO APPROACH AND MAKE LOTS OF FRIENDS!
I don't think I need to do that.
Come on, let's be super-popular together!
SHE'S REALLY THINKING ABOUT ME.
Okay.
Yay!
ゴゴゴ
RUMBLE
SO THIS IS IT, HUH?
ちゃんとした眼科
コンタクトするよ
SIGNS: A REAL OPTOMETRIST (TOP), WE HAVE CONTACTS (BOTTOM)
※KOTORI WORE A BLAZER IN HIGH SCHOOL, BUT HERE SHE'S SHOWN WEARING A SAILOR UNIFORM, DUE TO AUTHORIAL PREFERENCE.

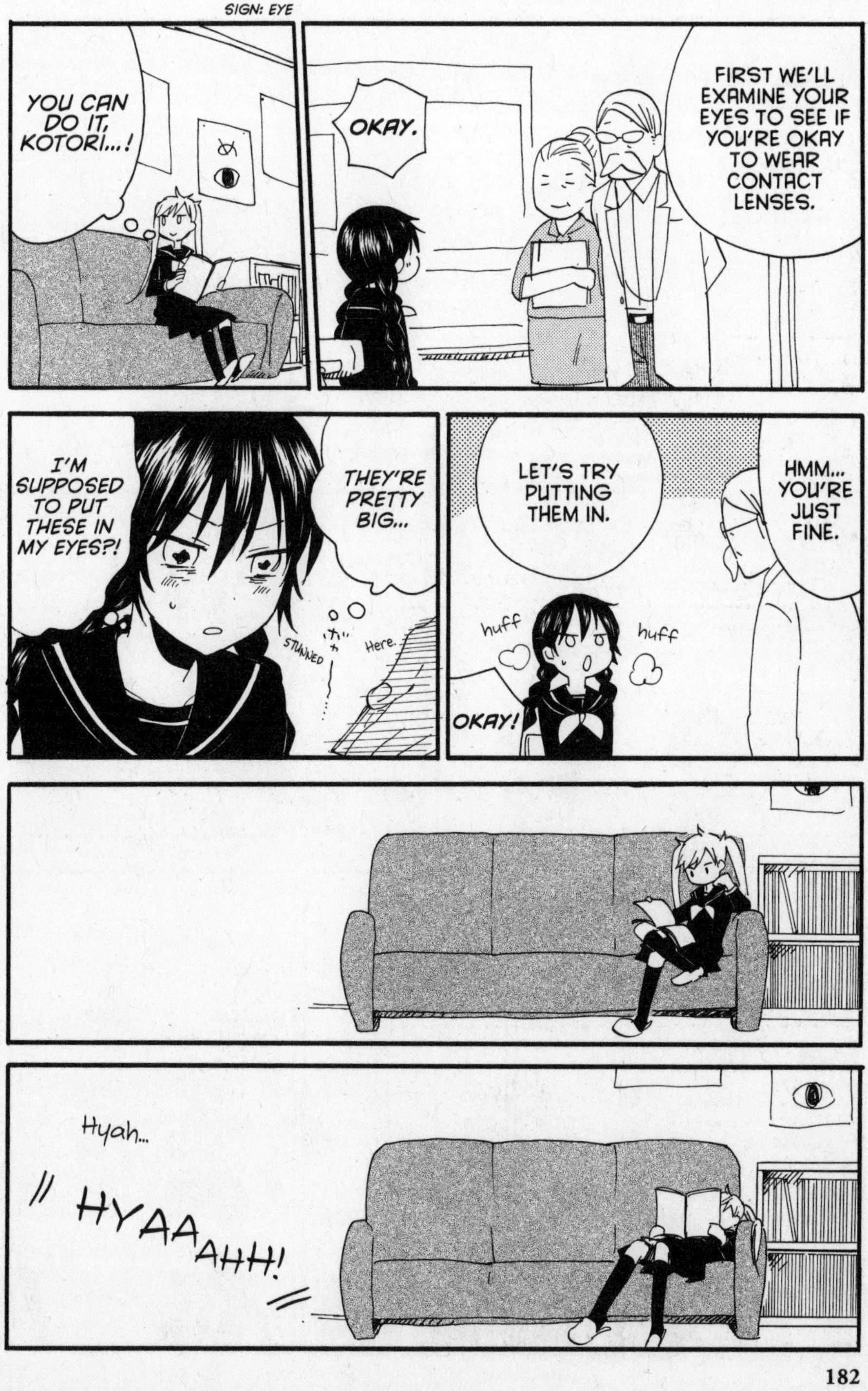
FIRST WE'LL EXAMINE YOUR EYES TO SEE IF YOU'RE OKAY TO WEAR CONTACT LENSES.
OKAY.
SIGN: EYE
め
YOU CAN DO IT, KOTORI...!
HMM... YOU'RE JUST FINE.
LET'S TRY PUTTING THEM IN.
huff
huff
OKAY!
THEY'RE PRETTY BIG...
Here.
STUNNED
I'M SUPPOSED TO PUT THESE IN MY EYES?!
Hyah...
HYAAAHH!

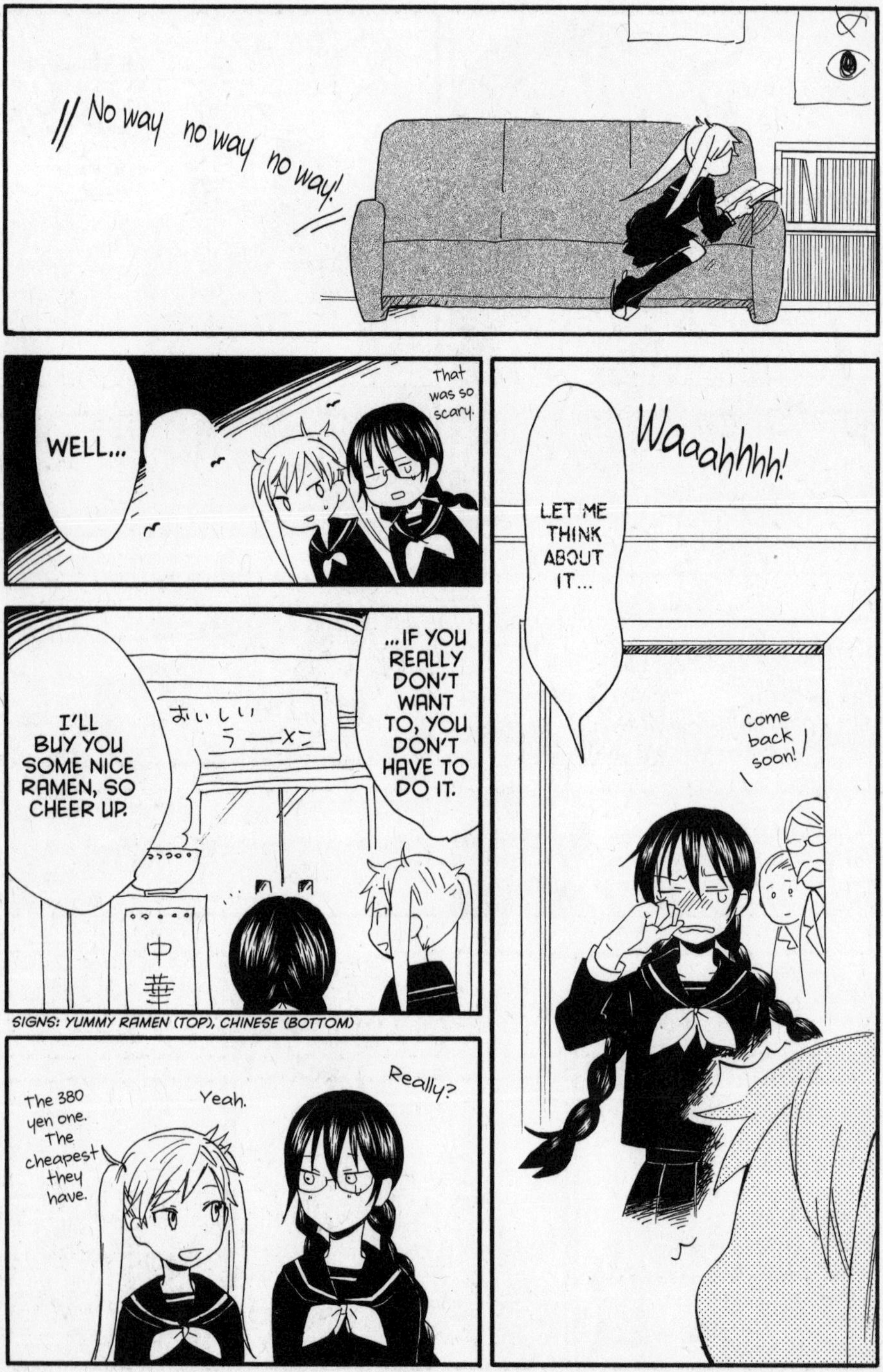
No way no way no way!
Waaahhhh!
LET ME THINK ABOUT IT...
Come back soon!
That was so scary.
WELL...
...IF YOU REALLY DON'T WANT TO, YOU DON'T HAVE TO DO IT.
おいしいラーメン
I'LL BUY YOU SOME NICE RAMEN, SO CHEER UP.
中華
SIGNS: YUMMY RAMEN (TOP), CHINESE (BOTTOM)
Really?
Yeah.
The 380 yen one. The cheapest they have.

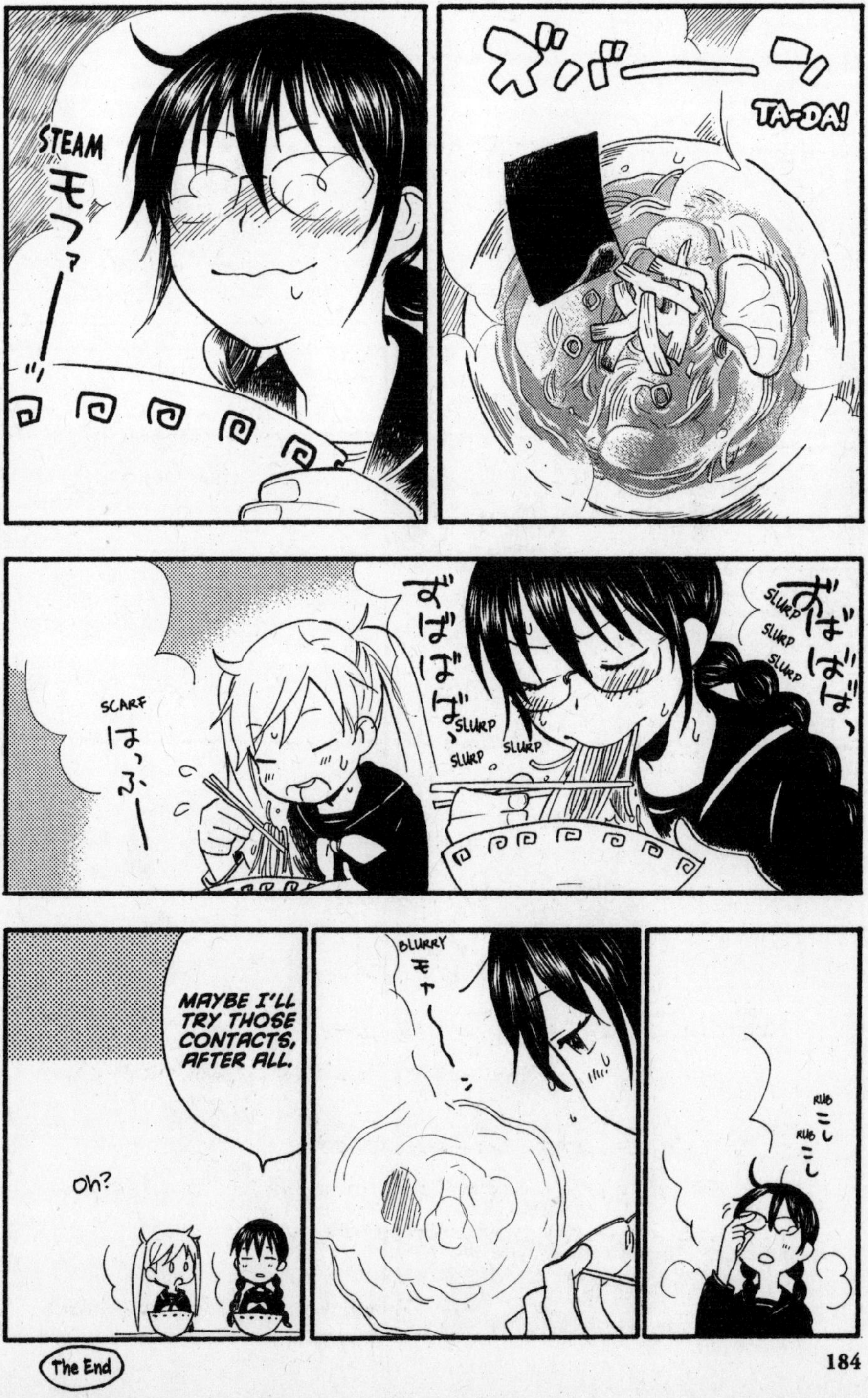
ズバーーン
TA-DA!
STEAM
モファーッ
SLURP SLURP SLURP
ずばばば
SLURP SLURP SLURP
ずばばば
SCARF
はっふー
RUB
こし
RUB
こし
BLURRY
モャ〜
MAYBE I'LL TRY THOSE CONTACTS, AFTER ALL.
Oh?

The End

Afterword

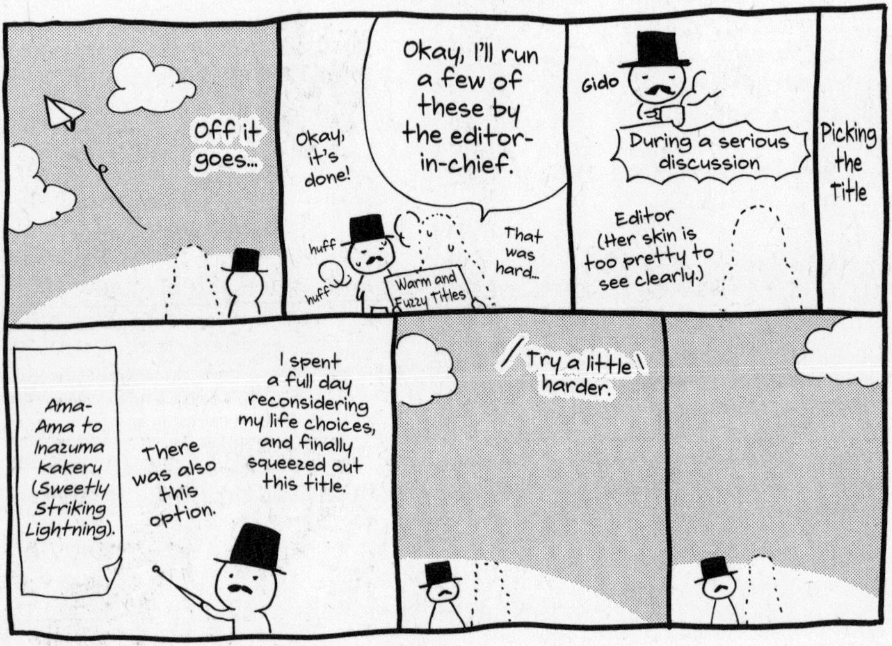

Picking the Title
Gido
During a serious discussion
Editor (Her skin is too pretty to see clearly.)
Okay, I'll run a few of these by the editor-in-chief.
That was hard...
Okay, it's done!
huff
huff
Warm and Fuzzy Titles
Off it goes...
Try a little harder.
I spent a full day reconsidering my life choices, and finally squeezed out this title.
There was also this option.
Ama-Ama to Inazuma Kakeru (Sweetly Striking Lightning).

See you next volume!

雨隠 ギド
Gido Amagakure

Thank you!

Koz, Gon-chan, Tsuru-san, W-yama-san
O-hara-san, M-chan, E-san, Nori-chan

T-shiro-sama, Jun Abe-sama
Research Support: Tabegoto-ya Norabo-sama
Cooking Advisor: Yo Tatewaki-sama

Thank you for all for your help!!

Translation Notes

Flower viewing, page 10: Flower viewing refers to Hanami, the Japanese tradition of viewing flowers in full bloom. Though this may include any type of flower, it mostly refers to cherry blossoms and, less often, plum blossoms. Hanami is typically done in spring and is often enjoyed as a picnic-like activity where friends, family, and coworkers eat prepared meals while observing the beauty of flowers in bloom.

Donabe, page 26: A special type of clay pot used for cooking over an open flame.

Nozawana, miso beef, and iwanori seaweed, page 39: Nozawana is a type of Japanese mustard leaf that if often pickled. Miso beef or *nikumiso* is a mixture of ground beef and miso. Iwanori (rock seaweed) is a type of seaweed found between rocks that is typically dried for consumption. All three of these foods are typically used as condiments or rice toppings.

The role of a teacher, page 54: In Japan, the role of a teacher can sometimes be a little different from that of their Western counterparts. Japanese teachers may be more directly involved in the life of students inside and outside school, almost functioning as second parents. Though there is a clearer line between teacher and student these days, in the past, the student-teacher relationship was much more intimate, and it wasn't uncommon for teachers to spend time with their students and their students' families outside of school.

Thumbprint, page 56: Though signing one's name has become fairly common in Japan, ink stamps/seals and thumbprints are still used to sign documents.

Salisbury steak, page 58: In Japan, this dish is called *hanbaagu* or may also be called hamburg steak. *Hanbaagu* is a standard of *goshoku* (Western-style cooking) and you'll find some version of it in almost every *famiresu* (family-style restaurant) in Japan.

Konnyaku, page 59: A starchy plant also known as "devil's tongue." It's made into a gelatin form and used as an ingredient in Japanese dishes.

Golden Week, page 113: In early May, a series of holidays form a week of vacation, allowing many students and families to travel or spend time together.

Shirasu, page 117: Dried baby anchovies.

Chikuwa, page 117: A tube-shaped food product made from fish paste, starch, and other ingredients.

Konbu, page 122: A type of thick kelp that is often dried and used in the preparation of soup stock.

Tatami mats, page 140: A type of traditional Japanese flooring tupically made of rice straw.

Chawanmushi, page 164: A savory, steamed egg custard eaten as a main dish in Japan. Chawanmushi directly translates to "steamed (in) tea bowl" and the dish itself is traditionally served in a tea bowl.

Nyuumen, page 166: Thin wheat-flour noodles in a broth with vegetables, meat, and any number of other ingredients.

Katsuobushi, page 167: Dried, fermented skipjack tuna that is typically shaved off into flakes. It is also used to prepare soup stock.

Kamaboko, page 171: A type of processed fish paste primarily made from pureed whitefish and formed into a loaf that can be sliced i.

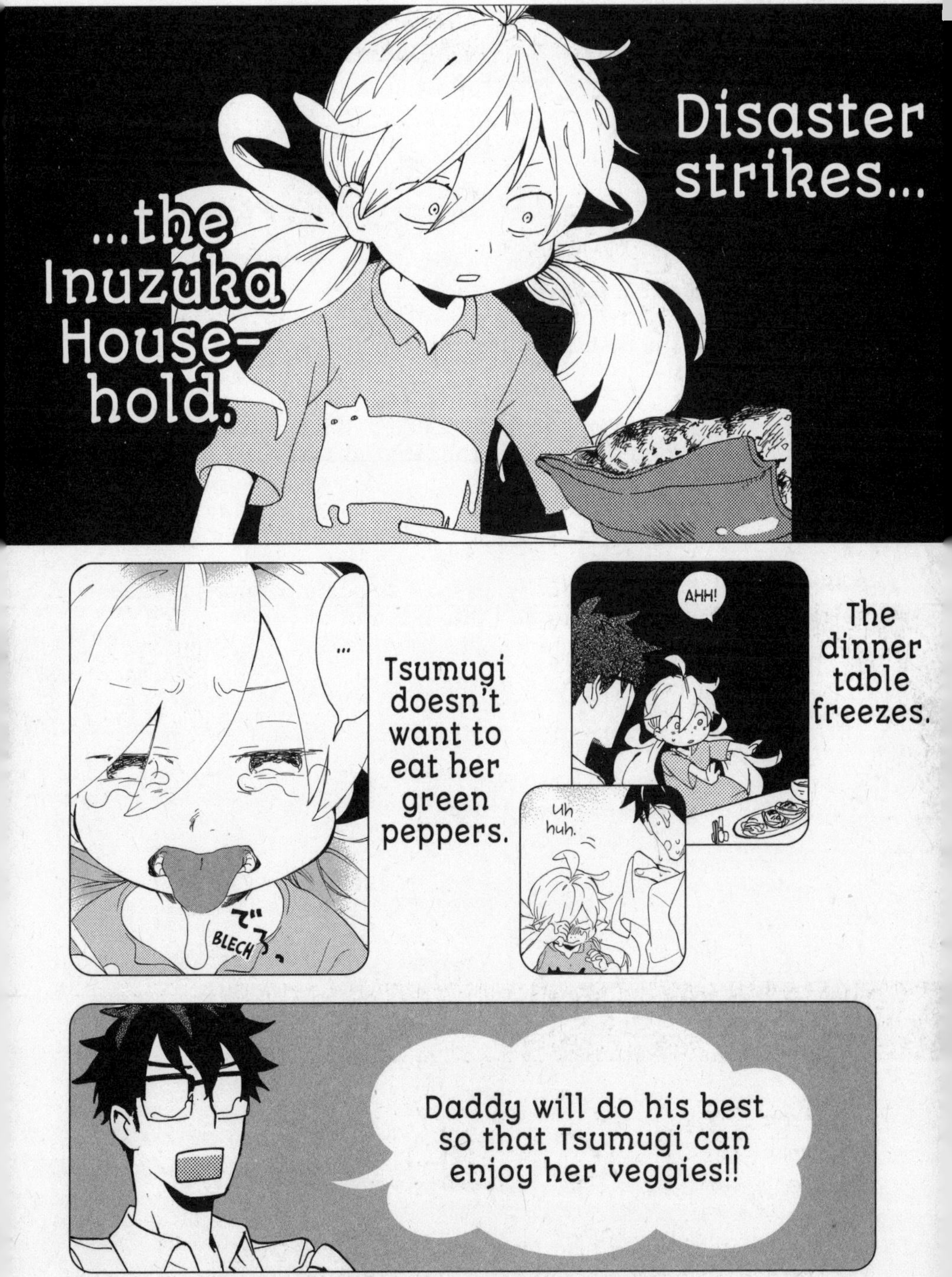
Disaster strikes...
...the Inuzuka Household.
The dinner table freezes.
AHH!
Uh huh.
Tsumugi doesn't want to eat her green peppers.
...
BLECH
Daddy will do his best so that Tsumugi can enjoy her veggies!!

A gratin filled with veggies.

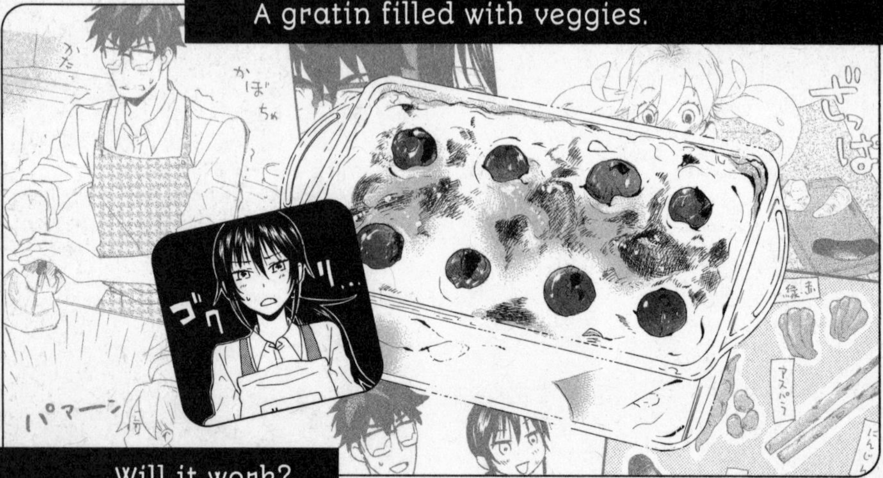

かぼちゃ
ゴクリ…
パマーン
アスパラ

Will it work?

Will Tsumugi smile...

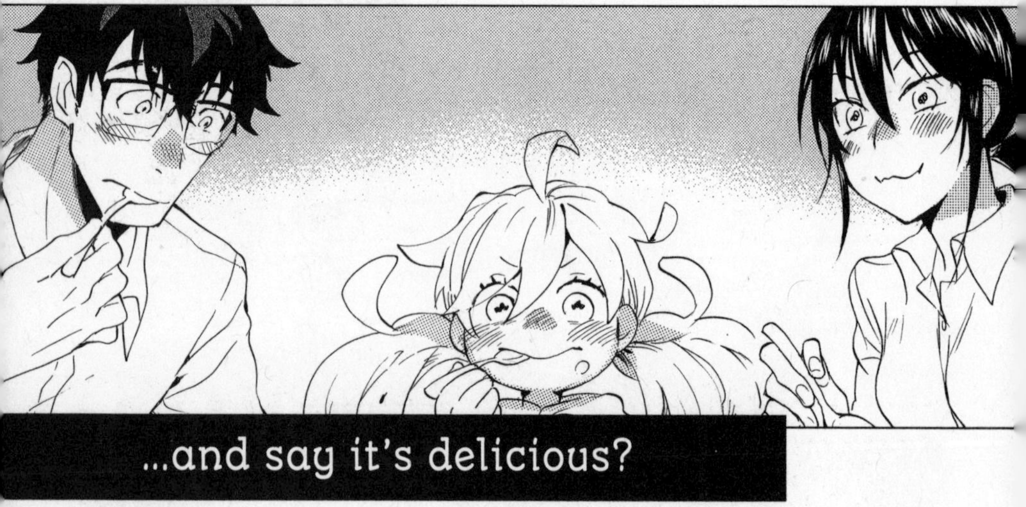

...and say it's delicious?

甘々と稲妻 Sweetness & Lightning 2

On Sale September 2016!

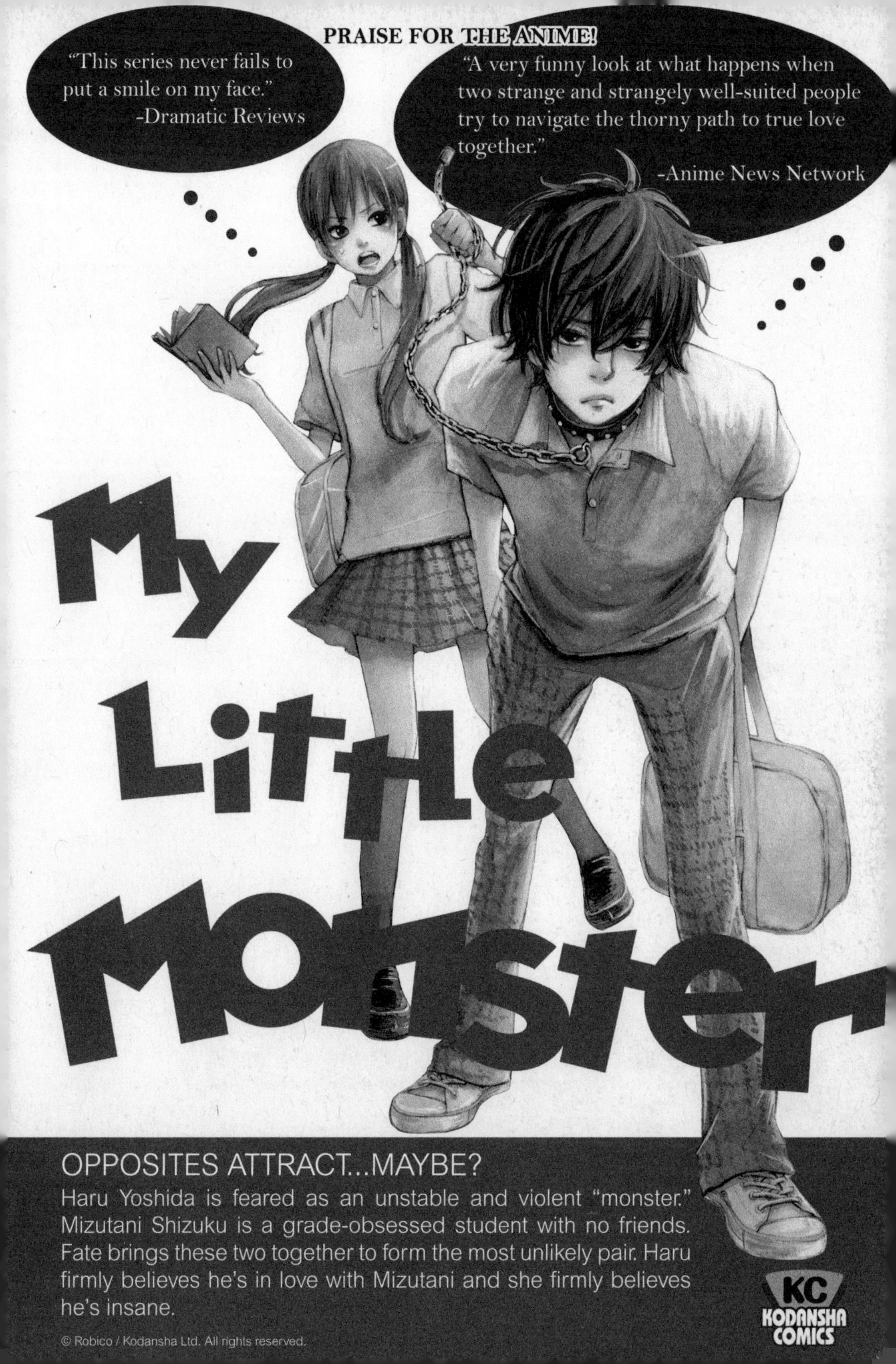

My Little Monster

OPPOSITES ATTRACT...MAYBE?

Haru Yoshida is feared as an unstable and violent "monster." Mizutani Shizuku is a grade-obsessed student with no friends. Fate brings these two together to form the most unlikely pair. Haru firmly believes he's in love with Mizutani and she firmly believes he's insane.

KC KODANSHA COMICS

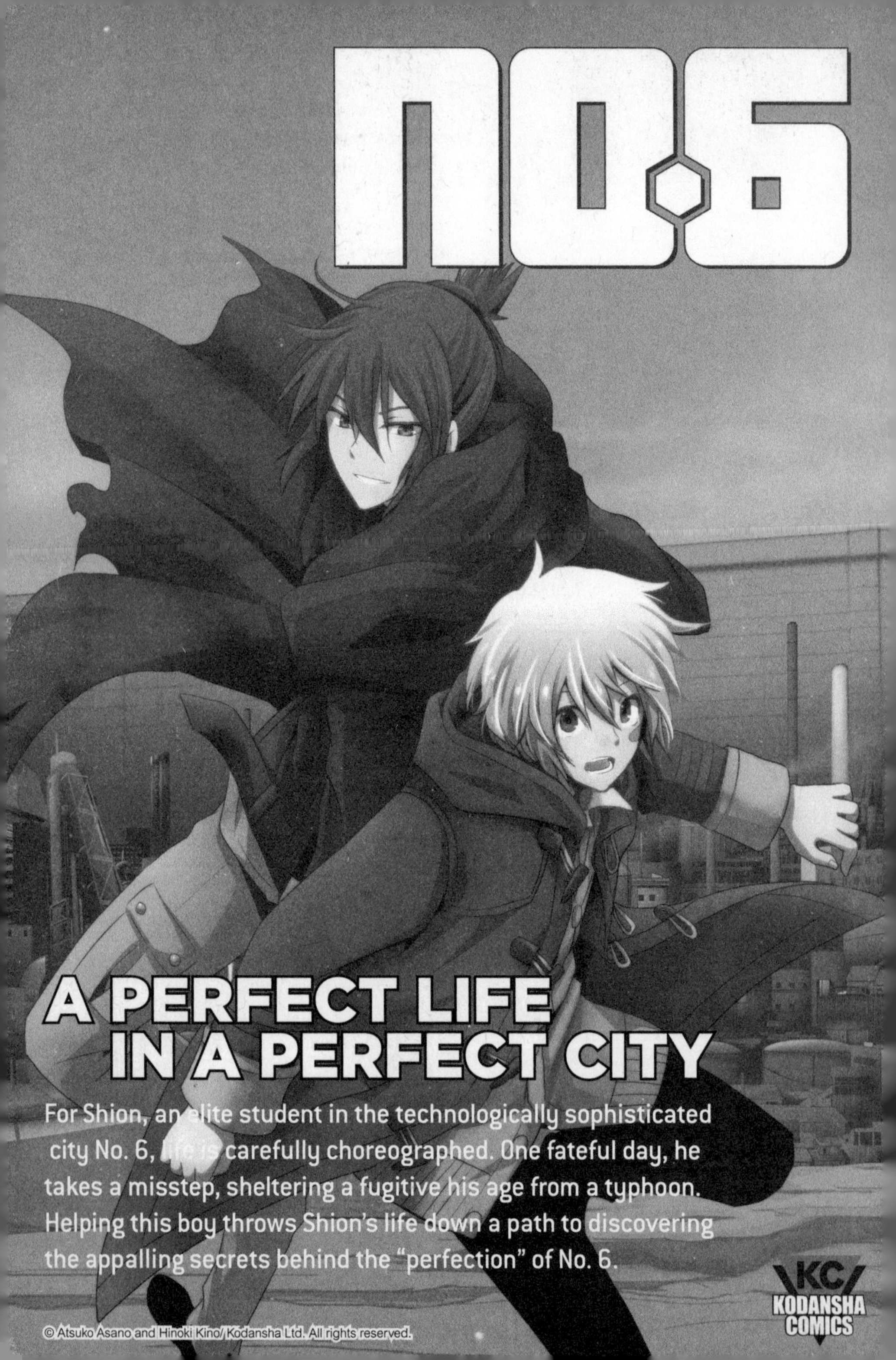
NO.6
A PERFECT LIFE
IN A PERFECT CITY
For Shion, an elite student in the technologically sophisticated city No. 6, life is carefully choreographed. One fateful day, he takes a misstep, sheltering a fugitive his age from a typhoon. Helping this boy throws Shion's life down a path to discovering the appalling secrets behind the "perfection" of No. 6.
KC
KODANSHA COMICS
© Atsuko Asano and Hinoki Kino/Kodansha Ltd. All rights reserved.

Say I Love You.

KC
KODANSHA
COMICS

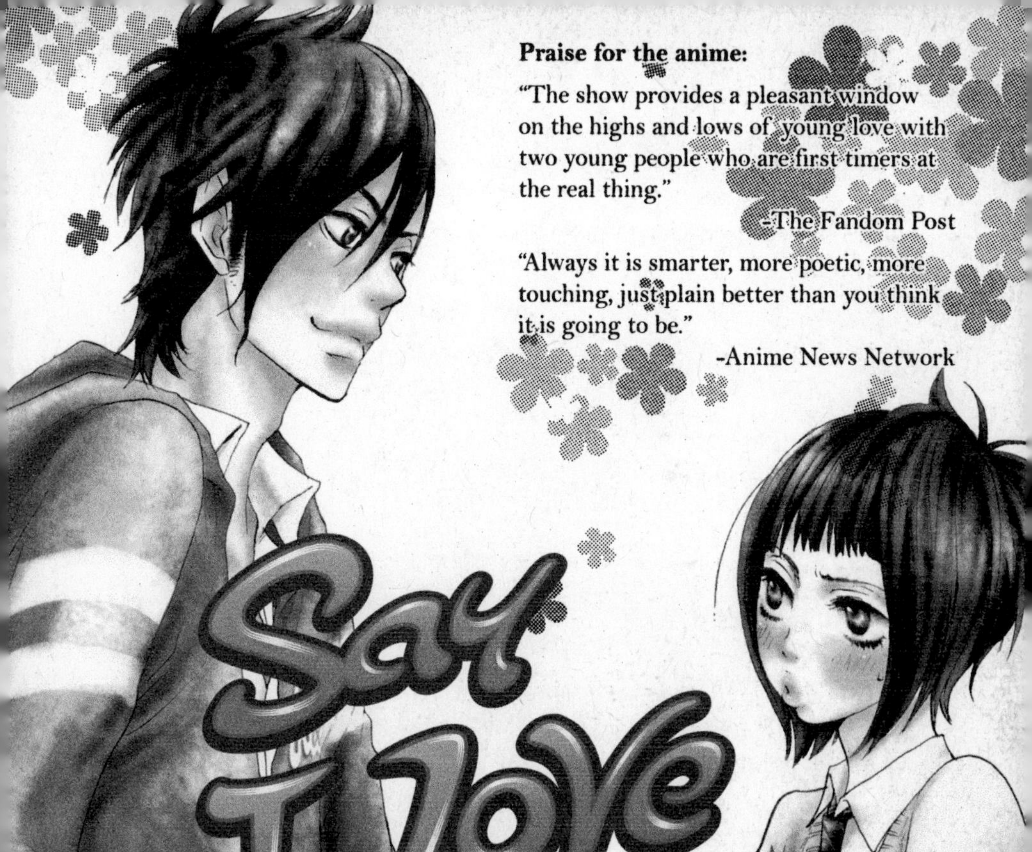

Mei Tachibana has no friends — and says she doesn't need them!

But everything changes when she accidentally roundhouse kicks the most popular boy in school! However, Yamato Kurosawa isn't angry in the slightest— in fact, he thinks his ordinary life could use an unusual girl like Mei. But winning Mei's trust will be a tough task. How long will she refuse to say, "I love you"?

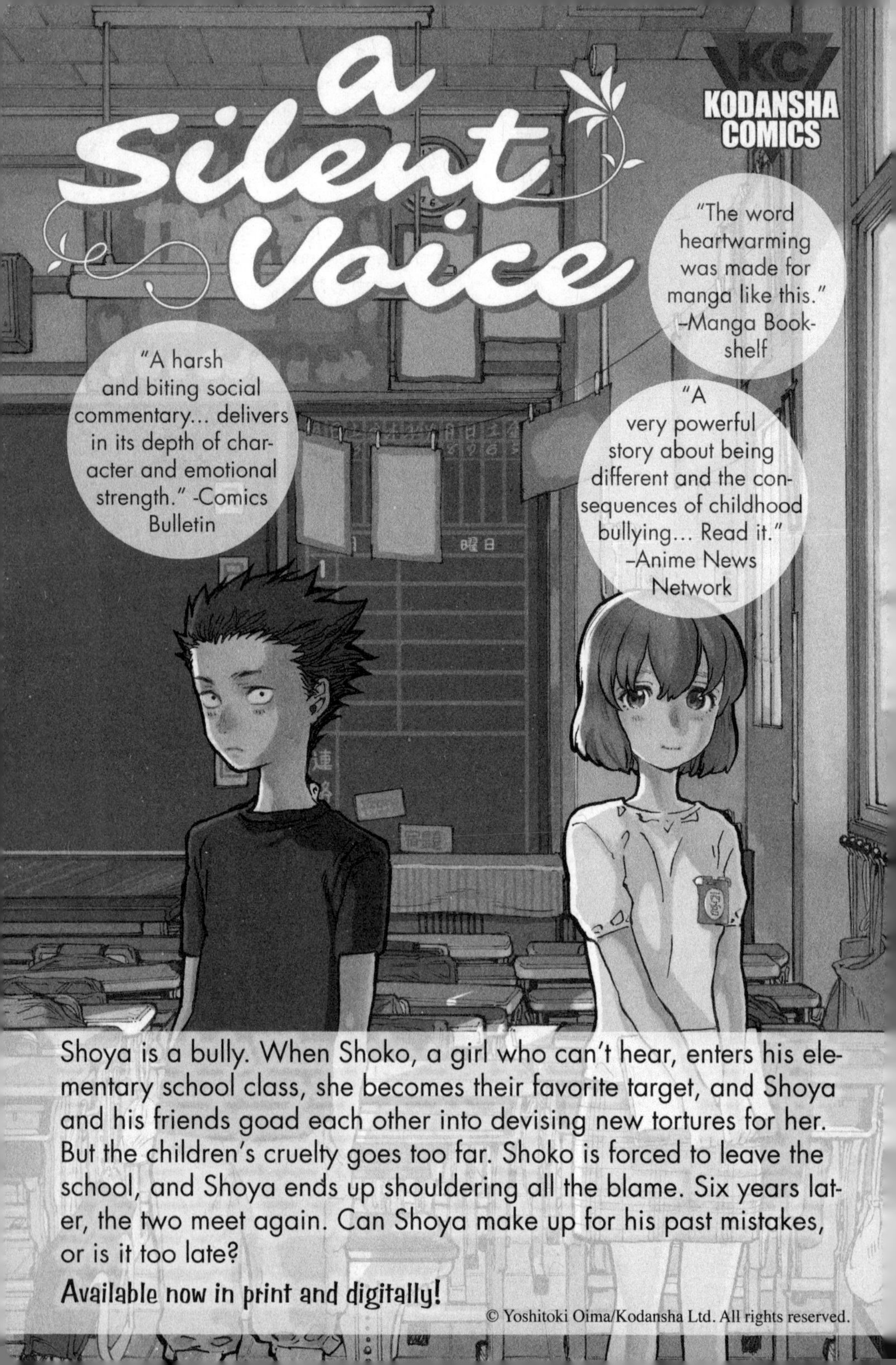
a Silent Voice
KC KODANSHA COMICS
"The word heartwarming was made for manga like this." –Manga Bookshelf
"A harsh and biting social commentary... delivers in its depth of character and emotional strength." -Comics Bulletin
"A very powerful story about being different and the consequences of childhood bullying... Read it." –Anime News Network
Shoya is a bully. When Shoko, a girl who can't hear, enters his elementary school class, she becomes their favorite target, and Shoya and his friends goad each other into devising new tortures for her. But the children's cruelty goes too far. Shoko is forced to leave the school, and Shoya ends up shouldering all the blame. Six years later, the two meet again. Can Shoya make up for his past mistakes, or is it too late?
Available now in print and digitally!
© Yoshitoki Oima/Kodansha Ltd. All rights reserved.

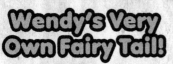

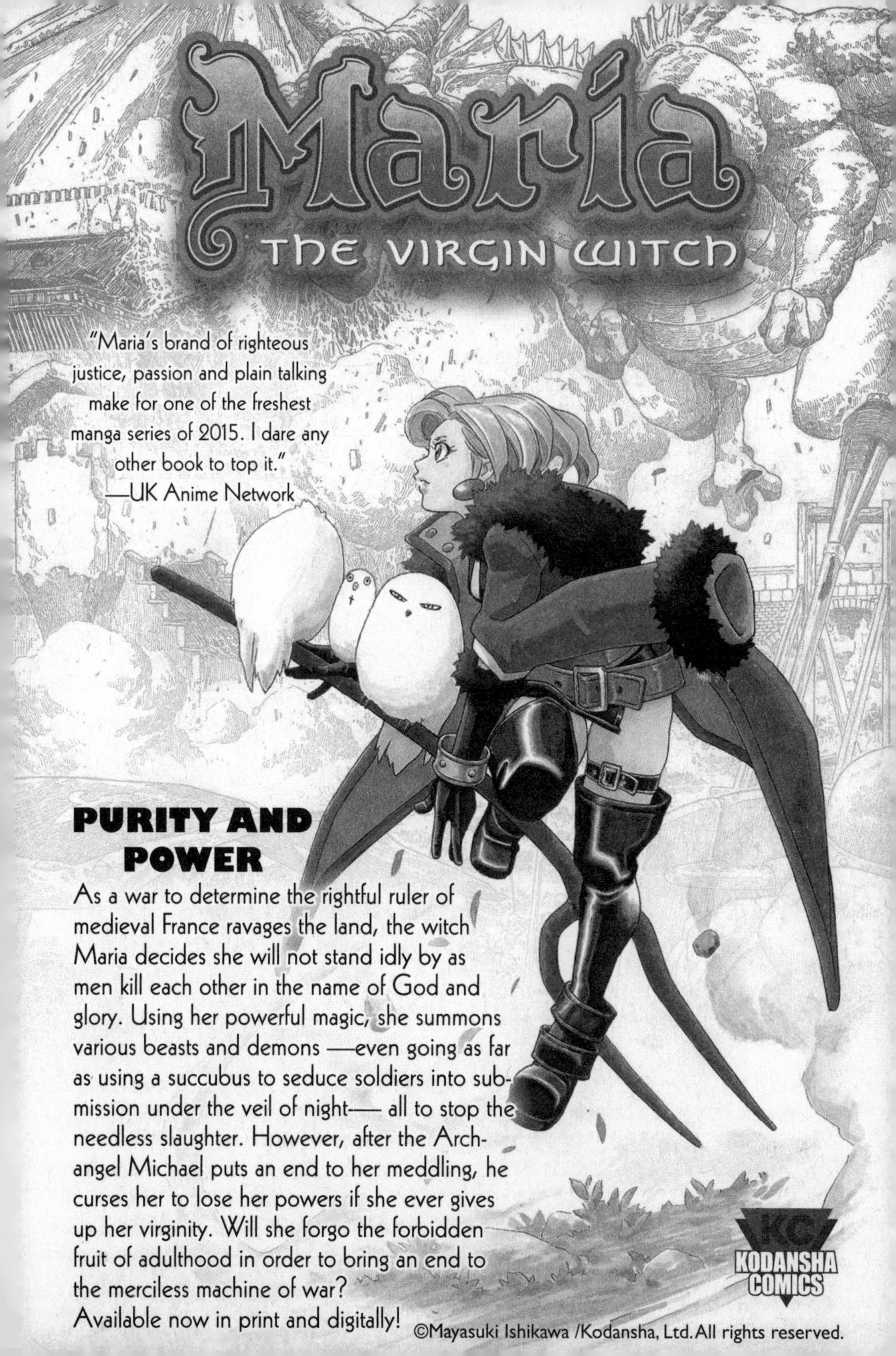
Maria
THE VIRGIN WITCH
"Maria's brand of righteous justice, passion and plain talking make for one of the freshest manga series of 2015. I dare any other book to top it."
—UK Anime Network
PURITY AND POWER
As a war to determine the rightful ruler of medieval France ravages the land, the witch Maria decides she will not stand idly by as men kill each other in the name of God and glory. Using her powerful magic, she summons various beasts and demons —even going as far as using a succubus to seduce soldiers into submission under the veil of night— all to stop the needless slaughter. However, after the Archangel Michael puts an end to her meddling, he curses her to lose her powers if she ever gives up her virginity. Will she forgo the forbidden fruit of adulthood in order to bring an end to the merciless machine of war?
Available now in print and digitally!
KC
KODANSHA COMICS
©Mayasuki Ishikawa /Kodansha, Ltd. All rights reserved.

Yamada-kun AND THE Seven Witches

"A very funny manga with a lot of heart and character."
—Adventures in Poor Taste

SWAPPED WITH A KISS?!

Class troublemaker Ryu Yamada is already having a bad day when he stumbles down a staircase along with star student Urara Shiraishi. When he wakes up, he realizes they have switched bodies—and that Ryu has the power to trade places with anyone just by kissing them! Ryu and Urara take full advantage of the situation to improve their lives, but with such an oddly amazing power, just how long will they be able to keep their secret under wraps?

Available now in print and digitally!

Sweetness & Lightning volume 1 is a work of fiction. Names, characters, places, and incidents are the products of the author's imagination or are used fictitiously. Any resemblance to actual events, locales, or persons, living or dead, is entirely coincidental.

A Kodansha Comics Trade Paperback Original.

Published in the United States by Kodansha Comics,
an imprint of Kodansha USA Publishing, LLC, New York.

Publication rights for this English edition arranged through Kodansha Ltd., Tokyo.

First published in Japan in 2013 by Kodansha Ltd., Tokyo, as *Ama-ama to Inazuma* volume 1.

ISBN 978-1-63236-369-5

Printed in the United States of America.

www.kodanshacomics.com

9 8 7 6 5 4 3 2 1

Translation: Adam Lensenmayer
Lettering: Lys Blakeslee
Editing: Ajani Oloye
Kodansha Comics Edition Cover Design: Phil Balsman